The Gospels and Christian Life in History and Practice

The Gospels and Christian Life in History and Practice

Richard Valantasis, Douglas K. Bleyle, and Dennis C. Haugh

ROWMAN & LITTLEFIELD PUBLISHERS, INC.
Lanham • Boulder • New York • Toronto • Plymouth, UK

ROWMAN & LITTLEFIELD PUBLISHERS, INC.

Published in the United States of America
by Rowman & Littlefield Publishers, Inc.
A wholly owned subsidary of The Rowman & Littlefield Publishing Group, Inc.
4501 Forbes Boulevard, Suite 200, Lanham, Maryland 20706
www.rowmanlittlefield.com

Estover Road
Plymouth PL6 7PY
United Kingdom

British Library Cataloguing in Publication Information Available

Library of Congress Cataloging-in-Publication Data
Valantasis, Richard, 1946-
  The Gospels and Christian life in history and practice / Richard Valantasis, Douglas K. Bleyle, and Dennis Haugh.
    p. cm.
  Includes index.
  ISBN 978-0-7425-5922-6 (pbk. : alk. paper)—ISBN 978-0-7425-5921-9 (cloth : alk. paper)—ISBN 978-0-7425-7069-6 (electronic)
  1. Bible. N.T. Gospels--Criticism, interpretation, etc. 2. Bible. N.T. Acts—Criticism, interpretation, etc. 3. Christian life—History—Early church, ca. 30-600. I. Bleyle, Douglas K., 1967- II. Haugh, Dennis, 1942- III. Title.
  BS2548.V35 2009
  270.1—dc22   2009002909

Printed in the United States of America

∞ ™ The paper used in this publication meets the minimum requirements of American National Standard for Information Sciences—Permanence of Paper for Printed Library Materials, ANSI/NISO Z39.48-1992.

For Marian, Jennifer, and Janet—the trinity's holy trinity

Contents

※

Acknowledgments

This book grew out of a series of seminars on the gospels led by Richard Valantasis at Iliff School of Theology in Denver, Colorado. The enthusiastic and energetic engagement of the students in those seminars, as well as their ability to think about the gospels and their contexts in new and different ways, formed the content of this book. Richard Valantasis's two best students, Douglas Bleyle and Dennis Haugh, his coauthors of this book, took that creative seminar work and turned it into exciting stories about how the gospels formed Christians in their own times and contexts and with unique perspectives on community formation. The greatest delight of a professor is teaching students eager to explore new ideas and to challenge the professor's capacity to respond to new questions and issues. Valantasis's students at Iliff School of Theology provided that delight and challenge with gusto, and he thanks them all for their part in generating this book. Valantasis also thanks his students at Candler School of Theology and the Graduate Division of Religion of Emory University who were eager to learn about the ascetical and contemplative formative practices of the early church. Robyn-Michelle Nevill and George Branch-Trevathan in particular helped conceptualize ancient formation.

Working collaboratively on a writing project, although challenging at points, also provides delight. The hours spent imagining the contexts and practices of the communities that produced the gospels opened new ways of conceptualizing their lives. The coauthors prompted each other to throw out old ways of thinking and to explore deeply new ways. The creative process of their conversations led to great and often intense times of reading each other's work and writing (and rewriting) chapters to capture the creative energy of each gospel in its own right. Although Bleyle and Haugh want to thank Valantasis for inviting them to write this book as a team, Valantasis wants in turn to thank them for the wonderful time of collaboration and cooperation in creating this book. Our face-to-face meetings were electric, and they invigorated us for great thinking and even better writing.

Bleyle and Valantasis thank the students of the Anglican Studies Program at Candler School of Theology of Emory University in Atlanta, Georgia, especially Justin Yawn, Liz Schellingerhoudt, Buddy Crawford, and Justi Schunior. They all heard and read parts of this book as it was being produced, enthusiastically received it and even used it in their preaching, and encouraged us to keep going on the unusual tack we were taking.

Bleyle and Valantasis also thank the participants in our Monday evening home Eucharist, especially Maria Artemis whose artistic and mystic sense of the way religious people live made the gospel communities we were studying come to life before our eyes, the Schellingerhoudt family (Kees, Annelies, and Witner) whose enthusiasm for entering into the gospel brought life to our work, Nancy Baxter whose tender and direct honesty about the Christian life challenged us to be honest about the difficulties these gospel communities faced, and Alice Rose whose eager spiritual searching after authentic Christian living made us write to the mind and the heart at the same time. Without them our ideas and writing would probably have been very dry. We owe them all a great debt.

Valantasis and Haugh thank Bleyle for opening the world of film and television as a bridge to the gospels and their world. We had fun, probably too much fun, thinking about our contemporary world and its correlates to the gospels, even the ones we decided not to use in the book. Bleyle's vast knowledge and wide experience of popular culture helped us enormously and energized our efforts to communicate in a relevant way with our audience.

During the writing of this book, Valantasis and Bleyle were developing the idea for their Institute for Contemplative Living. The formative practices of the gospels fed their vision and their vision led to new ways of reading the gospels as formative documents. The two projects were joined at birth. Three people in particular captured the vision. Neil Alexander, the bishop of the Episcopal Diocese of Atlanta, and John Bolton, the rector of Our Saviour Episcopal Church, supported the exploration of formative practices both in the gospels and in the church at large. Mark MacDonald, the bishop of Navajoland, whose vision of a truly indigenous Navajo Christianity arising from the retelling of the stories of Jesus, spurred us to consider how the gospels could be refracted in our times and in different cultures. We look forward to supporting him in his vision, and to the way this book might help that process of remaking the gospels in our own times. We thank them all for their encouragement to explore new ways of formation based on ancient models.

Bleyle and Valantasis could not have finished the writing and revising of this book without the aid of the staff at Java Joe's in Santa Fe, New Mexico. Their coffee kept us awake and energized. Special thanks to Mark, our barista, and Dave, the owner.

All three of the authors thank Pamela Eisenbaum at Iliff School of Theology for her support for this project. Pam brought Dennis Haugh into the academic study of the New Testament, encouraged Douglas Bleyle to pursue his academic passions, and provided rich intellectual vitality to Richard Valantasis, her colleague in the department. We hope Pam will use our book every semester in her classes!

Haugh acknowledges warmly the support and eager attention of his parish community, the Pax Christi Catholic community of northern Douglas County who have formed a community of faithful and honest seekers for the way to be Catholic Christians today. When Haugh presented the material, his parish community listened carefully and challenged him more and more to bring out the heart of the gospel for them.

Bleyle could not have written this book without the support of a host of people. His family, especially his parents Don and Mary Ann Bleyle, brother Jeff and sister Jeanie, and his extended family continually checked in on the progress and were eager to read the result. Their encouragement gave the writing energy and kept him on track. His former parish community, the Lakewood United Methodist Church, especially Melanie Rosa and Gordon Benesh who read an early version of one of the chapters, sustained him during the inception of this project and pushed him to articulate clearly the formative practices then so they could use them today.

All three of the authors thank Janet F. Carlson for her work in making the book sound like it was written by one person. This was not an easy task. Each author has a style of his own, and a way of writing sentences that challenged and often frustrated her. But Janet rose to the task, smoothed out the rough places, queried what we really meant, checked our sources, and in every way helped us to turn out the finished book. In many respects, she became a coauthor, and we thank her for her many hours of reading and responding to draft after draft and to what we thought was the final version. Bleyle now has a more sensitive and less fearful appreciation for red pencil queries and comments!

All three authors also acknowledge our first editor, Ross Miller. He responded quickly to our initial proposal, sent gentle reminders that we were very late in sending him the manuscript, and congratulated us enthusiastically for finally finishing the book. We appreciate his vision and enthusiasm. We also thank our second editor, Sarah Stanton, who guided us through the final editing and production of this book. Her grace and attention to detail (and schedules!) spurred us on to careful writing and revising.

But this book would not have been possible without the gentle, persistent, sometimes frustrated, but always enthusiastic support for the project from our partners. Marian Haugh, Jennifer Bleyle, and Janet Carlson paid a high price for letting their spouses loose on a book project together. The hours spent writing were hours spent away from family, and we all three honor them for their support throughout the seemingly endless years of writing by dedicating this book to them. We were not a very holy trinity in writing, but they all were a very holy trinity in support and encouragement.

CHAPTER ONE

Introduction:
Good News Everywhere

Imagine with us an early Christian builder leaving his birthplace, Berytus (modern Beirut), to follow the Roman roads to Rome, the center of empire, where he will help beautify the public buildings with marble. Our Christian, named Theodore ("gift of God") is an expert in building in marble, and Rome has been intent in the last hundred years to make the city sparkle with the beauty of marble facing in order to display not only Rome's wealth but also her splendor and power. Theodore has been a Christian now for twenty years and is proud to say whenever he can witness to another, "I am a Christian" (Christianus sum), a phrase later often repeated by the Christian martyrs before their accusers, but which Theodore uses as a marker of his true identity.

As he walks along the roads the Romans built for their armies, Theodore encounters many different kinds of Christians. Many of them seem very strange to his way of thinking about Christianity, but to him, as long as they can say "Christianus sum" that is all that matters to him. Passing through Antioch, Theodore, a Gentile Christian, encounters many Jewish Christians who still observe Jewish customs and who simultaneously honor Jesus as the Son of God. Their weekly Eucharist seems more like a Passover meal, the Jewish festival meal that commemorates the liberation of the Jews from Egyptian servitude. These Antiochian Christians celebrate their "passover" into eternal life through Jesus's death and resurrection at a passover meal with wine, lamb, flat unleavened bread, and herbs of all sorts. Theodore considers how these Christians seem to have held onto their old roots in their observance.

At a village in Syria, Theodore encounters yet a different Eucharist. Entering the village, he finds that the men and the women of the village do not marry, but remain virgins for life after their baptism. They proclaim proudly "I am a Christian" and "We are a Christian community." Their challenging way of life is symbolized by the humble

1

Eucharist they celebrate every day with bread and water, since wine is forbidden to those dedicated to God. Theodore wonders at their ability to live so harsh a life filled with such intense prayer.

Theodore walks to Byzantium (Constantinople, now Istanbul in Turkey) where he will pick up the Egnatia Road, the famous Roman road that traverses Greece, Macedonia, and Albania and connects with the road to Rome. Here those who say "I am a Christian" seem far wealthier and worldly. They have large homes in which to gather and lavish communal meals on the Lord's Day. They chant the psalms with strange melodies, the men chanting the first verse and the women chanting the second. Their leaders wear rich clothing befitting Roman senators as they preside at the worship service, and there are many deacons who serve them at the table both for the Eucharist and for the festive meal that follows.

Walking the Egnatia Road, he reaches Philippi, a city that Paul had visited a few years before and where he founded a Christian church. There those who say "I am a Christian" seem to be very dignified and wealthy. They are proud of their contribution to Paul's ministry and they use their wealth to help others in their Christian path. They offer to give Theodore work there for him to live with them and adorn their city, but Theodore was called to Rome. Theodore loved their Eucharist: a rich and sweet bread is offered and a fine wine mixed with water. Their Eucharist is celebrated in the morning, and they gather at night for singing psalms and hymns and for a festive love-feast open to all Christians. After eating well, and sleeping better, Theodore leaves the Philippian Christians and moves on.

Arriving at Thessalonika, Theodore encounters yet a different group of people who say "I am a Christian." These Thessalonian Christians expect the end of the world at any time. They watch and wait for the time when Christ will appear in the heavens. Their eucharistic meal is one of anticipation of the end-times, the heavenly feast at which Christ will preside after he returns to judge the world, and it is a meal filled with judgment of the evildoers and praise of the sanctified. Their wine and bread at the Eucharist mark the very blood and body of Christ, the body that was sacrificed for them and preserves them as safe and sanctified until the end-times. Theodore, who believes that the end-times are far off (else why would he go to Rome to build majestic buildings?), finds the Thessalonians too intense for his taste. He is eager to move on.

Theodore travels next to Lychnidos (modern Ohrid in Macedonia) where he finds many shepherds who say, "I am a Christian." Theodore was thrilled to be in the rocky and high mountains among so many humble people. Living on the outskirts of town, these Christians gather weekly for the Sunday Eucharist in the evening. After reading parts of the Bible and singing psalms, their leader offers a crusty bread, cheese, and olives for their Eucharist, a feast that anticipates the wonderful feast when the Great Shepherd Jesus will gather people from the whole world to the heavenly banquet and they will no longer be shepherds but the Lord's sheep. Theodore loves their understanding of themselves as Christians and longs to stay with them for a while, but his journey is soon coming to a close and he presses on.

Stopping briefly at Claudiana (modern Peqin in Albania), Theodore seeks out the Christians there. He finds very poor people living in small mud homes clustered on the outskirts of the village. Their leader welcomes Theodore as if he were Christ himself and asks him if he were a prophet carrying the words of the Lord, but Theodore admits that he is simply a Christian worker going to find work in the empire's great city. Their leader gives thanks in a Eucharist of bread and fish, and having fed Theodore with the presence of the risen Jesus in their midst, they send him on to Rome.

When Theodore finally arrives in Rome, he is amazed where he hears of Christians. Some are Roman nobles who gather at the grand mansions of the rich and celebrate the Eucharist as he saw it at Byzantium, with all the trappings of Roman wealth and privilege. Others are communities of freedmen, meeting in the apartment buildings called "insulae" and celebrating the Eucharist with humble, coarse bread and inexpensive wine. Some are communities of those who were friends of the apostle Paul and they celebrated the Eucharist in which the presence of Jesus was made known among very diverse people, rich and poor, young and old, slave and free, Jew and Gentile. Theodore chooses this Pauline community to attend the Eucharist. He is overjoyed at the spirit that permeates their meeting, and he is well-fed at the meal that follows.

Theodore reflects on the many different ways that Christians lived their lives under the singular banner "I am a Christian." At times it was difficult for him to understand the ways his fellow Christians lived and it made him feel uncomfortable: some never married and never drank wine; others were rich, many were poor; some were shepherds and others city leaders; some celebrated their Eucharist with bread and wine, others with cheese, olives, and fish. But somehow at its core it was all the same thing: people following Jesus as their Lord and following the way of life that Jesus taught in whatever part of the world in which they lived.

Our imaginary traveler Theodore encountered many different expressions of Christian living as he crossed the Roman Empire from east toward the west to Rome, the center of the empire. We used the example of the different ways of celebrating the Eucharist as a point of comparison and to show the great diversity of practice that marked Christians throughout the earliest centuries of Christian expansion and formation. We know it is shocking to think of such diversity in early Christianity, because we all seem to assume that Christianity started as something unified and cohesive and diversity crept in later. But that is not really the case. Diversity in Christianity preceded the uniform way it became generations later. Think of early Christianity in the first few centuries of its existence as a huge kaleidoscope refracting one stream of light through a prism that makes many different shapes and colors appear. That is what Theodore encountered: Jesus Christ refracted through many different communities, people, parts of the empire, expectations, and understanding. Their kaleidoscopic perspectives found expression in the various ways they celebrated the Eucharist—in that sacred meal different theologies, social organization, models of church leadership, ethics, values, and understanding of the "good news of Jesus Christ" found concrete expression.

Each of the communities that Theodore encountered was very different from one another. This great diversity is the hallmark of earliest Christianity. The question that has fascinated us and propelled us to write this book is "How were individual people trained as Christians in these diverse communities?" We wanted to understand the processes that communities created to make a Christian woman or man capable of living in their communities. What did they need to know? What practices were central to the community's life? What understanding of Jesus did the community hold? What attitudes did each community express about who should lead them and how that leadership should be honored by their members? Who should eat with the community? Who should be included in the ritual life of the community and what understanding should they have of the rituals the community performed? How did the community understand the Christian values and mores that held their community together? What was the community's attitude toward wealth, social status, ethnicity, gender, other Christian communities, and the wider world in which they lived out their Christian life?

These are all questions of formation, the processes that communities employ to integrate new members into their lives and to empower their members to participate fully in the community's life. Every community, both then and now, has such systems of formation in operation, but they are not always made explicit. In order to function as a fully empowered member of a community, a person needs to be initiated into a particular way of living, and formation provides that initiation. Certainly in the writing of the four gospels we study in this book, the authors, whoever they were, did not address the question of formation directly, so it demands that we tease out those formative practices from their finished books. So we turned our minds and attention to exploring the systems of formation that animated the communities that produced the four canonical gospels, Mark, Matthew, Luke/Acts, and John. In other words, we read each of the gospels as a manual, a written resource, for the formation of each of the different communities that produced it.

This book is about those concrete expressions of the life that early Christians lived. It is a book about the way Christians lived and integrated into their lives the way they thought, read scriptures, prayed, ate, lived together in community, and formed their communities of faith. It is a book that explores the diversity of Christian formation in the four different places where the gospels (Mark, Matthew, Luke, and John) were produced to help the people in their communities to live their lives saying, "I am a Christian."

An Overview of Christian Literature

To make sense of the great diversity of Christian expressions throughout the Roman Empire, our imaginary traveler Theodore would probably have had to take a course in early Christian literature to explain all the differences. It is no different for us. The gospels were written in a particular time in the history of the Christian religion, and we need to understand both what went before their composition and what followed. (All the gospels were written in the Roman Empire, so we use the term "Roman" to refer to all the people who lived in the Roman Empire, not simply to those who lived in Rome.) So we will begin our journey through the gospels with a brief overview of the earliest Christian writings in the first two centuries of the Christian religion.

We start with Jesus who lived from about 4 BCE until around 29 CE. Jesus was a Jew who lived in Palestine, which then was a Roman province. He is remembered as announcing the reign of God, first in this outlying province and extending over all the world. We have no evidence of Jesus traveling farther afield into the Roman Empire. Jesus did not write anything. Later Christians portray him as primarily teaching orally and performing miraculous deeds, but all these traditions were written down much later—at the earliest about forty years after Jesus's crucifixion and resurrection, when Mark wrote his gospel. Jesus was in all likelihood bilingual, speaking the native Aramaic of Palestine and also speaking Greek, which was the common language of all peoples in the eastern Roman Empire from the time of Alexander the Great onward. Only a few traditions record Jesus speaking Aramaic; most of the traditions of Jesus passed down to future generations preserve his sayings and deeds in the Greek language, and so we assume that Jesus was indeed bilingual. That bilingualism suggests that Jesus probably extended his initial teaching and deeds to include the Roman dominators of his time, or at least that his teaching and deeds very quickly took root in the Roman context. There were many Jews in the time of Jesus who were fully bilingual, and so Jesus was not unusual in that respect. But we must remember that we have little that we can directly connect to the historical person Jesus; most of the information about him comes from later times, after years of oral transmission of his sayings and deeds.

The first period of Christian writing begins with the letters of Paul. Paul, an apostle of Jesus who did not know him when Jesus was alive, received a vision of Jesus around 35 CE—a vision that changed his life and started him on his way to proclaiming Jesus as the inaugurator of a new age. In this new age, God would graft the Gentiles (non-Jews living in the vast Roman Empire) onto the branch of Israel and they would become coheirs with Israel in the fulfillment of God's promises to Israel. Paul's letter to the Galatians, where he tells the story of his life in the church, relates that he spent a few years (probably 35–38 CE) in Arabia preaching the gospel, the announcement of the new age inaugurated by Jesus (Galatians 1:17). In 48 CE, roughly thirteen years after his vision of Jesus, Paul met in Jerusalem with known associates of Jesus during his lifetime: Peter, James, and John. This Jerusalem meeting, as Paul recounts it in the first chapter of Galatians, was a stormy meeting with lots of suspicion about Paul and his mission to the Gentiles and genuine conflict about whether the movement Jesus began really applied to anyone beyond the Jews. In the end, the Jerusalem Christian leaders approved of Paul's mission to the Romans. This was an important moment for Paul and for Christianity, because Paul began planting churches throughout the region in Asia Minor and on the Greek peninsula. But the relationship between Paul and these leaders was always a stormy one, because even after this Jerusalem meeting, Paul reports that he had an altercation with Peter around 48 or 49 CE in Antioch, when Peter refused to eat with non-Jews in a community Paul was nurturing (Galatians 2:11–12). Paul's churches, mostly urban, took deep root, and his mission was a very successful one.

In the process of planting his churches and nurturing the Christian communities in this vast region of the world, Paul wrote letters addressing issues that arose after he planted the church. Paul's earliest letter, written about 50 CE, is to the church in Thessalonika, a major Roman city on the Greek peninsula. Paul wrote his last letter, to the Romans, in about 58 CE, so that the roughly eight-year period of his letter writing came at the end of his ministry of proclaiming the gospel. In these years, he wrote a number of letters to the Corinthian churches, as well as those in Galatia in Asia Minor, Philippi in Greece, Thessalonika in Macedonia, and a letter to a friend about a servant named Philemon. The letter became Paul's primary means of staying in touch with his communities and of providing continued leadership to the churches he founded as they struggled to live out their new lives in the new age Jesus's death and resurrection inaugurated. The tradition holds that Paul was arrested, tried, and sent to Rome where he was martyred about 60 CE.

While Paul engaged in his mission, that is during this first Christian period, ranging roughly from the crucifixion and resurrection of Jesus until the time of the destruction of the Temple in Jerusalem by the Romans in 70 CE, people began to collect the sayings of Jesus and to create catalogs of his deeds. These collections probably reflect the formative practices and interests of the people who gathered them. Sources that the later gospels used seem to indicate that, prior to the gospels' composition, there were already oral and written sources that circulated among the various and diverse Christian communities. These communities used those early sources to support and form their communities. The later Gospel of Thomas, for example, collected sayings of Jesus, some of which have been argued to be the very words of the historical Jesus. There also seems to have been collections of stories about Jesus's miraculous healing of the sick and raising of the dead. These collections, which were very fluid and easily added to by later followers of Jesus who began to speak and to act in the way Jesus did during his lifetime, continued long after the first gospel was written, but the heyday of gathering them took place in these thirty years or so from the crucifixion of Jesus and the composition of the first gospel. In that same time period, we have only the letters of Paul to document the growth and expansion of the religious movement Jesus began.

Paul's visit to the Christian leaders in Jerusalem preceded a serious Jewish uprising in Palestine that began in 66. In that year, fighting erupted in Palestine that aimed to free the Jews from Roman domination. In 67, the emperor Nero appointed Vespasian, a general who was soon to become emperor, to suppress the Jewish revolt. In 69, the Roman army proclaimed Vespasian emperor while in Palestine, and he left Palestine for Rome to take up his rule as Nero's successor, appointing Titus, his son, to continue the Jewish war in 69. In 70, Titus destroyed the Temple in Jerusalem and took the spoils of the Temple as well as many Jewish slaves to Rome. This failed Jewish revolt had serious consequences for both Jews and Christians. Judaism, now without a temple in which to offer the required sacrifices and without a center for the faith, had to find a new road. Any hope of keeping Christianity closely tied to Jerusalem and Palestine, as the Jerusalem leaders who met with Paul earlier had hoped, died with the destruction of the Temple. Both Judaism and Christianity had to find new directions for their movements. After the destruction of the Temple, what we now call Rabbinic Judaism (about which we will speak later in this book) began to mold Israelite religion into the form which we know as Judaism today.

Following this Jewish uprising, the period of Paul's letter writing, and the collection of traditions about Jesus (whether they came from Jesus or from his followers), we begin the period of the writing of the gospels (68 CE until about 110). We do not actually know the names of the people who wrote the gospels. Early in Christian history, traditions attached names from among the known associates of Jesus to the gospels. That later attribution to a known associate is why the gospels are always "the gospel according to" Mark, Matthew, Luke, or John, and students of the New Testament simply refer to them by their traditional attributions. So Mark wrote the first gospel in Rome around 68 CE. Matthew wrote around 80 CE. Luke wrote his first volume, which we call his gospel, around 90, and John wrote his around 110. The four gospels in the New Testament were written during a roughly forty-year period. The time of Jesus and the time of the gospels were separated by a serious military conflict and a tumultuous period of religious redefinition. In many respects, the gospels reflect various responses to this problem of redefinition, and they reflect the new and various ways that Christian communities found to understand Jesus, themselves, and the new way of living Jesus announced. The formative practices shifted and changed as the political, religious, and social environment changed over time.

During this same period we have letters written by followers of Paul in his name, extending the ministry of Paul to other communities after his death. The letter written pseudonymously, that is under the name of Paul, to the Colossians was written in 80, while the pseudonymous letter to the Ephesians was written around 95 CE. Both the later Pauline communities and the communities that produced the gospels were struggling to find their way, to articulate their new way of living in a decidedly Roman context, and to find ways of incorporating new members in a time of redefinition and discovery.

That period of redefinition and discovery, however, did not end with the books that we now have in our New Testament. There were many other Christian writings that emerged in the beginning of the second century, following the writing of the Gospel of John. We have the Gospel of Thomas, a collection of sayings of Jesus, published around 110 CE. We also have the letters of Bishop Ignatius of Antioch written at the same time. Christian novels, called the "apocryphal acts of the apostles," were composed during the second century. These novels describe the sayings and miraculous deeds of various apostles (Peter, Paul, Thecla, Thomas, Andrew, and Phillip among others) as they took the Christian religion to the far reaches of the Roman Empire and beyond, as far as India. Christians also began to speculate about the infancy of Jesus and his family life, the years before the beginning of his public ministry. We have infancy gospels attributed to James, Thomas, and Matthew, which all explore the young years of the God-man Jesus, information not contained in any of the gospels we now have in our New Testament. And there were many other kinds of gospels: the Gospel of Mary Magdalene, the Secret Sayings of James, the Gospel of Judas, and others, which explored the various postresurrection appearances of

Jesus and the teaching that he continued to provide Christians long after his embodied life on earth. Christians were prolific writers whose imaginations and interests seemed only to grow over the years. And, each of these gospels, whether in the New Testament or not, expresses different formative practices, different systems of formation.

It was at the end of the second century that the books we now have in the New Testament were beginning to take shape as we know them. From among these various and diverse sources, Christian leaders began to decide which books were the most basic for all Christians to read and revere. Four gospels were selected from the array of options (Mark, Matthew, Luke/Acts, and John), as well as the authentic letters of Paul, and other letters written under Paul's, James's, and Peter's names. The book of Revelation was slower in being accepted, but in the end it was included among those books that would constitute the New Testament. Although the process of creating a canon of the Bible is a complex one that we will not explore here, we can safely say that the process of forming the canon also reflects a concern for Christian formation. The bishops of the church from the second through the fourth centuries wanted to create a body of literature that would form communities in specific ways around correlative traditions about Jesus. Even though the four canonical gospels differ greatly from one another, they were forged into a cohesive story that every Christian community could employ as the basis for their lives. At the same time the bishops also wanted to rule out other formative practices that they found problematic. Some gospels, such as those of Thomas and Mary, were found to form people in ways the bishops found objectionable, so they were not included in the New Testament. It was this process of formation that guided the bishops in their decisions about the canon of the New Testament.

This book, however, only deals with the formation of the four gospels included in the New Testament. From this brief overview, it is evident that these gospels were composed under very different and often conflicted circumstances. They reflect the creative energies of people and communities across the Roman Empire as they sought to understand Jesus, the reign of God that Jesus announced, the new age that Paul preached, and the new way of life to which they were called to live out their faith. It is to those gospels that we now turn.

Reading Jesus, Reading Gospels

In our times, readers go to the New Testament to find out about Jesus. Readers want information about Jesus because they believe in him, or are curious about what he taught, or are a person of another religion wanting to understand the faith of colleagues or friends. Modern readers assume that the proper place to find information about Jesus is the Bible, specifically the New Testament, yet more specifically, the gospels. This has not always been the case, though. In the Middle Ages, people went to the Bible to learn about the moral and spiritual messages hidden in the text of the Bible: they knew about Jesus through the liturgical cycle of the church year (Christmas, Easter, Pentecost, for example), through stories told in preaching and in the art that adorned their churches, through chancel plays that dramatized stories from the Bible, and through the monks and nuns who taught them the faith. During the Reformation, theologians went to the Bible to learn about justification by faith and to counter theologies that stressed the more Catholic emphasis on works: they knew about Jesus through preaching and education. Even today, people often look to the Bible to "prove" what they already believe, whether that is about the justice of feeding the poor or the wisdom of respecting the environment. Each generation uses the Bible in different ways to gain the knowledge and information they need to live their lives.

In the early days of the church, however, before there was a New Testament or even gospels, people learned about Jesus and the Empire of God (a term we consider a more accurate rendition of the familiar "Kingdom of God") about which Jesus preached in different ways. Most often, people heard about Jesus's Empire of God from wandering prophets and teachers who moved from village to village and from town to town in order to spread the news about it. Some very few of these wanderers might have actually known Jesus in person, but most of them probably only had a visionary experience of Jesus that propelled them to begin telling the story of Jesus, and the Empire of God that Jesus proclaimed. In fact, *most* of the early participants in Jesus's Empire of God were probably this visionary type.

The apostle Paul, whose writings make up a significant part of the New Testament, stands as the best example of this sort of wandering announcer of the divine Empire who did not know Jesus in person, but who had a vision of Jesus after Jesus's resurrection. Paul moved from city to city, founding communities of those who entered the new life God opened through Jesus Christ, nurturing them through letters, and continuing to connect with them through various visitors and colleagues. After the wanderers like Paul did their work, there were probably also local leaders, both women and men, who kept information about Jesus and the Empire of God in order to teach others, to lead worship, and to train new generations in the Christian way of life. Before there were written gospels, people relied upon information communicated orally for their knowledge of the Empire of God that Jesus proclaimed. Eventually Christians would begin to write down these oral traditions, but at least for the first thirty or forty years the participants in the Empire relied upon these wandering prophets to bring and to produce for them the words of Jesus about the Empire of God, a process that continued in Christian books not included in the New Testament for at least another century.

So what were these formative visionary experiences? What did they see that propelled them into the Empire of God? What they saw was a divinely inspired revelation of a new way to live organized around a different way of understanding God. In the resurrected Jesus, the holy man whose death God made effective for salvation by raising him again to life, they saw the reality of the Empire that God was in the act of creating among both Jews and the other people of the Roman Empire. They knew the Empire of God was a reality because Jesus was crucified and died, but then God raised him from the dead to continue the miraculous work of the Empire of God among both Jews and others. For these visionaries, both itinerant and stable communities, God was not far-off, distant, vaguely related to the fate of the people living in the repressive Roman Empire. God was present, active, engaged, and putting in place a new world order that centered on God as the emperor of the world and Jesus as God's earthly representative. Jesus's ministry, death, and especially his resurrection, pointed to this new Empire. Jesus did not point to himself as the center of his work, but to the Empire of God that was breaking into the world. Jesus was the messenger of a divine, glorious Empire, albeit a very important messenger. In his mission, Jesus initiated the Empire, but during his lifetime and especially in his postdeath appearances Jesus authorized and empowered women and men to continue building that new divine Empire until the entire world was under divine authority. The wandering prophets and the local leaders such as teachers, bishops, and deacons were those people who had experienced the empowerment from Jesus and who continued Jesus's work for generations following Jesus's death.

Although it seems pretty strange to us today, the earliest participants in the movement begun by Jesus to live in the Empire of God were not so much interested in Jesus as they were in the Empire Jesus announced. We, of course, find Jesus infinitely interesting, but the early followers of the divine Empire were more interested in the Empire and the way to live in it than about real, hard facts about Jesus. Paul, for example, actually tells us very little about the person of Jesus: he writes that Jesus was born of a woman (that is, that he was a real human being, and not a phantasm of some sort), born a Jew (Galatians 4:4; Romans 1:5 and 9:4), suffered, died, and was resurrected (Romans 4:24), and then appeared to many people at one time (1 Corinthians 15:5). That is all that mattered to Paul about the person of Jesus. The death and resurrection of Jesus were important to him, but not the manner of his death nor the manner of his resurrection. Paul was not even interested in what Jesus said or taught, but just the fact that God had raised him from the dead in order to announce the new Empire of God and to build a new world order based in God's Spirit. What was important to Paul and to other early participants in the divine Empire was the new way of living that Jesus instigated and the door to that Empire that Jesus opened to both the Jews and others.

As time wore on, stories about the Empire that Jesus told, or more accurately that Jesus inspired people under the power of the Spirit to tell, began to be repeated over and over again in different contexts. Certainly some of the words spoken in Jesus's name by these emissaries of the Empire of God had actually been spoken by Jesus; they were his very words. But many of the things attributed to Jesus actually came from these authorized people and wandering prophets, the bearers of the news of the divine Empire. They spoke to people in Jesus's name, with Jesus's authority, with Jesus's Spirit within them. Their words came directly from Jesus in a different way, not from the historical figure, but from the divine inspiration emerging from the movement begun by his presence. But the source of the sayings about Jesus did not matter to the early participants in the movement Jesus inaugurated. Jesus was Jesus no matter how he was made present: either through words preserved in his memory; or words produced by prophets who in turn created words of Jesus to accommodate new circumstances not addressed by Jesus himself; or whether through a kind of thinking that brought Jesus's mind to bear on new situations. Ultimately all the teachings came from God, through Jesus, to the world—whether by Jesus's direct speech, or by speech inspired by a vision of Jesus to inaugurate the Empire of God, or proclaimed by Paul, or even refracted and rewritten by the later gospel writers. The presence of God's Empire was what really mattered.

Not everyone heard the story about the Empire of God in the same way, however. These early participants in the Empire Jesus preached, especially in the long period of oral transmission, lived in vastly different communities and contexts and heard the message in different ways. Some communities, like the Thessalonians to whom Paul wrote, heard the message about the Empire of God as something happening immediately. These Thessalonians assumed they were living in the end-times when Jesus would come down from the sky and bring judgment to the world. They waited eagerly for this immediate second coming. These are called "apocalyptic Christians," because they awaited daily the final apocalypse that would bring the Empire of God into physical reality.

Other people during the period of oral transmission heard the Empire of God inaugurated by Jesus as God sending yet another sage, a speaker of divine wisdom. We read in the Israelite scriptural books Wisdom of Solomon (chapters 6 through 10) and Proverbs (chapter 8) that God sends God's divine mind down to each generation to instruct them in God's law, in the way that God would have God's people live and relate not only to each other but also to those outside Israel. The sage, coming to each generation, carries God's wisdom and interprets it for the people. Many participants in Jesus's Empire of God thought of the Empire as embodying a new wisdom, a new way of living, a new instruction from God about how to conduct one's personal and corporate lives. Many participants considered Jesus to be this Wisdom of God, the Word of God made flesh as John's gospel calls him (John 1:14), this conveyor of the divine mind to the people. Since parables and other wisdom sayings were produced both by Jesus and by those Jesus empowered in later generations, this interpretation of Jesus's status as the Wisdom of God made perfect sense. These participants in the Empire of God might be called the "wisdom followers" and they were not necessarily completely distinct from the apocalyptic. In other words, participants might have multiple lenses through which to understand the Empire and the role of Jesus in inaugurating the Empire.

Yet another group of these early participants in the Empire of God heard the message of the divine Empire through the filter of healing. Jesus and his followers were known for their healing of the sick without asking for payment (expecting payment was common in the ancient medical professions). People interpreted miraculous healing as a sign of God's presence, or for a Roman, as a sign of an intervening divine power. In an age when medicine was expensive and mostly reserved for those who had financial means, these healing miracles spoke loudly to the common people. That Jesus healed, and that participants in the Empire of God healed others, spoke loudly of the power and energy of the divine Empire. Jews had traditions from the prophets like Elisha and Elijah who healed the sick, so when they heard of the healing miracles of Jesus and his followers, they interpreted those miracles within the context of the prophetic healing in their scripture. The Jewish lens correlated the Empire's healing to the prophetic tradition. Likewise, Romans and Greeks had traditions about the god Aesclepius who could heal the sick with great power, and so when they heard the stories of healing miracles by Jesus and his followers, they correlated them to the god's healing power and authority. Both heard the stories of healing miracles, but each interpreted them from within their own cultural frame.

In this pre-gospel early period, there were also participants in Jesus's Empire of God who had a more school-like perspective. These junior scholars took the wisdom sayings of Jesus and elaborated them with stories that showed how these stories could apply to different circumstances. The process of elaborating sayings formed an important part of the education of the young, so it is logical that these more educated people would use their familiar techniques on the sayings they had received—sayings either directly from Jesus or indirectly from Jesus through other empowered emissaries. The test of the veracity of these elaborated stories rested on the perceived accuracy of the context of the story to the life and times of Jesus and his earliest participants in the Empire. If the story sounded plausibly like Jesus would have acted and spoken, then the story was true for those hearers. Hearers deemed the elaboration true if the story about Jesus or his followers correlated to their understanding of Jesus and the Empire of God. These elaborated stories are called "pronouncement stories" (or *chreiai* in Greek). These participants in Jesus's Empire of God worked with the sayings so that they made sense to their communities.

Another important lens for both Jesus and the Empire of God demands mention: the Israelite scriptures. Roman and Jewish Christians (then as now) turned to the Israelite scriptures as an important and formative source for what God was doing in their midst through Jesus. The Psalms of David in particular became a constant motif not only on the lips of Jesus and the early participants in the Empire of God, but these psalms were also supplemented with the writings of the Israelite prophets, stories about Abraham and his covenant with God, Jonah and the whale, stories about Moses parting the waters of the Red Sea to let the Israelites pass through on dry land. Christians wove these and many other references into their understanding of Jesus and the Empire so that the story of Jesus, the significance of the Empire, and the early work of the church became one interwoven fabric.

Although oral teaching continued for more than two centuries following the death of Jesus, during the heyday of oral traditions (roughly 30–70 CE), some of these stories and traditions about Jesus and the participants in the Empire of God began to be collected. Some folks began to collect stories about Jesus's and his followers' miraculous healing of the sick. Jewish hearers would mold these stories to fit the way Elisha and Elijah healed, while Romans might tell the stories in the same way that Aesclepius healed. Either way, the stories of miraculous healing began to be written down in collections of healing stories.

Still other communities and individuals began collecting sayings spoken by the person or in a vision of Jesus as the sayings of a sage (a wise man). These collections of the sayings of the wise-man Jesus were very popular, because they were the most familiar way for a teacher to teach new followers. In 1945 in Egypt the Gospel of Thomas was discovered and this gospel consists of 114 sayings of Jesus without any stories attached. The sayings begin with "Jesus said" and then a series of sayings and parables, most of which are familiar to us from the New Testament gospels follows. So, we have examples of these sorts of collections, and we know that Matthew and Luke used yet another collection for the composition of their gospels.

Still other communities and individuals began to elaborate these collected sayings into stories that showed the way Jesus and the early participants in the Empire of God applied their knowledge and engaged with other schools of religious and philosophical thought. These expanded and contextualized sayings began the process of putting the words and deeds of Jesus and those engaged in the Empire of God into narrative form. Early on Christians began weaving stories and sayings together, presumably to remember them and to arrange them to make the biggest impact on their hearers. These early narratives probably served to help form their communities.

And many early participants in the Empire began to collect stories and references from the Israelite scriptures that seemed to connect with their experience of the Empire of God. Some of these collections of scriptural references related to Jesus, like the Suffering Servant poems of the prophet Isaiah (chapter 42); still others related to miraculous events from the Psalms, and from Wisdom. These collections of references helped the participants in the Empire of God to understand how their experiences related to the past deeds of God among God's people. These collections emerged from a kind of meditation on their current experience of Jesus's Empire against the background of their knowledge of the Israelite scriptures.

So now we have two different kinds of material that were available to later participants in the Empire of God. One kind of material related to the elements of the life of Jesus for whom Paul is the best early recorder. These elements included the information that Jesus was born of a woman, that he was born a Jew, that he had a meal with his followers on the night before he was handed over to trial (1 Corinthians 10 and 13), that he was crucified, died, resurrected, and appeared to many people at one time. Later Christians also had this information about Jesus, the one who inaugurated the Empire of God, for their use as they lived out the Empire of God in their own contexts. The information in their writings is sketchy about the details of Jesus's life, perhaps because people simply were not interested in those details. Later (probably beginning around 65 CE, or roughly forty years after the death of Jesus), people wondered about the announcer of the Empire of God and focused on Jesus as the central voice of that Empire, but early on, there was little interest in the details of Jesus's life and ministry.

Later Christians began to write their gospels, nearly forty (the Gospel of Mark) to seventy (the Gospel of John) years after the death and resurrection of Jesus, and they used a second kind of source material to relate to the elements for the construction of their gospels. Here the collections of miracles, sayings, pronouncement stories, the Israelite scriptures, and the letters of Paul form the earliest written sources for later writers. Mark, in fact, used all of these sources in composing his gospel. And after Mark's gospel circulated widely, Matthew and Luke used Mark's gospel as a source, in addition to the sources Mark himself had used. We will return, later in this introduction, to explain this process more fully.

The Function and Context of the Written Gospels

So if early participants in the Empire of God got their information about Jesus and the Empire of God from these sources, then why would they write gospels? What purpose did the written gospels serve in a context where oral traditions (both those stemming from Jesus and from those who had a vision of Jesus) formed the primary means of communicating information about the Empire and the person who inaugurated it? This is where our expectations about the gospels differ from early Christian expectations. Whereas we go to the gospels as a primary means of information about Jesus, early Christians used the gospels as means of forming their communities in the particular way of living in the Empire of God appropriate to their circumstances. We go to the gospels to find out *what* should be believed, while the early Christians developed the gospels to figure out *how* they should *live* in their particular Christian community, to *understand* the Empire of God from their particular community's perspective, and to *interpret* the significance of Jesus who inaugurated the Empire as Jesus is to be understood in their own communities. Communities produced the gospels to help them train their own and future generations in a particular way of living, understanding God, and making sense of Jesus's role in the Empire of God. In this way, the writing process itself became a formative process, and the gospels became formative documents.

To understand the difference between how we approach the gospel and how the early church approached the gospel, we need carefully to attend to the chronology. But we will begin with a correlative situation that will help explain the difference. The American civil rights movement centers in the mind of most twenty-first century Americans on the life of Martin Luther King, Jr. (1929–1968). King served as the central spokesman for the civil rights movement at a crucial point in its history and his magnetic personality dramatized the African-American struggle for equal rights. But the history of the civil rights movement extends further back into American history. At one level, it began even before the American Civil War with the movement to abolish slavery. The later nineteenth century also witnessed the growth of the suffrage movement to give equal voting rights to women. In the twentieth century, however, the civil rights movement extended outward to include the work of many other people and organizations that had worked for many years for the civil rights of minority and African-American communities. Some examples include: the executive order of July 26, 1948, integrating the Armed Forces; the May 17, 1954, Supreme Court ruling in *Brown vs. the Board of Education of Topeka, Kansas,* that ruled racially segregated schools unconstitutional; the December 1, 1955, refusal of NAACP member Rosa Parks to give up her seat on a Montgomery, Alabama, bus for a white person; the 1957 founding of the Southern Christian Leadership Conference; the federal intervention that same year by President Eisenhower forcing the Little Rock, Arkansas, Central High School to allow nine black students to matriculate; the formation in 1966 by Stokely Carmichael and others of the Student Nonviolent Coordinating Committee; the organization of the Black Nation of Islam and the Black Panthers; and many other people and organizations working toward civil rights for African-Americans. But for most Americans the real story of civil rights focuses on Martin Luther King's "I have a dream" speech during the March on Washington in 1963. From that speech onward, the civil rights movement merged with the life and death of Martin Luther King, who was assassinated in 1968. The story of American civil rights can certainly be told from the perspective alone of Martin Luther King's work, life, and martyrdom, and that story would tell the big picture of the struggle for equal rights for minority populations in the United States. That story remains a true and powerful story, but in telling that story other elements of the civil rights movement, equally important in the history, have been eclipsed. The large story of Martin Luther King overshadows the story of other important people and events in the struggle for equal rights. These other stories become subsumed under the story about Martin Luther King. The same story takes on different meanings according to how the story is told, who tells the story, the context in which the story is told, and the purpose of the storyteller in telling the story. All the stories relate the same larger story, but they tell it from different perspectives, at different times, and for different purposes. The same has occurred in the collection of materials for the New Testament: a particular story of Jesus has been used as the central focus of a story that had a history before the gospels were written.

So now let's look at the chronology more carefully. Jesus was born around 4 BCE and died in 29 CE; he was born under the emperor Augustus and was condemned and crucified under the emperor Tiberius, who ruled from 14–37 CE. Jesus's birth occurred during a kind of renaissance time for the Roman Empire, when it was at peace, experiencing economic prosperity, and exercising extensive power over a large empire. Jesus was born when the concept of empire took deep and abiding interest, since the imperial period of Roman history began with Caesar Augustus. In an ironic sense, Jesus's and Augustus's empires were born at the same time. Jesus's positing of a new Empire, just as Augustus had, could certainly be interpreted by the Roman authorities as a threat to Roman hegemony, and it was. That threat led to Jesus's crucifixion as the "Emperor of the Judeans," whom the Romans ruled with great force.

Paul received his revelation of Jesus in about 35 CE, began to found communities throughout Greece and Asia Minor for over a decade, and wrote his letters to various Christian communities in the eight years between 50–58 CE, during the last years of the emperor Claudius and the first four of the fifteen-year reign of Nero. These were troubled years for the Christians. Paul seemed constantly to be getting into trouble with political authorities, who apparently attempted to arrest him a number of times, as well as with the Jewish religious authorities who were not pleased with his proselytizing and preaching about Jesus. Nero openly persecuted the Christians and blamed them for burning Rome.

The Roman historian Tacitus even says that Nero used Christians as human candles to provide light for a garden party (*Annals* 15:44). When Paul wrote his letters, the times had changed significantly from the earlier Augustan time of Jesus. The difference in context is noticeable in the letters.

The first gospel, Mark, was composed in 68 during Nero's principate. While Paul wrote at the beginning of Nero's troubling rule for Christians, Mark wrote at the end, when Nero seemed far more volatile and hostile to Christians. The chaos at the end of his regime made the political, social, and religious context perilous for those perceived to be hostile to the Roman people and the emperor. It was not a happy time for Christians, although Christian communities clearly seemed to have grown and developed in these perilous times. But the times demanded caution and, as we will see, Mark's community used great caution and skill in presenting their story about Christianity.

Matthew composed his gospel during the reign of Vespasian (69–79) and his son Titus (79–81). Vespasian was proclaimed emperor in Palestine by his army during the Jewish wars, and it was Titus who, upon Vespasian's return to Rome to become emperor, continued the war, destroyed the Temple in Jerusalem, and brought the spoils of the Temple to Rome in a triumphal entry. Titus's triumph has been memorialized in the famous "Arch of Titus" (built in 81 CE) that celebrates the victory of Rome over the Jews. The Jewish world as Matthew knew it had ended. The Temple was no longer, and the Jewish religious rites that centered on the Temple could no longer be performed. Without the Temple, Judaism as it had been practiced could no longer exist. Therefore Rabbinic Judaism itself came into being as the rabbis attempted to translate Temple practice into daily household practices for Jews, who could no longer fulfill their obligations in the Temple. The rabbis inaugurated a new formation for a challenging time in Jewish history.

Luke composed his gospel, the first book of his two-book project that includes Acts of the Apostles, during the stormy reign of Domitian (81–96), another son of Vespasian. Domitian's response to different ways of living and thinking was execution. He executed philosophers, political opponents, and he persecuted Christians—all out of a sense of maintaining and developing the public moral stature of the Roman people. Although ruthless, he maintained high ideals for the people, while at the same time entertaining a very non-Roman sense of his own superiority that demanded a kind of personal adulation by his people. Luke's gospel reflects the high moral standard set by the emperor.

Luke's second book, Acts of the Apostles, and John's gospel were composed during the reign of Trajan (98–117). These books present two very different perspectives on the organization and theology of the Christian communities. During Trajan's reign, the Romans completely decimated Jerusalem, renaming it *Aelia Capitolina*, and brought to a conclusion the long Jewish Wars. From yet

•

another part of the Roman Empire, we know more about Christian practices in this period than any other because we have a letter from Pliny, a Roman governor, to Trajan asking what should be done to people professing Christianity in his Roman province. Trajan had outlawed secret organizations, and Christians appeared to Pliny as one such secret organization. Trajan did not advocate the execution of Christians merely for calling themselves Christians, but only if they were recalcitrant and obstructive, when, for example, the Christians refused to offer worship to the emperor. Not necessarily a fun time for Christians! Both the Acts of the Apostles and the Gospel of John reflect this time of growth and renewal of the Christian faith: Acts develops the apostolic authority of the leaders of Jesus's movement, while John refers back to an earlier model of church organization and revelation with diverse leaders and modes of revelation.

Even this cursory chronological outline within its Roman context shows how important it is to read the New Testament in its historical context in order to understand the message that each piece of literature communicates. The Roman history of this period, like the history of the American civil rights movement in our own times, shifted and changed dramatically over the course of the four decades during which the gospels were written. These dramatic shifts over time meant that the early Christian churches organized themselves and produced their gospels in significantly different times and places over a short period of time from about 68 until 110 CE. There was not a unidimensional Roman Empire against which the Empire of God was articulated, but many different empires over the course of the years. As the context shifted and changed, so did the story about the Christian communities, the Empire of God, and Jesus.

In order of composition (the order we follow in studying the history of Christianity and the history of Christian practice), we begin with Paul's letters written 50–58 CE and we read the gospels as later literature reflecting different and later times (from 68–110 CE). So we begin with wandering prophets carrying the word about the Empire of God, beginning sometime during Jesus's lifetime (about 4 BCE–29 CE) and move toward reading the gospels in their historical contexts. Most modern people, however, read the other way. They begin with the gospels and try to fit the unusual Paul into the picture portrayed by the very different kind of writing in the gospels. They read the gospels first, then Paul; but in contrast the early church collected Paul first, then the gospels into the New Testament. The world of the early Jesus movements and the Empire of God look very different if they are read, chronologically, as following Paul. Not only does the chronological reading show the difference between the gospels and their environments, but it also points up the very great difference between the gospels' pastoral context of Jesus wandering about the Palestinian countryside and the urban and sophisticated churches that Paul founded and to whom he wrote his letters.

The difference between the images of the communities to which Paul wrote and the images of Jesus in the gospels has significant impact on how we read the gospels. If we read the four gospels first, and then read Paul's letters, we have an image of a very simple collection of uneducated people following Jesus and eventually converting the whole Roman Empire in the next few centuries. The story from this perspective focuses on the details of Jesus's life, not on the information about the Empire of God that Jesus proclaimed. It is a pastoral and agrarian movement that began in the countryside and had little to do with city life.

If we read the letters of Paul first and then read the gospels (which were written after Paul), we immediately find ourselves in a sophisticated, reasonably literate, rhetorically knowledgeable urban society brimming with energy about the Empire of God. Paul's letters describe messengers moving from large city to large city in the Roman Empire. Paul himself has a staff to whom he dictates his letters, who prepare the letters for distribution, and collect copies for future reference and use. Paul also connects with a large number of people who have various specific functions within the organization of the churches. Just a cursory reading of Romans 16 tells that story loudly: coworkers, leaders of house churches, other apostles, messengers, friends—all relate as people known to Paul in various cities in the Empire. Any interest in Jesus's life was later satisfied with the composition of the Gospel of Mark (68 CE).

One kind of reading based on the gospels argues for a Palestinian rural origin for Christianity among largely agrarian people; the other, following Paul's letters, argues for a more sophisticated urban and educationally advanced origin for Christianity among mostly urban poor and middle-class people. The one reading focuses upon the Jewish and Israelite context; the other focuses on the Greek and Roman context. Both are present in the New Testament, but how we read it becomes an important lens through which to see the development of Christian practice and formation.

The Synoptic Problem

The lenses become even more complicated when we ask why the four gospels in the New Testament were written the way they were. If, as we argue, earliest Christianity was of the Pauline variety, an urban and urbane movement, why do the gospels portray Jesus as a Palestinian peasant leading a largely rural movement? Why did they write like that at a time when that idyllic, rural story contrasted so much with the life experience of urban Christians often living in dangerous circumstances? These are interesting questions. For a variety of reasons that will be addressed in the chapter on the Gospel of Mark, Mark, the first gospel, created the literary fiction of an idyllic time in the history of the

Empire of God, when Jesus walked around as an itinerant prophet and sage of the new world order. This literary fiction became a literary tradition in the gospels that were written later. Matthew, Luke, and John wrote long after the Romans razed the Jerusalem Temple, an important center of the story about Jesus and the Empire. So Mark created the story line that the other gospels followed. So what is the relationship of Matthew, Luke, and John to Mark. The answer to that question relates to a problem of the literary relationship of the gospels. The later gospels, using Mark's gospel, continued Mark's literary fiction; that is, they are literary dependents of Mark. This leads us to something scholars call "the synoptic problem": why do Mark, Matthew, and Luke read so much alike, even though they were written at different times? We turn to the explanation of that problem now.

New Testament scholars have long known that Mark was the first gospel written. We date Mark to a time before the destruction of the Temple in 70 CE. When you lay the gospels side by side in order to view them together (a synopsis or a "looking together"), you discover that Matthew and Luke follow Mark's narrative order. Not only do Matthew and Luke follow Mark's order, most of the words in Mark are found word for word in Matthew and Luke. Matthew and Luke sound like they are telling the same story not because they are independent sources for information about Jesus, but because they use the same source document, the Gospel of Mark, as the basis for their gospels. These three gospels, because they show both narrative and verbal similarities that can readily be seen when they are placed side by side synoptically, are called "the synoptic gospels." What makes the stories of Mark, Matthew, and Luke similar is the fact that two of them (Matthew and Luke) use the other, Mark, as the source for their writing.

But there are also verbal agreements between Matthew and Luke that show that they used another similar source in writing their gospels. These verbal agreements and overlapping stories emerge in the sayings and parables attributed to Jesus. Matthew and Luke seem to have used another similar, if not common, source. The two-source hypothesis, an explanation of the sources used by Matthew and Luke to develop their gospels, argues that in addition to Mark, Matthew and Luke each used a similar collection of the sayings of Jesus (often designated by Q, the first letter of the German word *Quelle*, which means "source") to supplement the narrative they found in Mark. These sayings portray Jesus as a sage, a wise person who brings the mind of God to new generations. Matthew and Luke clearly thought that the story they inherited from their written source, Mark, was not sufficient for their purposes. So Matthew and Luke used two sources: the Gospel of Mark provides the outline; the Sayings Source Q provides additional teaching material to fill out their understanding of the Empire of God through the sayings attributed to Jesus. Recall that we said that these sayings collections were not the exact words of the historical Jesus alone, but also authorized sayings produced by prophets who interpreted the Empire of God in different contexts and periods of time and who spoke in Jesus's name to distant people.

What is interesting about this use of similar sources is the freedom that each community had in rewriting the story. Matthew and Luke freely used and adapted Mark for their own purposes. They changed his language a bit, adjusted the way Mark presented Jesus, supplemented Mark's short sayings and the small collection of parables (mostly found in chapter 4) with a full-fledged and extensive collection of sayings from another source (the Sayings Source Q), and in many ways changed the story significantly to fit their own communities, interests, and understanding of Jesus and the Empire of God. Once again, it is the differences between the gospels, and not their similarities, that leads the way to understanding the communities that produced, read, and worshiped with these gospels.

John's gospel sticks out as something even more different. John's gospel seems to be aware of the story as Mark, Matthew, and Luke have developed it, but seems resistant, if not hostile, to it. John's gospel changes the order of the Markan narrative, reinterprets the healing miracles as signs of the presence of God in Jesus, elevates minor characters in the synoptic gospels to major roles, and portrays Jesus as giving long and involved revelation speeches to a wide assortment of people both inside Jesus's inner circle of followers and outside to Romans and Jews of all sorts. What enabled John to tell such a different story? Why was it possible for John to be different from the others?

Again, when looking at the differences between the gospels, keen observers note the very different perspectives given to familiar things. Clearly each of the communities that produced these four gospels perceived themselves authorized and empowered to tell the story in a different way. Mark, as the first writer of a gospel, produced a remarkable story about Christian origins that at once was idyllic, rural, mostly uneducated, and only occasionally involved in the cities under Roman rule. We will understand more about Mark's amazing skill in producing this image in the next chapter when we study the first gospel, but in the meantime we simply observe that Mark creates an idealized itinerant rural explanation for Christianity with disciples and followers who seem not to understand what Jesus and the Empire of God is really about.

Mark created the story line. Matthew and Luke, however, inherited that story and began to change it to suit their communities. Matthew builds the story into various educational regimes because Matthew's gospel emerges from a kind of Christian rabbinic school, schools that made it possible for Judaism to exist after the destruction of the Temple in 70 CE. Luke goes even further than Matthew. Luke not only reframes Mark's story by adding long speeches of Jesus taken from the Sayings Source Q, but Luke adds a whole second book, the Acts of the Apostles, to supplement the gospel. The story of Jesus was not sufficient for Luke to explain Christian origins; he needed to expand the story to include the development of the church. Whereas Matthew takes on a more Jewish flair, Luke/Acts takes on a more Roman persona. John takes yet another perspective. We argue that John does not like the directions that Luke/Acts and Matthew have taken and that John's gospel at once criticizes the state of the church in the first decade of the second century CE, and also returns to an image of the earliest Christian communities as communities of prophets who have visions of Jesus and speak in Jesus's name to the whole world. So John's gospel is a kind of second-century renewal movement going back to a different model of Christian origins and a different understanding of the Empire of God and the church that encapsulates it.

The synoptic problem, the two-source hypothesis, and the uniqueness of the Gospel of John all point to an understanding of Christian empowerment that is central to our understanding of Christian origins. The reason we have four very different gospels that use their sources in unique and diverse ways is that each different community understood themselves as empowered to enact the Empire of God in ways appropriate to their context. Jesus did not proclaim a single Empire of God that was uniform in every context, but he authorized people to enact the Empire of God in whatever way they knew how. Jesus empowered the diversity of expressions of the Empire of God, and the proof of that empowerment rests in the diversity and unique perspectives of each of the gospels found in the New Testament. The diversity and the unique perspectives speak of the rich diversity that lay at the heart of the Empire of God that Jesus inaugurated.

The Gospels and Formation

We argue that the diversity and unique perspectives of each of the gospels relate to their community's systems of formation and religious practices that emerged for their particular location and historical context. Historical context as well as regional differences, as our traveling marble-builder Theodore realized, made possible regional variations that had an important impact on the way Christianity developed. The vastness of the Roman Empire combined with the unique environment of every community's enactment of the Empire of God meant that communities at great distances from one another would not necessarily grow and develop in the same way. Variations and differences would develop in response to each community's history and context. Theodore saw this close at hand. Practices such as the Eucharist or baptism might take on local character and express different aspects of tradition. The outline of the actions (eating or washing) might be the same, but the manner of performing them, the language used, the associations and interpretative systems would vary greatly. Like the diverse practices, there were different Christologies (understandings of Jesus), different ways of reading scripture, multiple philosophical perspectives, and creative ways of reflecting theologically. Christianity in the Roman Empire began and continued to be a very diverse religion for many centuries.

Another way of describing this diversity emphasizes Jesus's authorization for the enactment of the Empire of God. The gospels, both those found in the New Testament and those other early Christian gospels, describe a community's understanding of the enactment of the Empire of God through their teaching about the birth, life, ministry, death, and resurrection of Jesus. Here, like the relationship of Martin Luther King, Jr., to African American civil rights, Jesus became the occasion for talking about a larger movement as it unfolded in a particular location. Although the gospels talk about Jesus, they are really describing how their communities formed people to live the life Jesus called them to live in the Empire of God. In this sense, the gospels are not about Jesus, but they use Jesus as the occasion for working out their particular theology and practices as a community. Each community seemed to understand themselves as capable and authorized to change written and oral sources to reflect their own lives, needs, understanding, location, culture, religious traditions, sacred texts and events, and historical circumstances. This is what we mean by saying that the gospels are formative texts.

Formation stands at the heart of the production of each of the gospels. The primary function of each of the gospels is not to convey information about Jesus, but to provide a manual for training and enculturation in the practices of Christianity for their particular community's context and needs. Enculturation is the process whereby individuals learn their group's culture through experience, observation, and instruction. The gospels are replete with these: we observe as people experience the Empire through healing, conversation, and confrontation with Jesus. Readers observe how Jesus himself inaugurated and enacted the Empire of God and it serves as a model for them in their own lives. And Jesus gives instruction, lots of instruction, through his sayings, pronouncement stories, and in his martyrdom and resurrection. Teaching pervades the gospels. The gospels are a site for just such enculturation and the differences between gospels show the differences in the communities' systems of enculturation.

The gospels also provide direct training. Throughout the gospels, in the voice and actions of Jesus as well as the other characters narrated, readers receive explicit teaching and learning in living a particular lifestyle. Readers are trained to drop everything about their familiar daily life and follow the way Jesus leads. They receive instruction about how they should live, with whom they should eat, how they need to be cleansed (if at all), what is good action, how they should relate to the poor, how they should take revenge (if at all). In other words, the gospels provided training for communities in specific actions and practices that defined their communities. It was not the same for each community that produced a gospel, even though there may be some overlap. The same saying can be interpreted in one gospel to mean one thing and applied in another gospel to mean another.

Let us provide one example of this training in a familiar passage from the Lord's Prayer. We would assume that something as important as the Lord's Prayer, which was prayed daily by early Christians, would not reflect regional or contextual differences. But it does. Luke relates the prayer as "forgive us our sins, as we have forgiven those indebted to us" (Luke 11:4, our translation) while Matthew has "forgive us our debts, as we have forgiven those indebted to us" (Matthew 6:12). Luke, whose community seems to consist of more wealthy folks, wants to train his people in a spiritual sense: to forgive sins the way they forgive debts. Money is important to his community, so spiritualizing forgiveness "of sins" rather than debts makes sense. Matthew, however, who probably has a more Jewish sense of the Jubilee year, when Jews forgave the debts of those who owed them, trains his community in a Christian version of the Jubilee: God will forgive debts in the same way as those who have forgiven debt in the Jubilee year. Money, here, is not as important as the process of continuing a valued Jewish practice of forgiving monetary debt within Matthew's Christian community. Clearly Matthew's and Luke's communities felt that they could change the prayer to reflect their own practices and values regarding forgiveness—and they did. What was important to them was not the exact words that Jesus might have given in the prayer, but the way the practice of forgiveness was to be lived in each community even if that practice did not jibe with other Christian communities.

This is one example of how the gospels use Jesus to provide training to their communities. As you will find in each of the following chapters, there is a rich treasure trove of such practices that provide a wealth of information about Christian formation. The community's gospel encapsulated and embodied the systems of enculturation and training necessary for a person to live authentically in their church.

The formation each gospel presents depends upon the community that produced it. Before the gospels were written, each community had information about the Empire of God and Jesus. This information would have been different for each community depending upon which itinerant prophet had visited them and what traditions they had heard about Jesus. Early Christianity had no means of getting the same information to every corner of the Roman Empire stretching from Persia (modern Iran) to Spain, from Libya in North Africa to Scotland. Each community had their own traditions that they believed were given under the guidance of the Spirit. So each community had a different sense of the way they should enact the Empire of God, a particular sense of the person of Jesus who announced the Empire, and a different way of making sense of the development of the religion from its earliest days. Those particularities and unique perspectives found in each community were important. A Christian, like our imaginary marble-builder Theodore, could recognize elements of what he knew in other communities, but he also saw significant differences. There was not yet any sense of uniformity to the Christian life. Variety, difference, and regional contexts played an important part in the way the Empire was lived, understood, and communicated.

Each written gospel, then, provides a window into the beliefs and practices of one of those particular communities. Mark's gospel is a window on the Roman church during the chaotic time of the emperor Nero. Matthew provides a window on a community in Antioch of Asia Minor during the reign of the emperor Vespasian and his son Titus, who destroyed the Temple in Jerusalem in 70 CE. Luke shows us a Roman community somewhere in Asia Minor or Greece during the reign of Domitian. John provides us with information about another Asia Minor community during the reign of the emperor Trajan. Communities produced the gospels at different times and in different places. The gospels reflect these different locales, historical contexts, and understandings of the Empire of God and Jesus's role in it. When reading the gospels, then, it is important not to look for what is the same in each one, but to look for the differences. It is the differences between them that speak loudly about how each community understood themselves, Jesus, and the Empire.

Reading this Book

Our perspective on the gospels, taken from the manner and chronology of their production, differs from the perspective given in a traditional introduction to the New Testament. We look to the formative practices articulated and promulgated by the gospel texts at a later historical time than the lifetime of Jesus. We also highlight the differences between the gospels to mine those differences for an understanding of the kind of Christian community that produced and used the gospel as a formative document in their corporate lives. This means that this book is not a verse-by-verse commentary on the gospels, but rather a study of the formative practices in the gospel.

This book also breaks new ground. It explores the practical theology of the gospels. We study the way the gospel writers read sacred texts of the Israelite scriptures; read other gospels; conformed traditions to the needs of their community; produced social and liturgical structures to sustain their communities; received divine revelation; maintained themselves in an often hostile political and religious environment; lived out the implications of the Empire of God in their particular location and time; and refracted the life, ministry, teaching, death, and resurrection of Jesus in ways their particular communities could understand. Although we base our study on a thorough engagement with the scholarship on the gospels, we have not attempted to make this a scholarly treatise on the gospels as formative documents. Rather we have laid out a reading of the gospels that honors critical scholarship, but moves in significantly different directions to see how Christians lived out their lives and how the gospels helped them train others to live in their communities. This book is, in that way, a manual for training contemporary readers in ways of understanding ancient Christian practices of formation and training for possible use in their own contexts. We hope other scholars will benefit from our perspective, but our goal is to shift gospel studies away from the strictly historical and exegetical scholarly approach to one that makes gospel formation accessible to a wider audience.

The shift in understanding the gospels emerged from a specific practice we employ in reading the gospels. Rather than breaking down the gospel into its constituent parts (paragraphs, sometimes called "pericopes," or selected verses), we read the gospel through in its entirety. In reading the gospel straight through from start to finish as a dramatic reading (this is what would have happened in antiquity), the gospel takes on a new meaning because the parts cohere, relate, connect in different ways throughout the reading. In reading the gospels as a whole in one sitting, we observed themes, correlation of stories, and oral structural connections not discerned simply by close reading of small textual units. We recommend a similar practice for those reading this book. Read the gospel aloud at one sitting, preferably even with an audience. It will seem strange at first, because most Christians are accustomed to hearing the gospels in small units read during worship, but the reading of the whole text aloud as a performance opens the text to significantly more subtle and cohesive readings.

The primary questions that emerge from this kind of dramatic reading of the gospels are these: what does the gospel say it means to be a Christian? What are the practices the gospel promulgates to help listeners live the Christian life? In reading the text aloud we literally hear and experience anew the kind of formation that the gospels were intended to produce in the hearer. We begin to sense the way the gospels led their hearers to understand what it meant to be a Christian and what spiritual practices, emotions, social structures, moral values, liturgical expressions, financial arrangements, and social concerns that Christian life demanded. So the practice of reading aloud leads to different questions—in other words the practice of reading the entire text aloud opens the text to new interpretations, and this book is an example of those possible new interpretations.

Although we read the gospels aloud both in their original Greek and in English translations, we understand that our readers will only be using an English translation. Throughout this book we have used primarily the Roman Catholic *New American Bible*. We chose that translation because we consider it a fine translation, because we agree with the way that it renders the Greek text faithfully in English, and because it is not the familiar sounding text of other translations that normally might be used in classroom and study. It is important to remember that you are reading a translation. In English, the translation evens out the text so that it all sounds the same. A translation cannot capture the fact that Mark sounds more like a truck driver speaking Greek, or Luke speaks in elegant and upper-class Greek, that Matthew sounds more like a New York rabbi, or that John writes in a kind of New Age seductive Greek. These nuances cannot be rendered in English, but they are essential to understanding the text. So keep in mind as you read the text that under it are dialectical nuances that you cannot hear in English.

Four chapters of our book take up the gospels. We also provide a "portal" chapter for each gospel, an entry point of information we think you need to understand the gospel itself. We introduce each portal with a fictional dramatization of some early Christian, Roman, or Jewish situation likely to occur at the time of the composition of the gospel. In Mark we introduce you to a Roman miracle-working philosopher named Apollonius, in Matthew to a philosophical community, in Luke/Acts to a Roman letter writer, and in John to the *Didache*, a late-first/early-second-century book that describes the work of early prophets. The portals describe important information necessary for reading the gospel as a formative document.

Each gospel chapter begins with a reference to popular culture (*The Colbert Report* on Comedy Central, the films *The Matrix* and *Almost Famous*, and the television program *Queer Eye for the Straight Guy*). These popular cultural events elucidate in modern terms aspects of the formative practices we find in the gospels. Then each gospel chapter takes up the formative practices of the community that produced it.

We conclude this book with a chapter that explores the implications of reading the gospels as formative documents for contemporary religious folks. Here we suggest ways of using this study as a means of exploring religious faith not only in Christianity, but in any religious context.

So now, like our wandering builder Theodore with whom we started this chapter, we invite you to wander through the gospels to discover the riches of the different ways of living the Christian faith that they reveal. Like Theodore, you may find yourselves surprised by what you see, sometimes shocked and, we hope, always fascinated by the practices these gospels promulgate.

Questions for Discussion
1. In modern societies, we often experience a dichotomy between urban and rural settings, politics, and culture. A popular narrative fictional arc has a sophisticated urbanite moving to a rural setting. After a series of mishaps, the heroine herself is converted to the habits and norms of her rural neigh-

bors (see *Sweet Home Alabama* or *New in Town*). Similar urban fantasies about an idyllic rural existence flourished in antiquity. What do you think is the impetus for these fictions? What difference does location make?

2. Whenever we go to see a production of Shakespeare's play *Romeo and Juliet*, we know beforehand that things will turn out badly. In part, this is because we are dealing with a fixed, written text. The earliest Christians did not have such a text in front of them, and they relied on oral—often fluid—traditions about Jesus. What difference would the use of these traditions make in forming Christians who follow Jesus?

3. We see the gospels as forming Christian identity. How were you formed as a citizen?

Resources for Further Study

There is a difference between the history of Christianity and the history of Christian literature. The early history of Christianity must begin with the construction of the life and mission of Jesus that in turn depends upon reconstruction of the early sayings of Jesus and an imaginative portrayal of the life and deeds of Jesus. For a reading of the sayings of Jesus, see Richard Valantasis, *The New Q: A Fresh Translation with Commentary* (New York: T. & T. Clark, 2005). John S. Kloppenborg, *The Formation of Q: Trajectories in Ancient Wisdom Collections* (Philadelphia: Fortress, 1987) portrays the history of the communities organized around the sayings of Jesus. For a portrayal of the early history of Jesus's mission, see Steven J. Patterson, *The God of Jesus: The Historical Jesus and the Search for Meaning* (Harrisburg, Penn.: Trinity Press International, 1998). The classic work on the historical Jesus is John Dominic Crossan, *The Historical Jesus: The Life of a Mediterranean Jewish Peasant* (San Francisco: HarperSanFrancisco, 1991).

The history of Christian literature, however, begins with the letters of Paul. Our introduction to the gospels takes very seriously the chronological priority of Paul. For an introduction to Christian literature that takes a strictly historical and chronological development beginning with Paul, see *The Chalice Introduction to the New Testament*, ed. Dennis E. Smith (St. Louis, Mo.: Chalice Press, 2004) and David L. Barr, *New Testament Story: An Introduction*, third edition (Belmont, Cal.: Wadsworth/Thompson Learning, 2002). For a critical introduction to the New Testament that recognizes the priority of Paul and yet starts with the gospels, see Bart D. Ehrman, *The New Testament: A Historical Introduction to the Early Christian Writings*, fourth edition (New York: Oxford University Press, 2008). A still useful, but older history of Christian literature and the Jewish and Christian backgrounds may be found in Helmut Koester, *History and Literature of Early Christianity* (New York: Walter de Gruyter, 1982) and his *History, Culture, and Religion of the Hellenistic Age* (New York: Walter de Gruyter, 1982).

Helmut Koester's *Ancient Christian Gospels: Their History and Development* (Philadelphia: Trinity Press International, 1990) is a comprehensive analysis of the history of the canonical and noncanonical gospels. Lawrence M. Wills's *The Quest of the Historical Gospel: Mark, John, and the Origins of the Gospel Genre* (New York: Routledge, 1997) studies the way the genre of the gospel developed. See also Pheme Perkins, *Introduction to the Synoptic Gospels* (Grand Rapids, Mich.: Eerdmans Publishing, 2007).

On the synoptic problem and the methods of interpreting it, see E. P. Sanders and Margaret Davies, *Studying the Synoptic Gospels* (Philadelphia: Trinity Press International, 1989). Any of the introductions to the New Testament listed above will provide a thorough analysis of the problems presented by the similarities and dissimilarities of Mark, Matthew, and Luke.

Walter Bauer was the first and most influential scholar to argue for the original and early diversity of early Christianity. In his *Orthodoxy and Heresy in Earliest Christianity*, trans. Robert A. Kraft and Gerhard Krodel (Philadelphia: Fortress, 1971), Bauer argues that early Christianity teemed with diverse ways of living and thinking and only later did a uniform and orthodox Christianity emerge. We find the same teeming diversity in the formation of the gospels themselves.

The literature on Paul is enormous. On the relationship of Paul to Roman philosophy, see Troels Engberg-Pedersen, *Paul and the Stoics* (Louisville, Ky.: Westminster John Knox, 2000) as well as Abraham J. Malherbe, *Paul and the Popular Philosophers* (Minneapolis: Fortress, 1989). Pam Eisenbaum's work on Paul is significant; see her *Invitation to Romans: A Participant Book* (Nashville: Abingdon, 2006) and her forthcoming *Paul Was Not a Christian* (San Francisco: HarperOne, 2009). For an intriguing new reading of Paul that emphasizes his rhetorical skill, see Stanley K. Stowers, *A Rereading of Paul: Justice, Jews, and Gentiles* (New Haven: Yale University Press, 1994).

The fascinating history and process of delineating the canon of the New Testament is explored by Lee M. McDonald who edited the papers in *The Canon Debate* (Peabody, Mass.: Hendrickson, 2002). The classic work on the formation of the Christian scriptures is Hans von Campenhausen, *The Formation of the Christian Bible*, trans. J. A. Baker (Philadelphia: Fortress, 1972).

The question of formation is central to our argument in this book, and we are dependent upon the work of one of our coauthors, Richard Valantasis, for understanding the practices that made communities work and incorporated new members into them. His essays on asceticism, the ancient word for formation, may be found in *The Making of the Self: Ancient and Modern Asceticism* (Eugene, Ore.: Cascade Books, 2008). See also his *Spiritual Guides of the Third Century: A Semiotic Study of the Guide-disciple Relationship in Christianity, Neoplatonism, Hermetism, and Gnosticism, Harvard Dissertations in Religion* (Minneapolis: Fortress,

1991), as well as his *The Gospel of Thomas* (New York: Routledge, 1997). Since religious practice forms such an important part of our reading of the gospels, see also his edited volume of religious texts in *Religions of Late Antiquity in Practice* (Princeton, N.J.: Princeton University Press, 2000).

For those students intrigued by the differences in the Lord's Prayer and who want to study further, see Nicholas Ayo, *The Lord's Prayer: A Survey Theological and Literary* (Notre Dame, Ind.: University of Notre Dame Press, 1992). An older but very interesting reading of the Lord's Prayer may be found in Joachim Jeremias, *The Prayers of Jesus* (London: S. C. M. Press, 1967).

CHAPTER TWO

Portal to the Gospel of Mark: Nero's Frantic Rome

It was no small matter, my dear empress, to assemble this life of our famous teacher Apollonius, since I, the humble writer and biographer, needed to assemble from such disparate sources and widely distant places the stories of our beloved teacher's sayings and deeds. His magnanimity and wisdom so far exceeds my ability to write and describe that I find myself deeply humbled by your request to assemble a narrative that preserves many of the things that people have reported about him, both in his life here on earth and in his teaching of his disciples after his death. Apollonius was indeed, my dear empress, a man of our times, a guide, a teacher, a healer, a prophet, and a window on the divine world in which he truly lived.

Apollonius led many people throughout the empire to a proper worship of the gods. He railed against animal sacrifice, teaching that the killing of an animal did not in any way appease or please the gods who needed neither animal blood nor sacrificial cults to look favorably upon the multitudes. Instead, he taught that a proper reverence for the gods involved an upright and moral life, an offering of the virtues developed in the soul of the person and presented as a royal gift to the gods. The priests, he would argue, should be moral guides, not butchers of animals, and although many priests opposed such a radical view of moral sacrifice and offering because their livelihood depended upon them, they found his teaching worthy and commendable.

Once in the city of Amphipolis, our blessed Apollonius came upon a young child who had just died of a high fever brought on by an evil demon. The parents went to him, crying uncontrollably, saying, "If you had been here, our child would not have died!" Apollonius exhorted them to control themselves and to put their trust in the gods, but they could not. And so our beloved Apollonius went into the upper room where the child had been laid out for burial; he prayed to the gods using strange words in foreign languages, invoking gods of whom the parents had not heard, and yelled in a loud voice, "Child, live again!" Immediately the child opened her eyes, took deep breaths, blinked her eyes, and began to smile at the man of the gods who had restored her to life. Her parents, overjoyed at the wonder of their child living again, brought gifts to our beloved Apollonius and began to tell all the villagers of his miraculous power. But Apollonius simply went on his way.

It was the custom for our beloved Apollonius to live simply. He wore only linen tunics, owned only one pair of cheap sandals, had no walking stick, no change of clothes, no purse to hold his money. He walked about from village to village, teaching and healing, and voicing prophesies and warnings about the dire things that were to begin happening in the world. He saw the cosmic effects of human wickedness on the course of events in the future.

Apollonius once came to Chios where the demons cried out against him. He stood his ground against them, but they continued to attack the people of the island. One man, an elder of fifty years who had been troubled by demonic attack throughout his life, fell at Apollonius's feet pleading for release from the bondage of his demonic oppression. Apollonius, filled with ire against the demons and full of the power of the gods, spoke sternly to the demons: "Why do you, wicked demons, oppress this innocent man and thwart his life and confuse his mind?" The demons answered, "You have no power over us! Go your way!" But the blessed Apollonius looked up to the heavens, lifted his hands in prayer, and ordered the demons to depart, saying "Be gone, evil spirits, and let health of mind and body be restored to this man! Do not enter him again, but go to the desert places and be lost!" The man fell down upon the ground, the demons having departed from him and leaving him half-dead. Apollonius lifted him up, telling him to live a virtuous life and to dedicate himself to the good of the people. The healed man left in joy, rejoicing at the new life that had been given him.

There are many stories such as these, dear empress, so many that I could recount them for days. But the true mystery resides in his death and translation to the heavenly world from which he continues to teach. This story truly astounds us. Our beloved teacher opposed the tyranny of the despotic emperors Nero and Domitian. Nero expelled him from Rome, castigating him and accusing him of the most serious sedition, but Domitian, who found himself compelled to listen to this holy man, at first supported our beloved Apollonius. Later, however, the emperor objected to the vigor of his tirades against despotic emperors, and he had the blessed man arrested and brought to court. In the midst of his defense Apollonius railed against the abuses of power—the deaths, the murders, the seizure of property, and the compulsive desire for pleasure that he saw in the imperial courts. The jurors were astounded that his defense provided the imperial lawyers with their argument. As Apollonius was speaking, however, he began to ascend as in a cloud. Slowly his body was lifted from the courtroom, rising high into the heavens until we could no longer see him, and he disappeared. The gods had taken him up. But from the heavens he continued to teach his followers in visions *about the immortality of the soul and the need for virtue, about the power of the gods and the ineffectiveness of animal sacrifice, and about the horrible things that were about to happen to humans because of their unfaithfulness and greed.*

This my dear empress is only a start of the life and teaching and deeds of our beloved Apollonius. I am not capable of writing more; his greatness exceeds my strength and ability, but the wonder of his life fills my soul with delight. And so I send this to you as the start of a narrative of the most holy life of Apollonius, the man of the gods.

This fictive life of the real person of Apollonius provides a window into the ancient process of writing biographies. Although this account is not from an ancient source, the stories it tells are all taken from ancient texts, which are available to us today. The historical Apollonius, whose life paralleled the time of Jesus, had many followers throughout the Roman Empire. Stories about him abounded, as they did about Jesus. Since many people wanted to hear the stories, there was great popular demand for biographies and narratives relating the life, teaching, and deeds of holy teachers. The ancient world wondered and enjoyed the lives of holy men who could teach, heal, confront the abusive powers of the day, and predict the future.

Ancient Biographies

Ancient biographies, most often written by a devoted disciple, were interesting documents that gathered very wide-ranging material, often from disparate parts of the world, to produce an entertaining and instructive story of a model person's life. Frequently these biographies included extended teaching of the philosophy of the person, usually embedded into short stories that gave some context to the saying or deed of the person. Also, these biographies described the manner of life of the famous person, emphasizing the particular lifestyle that the person modeled, such as itinerancy (going about from place to place without a permanent home base), diet, dress, and provisions. The biographies related the (often made-up) particularities of the birth of the person, emphasizing the presence of divine forces and agents attending the birth, as well as the (often miraculous and significant) deaths of the person. The point of the biography was to entertain while instructing, or more precisely, to instruct while entertaining.

But what was the instruction that the biographies provided? This is important. The biographies modeled a way of life through the narrative. For ancient people, the biographical account gave a snapshot of a particular pattern of living that was comprehensive. Biographies, especially those of holy men and women, described the diet, itinerancy or permanent living place, dress, personal hygiene, and personal habits of the person. The biographies described these details of living to give the readers a model of a particular way of life lived by the famous holy person. But the biographies went much further in describing social relationships and the manner properly to socialize with followers, opponents to the philosopher's way of life, and incidental others.

The biographies modeled for readers proper social relationships for those choosing the holy person's way of life: attitudes toward biological family, close connections to students and disciples, relationships of those providing lodging or food or monetary support, connections to cultic and religious centers and priests, and general attitudes toward the predominant social arrangements of the day. The holy person became an exemplar of a whole set of social relationships consistent with the holy person's way of life. And the biography provided a model in the life of the holy person for attitudes toward the emperor, the Roman military, Roman society, the Roman Senate, and all official agencies of the imperial administration. This is where many philosophers, including Jesus, probably got into trouble: most railed against the abuses of power and authority in the imperial administration as well as in the religious establishment, and they were expelled from cities, put into jail, crucified, and in some cases asked to commit suicide. The holy person's way of life was not neutral, or merely pious, it had serious personal, social, religious, and political implications for those readers called to imitate the model presented in the biographies.

The truth of the portrayal of the "facts" of the philosopher's life in ancient biographical narratives was not the point. This is difficult for us in the modern age to understand. Neither biographers nor their readers had news reports, video footage, or paparazzi to take candid shots. They had stories that were told over and over again, elaborated and changed over time and through transmission, and these stories began to develop a sense of the person's life, deeds, teaching, and death. And the biographies of both Apollonius and Jesus gathered disparate materials and stories in order to memorialize these exemplary persons, so that the biographies became a sort of repository of traditions that modeled a new way of living. Both Apollonius's and Jesus's biographies were written by adherents to the way of life they espoused.

Imperial City—Imperial Power—Imperial Disarray

The political tone of our fictive story about Apollonius is true to the times. Philosophers were perceived by imperial authorities to be dangerous people who often advocated sedition against the emperor. The times were indeed perilous, and that brought trouble for the followers of these holy men. But to understand this political climate, we need first to understand Rome and the Roman context.

We should visualize Rome as a big, "world city" (population nearly a million), like modern-day New York, London, Buenos Aires, or Tokyo. It was the capital of an empire that stretched from the Straits of Gibraltar in the west to Persia in the east, from Scotland in the north to the Sahara in the south. To display their wealth and power, emperors and major politicians competed to initiate, design, and fund major construction. As a tribute to themselves and as a way to win favor with the poor among the Romans, the wealthy emperors (and often wealthy noblemen on their own) built temples to their favorite gods, arches to remember important victories, arenas for plays and sports, forums for gatherings of citizens, aqueducts for carrying water from the mountains to the city, and baths where Romans refreshed themselves. The first emperor, Caesar Augustus, boasted that he found the city in clay and left it in marble. With all of this construction, the glory of the Roman Empire was on perpetual display in the city. Its magnificence, its architectural and engineering skills, and its permanence even today give the impression of unchallengeable, overwhelming, inevitably victorious strength.

The arts solidified this notion of glorious inevitability as poets, dramatists, and historians produced work that extolled the founding mothers and fathers for their diligence, honesty, and sober judgment and the divinely inspired progression from an agrarian village to leading the greatest empire then known. Writers went out of their way to find the virtues of the ancestors in the first emperor, Caesar Augustus, who reigned for forty-one years, from January 27 BCE to his natural death in August 14 CE. Caesar Augustus took power after almost exactly one-hundred years of near-constant civil wars, as first one and then another Roman politician-general vied for ultimate power. His reign began what has come to be known as the *Pax Augusta*, or the Augustan Peace, because of the relative quiet in the countries surrounding the Mediterranean Sea.

Whether Roman or Jew, only men enjoyed full human and civil rights in first-century Rome. Roman law did afford women a number of important rights, particularly the rights to inherit and control wealth from their birth families and to divorce their spouses. Beginning in ancient Rome and continuing until Rome's power faded in the fifth century CE, a relatively few wealthy and well-connected women could play an important part in the affairs of state. Six well-connected women served the goddess of the hearth, Vesta, as priestesses; these Vestal Virgins were the only women to participate in the Roman priesthood. In 195 BCE, wealthy Roman women successfully fought the "sumptuary laws" that limited a woman's ability to display wealth in public. The wife of Caesar Augustus had served as his regent while he was out of Rome. Agrippina, the mother of Nero, clearly played an important role in the politics of her time. But the lives and influence of women even in Rome were circumscribed by their exclusion from the military and political life and the expectation that they would function only within the home. It is not obvious whether wealthy, formally educated women had more or less freedom than the great mass of women. It is reasonable to suspect that in a family struggling to survive, a clever, financially astute woman might well create for herself a position of freedom and authority quite beyond expectations.

Because of the power that resided in Rome, the city attracted all kinds of persons from around the world: prosperous merchants, ambitious politicians like the philosopher Seneca, religious figures like the apostle Paul, and eventually the Christian religion itself, which first came to Rome from Jerusalem through the commercial and political ties between the two cities.

Not all of Rome's immigrants came willingly, but many came as slaves of the households of the prosperous or as slaves from the conquests of the Roman army. Slaves served an important function in Roman society: they were teachers to the young, household managers, servants, carriers, and those who performed the most servile functions for the Romans. Everyone who could afford a slave owned one or more, and slaves were a sign for other Romans of a person's rising and increasing wealth and authority. Some slaves, especially the more well-educated, were emancipated a year or two after being purchased, joining the large rank of "freedmen" in the Roman cities and countryside. Freedmen were still socially and often economically marginal figures, but at least they were free of a master and no longer had to perform servile duties for autocratic overlords. Freedmen could own slaves, if they could afford to buy them.

Most of the Jews in Rome appear to fit this description of those who were first brought in as slaves and many of whom were freed. The earliest extant record of Jews resident in Rome comes from a legal notice in 139 BCE, which says that the Jews, along with astrologers, were banished from the city. The expulsion, of course, would only apply to freed slaves and free people. The major influx of Jews came in 63 BCE when the Roman general Pompey brought back slaves from his actions in Judea. Roman customs and laws insured that most of the original slaves were freed and received Roman citizenship within a generation of their capture.

While the Roman armies maintained the external peace, the political scene in Rome was in chaos. Augustus had been able to ensure that his chosen successor, Tiberius Caesar, succeeded him on his death. From the time of Tiberius on, however, succession became a deadly game. Tiberius was followed by Caligula, widely thought to be crazed, and noteworthy as the first emperor who demanded that he be worshipped as a living god. He was assassinated and succeeded by his uncle, the elderly Claudius. Claudius took as his fourth wife Agrippina, his niece, who was also the sister of the late emperor Caligula and mother of the teenaged boy Nero. At Agrippina's urging, Claudius adopted Nero as his son, putting him in the line of succession ahead of Claudius's birth son. To further solidify his aspirations, Nero married Claudius's daughter, Claudia Octavia, his cousin, stepsister, and now wife. Both of these marriages, Claudius's to Agrippina and Nero's to Claudia Octavia, flaunted strict Roman marriage laws and required special legislation by the Senate. Claudius died in October 54 CE, perhaps as a result of poisoning by his wife Agrippina, and was succeeded by Nero. The fourteen-year reign of Nero provided the principal political context for the author of the Gospel of Mark.

The Praetorian Guards, the elite army unit charged with protecting the life of the emperor, proclaimed Nero emperor when he was sixteen years and ten months old. Nero took as principal advisors two men seemingly cut from the cloth of the ancestors: Seneca, the Stoic philosopher, and Burrus, head of the Praetorian Guards. Under their tutelage, Nero gave increased power to the Senate, an assembly of aristocrats, providing some semblance of republican democracy once again to Rome. Seneca and Burrus also helped Nero move away from the influence and control of his mother Agrippina. She then became a supporter of others aspiring to the throne, including his stepbrother, whom Nero then poisoned. Finally, in 59, Nero had his mother killed. It took two efforts as she survived the first, a deliberate shipwreck.

At the same time that Nero began moving away from his mother's influence, he also reduced the role of Seneca and Burrus, accusing them of embezzlement and treason. With the waning of their influence, Nero became increasingly arbitrary and self-indulgent. Rather than further increasing the role of the Senate, Nero progressively reduced its real power. After entering into an affair with Poppaea, the wife of his friend and general Otho (himself a future emperor), Nero divorced his very popular first wife Claudia Octavia and exiled her. That provoked enough of an outcry that he was forced to bring her back, which proved to shorten her life considerably: Nero had her executed.

The event most often recorded about Nero's reign was the fire in July 64 when Rome burned for five days. About a third of the city was destroyed and another half was heavily damaged. While Nero is often portrayed as "fiddling while Rome burned," in fact he was out of Rome at the time. On his return, he led the relief and reclamation efforts, apparently with energy, skill, and vision. The rumor persisted, however, that he personally had set the fire in order to clear land for his proposed new palace. To deflect these rumors, Nero accused the members of a new religious sect in Rome, called Christians, of starting the blaze. To identify all the members of the sect, the authorities rounded up known Christians, interrogated—that is, tortured—them and on the testimony of their fellow Christians arrested still more. The Christians were executed not for the fire but for the crime of "hatred against mankind," probably related to their refusal to offer sacrifice to the emperor or the goddess Roma.

In his later years, Nero systematically and almost irrationally undertook the eradication of his "enemies," including the philosopher Seneca. This certainly engendered fear on the part of political Romans and, with his consistent denigration of the Senate, built up resentment against Nero on the part of the upper classes.

The mass of citizens in Rome, whose support was critical, never really wavered in their support for Nero, however. To maintain their support, Nero mixed public and personal expenditures for the purchase and distribution of wheat and the production of gladiatorial and other entertainments for the citizens: these came to be called "bread and circuses." While Nero provided enormous gladiatorial shows, including the reenactment of naval battles on artificial lakes with naval ships and condemned men fighting to the death, he is remembered most for his support of the dramatic arts, cannily combining his own love of the entertainment arts with political necessity. He built a number of gymnasiums and theaters and supported dramatic performances with actors dressed in Greek clothing. Nero himself appeared in dramas and read his own poetry in public demonstrations.

Roman historians point out that the upper classes disdained the theater, thinking it was for the lower class, leading to immorality and laziness. The apparent Greek influence in all of this was suspect, as the Greeks of the first century, after all, were the conquered people, not the victors. Participation in and support by the emperor of these entertainments, therefore, were regarded as particularly demeaning of the office. As a consequence, the upper classes of first-century Rome were pretty unhappy with this level of expenditures.

In the end, more than his arbitrariness or love of the stage, what brought down Nero was money. His "edifice complex" became too much for even the Roman Empire to sustain. A tax revolt began in Gaul, spread to Spain, and led to Nero being declared an enemy of the state by a rejuvenated Senate. In June 68, at the age of thirty years and six months, Nero committed suicide.

From the time of his death to January 70, four different generals stationed in the provinces were acclaimed emperor as the empire once more fell into civil war. In December 69, the forces of Vespasian, who had been in Palestine putting down the Jewish revolt, entered Rome and restored order. He and his sons Titus and Domitian reigned for the next twenty-seven years, a new period of relative political stability.

This was the empire of Rome. From an outsider's perspective, the Romans built the largest and most successful empire in Western history and held it together for six centuries. While its power was indisputable, the empire was run by arbitrary, greedy, rapacious, lascivious men. Furthermore, Nero enacted treason and sedition laws that subjected to punishment (usually including torture) any disparaging, hence treasonous, comments about the emperor or the Senate.

As witnessed in our fictive biography of Apollonius, the Roman situation suggests an attitude of caution would have been appropriate for any writer. These were perilous times for writers, philosophers, and teachers—times that demanded care and subtlety. The way of life philosophers advocated had personal, social, religious, and political implications and often challenged imperial power and authority and traditional Roman customs.

Nero and the Arts

Nero's love for the arts is legendary, and yet it had important political implications during his principate. Nero wanted to be known as an artist and as a patron of artists. The Roman historian Tacitus, himself a young man when Nero died, reports:

Nero however, that he might not be known only for his accomplishments as an actor, also affected a taste for poetry, and drew round him persons who had some skill in such compositions, but not yet generally recognized. They used to sit with him, stringing together verses prepared at home, or extemporised on the spot, and fill up his own expressions, such as they were, just as he threw them off. This is mainly shown by the very character of the poems, which have no vigour or inspiration, or unity in their flow. He would also bestow some leisure after his banquets on the teachers of philosophy, for he enjoyed the wrangles of opposing dogmatists. And some there were who like to exhibit their gloomy faces and looks, as one of the amusements of the court (Tacitus, *Annals* 14.16).

This image of a youthful patron of the arts, gathering other young artists for sessions of creative writing (even if Tacitus did not find the product of these sessions to be of high quality), and of holding banquets primarily oriented to the creation and performance of literary and dramatic productions, pervades the pages of Tacitus's description of Nero's principate.

Nero's patronage of the arts, however, came with a high price both to artists and to the Roman aristocracy. Artists, as well as the crowds both noble and common at the various performances, were required to be profusely adulatory of the emperor and his performances. Tacitus described such an occasion in this way: "Soon he [Nero] actually invited all the people of Rome, who extolled him in their praises, like a mob that craves for amusements and rejoices when a prince draws them the same way" (*Annals* 14.14, p. 328). Nero thrived on the free and enthusiastic response of his audience, even though the enthusiasm often may have been feigned. Those who denied the emperor his praise often ended up in dire circumstances. Lucan, Seneca's nephew and himself a prominent writer, produced among other works the *Bellum civile*, an epic poem in multiple books that contains a flattering portrayal of Nero. Lucan's writing, though popular with Nero, was too successful, and therefore Nero prohibited Lucan both from performing and publishing any of his work. At times the Senate colluded with the emperor to punish those who composed literary pieces criticizing Nero. The Senate acted to punish an author for producing literature critical of the emperor, calling it treason, and returned to the dreaded practices of Nero's predecessor Claudius. The punishment was often exile, execution, or the demand that the person commit suicide.

The mixture of politics and literary production in Nero's court, however, is clear: to write political verse was to invite imperial, if not senatorial, condemnation leading to death. Indeed Nero put to death many of the artists whom he had encouraged and supported in their artistic endeavors, because he sensed the ironic and antiestablishment subtext. Even though the senators attempted at times to collude with the emperor, in the end Nero's will prevailed—the good artist, and especially the good artist critical of the emperor, would probably end up at worst being forced to commit suicide or at best in exile. The rift between Nero and the aristocracy was serious.

The seriousness of the circumstances becomes clear in the aristocratic response to Nero's performances. While Nero thrived on the public adulation showered upon him at the games, most Roman aristocrats and Senators were embarrassed and humiliated by his performances. The language of shame and degradation at both Nero's performances and Nero's insistence on the performance of other aristocrats pervades Tacitus's account of Nero's principate. Traditional Romans and the Roman aristocracy clearly found the performances to be degrading, disgraceful, and lacking the proper dignity for both emperor and nobility. Such perceived moral degradation by the Roman nobility led to Nero's downfall.

Nero loved Greek art. He wanted to live the life of a Greek artist among a Roman aristocracy that did not appreciate the apparent abandonment of Roman literature and customs. Naples, the most Greek city of the Italian peninsula, became Nero's favorite place precisely because there he could live and dress the Greek life among Romans in a relaxed and supportive environment. It was indeed Nero's love of Greek writing and mores that most disturbed his peers among the leadership and the aristocracy of Rome.

The love of things Greek, however, had a long history in Rome. Greek had been a second language to the Roman aristocracy and educated people for many years. The presence of the Greek language in Rome, in that sense, is not unusual. Certainly many religious sectarians from the eastern reaches of the Roman Empire, of all social and intellectual levels, continued to speak Greek, including the Jews of Rome and their Christian sectarians. But under Nero's influence and guidance, this interest in Greek literature and philosophy flourished.

Nero's practical knowledge of Greek enabled him to make speeches in Greek. And in addition to his own knowledge of Greek language and literature, Nero cultivated Greek genres of literature among his coterie of artistic courtiers: Greek epigrams, Alexandrian verse, and especially Greek epics and tragedies. Nero's favorites (at least until he forced them to commit suicide or to be banished) included Seneca, who wrote tragedies in Latin; Lucan who wrote an epic in Latin; and Musonius Rufus who wrote philosophical treatises in Greek. Nero's intellectual court was thoroughly bicultural, if not in fact bilingual. Enthusiasm for Greek literary and philosophical genres as well as Greek performative arts became a dangerous touchstone in Nero's principate—dangerous, because it could lead to dire circumstances; a touchstone because the Greek arts pervaded the imperial household. It is clear, however, that to be engaged with the Greek arts during the principate of Nero was a political statement not only within the household of the emperor, but also among the Roman aristocracy. Artistic pursuits had serious political consequences and were not in any way a neutral activity.

The literary and intellectual life of the Roman Empire changed significantly during the Principate, when a series of autocratic emperors with all the power and authority of government vested in them replaced the more representative and corporate republican form of government of the first emperor Augustus. The Roman literary correlative to this political shift is known as the Latin Silver writers, which developed during the Principate in the period from 17 to 130 CE. It was the previous Golden Age, the age of the self-designated renewal of the republican era under the emperor Augustus—a Golden Age that encouraged the likes of Virgil, Cicero, and Livy—that spawned the less-valued, more corrupt, and debased Silver Age of Lucan, Seneca, and Tacitus. It was a highly rhetoricized age, creatively exploring original styles of writing, and eager to endear a public audience through the display of rhetorical ostentation and flourish at public readings. The Gospel of Mark was written in Greek and developed a new genre called "a gospel"; it was composed in this shifting literary scene in Rome, and it may well be considered against the background of the Latin Silver artists.

Nero and Dissimulation

Our fictive story about Apollonius's relationship to emperors points to the real danger a holy person faced. The principate of Nero was complex; it could certainly be described as simultaneously theatrical, literary, bloodthirsty, and chaotic. Nero's tastes, propensities, interests, modes of support for the arts, combined with his ruthless murder of those whom he perceived to be a threat or to be critical of his life and art, created a peculiar and dangerous atmosphere for his various constituencies. The plebeians, the common people in Rome, clearly loved the shows and the emperor's performances. The patricians, the elite Romans, being very critical of immorality and impropriety, not only had to support the emperor, but were also required to perform before him and with him. Those many literary authors producing their poems, plays, novels, and philosophical lectures in this context were caught in a complex emotional, intellectual, and political spiderweb that could either lead to their political and social advancement or to their banishment or death.

The response of the educated class to Nero's person and court was also complex. One needed to be very careful not to reveal one's real thoughts or responses to Nero for fear of being brutalized. This situation demanded that one disguise or hide one's true reactions and thoughts from the emperor and his informants, since the consequences were potentially so brutal or bizarre. Even those, like Seneca, who were trusted friends of the emperor continued under scrutiny by opposing factions and political rivals.

In the great teaching of the rhetorical masters of Rome, literary authors found a way to say what they wanted to say, but not in an obvious way that would get them into trouble. They began to write using the rhetorical practice of *dissimulatio* (dissimulation), the rhetorical strategy of "masking" one's "real designs" by concealing eloquence (*dissimulatio eloquentiam*) in order to curry the favor of the listener (Quintilian, *de Oratore*, XII.ix.5). Quintilian, quoting Cicero, describes *dissimulatio* in this way:

> There is also the device of dissimulation, when we say one thing and mean another, the most effective of all means of stealing into the minds of men and a most attractive device, so long as we adopt a conversational rather than a controversial tone (Quintilian, *de Oratore*, IX.i.29, quoting Cicero, *de Oratore*, III.ii.201).

The force of dissimulation revolves about concealing one's artifice and thoughts in order surreptitiously and inconspicuously to change the hearer's way of thinking, perceiving, and understanding. It is a kind of "stealth" literature intended to persuade the audience without having to address problematic issues directly. Dissimulation was the only way of surviving the autocratic rule of the emperor and to continue writing. In the end, it was dissimulation that enabled the moral fabric of the Roman literati and society at large to survive Neronian persecution and that enabled the author of the Gospel of Mark to write his gospel.

Religion in Rome: Philosophers, Demons, and Gods

The "typical" postmodern sensibility considers religion a private, personal matter: a matter of personal conscience and activity. In contrast, religion in first-century Rome was first a political activity. Romans were convinced that their success in international conquests was not because of any innate superiority but because of their reverence for the gods. The primary reason to be religious, to do proper reverence to the gods, was to preserve and expand the Roman Empire. This same link between proper reverence of the divine and political success could be found in the Israelite scriptures, in which the prophets and psalmists argued that Israel would be successful only while the people were faithful to their agreement with the Lord, the God of Abraham, Isaac, and Jacob, the God who led the Hebrew people out of slavery in Egypt.

The world of first-century Rome, as we indicated earlier regarding the political situation, was unpredictable. Sensible people then as now looked for reassurance on the significant issues facing humanity: what is the life well-lived? How should the individual relate to the rest of society? Does the divine exist and what is its nature? These are such huge questions that we moderns divide them up among philosophy, sociology, cosmology, and theology. Philosophers in antiquity saw neither a need nor a way to compartmentalize these questions: they were all of one cloth.

Romans, Greeks, Egyptians, Syrians, Spaniards—people from around the world had been engaged in serious thought and debate on these central issues, which were recorded for at least eight centuries before Jesus of Nazareth was born. Faced with a capricious police state, scant medical knowledge, and subject to the vagaries of violent, unpredictable natural phenomena, one of the most pressing questions for the thinkers of Mark's time was "How shall we face death?" Usually we think of the flip side of this question: "How shall we live?" In the end, of course, they are the same question, for all thinkers agreed that as one lives so shall one die.

Three of the most important schools of philosophers, arguing from very different assumptions about the nature of the world, concluded that death itself was to be faced with equanimity. Epicureans denied the existence of personal gods who controlled the universe or judged humans; fear of death was irrational and could be overcome through careful study of the teachings of Epicurus. Stoics believed that the world was in an infinite, perfectly repeated, cycle of growth, decay, conflagration, and rebirth. One's own fate was inescapably tied to this cycle and the sage should accept all circumstances, good or ill, with equanimity. Death was inevitable and should not be feared. Platonists, intellectual descendants of a third Greek philosopher, Plato, taught that the goal of life was to join the individual human soul to the divine. The human being could take on the mind of the divine after death, so death itself should hold no fear.

As to the individual and society, the principal philosophical schools recognized, at a minimum, that the happiness of the individual required a safe and secure environment. They looked for governments to provide the minimum security of their own communities. Some developed the notion of the "common good," the greatest benefit for the greatest number in society, and argued that the individual should work to promote the common good. The Roman stories of the founding ancestors stressed their involvement in the affairs of state, in order to advance the welfare of the city and the Empire. The Israelite scriptures, particularly the prophetic schools, clearly saw a link between justice in the community and the fulfillment of the covenant with God. The prophets demanded justice for the poor and the oppressed, and resisted actions by the powerful to harm the powerless. Both Romans and Jews believed that the place of the individual was to support the larger social units: the extended family, the tribe, the nation. An individual's personal salvation, as that might be understood in modernity, was far less important in antiquity than enhancing the life and well-being of these social units. When first-century Christians heard philosophers, prophets, and interpreters of Jesus speak of salvation, a societal context was understood: only in and with the society could one attain salvation.

As to the divine, starting six hundred years before Jesus was born, most philosophers held that there could be only one supreme, creator God, though a minority denied the existence of any god. For those who did accept a single god, the mythic tales from their antiquity about such gods as Zeus (Greek), Jupiter (Roman), and Venus presented something of an embarrassment. On the one hand, such texts as Homer's *The Iliad* and *The Odyssey* reporting the scandalous comings and goings of the gods, were studied as texts that defined the character of the Greek people, that is to say, all civilized people. On the other hand, the scandalous behavior of the gods could not be held up as a model for students. One solution to the problem was to argue that the stories were completely alle-gorical, extended literary works in which the literal meaning was not the mean-ing intended by the author. Minimally it holds that no single literal meaning can stand alone, but that a valid utterance must possess a transcendent meaning as well, a symbolic surplus beyond the literal level.

The gods were sometimes described as aspects of the personality of the one God, symbols of the divine or, perhaps, lesser gods, beings intermediate to the one God and humans. Many accepted the existence of "demons," who may be lesser gods or the manifestations of souls of humans that are in the process of journeying from human life to some form of an afterlife. Some of the demons were considered beneficial, including the one whom many thought created the universe at the behest of the one God. Other demons, however, were harm-ful to humans. Demons literally might seize a person's body and personality, a viewpoint recounted in several of the miracle stories in the gospels and in the biographies of Roman holy people.

Just as some Greeks and Romans had concluded that there was only one supreme god, the Jews too arrived at the conclusion that their God, the God of their ancestors Abraham, Isaac, Jacob, Sarah, Rebecca, and Rachel, Moses, and Miriam, was the one creator God of the universe and, therefore, the God of all nations, of the Egyptians, Greeks, and Romans as well as of Israel. The book of Jonah describes the power of the God of Israel to punish the city of Nineveh, the capital of the Assyrian Empire. The Israelite scriptures describe angels sometimes as manifestations of the divine present in the world and some-times as intermediate creatures called upon to act out the will of God within the universe. Angels intervene in the life of Abraham described in the book of Genesis (chapter 18) and bear coals from the throne of the Most High to touch the tongue of the prophet Isaiah (Isaiah, chapter 6).

In antiquity, even though there was great variety in interpretation, the answers to the pressing issues about the meaning of life, the place of the individual in society, and the existence and nature of the divine, formed a surprisingly strong consensus among the philosophers. There was, however, a distinct difference be-tween the Jewish response to a plurality of gods and that of the Romans.

Perhaps because of an innate sense that the multiple gods of story and state—the likes of Jupiter, the chief god, Juno, his wife, and Mars, the god of war—were less than real, the Romans were perfectly willing to add the gods of the conquered peoples to their lists. Temples, places for sacrifice and petition to the gods, were built for the gods as they were adopted by the Romans. As a result, Rome became a religiously diverse city. In addition to the Roman gods and their traditional rituals, Romans also supported the worship of Eastern gods, like the Egyptian goddess Isis, the Greek god Dionysus, or the Great Mother from Asia Minor. As commerce, trade, and tourism grew following Rome's pacification of the Mediterranean, such cults moved throughout the Empire, so that, for instance, the Dionysiac societies flourished throughout the whole Empire—in Greece proper, on the Greek islands, in Asia Minor, along the Danube River, and especially in Italy and at Rome.

The religion of Israel did not work this way. When conquered, neither Jews nor Romans built a new temple in Rome to the God of the Hebrew people. The Temple in Jerusalem was the only place where sacrifice and prayers could be offered. Synagogues where Jews settled in the cities around the Mediterranean were first and foremost gathering places for the expatriates. Then they became schools where the Israelite scriptures were read and commented upon. They were not places for sacrifice.

In addition, the covenant between the Jewish people and their Lord, which is how they referred to their God, required the people to be exclusive, to be monotheistic in their relationship, and to recognize and worship only the Lord. The Lord, they were told, is a jealous God. This became an issue when the emperors were declared—or declared themselves—gods. The Roman Senate declared Julius Caesar, who died in 44 BCE, divine shortly after his death. At that point, his heir and the first emperor, Caesar Augustus, took the title "Son of God." While both Augustus and Tiberius were deified only after death, we have already commented that Caligula, the third emperor, had himself declared divine while he was alive. All Romans, throughput the Empire, were to worship this emperor. The monotheistic Jews finessed the issue by offering daily sacrifice in the Jerusalem Temple to the well-being of the emperor, rather than to him directly. The annual Temple tax, paid by observant Jews throughout the Empire for the support of the Jerusalem Temple, supported this practice as well.

Reading Scriptures

Much of the religious scene for Romans and Jews revolved about a set of documents or practices that informed their religious sensibilities. Both Romans and Jews had their own versions of what might be called "scripture." Very simply, a text becomes scripture when a community agrees that it will order and give meaning to their lives, as individuals and as a group. In Rome, after its publication and reception, the Christians considered the Gospel of Mark as part of their scripture. For centuries, the Greeks regarded the epic poems of Homer, *The Iliad* and *The Odyssey*, as providing important guidance for their lives. Since the invention of the printing press, the term has more often than not been restricted to written or printed texts, but this need not necessarily be so. Secret societies, for instance, may refuse to commit their rules and regulations to paper lest they fall into the wrong hands. Many first-century Jews accepted as scripture the oral tradition of their fathers. They understood this to be teaching that God gave orally to Moses on Mount Sinai at the same time that God gave the written law, the Ten Commandments. The tradition held that the oral tradition was handed on orally—exclusively—so that it would be memorized and become a part of the student. For these Jews, this oral tradition must be considered scripture.

Scripture as we use the term included philosophical texts as well as what we would include as religious texts. Philosophical schools revered their founders as those who, through the acquisition of full knowledge of the gods and acceptance of a proper role in the state, had developed the proper state of mind to face life and death with equanimity. Their writings, often including transcriptions of their lectures, transmitted this knowledge to successive generations. The student's goal was to appropriate these texts so as to take on the mind of the master, to so thoroughly assimilate the master's teaching as to be able to replicate the master's thinking process, in order to achieve that same equanimity. On a particular subject, the student would memorize the master's words along with a brief, linking saying. Then in a moment of crisis the student would recall the saying of the master and bring to mind the entire teaching. So, for example, a student of Mark debating on the question of the necessity of wealth for the happy life might recall Jesus saying: "It is easier for a camel to pass through the eye of a needle than for one who is rich to enter the kingdom of God" (Mark 10:25). Recalling this saying about wealth and riches first brings to mind the story of the rich young man whom Jesus loved and then all the teachings that Mark recorded about wealth. In this way, the student began to understand how Jesus, the Master, would argue in the debate. Thus the student took on the mind of Jesus about wealth. We note that this process does not require that the student be literate, only that the student devote sufficient time to memorize large tracts and sayings read or recited by another disciple.

To strengthen their positions, Greek and Roman philosophers also looked to general literature—the Homeric epics, plays by classical writers, and poetry—as providing valuable insights and models for the philosophic arguments being made. Of course the philosopher realized that the cited work was fiction, and not of the same genre as the base work, but nevertheless philosophers recognized that their students would be familiar with these general works and sympathetic to the points they made.

Greeks, Romans, and others following traditional religions would also look to auspices, revelatory rituals intended to help understand the will of the gods about the proper course to be taken at a moment of judgment. One of the classes of Roman priests were the *augurs* who read the future from the entrails of chickens and the flights of birds. In fact, Roman officials were not supposed to take any major course of action—declaring war or passing legislation, for example—until the augurs judged the time to be auspicious. Also providing input were any extraordinary events in nature. A star shining especially brightly was thought to herald the coming of an emperor. Earthquakes were not only destructive on their own but they were also natural premonitions of worse things to come. Ancient peoples also consulted oracles. First Greeks and then Romans traveled to the oracle at Delphi for advice on which of two or more courses to take.

Thus, in its fullest sense, Greeks and Romans had many scriptures on which to rely: the philosophical writings of their schoolmasters, classical literature, histories of great people, Delphic pronouncements, and the auspices of nature. Many similar sources were available to the Jews in Rome from their Israelite scriptures. In the first century, these were often referred to as "the Law and the prophets." "The Law" would refer to the first five books of what is generally known as the Hebrew Bible: the books of Genesis, Exodus, Leviticus, Numbers, and Deuteronomy. These books start from a portrayal of the creation of the world, continue through the journeys of Abraham and his offspring, ending in Egypt from where the Lord eventually rescues them, their wanderings in the desert on their journey back to the promised land of Canaan, and the directives that God gave them on how to live and worship in the promised land. "The Prophets" probably included the texts describing the developments in the promised land from the time of the entrance of Abraham's descendants until their exile in 587 BCE to Babylon, plus the texts named for particular prophets, the books of Isaiah, Jeremiah, Ezekiel, to name the major ones. In addition, writers frequently cited Psalms that are not now included in either compilation of Law or Prophets. The whole together would provide a rich resource including mythological narratives, recitations of important historical personages and events, poetry, oracles, speeches, and laws.

If we were to characterize the use of scriptures in antiquity, it would be very similar to the way we see scriptures being used in contemporary settings, like the early morning Bible study groups meeting in coffee houses. The participants are seeking direction on how to live their lives. When as a candidate for the office of president of the United States, Texas governor George W. Bush declared that "Jesus is my favorite philosopher," his was an attitude that could have been pulled from the first century. Philosophers, after all, were supposed to help others learn how to live wisely and their students more often than not produced texts to lead those with whom they had no immediate contact to take on their mind.

Seneca and Spiritual Direction

In addition to consulting and interpreting their scriptures, Romans also turned to spiritual guides. The first three centuries of the common era betray a remarkable interest in consulting spiritual guides. Often these guides were written sources, that is, they were the writings of sages who provided Romans with philosophical and spiritual advice. Seneca, Nero's tutor for many years, is a prime example of the process.

Seneca was brought out of exile by Nero's mother, the infamous Agrippina, in 49 CE and was made Nero's tutor in 51. Together with Burrus, who was leader of the Praetorian Guard under Claudius and Nero, Seneca virtually ran the empire from 54–59 CE, during Nero's youth. To the historical mind, Seneca remains a twisted figure whose philosophical writing and manner of life were so divergent that all the historical sources portray him as a hypocritical teacher who taught Nero not philosophy and the good, but vice and tyranny. His final letters, the letters to Lucilius, a wealthy younger gentleman striving to advance his career in the Roman aristocracy, were written ostensibly to guide him on his political, philosophical, religious, and social ascendancy.

When Seneca was forced from Nero's court, he retired and turned his attention to writing the letters to Lucilius. The letters are fictions in that, although addressed to a person, there is nothing in them that indicates that they are personal correspondence. The letters are a literary creation in a conversational tone intended to create the illusion of a master teacher and director of souls speaking to a younger man in order to train him in the proper way of living and of dying.

Seneca describes his spiritual formation as a therapeutic process. In his letters to Lucilius, Seneca presents (*Epistles* 80:23) the analogy between physical and mental training. This analogy is commonplace in Hellenistic and Roman educational circles, and it becomes a primary tenet of Greek and Roman spiritual practice. The mind, like the body, may be prepared for superior things through training. Like the body, the mind and the person may be sculpted to reflect its superior status and its superior state of preparation for philosophical, political, and intellectual effort.

Even though the letters are not real letters to a real Lucilius, they give the impression of intimate and personal conversation. This appearance lends credence and gives validity to a confession that Seneca makes regarding his own formation as a person: "I feel, my dear Lucilius, that I am being not only reformed, but transformed" (*Epistles* 6:1). This reformation and transformation articulates a goal toward which the philosopher aims in his philosophical practice.

Again, the fiction of personal correspondence lends credence and depth to the prospect of achieving this goal. The personal and corporate transformation involves a kind of mentoring, or spiritual direction, that helps another to be formed anew. The director takes an active role in the exhortation and encouragement of the seeker after nobility:

> I claim you for myself; you are my handiwork (*meum opus es*). When I saw your abilities, I laid my hand upon you, I exhorted you, I applied the goad and did not permit you to march lazily, but roused you continually. And now I do the same; but by this time I am cheering on one who is in the race and so in turn cheers me on (34.2).

The benefits of that transformative relationship between director and seeker remains mutual to the extent that each participant benefits from the transformative process. Although the seeker specifically receives the attention of the director, the director in turn also moves toward transformation at the behest of the seeker. The formative practice here is reflexive in that both participants improve through training, although the manner of each seems to be different. The seeker is exhorted, fabricated, directed, encouraged, and kept to the proper path, while the director also advances as a participant in the process. Seneca and his fictional epistolary friend Lucilius form a community for mutual transformation.

The process of training, however, is not simply an ideal. It begins with a realistic assessment of the capacity of the person to change. Seneca's letter instructs that each person is to begin to perfect that which relates to each person's natural ability and in each environment in which the person is found. Seneca uses the example of the famous classical Greek sculptor Phidias to make his point:

> It was not of ivory only that Phidias knew how to make statues; he also made statues of bronze. If you had given him marble, or a still meaner material, he would have made of it the best statue that the material would permit. So the wise man will develop virtue, if he may, in the midst of wealth, or, if not, in exile; if possible, as a commander—if not, as a common soldier; if possible, in sound health—if not, enfeebled. Whatever fortune he finds, he will accomplish therefrom something noteworthy (85:40).

The social and political environment and the natural capacities of the person, expressed in the commonplace about the kinds of materials available to artists, combine to provide the starting point for reformation and transformation.

Seneca recognizes that natural ability affects the capacity for change, and may even provide the impetus to begin the process of transformation. By training, the seeker may advance beyond what nature limits, but the seeker will never completely transform the self:

> That which is implanted and inborn can be toned down by training, but not overcome. . . . Training and experience can never shake off this habit; nature exerts her own power and through such a weakness makes her presence known even to the strongest (11.2).

This attitude at once impels the person to attempt to overcome nature, and encourages activity toward transformation, while at the same time accounting for the frailty and difficulty of progress. Seneca acknowledges that it is more difficult for an old man to change than for a young man: "Such a man cannot be re-shaped; only young minds are molded" (25.2). Nature is a strong force, but not an insurmountable one—progress may still be made despite nature: "At our birth nature made us teachable, and gave us reason, not perfect, but capable of being perfected" (49.11–12).

The training, however, has a deeply religious base. It is not simply the training in nobility for its own sake, or for the sake of the state and society, but for the religious transformation of the person:

> When a soul rises superior to other souls, when it is under control, when it passes through every experience as if it were of small account, when it smiles at our fears and at our prayers, it is stirred by a force from heaven. A thing like this cannot stand upright unless it be propped by the divine. . . . [T]he great and hallowed soul, which has come down in order that we may have a nearer knowledge of divinity, does indeed associate with us, but still cleaves to its origin; on that source it depends, thither it turns its gaze and strives to go, and it concerns itself with our doings only as a being superior to ourselves (41.5).

The process itself is simple. It involves daily effort to reform the self: "For what else are you busied with except improving yourself every day, laying aside some error, and coming to understand that the faults which you attribute to circumstances are in yourself?" (50.1).

Turning to the Gospel of Mark

The author of the Gospel of Mark wrote during the very troubled times of Nero's principate and may well have been part of the literary movement of the Latin Silver authors. It was a dangerous time, but also one of great creativity, religious and philosophical thinking, and practical exploration of new ways of living a morally and spiritually fulfilling life. It took skill to maneuver the various pitfalls placed by the emperors, and it was a time of great literary production that maneuvered the political situation well. Mark's gospel was just such a literary production, as was the life of Apollonius with which we began this chapter.

Questions for Discussion
1. Why is it important to know the original political and social context of the writer and the original audience to understand a written text? What difference does it make in reading it? Think about *The Lord of the Rings*. What difference does it make that it was written during World War II?

2. Why is it important to understand the literary and rhetorical tactics of an artist in order to understand the artistic work? Consider Michael Moore's documentaries, such as *Fahrenheit 9/11* and *Sicko*. What are his tactics? How is it a true "documentary"? Does he express a particular ideological perspective? What happens to a viewer who does not understand his tactics or ideology?

3. Can you identify in your own cultural context an artistic creation that uses dissimulation? Think about such popular songs as Leonard Lipton and Peter Yarrow's "Puff the Magic Dragon," John Lennon and Paul McCartney's "Lucy in the Sky with Diamonds," Lou Reed's "Sweet Jane," Wilco's "Company in My Back," and U-2's "Running to Stand Still." What are they really talking about? How do they hide one message in another?

Resources for Further Study

The literary legacy of the Roman Empire is rich and diverse during our period of interest. Important works can be found in the Loeb Classical Library (Cambridge, Mass., Harvard University Press) in original languages with an English translation alongside. For this chapter, Loeb includes the works of Philostratus (*Life of Apollonius*), the Roman historians Tacitus, Suetonius, and Dio Chrysostom. Cicero's works include lengthy essays on the traditional Roman religion (*de Natura Deorum* [*On the Nature of the Gods*], *de Divinatione* [*On Divination*], and *de Fato* [*On Fate*]), on the major philosophical systems (*Academica* and *de Finibus Bonorum* describe the positions of major philosophical schools on important points), and on oratory (*de Oratore*). Quintilian wrote his *Institutio Oratoria* as a handbook for aspiring rhetoricians. Included there are his instructions on the use of *dissimulatio* and the various styles of writing. Working at the same time Paul was writing letters to the Corinthians and Romans, Seneca produced 124 letters of moral suasion to Lucillus (*Ad Lucium Epistulae Morales*). These might profitably be read with his *Moral Essays*.

It is often useful to have ready at hand a general reference for Roman history. There are many studies available; one we have found useful is Marcel Le Glay, Jean-Louis Voisin, and Yann Le Bohec, *A History of Rome*, trans. Antonia Nevill (Oxford: Blackwell, 1996). Edward Champlin produced a biography of Nero, which includes a good deal of helpful information on the general state of the dramatic arts during his reign, *Nero* (Cambridge, Mass.: Belknap Press, 1996). The tumultuous year 69 CE, the year of the four emperors, is portrayed well in Kenneth Wellesley's book *The Long Year: A.D. 69* (Boulder, Colo.: Westview, 1976).

All the translations of Tacitus are from *The Complete Works of Tacitus*, Modern Library College Editions, trans. Alfred John Church and William Jackson Brodribb, ed. Moses Hadas (New York: The Modern Library, 1942).

A complementary study to our description of *dissimulatio* is Jerry Camery-Hogatt's *Irony in Mark's Gospel: Text and Subtext* (Cambridge: Cambridge University Press, 1992). He argues that Mark's use of irony (a literary tactic of double meanings) is a strategy crafted to lead the reader-listener to make a decision for Jesus. The reader can see both the similarities and the points of difference that we have with this reading of Mark. Vasily Rudich, in *Political Dissidence Under Nero: The Price of Dissimulation* (London: Routledge, 1993), thoroughly examines the rhetorical strategy of *dissimulatio* in the Latin Silver authors.

We have combined into one section our discussions of the salient features of the traditional Greco-Roman religions and the philosophical systems that interacted with them. The two-volume work by Mary Beard, John North, and Simon Price, *Religions of Rome* (Cambridge: Cambridge University Press, 1998) provides in the first volume a history of the development of religion in Rome and in the second primary sources for the work. There are a number of summary works about the philosophic schools of this time. R. W. Sharples's *Stoics, Epicureans and Sceptics: An Introduction to Hellenistic Philosophy* (London: Routledge, 1996) provides an excellent introduction to these three schools. Alas, Sharples does not cover the development of Middle Platonism, a key to understanding Philo of Alexandria and, in certain contexts, Paul of Tarsus. John Dillon's work, *The Middle Platonists: 80 B.C. to 220 A.D.* (Ithaca, N.Y.: Cornell University Press, 1996) is the standard work in this field.

CHAPTER THREE

The Gospel of Mark:
A Gospel for the Underground

Stephen Colbert of Comedy Central's The Colbert Report reports nightly on the news of the day, bringing to light the critical issues of the day through humor and irony. Colbert addresses his television and live audience as "Nation," suggesting that he is the leader of a new people who gather nightly under his guidance to explore the significance of international and national news relating to politics, religion, social life, and international affairs. Colbert, presenting himself as a conservative, presents a liberal perspective by refracting information through his egocentric and self-oriented interviews with various specialists whom he invites to his show to shed light on interesting and critical issues of the day. Colbert's humor and wit, often misinterpreting and twisting what his specialists say, opens the world to laughter and ridicule, while at the same time providing critical assessment of important topics. He is very funny and his humor drives home the often ridiculous actions of politicians and other national and international figures.

In a sense, Colbert dissimulates—he presents his own opinion and perspective by forcing his audience, his "Nation," to explore his true meaning caught between his humor and the way he twists his facts to ridicule the apparent truth of a situation. By presenting himself as a conservative on the surface, Colbert uses humor surreptitiously to promulgate a very liberal social and political agenda. "Nation" is never clearly given a clue to his real position, but "Nation" simply receives irony, wit, sarcasm, and misrepresentation as a clue to his real values and attitudes, which, although never openly stated, become evident in the kind of witty response to current events and people.

Colbert's discovery of an aspect of his identity provides a good example. On August 13, 2007, Stephen Colbert interviewed Spencer Wells of the National Geographic Society's genome project. Wells informed Colbert that according to the statistical data of his research, Colbert had a seventy-five percent chance of being Jewish. Colbert, who claims not to be Jewish although he is a Roman Catholic, began to play with the idea, claiming in his usual witty way that he was seventy-five percent Jewish. He announced on his program the inauguration of the "Atone Phone" for Jews to apologize to him during the ten-day period of Jewish repentance between Rosh Hashanah and Yom Kippur. For observant Jews, this is indeed a time of repentance, but Colbert twists it to focus entirely on himself. Colbert's career started with Jon Stewart's comedy program on Comedy Central. Jon Stewart is Jewish, so Colbert says sardonically, that "I know many Jews," and he goes on to explain that some Jews (notably Senator and former vice-presidential candidate Joe Lieberman and Washington Post columnist Richard Cohen—both of whose pictures were displayed on screen next to Colbert) have not been willing to appear on his show. So Colbert's "Atone Phone" is a way to express his seventy-five percent Jewish identity by making himself the center of attention. The irony is that the Jewish holidays call for individuals to survey their own lives and to ask forgiveness from those whom they have harmed in any way. It is not a time to insist that someone asks for forgiveness on the order of another. Colbert twists this in an egocentric and self-focused way by demanding that certain Jews acknowledge the harm that Colbert attributes to them and then for them to call him on the "Atone Phone" to ask for forgiveness. Colbert uses his humor and egocentricity to reveal the true nature of the holiday, but that is not done in any overt manner.

Another incident displays Colbert's dissimulation and its difference from mere humor. In the 2008 presidential election night episode "Indecision 2008" Colbert appears with his friend and colleague Jon Stewart in a typical election night program format. In this episode, Colbert dissimulates, while Jon Stewart makes humorous and funny comments. They interview Charles Ogletree, a Harvard University Law School professor who taught Michelle and Barack Obama. Colbert asks Ogletree, "If Barack Obama is elected president of the United States, is that racist?" When Ogletree answers, "No," Colbert says, "But then everything changes," and Stewart says, "Because then he would be the Man." He also asks Ogletree, "Did you know back then [at Harvard Law School] that he was a socialist?" Ogletree responds, "No, back then they seemed pretty conservative. I thought they were Republicans." Colbert replies, "So this could be a big win for the Republicans tonight!" Colbert raises questions of racism and socialism, two accusations by Obama's Republican opponents John McCain and Sarah Palin, in such a way as to make you believe that he was indeed a supporter of McCain and Palin's perspective. Stewart, who had throughout the election made it very clear that he supported Obama, raised serious questions and engaged humorously with Ogletree. Stewart's humor was supportive, as when he raised the accusation about Obama that, after all the campaigning, "We don't know who he really is. People say that after winning he'll pull off his mask and reveal his secret self. What is his secret?" The question humorously pulls up the image that after two or more years of campaigning, the American public could not know the candidate and that, wearing a mask that could be removed, suddenly we would find an unrecognizable Obama. Stewart's directly supportive endorsement of Obama contrasts markedly with Colbert's dissimulative support. Colbert, under the guise of a conservative Republican voter, seems always to be critical of Obama and the liberals, repeating Republican political attacks, and yet the audience finds his perspective humorous. The audience sees through the dissimulation to what Colbert really believes.

Colbert and the Gospel of Mark work in a similar fashion. Colbert hides his liberal agenda under a facade of conservative ideology and in a self-centered understanding of the events of the world. The Gospel of Mark hides the true meaning of its message in a text that seems to portray Jesus's failed attempt to establish a new Empire of God. We say a "failed attempt" because Mark portrays Jesus as a simple wandering teacher who is crucified as a criminal by the Romans and whose disciples never really understand who Jesus is nor the significance of what he does. The only people who really "get" Jesus in Mark's gospel are the demons who acknowledge him as the holy one of God and the Roman soldiers at the crucifixion who name him a Son of God.

That it is others and not Jesus's disciples who understand Jesus is clear from watching the beginning of the gospel unfold. Mark introduces Jesus's gospel by connecting him to the work of the Israelite prophets and their successor John the Baptist (1:1–8). Then Jesus is baptized by John and God acknowledges that Jesus is God's "beloved Son" in whom God is "well pleased" (1:9–11). After forty days' temptation in the desert, Jesus begins his ministry of proclamation and calls the disciples to follow him (1:12–20). Although the prophets were read as pointing to Jesus's role as God's agent, and God affirms that Jesus is God's son, it is a demon in the very first healing that Jesus performs—the curing of the demoniac—who is the first agent in Mark's gospel to acknowledge and understand who Jesus really is: "What have you to do with us, Jesus of Nazareth? Have you come to destroy us? I know who you are—the Holy One of God!" (1:24). The disciples play a very subordinate role in the beginning of the gospel, while Jesus goes about the crowds healing and preaching. The disciples in the gospel seem passive and confused by Jesus's teaching and healing. The gospel continually affirms the demons' ability to know Jesus. Mark writes: "And whenever unclean spirits saw him they would fall down before him and shout, 'You are the Son of God'" (3:11). The first time the disciples interact with Jesus comes in the story of the calming of the sea (4:35–41): after the disciples wake Jesus to save them from the storm, Jesus calms the sea, acknowledges that his disciples were terrified, and upbraids them for having no faith. Mark characterizes their response to this situation in this way: "They were filled with great awe and said to one another, 'Who then is this whom even wind and sea obey?'"(4:41). The demons get who Jesus is, while the disciples who witnessed the various healing events seem perplexed. Why is this? Why do the demons understand and the disciples seem befuddled? The situation is even more dramatic when, at the end of the story, before Jesus's crucifixion, the disciples abandon him ("And they all left him and fled" [14:50]) and Peter denies him (14:66-72). Even the women who were at the tomb in which Jesus was buried, upon hearing of his resurrection, "went out and fled from the tomb, seized with trembling and bewilderment. They said nothing to anyone, for they were afraid" (16:8). What is happening in this gospel where the insiders and close companions of Jesus seem bewildered, fearful, ignorant of Jesus's significance, and incapable of responding appropriately to Jesus's mission, while the demons themselves continually affirm Jesus's divine status and mission?

To understand this dilemma in the gospel, we need to remember the circumstances under which the Gospel of Mark was produced, because, like Colbert's humor, the gospel's negative portrayal of Jesus's followers has a hidden purpose. Mark's story is a complex one, but one that is at the same time intriguing and fascinating.

The author of the Gospel of Mark wrote in Rome. This is the oldest church tradition about the place of the composition of the gospel, and it makes sense. We know from Paul's letter to the Romans (written about 58 CE) that the church in Rome had been in existence from earlier times (Paul wrote to already established communities of believers), that the church consisted both of Jews and Romans (whom Paul calls Gentiles), and that there seemed to be conflict between these two groups living in the Empire of God that Jesus proclaimed. There was probably conflict between those in Jesus's Empire of God and the Jews who did not also acknowledge that Empire. From earliest times, then, the Roman churches seemed diverse and often conflicted.

Mark's Community in Rome

If we imagined a gathering of all the participants in the Empire of God in Rome what would it look like? Who were the participants? What did they know about the Empire of God? What did they understand about Jesus? When the author of the Gospel of Mark looked around the various communities of believers, what did he find?

Colbert's "Nation" helps us to understand Mark's community. We do not really know who is a part of the "Nation." We assume that "Nation" includes a diverse live and television audience of greatly varying political, social, and economic statuses. By positing them as a single people, a "Nation," Colbert brings them into reality as a single entity gathering up their differences into a unity that he created and maintains through his designation of them as a community of viewers.

Mark's community, based on the reading of his gospel, would have been equally as diverse as Colbert's "Nation." We imagine that Mark's community was comprised of both Romans and Jews. Both Romans and Jews were immersed in the artistic, intellectual, and literary life of the Roman Empire, including the pervasive philosophical movements of the day with their orientation toward moral and spiritual reformation of the person and society.

Since Mark's gospel includes so many healing stories, we can assume that there were those in his community oriented toward the power to heal. Some of those miracle-oriented people were Jews who recognized in Jesus's healing the prophetic powers of the prophets Elisha and Elijah to heal the sick and raise the dead. Jesus's walking on the water (6:45–52) and his feeding of the multitudes (6:34–44 and 8:1–10) remind us of the miracles of the Exodus of the Israelites from Egypt, which Jews celebrate during Passover. Others of the miracle-oriented people were Romans who interpreted Jesus's miracles as indicative of the kinds of healing the god Aesclepius performed. The first cure of the demoniac resembles this aesculapian form of healing: "All were amazed and asked one another, 'What is this? A new teaching with authority. He commands even the unclean spirits and they obey him'" (1:27). The healing of the Gerasene demoniac (5:1–24), which we will discuss further in a little while, also displays a Roman healing orientation. So we can imagine people in Rome thinking about how the miracles of Jesus announced and propelled the Empire of God.

We also can imagine there were people in this community who knew of the Empire of God through the wisdom teachings of Jesus found in his parables, which show how the Empire of God operates in the world. Chapter 4 of the gospel has the parable of the seed sown on the various kinds of earth (4:1–9), the parable of the lamp on the lampstand and not under a bushel (4:1–15), the parable of the seed growing on its own (4:26–30), and the parable of the small mustard seed that becomes a large plant to shelter birds (4:30–34). We also have the parable of the tenants who tried to kill the owner of the vineyard (12:1–12) and the story of the fig tree that withered (11:20–25). These people understood the Empire of God as something mysteriously unfolding in their midst, a mystery that reveals the mind and will of God for doing new things for the people of God. The parables of Jesus revealed for them God's mind, for the Empire that God was building through Jesus's teaching.

Mark's community also consisted of students who took the sayings of Jesus about the new way of living in the Empire of God and created stories to elaborate them. These elaborations (*chreiae* in Greek) are numerous in the gospel, and they often revolve about conflict with other teachers, most notably those called Pharisees. A good example is the saying "No one sews a piece of unshrunken cloth on an old cloak. If he does, its fullness pulls away, the new from the old, and the tear gets worse. Likewise, no one pours new wine into old wineskins. Otherwise, the wine will burst the skins, and both the wine and the skins are ruined. Rather, new wine is poured into fresh wineskins" (2:21–22). This saying has been embedded into a question put to Jesus by John the Baptist's disciples about why Jesus's disciples did not fast. It is an elaboration of a story formed around a saying of Jesus about the Empire of God, a saying that was memorized and passed on to others, and it shows the superior teaching of Jesus in relationship to the teaching of John and others. The same process is evident in the story of the disciples and the Sabbath (2:23–28) where the saying "The sabbath was made for humans, not humans for the sabbath" (our translation) explains why the disciples of Jesus did not observe some of the Jewish laws. Again, we find the sayings and controversies embedded in an argument about why Jesus's followers did not follow the traditions of the Jewish elders (7:1–16). The Gospel of Mark is replete with such elaboration and conflict stories, and the people to whom they spoke were most likely students in the Empire of God.

Mark's community also had people who entered the Empire of God primarily through reading the Israelite prophets and other books of the Israelite scriptures. In fact, Mark identifies the origins of the good news of Jesus Christ, the gospel of Jesus Christ, in the prophetic books. The very first verse of the gospel says, "The origins of the gospel of Jesus Christ, the Son of God is as it is written in Isaiah the prophet" (our translation). Mark says that if one wants to know where the good news of Jesus began, read the prophet Isaiah, or look at a living prophet, John the Baptist. The prophetic books and psalms also form the accounts of Jesus's crucifixion, as we will see later. Many members of Mark's Roman community steeped themselves in the Israelite scriptures, read the Empire of God through the scriptures, and even used them to characterize Jesus.

Roman adherents to Christianity most likely came to understand Jesus as a type of Roman philosopher and holy man. Influenced by Stoic philosophy, they could image Jesus as a philosopher whose short and pithy sayings and his controversies with other teachers reflected the Roman school context where teachers vied for students and competed for attention. As a holy man, a holy teacher, Jesus displayed the Roman popular piety we see in the reverence for Apollonius. And these Romans needed to learn and understand the Israelite scriptures in order to understand how Jesus and his Empire of God connected to ancient traditions, which the Romans valued deeply.

There were probably also some Pauline believers in Mark's community, those who looked to the presence and reality of the Empire of God in eating the bread that was the body of Christ and drinking from the cup that was the blood shed for the people. For these believers the Eucharist provided a way to remember Jesus and to celebrate the Empire of God as a present reality for them. The supper made the Lord present in new times.

The Purpose of Mark's Gospel

So when Mark looked at the great variety of people in the Empire of God in Rome in his day, his head must have reeled at the diversity. What could he do to bring them together, to unite them, to unify them? How could he resolve the conflict between various kinds of participants in the Empire of God without becoming a divider or taking sides with any one group? That was the problem that faced Mark, and it was only amplified by the fact that the author of Mark was writing during the principate of Nero, when any such organized and unified alternative empire would have drawn fire from the Empire. It was a dangerous time to be gathering a "Nation."

Mark's response to the need to unify a diverse group of people during a threatening and hostile period of their history was a brilliant one. Mark decided to shift the emphasis from the Empire of God to the person of Jesus. Mark would write a biography of Jesus that would hold together all the elements familiar to the various kinds of believers in the Empire of God, but focus them on the person who inaugurated that Empire, Jesus, the Son of God. The focus on the life of Jesus—healer, prophet, sage, religious opponent, and teacher—would place all the disparate parts into one whole. Each group in Mark's community would be able to recognize their understanding of the Empire of God as they knew it, based in the life, teaching, and works of Jesus.

Perhaps the best way to understand how the author of Mark understood his role is to compare his task with Seneca's letters to Lucillius. As we have already indicated, Seneca wrote fictitious letters in order to provide Lucillius with a plan for living. Seneca's letters became an instrument of spiritual and religious (for him, philosophical) formation. Mark also became a spiritual guide to his diverse, and often conflicted, community of people who had chosen to enter the Empire of God inaugurated by Jesus, God's Son. Mark, however, chose not letters (this was Paul's chosen genre of literature) but a biography to structure the religious lives of his community. But the aim was the same as Seneca's: to provide a literary creation that would mold and transform his people. The purpose of writing, therefore, was not simply to document the traditions about Jesus, nor even to preserve memories of Jesus, but rather creatively and energetically to provide his community with an instrument of formation. For Mark, this instrument was the weaving of all the trajectories of the believers and participants in the Empire of God into one story, the life and ministry of Jesus. Mark's choice, as we know from the biographies of Apollonius, was not a unique one. Apollonius, as you recall, was also a teacher, an exorcist of demons, a healer, and a teacher of wisdom. So Mark followed the tradition of using biography as a means of community formation—a tradition that the readers and hearers of the gospel would know well.

If the Gospel of Mark, then, was not primarily oriented toward providing information about Jesus, then what is it? This is a complex question. The gospel, a genre of literature that the Gospel of Mark created, is a narrative in the tradition of the ancient biography whose purpose was to reveal the character of a person through the creation of exemplary incidents and sayings. A biography was an imaginative creation, calling upon the writers' capacities to imagine the life and circumstances of the person about whom they were writing. It is understood that the description of character in this genre of literature is neither biography nor history in any modern sense, but an imaginative, revelatory literary creation:

the purpose of the biography is to reveal the inner workings of a famous person's character. But Mark's gospel, while focusing on Jesus, really reveals the inner workings of those who would gather around Jesus to enter the Empire of God. It is not mere ancient biography, but a kind of exposition of the movement that Jesus inaugurated. Moreover, the Gospel of Mark is written in a popular style of Greek and this suggests that the gospel intended to engage a broad spectrum of society for entertainment and perhaps for instruction. The popular style, which is very rough and unsophisticated, seems a deliberate strategy to characterize the new genre as accessible to even the lowest strata of society. We say that it is deliberate precisely because parts of the gospel, most notably the passion narrative, seem to be written in a better, more fluid and sophisticated style. So the author of the gospel was choosing a style deliberately to appeal to the masses and to give the impression of a community whose Greek was not very good. Finally, the Gospel of Mark, precisely as a narrative in the popular tradition, displays a rhetorical organization which was intended to be read out loud as a whole and performed publicly as a literary production. We must, then, read Mark as a whole literary piece, that was performed publicly (as all Roman literature, both Greek and Latin was), and that had a rhetorical function both to entertain and to instruct. In other words, the gospel narrative provided the public a performative occasion for the interpretation and understanding of the community's life, based on the story cre-ated by the author of Mark, who in turn used elements from the oral tradition of the sayings and deeds of Jesus.

Let us state our thesis about the Gospel of Mark so that you will know from the beginning where we are going. The Gospel of Mark, written in Rome sometime in the 60s CE, is a variation on an ancient biography that served, among other things, as a narrative for the formation of the community. This means that the primary function of the gospel was not to communicate information about Jesus (that information would have come from other means in the community as we have already indicated), but rather to provide information about how people were to be trained to live out their participation in the community of adherents to the religion. The Gospel of Mark is a formative narrative intended primarily to train the community in the proper way of living and dying, and it was written to draw together into one unified literary piece the various disparate understandings of the Empire of God found in the Roman community in which it was performed.

Since the formative aspect of the Gospel of Mark emerges from a specific community, then the location and dating of the gospel become much more central items of information necessary to the proper reading of the gospel. The tradition, supported by recent scholarship, maintained that Mark was written in Rome following the death of Peter. Tradition places the composition of the Gospel of Mark in Rome in the period 65–70 CE, that is, during the troubled last few years of the principate of Nero (54–68 CE).

Our portal to the Gospel of Mark talked about the literary and intellectual life of the Roman Empire that had changed significantly during the very powerful principate of Nero, who supported literary productions. It was a time of highly developed rhetoric, creative exploration of new and original styles of writing, development of new genres of literature, and eagerness to entertain the public at readings of daring and new writings. The Gospel of Mark was composed in this shifting literary scene in Rome.

The Creative Energy of Mark's Gospel

The formation that the author of the Gospel of Mark presented had many dimensions. First, he taught the Roman Christians how to survive in a hostile environment by teaching them a particular way of telling their story about the Empire of God that would elude the attentions of the Roman authorities. Second, the gospel developed a portrait of Jesus similar to descriptions of Roman philosophical teachers, a portrait that created a Christianity Romans could understand and respect. Third, the gospel taught the community how to read the Empire of God in the life of Jesus as a refraction and extension of the Israelite scriptures. And finally, the gospel provided information and context for the ritual life of the community in their practices of baptism, Eucharist, leadership, and table fellowship.

To understand the very creative task that Mark's gospel accomplished, we should begin with an overview of Mark's project in writing his Roman gospel. Mark's gospel ostensibly employs the biography of Jesus written as a narrative novel as a means of providing the Roman Christian community with an instrument of formation that is as politically dissident and as theologically and philosophically sophisticated as Seneca's letters to Lucilius. The biography of Jesus conceals a system of political and religious formation under the narrative art of the biography of Jesus; in other words, the evangelist is not writing a biography of the past, but rather addresses issues in his own context and in his own community at the time of his writing of the gospel. His purpose is to make the gospel narrative relevant to his community by offering them a means of unifying diverse perspectives on Jesus into one common narrative frame.

But how can we say that the gospel is not primarily about the person and significance of Jesus? Prior to the composition of the Gospel of Mark, there was little interest in details of Jesus's biography. Paul's interest focuses primarily on the crucifixion, death, resurrection, and appearance of Jesus to followers with a single reference to Jesus being "born of a woman, born under the law" (Galatians 4:4). Moreover, in the collection of the sayings of Jesus, we find little interest in the death and resurrection of Jesus, and primary interest in the wisdom sayings he promulgated. In the collection of miracle stories, Jesus is metaphorized both as a new Moses and as a powerful Aesclepius, but neither metaphorical frame communicates anything about the biography of Jesus as a person. The controversy stories portray Jesus as a wise teacher, again with no interest in his biography, while he functions as a heavenly figure in apocalyptic scenarios of the Pauline letters and the apocalyptic vision predating the Gospel of Mark. Even the very historical and biographical sounding passion narrative resonates with extensive intertextual referencing to the prophetic books of Israel. All of these environments, collections, articulations (whatever we want to call them), image Jesus positively as a function, a role, a figure, and they take very little interest in his person. Prior to Mark's gospel, there was a wide diversity of ways of describing the significance of Jesus, none of them dependent upon the particularities of his life—all of them dependent upon the significance of his words and deeds in the context of people enacting the Empire of God. And it was the various enactments of the Empire that created diverse understandings of the figure of Jesus—as Wisdom, as Moses, as Elisha, as Son of Man, as Teacher, as Healer, and the list could go on. All these perspectives were present in the Roman communities for whom Mark wrote.

The narrative and biographical parts of this framework can be summarized in one paragraph: sometime around 28 CE, Jesus of Nazareth, an ethnic and religious Jew, began an itinerant ministry in Galilee, an out-of-the-way and rural place in the northern part of the Roman province of Palestine. In his ministry, Jesus proclaimed the coming of the Empire of God as a time of justice for all, healed the sick, and demonstrated divine control of nature. As part of this ministry, he formed a community of men and women from whom he selected twelve to receive special training. During this period, for reasons difficult to discern from the narrative of the text itself, Jesus attracted the active animosity of Roman and Judean leaders. Despite this, when his popularity in Galilee was assured, Jesus and his disciples journeyed to Jerusalem at the time of a Passover celebration. There Jesus engaged in further teaching, particularly about the proper use of the Temple. Powerful enemies were emboldened and had Jesus crucified. At Jesus's imprisonment, most of the disciples fled in fear of their own lives. A few days after his death, a group of women went to the burial site and found it empty. A white-robed young man told them to return to Galilee to there await a Jesus raised from the dead.

Once Mark shifted all these traditions to the narrative in the style of a biography, the history of Christianity as a religion shifted ground. In antiquity, there was no confusion between a novelistic life and reality: all biographies were constructed, they were fabrications created out of the details ascribed to a person's life in order to reveal the person's character. The author of the Gospel of Mark created a narrative of a real life of a real person whose actions were described through the literary device of using the historical present tense, thus giving the impression of an eyewitness report. But this is a fictional and narrative strategy that the author of Mark created artistically for some rhetorical purpose during the Neronian principate. Once Mark put all the parts into the whole, that is, once the author of Mark created the biography of Jesus in his novelistic narrative, it was no longer possible to look back to the older ways of understanding. Once Jesus was the center of the Empire of God, the understanding of the Empire of God shifted focus. This Markan story of Jesus the Christ, which began in the prophets and ends with a suggestion of a resurrection of the crucified prophet, became the foundation document for a new religion that was diverging slowly and inexorably from sectarian status within Judaism. It took on a life of its own, as we see in the revisions of the document by Matthew and Luke, but the various Christian communities had survived and grown for nearly forty years before a biographical narrative was produced. Mark's literary achievement was simply brilliant. He not only unified his local Roman community, but he also transformed Christianity as a religion by focusing Christians' attention on Jesus, in whom were reconciled competing and diverse practices.

The gospel provided the basis for a variety of different lifestyles dependent upon the needs and interests of its interpreters. The correlation of the manner of living and dying with the interpretation of the story of the gospel fascinated early Christians. It is not that the description of the life of Jesus did not matter, but that everyone probably knew that the narrative of the gospel, created with a preponderance of elaborated stories built into a kind of biography, did not present information about the historical Jesus as a model to be imitated. Rather, it provided the scriptural and textual basis for an exercise in interpretation that would result in a way of living, a manner of life and death. Since the community learned about Jesus Christ through a variety of other more effective means of communication, the Gospel of Mark became a handbook of community and personal formation in the Roman church.

Mark and Dissimulation

Whenever Colbert interviews a guest on his show, the guest becomes the fodder for his dissimulation. Colbert turns the interview into an interview about himself. He uses the interview to reflect back on himself, and to underscore his egocentricity. While interviewing authors, for example, Colbert covers all the important points of the book, while at the same time pointing out his apparent conservative ideology. The guests presumably know in advance that the energy and focus will be on Colbert, and they try to circumvent his egocentric comments and address the issues of their books. They always fail, because Colbert never allows the guest to best him, and that is part of the fun. The interview on the surface reveals the Colbert personality, while under the surface, the guest talks about his or her book and receives significant publicity among Colbert's following, Colbert's "Nation."

The author of Mark is like Colbert interviewing Jesus. The Markan narrative about Jesus was carefully crafted, as it had to be in the complex Neronian literary and political context. Here we see Mark's formative brilliance at work. Dissimulation was a rhetorical strategy identified by Roman orators to persuade the readers by being ambivalent and perhaps even deliberately deceptive about the speaker's true intent. This could occur either in the choice of linguistic style or in the choice of words. We find the author of the Gospel of Mark espoused both methods.

The Gospel of Mark is often characterized as the least literary of the canonical gospels. The vocabulary and the literary construction of the whole text are both relatively rudimentary. Long sentences with compound, complex clauses were encouraged by the best Greek stylists and mark a good deal of Luke/Acts and the letters written by Paul. But Mark's style is short and abrupt. Quick scene changes are marked by the frequent use of the formula "and immediately Jesus went . . ." While these observations may be taken as denigrating the style of the Gospel of Mark, in fact, one of the oldest of the ancient style books, used and imitated by students in antiquity in learning how to construct an argument, describes three styles of oratory: the Grand, the Middle, and the Simple. The Grand was to be a flowing, ornate composition using impressive words. The Middle was not to be as fancy, yet not completely colloquial either. We might liken the Grand style to the high-sounding pomp of a new president's inaugural speech and the Middle style to use in everyday business communications, whether letters or oral presentations. The Simple style referred to the colloquial, a street style of standard speech. The great Roman orator Cicero used different styles in his speeches depending on whether he was speaking to the Roman Senate or the general populace. In this way, orators were to choose the style that would be the most effective for advancing their argument or, in the case of the Gospel of Mark, the community's understanding and the community's adversaries misunderstanding of the way to enact the Empire of God. Using this Simple style, the narrator of the text sounds like a Jewish fisherman of the first century: relatively untutored in the best Greek styles but nevertheless a trustworthy guide to the requisite practices. Adopting that rhetorical style accomplished two things: it hid the artistry of the text while making it accessible to a large and uneducated audience.

Why adopt such a style? One persuasive explanation is that such a style would indicate a very unschooled gathering of religious practitioners. In a world dominated by royalty and proper ancestry, managed by cultivated orator-lawyers, how dangerous to the stability of the Empire could people be who could not even speak well? Their story of a Jewish carpenter, crucified by a Roman official in the furthest province of the Empire forty years before, who led an undisciplined group of Jewish fishermen and other lowlifes, is told in a style one might expect from barbarians on the fringes of the Empire. They need not be taken seriously. And so the Christians might stay below the notice of the protectors of Roman values and stability. Unlike the followers of the Egyptian goddess Isis or the astrologers of Babylon, these people pose no real threat to the morals and values of the Roman people. Nero's persecution a few years previously was the action of a deranged man searching for a scapegoat for the terrible fire; he found it among Christian people of no education, sophistication, or social status.

Mark turned to the rhetorical practice of *dissimulatio*, the rhetorical strategy described in our portal to the Gospel of Mark. Dissimulation hid the real significance of a person's thought and belief under a mask of socially and politically safe appearance. Recall that the rhetorician Quintilian maintained that dissimulation is "when we say one thing and mean another" as "the most effective of all means of stealing into the minds of men." And he argued that dissimulation was most effective "so long as we adopt a conversational rather than a controversial tone" (Quintilian, *de Oratore*, IX.i.29, quoting Cicero, *de Oratore*, III.ii.201). Mark's Greek is certainly very colloquial and common, and his story conceals the truth about Jesus and his followers under the guise of a failed movement with a crucified leader. Mark's dissimulation depends upon creating an "insider" who understands the true meaning of the story, and an "outsider" who sees only the surface of things. Mark's gospel conceals for the outsider and reveals for the insider. It is a masterful rhetorical strategy that would have been appealing to both his Roman and Jewish audience, who as insiders wanted to stay under the radar and as outsiders would have found the description risible.

Making the Outsider an Insider

We will consider here, in the context of "insider/outsider" texts, that a significant part of the passion narrative seems to fit this description. There are too many similarities in Mark's account between a Roman triumph, the entry of a victorious general into Rome, and Jesus's treatment by the Roman cohort to be coincidental. The whole action starts when the Roman soldiers take Jesus from the outside where their actions would be observed, to the inside, the main hall or *praetorium* (15:16). There the whole cohort—some five hundred soldiers!—dress him in purple, crown him, and "mock him." In these actions they mimic Roman legionnaires participating in the triumph of a Roman general. Triumphs were granted by the Senate to generals who had won significant victories. In the triumph, the general led his troops into the city of Rome wearing a scarlet robe and a crown. The Romans put an even more impressive purple robe and a crown on Jesus. The general's troops marched along alternately singing songs that mocked and praised him. One soldier went before the general with a switch, striking him and repeating "Remember that you are a mortal." The intent of the mocking was twofold: so that the gods would not be jealous of the honor shown to the general, nor would the general mistake himself for a god. Compare that with Mark's description of their treatment of Jesus.

> The soldiers led him away inside the palace, that is, the praetorium, and assembled the whole cohort. They clothed him in purple and, weaving a crown of thorns, placed it on him. They began to salute him with, "Hail, King of the Jews!" and kept striking his head with a reed and spitting upon him. They knelt before him in homage. And when they had mocked him, they stripped him of the purple cloak, dressed him in his own clothes, and led him out to crucify him (15:16–20).

We understand Mark's gospel to affirm that the Roman army in Palestine made a secretive statement about their worship of Jesus (15:19), which those outside, the crowd calling for his crucifixion, would not understand. On the surface, the soldiers indeed are mocking and torturing Jesus. Looking below the surface, one sees the Roman legionnaires as the first humans to acknowledge Jesus's sovereignty.

The insider/outsider strategy is reinforced by Jesus's insistence on hiding his true identity. Throughout the narrative, Jesus orders demons, those he has cured, and his disciples not to reveal his identity (3:11; 7:36; 8:29–30). As we said earlier, the demons expelled by Jesus in healing, and the Roman guards at the crucifixion, precisely as outsiders, proclaim the truth about Jesus. But Jesus often rejects that disclosure. For instance, after the Transfiguration, the appearance on a mountaintop with Moses and Elijah, the great Jewish leaders and ancestors in faith, Jesus charges the three senior disciples, Peter, James, and John who witnessed the appearance "not to relate what they had seen to anyone, except when . . . [Jesus] . . . had risen from the dead" (9:9). Jesus forbids disclosure by these disciples who have seen Jesus in his glory and have begun to understand who he is. These insiders must not reveal his identity yet. On the other hand, Jesus does order the Gerasene (5:2–20), an outsider cured of demonic possession, to acknowledge "all that the Lord in his pity has done for you" (5:19) and the cured man does so (5:20). Jesus forbids the insiders, the Jewish disciples, from revealing what they know, while encouraging the outsiders, the Romans, to tell all they know.

Why would Jesus, an itinerant preacher and miracle-worker, order those he confronts, those he heals, and those he teaches to hide his identity? It is as though Jesus kept his imperial status secret, or hidden. We propose that the whole secrecy motif be considered as a part of the author's use of dissimulation. In the Gospel of Mark, Jesus models dissimulation, for he speaks only in parables so that outsiders will not understand the message. In the same way, the more he tells those he has cured not to reveal his identity the more they ignore him, and the more his words commanding secrecy mean the opposite of their normal meaning.

The insider/outsider motif is one of the ways Mark tells the audience to dig deeper, to look below the surface for a guide to Jesus's identity. The gospel also relies on Israelite scriptures to provide a context for understanding Jesus. Since these texts were largely unfamiliar to anyone outside the Judean community in Rome, certain of the resonances of the images with royal, political themes easily would be missed by an outsider overhearing a public reading of the gospel. At the same time, Roman authorities would be generally familiar with the fact that the Judeans had handed down such scriptures for hundreds of years and hence the Romans assumed them to be valuable. Hearing scriptures recited, therefore, might be reassuring to the observer. On the other hand, armed with the scriptures and Jesus's own instruction to "dig deeper," we would expect the Jesus followers to pour over the gospel, commenting on the many scriptural allusions and deciding how these allusions affected their own understanding of the gospel.

Dissimulation for Survival

We believe Mark's Jesus modeled the use of dissimulation that then became a tactic for survival for the Roman community. Jesus of Nazareth may indeed be the new emperor, but the story is that he is a failed emperor whose teaching led to his death (8:32–33). During his active life, his disciples—barely literate fishermen, low class even, from a distant, disadvantaged province like Palestine—never understood the import of his message and fled at the moment of crisis (14:50, 72), leaving him to die on a cross (15:37). True, the gospel tells us that there was an empty tomb, but the gospel closes on the narrator's comment that women who were to convey that news to the apostles "said nothing to anyone for they were afraid" (16:8). The logical conclusion to be drawn from this narrative is that the very Roman soldiers who gave Jesus a triumph in the *praetorium* (15:16–20), crucified him, but then proclaimed him Son of God (15:39), were also the ones who spread the gospel of Jesus of Nazareth. On the surface, this appears to be a ridiculous conclusion, but for first-century Romans, it may not have seemed far-fetched.

The community that read or performed the gospel, having lived through a period of political and social turmoil, having experienced persecution themselves a few years before, are now empowered to use dissimulation themselves. Within the community there were texts, including this gospel, with multiple levels of meaning. Jesus instructs the Christians in Rome to look for the deeper meaning in these texts. The gospel gives authorization for similar linguistic strategies on the part of the community. There is no need to wear one's religious commitment on one's sleeve. Blend in with the crowd and find ways to say one thing but really mean something else. Bumper stickers today carry the symbol of a fish as a sign of a Christian. The symbol first represents a fish but to the eyes of the insider it indicates the commitment of the individual to a life following Jesus.

Decoding Dissimulation

The student of the Gospels will then ask: how can anyone know what the author meant to say? What was the message supposed to be? After all, if the whole gospel is a dissimulation, how can we tell what the real message is? How can we tell when Jesus is speaking in a straightforward, declaratory manner and when Jesus expects his followers to dig deeper?

To answer the question, consider how Colbert's "Nation" decides what is "true" and what is "comedy" on *The Colbert Report*. First of all, they do not doubt that the "hard news" events really happened. There is a war in Iraq; Democrats and Republicans do compete in elections; elected officials can be counted on to make complete fools of themselves. The show's directors and producers regularly use tricks to create comical connections between what Colbert says and the real person or situation he discusses. "Nation" is well aware of, but untroubled by, the deceptive nature of these practices. That is not the point, to them. They do not look to *The Colbert Report* for a recitation of events—CNN does that admirably (and even a Rupert Murdoch tabloid does it adequately)—but for a commentary on the absurd truth and underlying meaning of these events. Thus, for "Nation," dissimulation is a form of entertainment and, at the same time, a way to raise awareness of the chaotic state of the world.

The practice of dissimulation also serves as a coded language for oppressed people, such as during the experience of slavery by African Americans. The oppressed develop a coded way of speaking. During slavery, the spirituals created by the slaves sounded to their masters like hymns to the Christian God imposed on the slaves. To those singing, they were prayers of hope and faith in their ultimate deliverance from bondage. The slaves, largely illiterate like the Christians in Rome, had no trouble constructing hymns with sophisticated multiple levels of meaning. Viewed in this light, the use of dissimulation would not have presented an insuperable impediment to the understanding of the gospel Mark composed. The hearers of the gospel could learn more about Jesus and about his practices by becoming insiders, and by reading Jesus in light of their scriptures . . . and their scriptures in light of Jesus, as they became insiders on how to read Israelite scriptures as well.

A Portrait of Jesus as a Roman Jew

First-time viewers of *The Colbert Report* are challenged to figure out who Colbert really is. It is the first task of the viewer to decode the images and to analyze for themselves which messages really portray the true Colbert. Is Colbert the reactionary conservative? Does Colbert's laughing at his own conservative statements reveal that he does not really believe them? Before a viewer can understand the program, the viewer must come to grips with the real Colbert.

In a similar way, for the audience to understand the Gospel of Mark, they need to decipher the real Jesus in the narrative. This deciphering is Mark's second formative strategy. Was Jesus a completely uncivilized Palestinian revolutionary like those others who were battling the Roman army in Palestine? Or was Jesus a Greek philosopher, perhaps debunking all the achievements of society? In fact, how civilized could this untutored Galilean have been? The Gospel of Mark establishes Jesus as a Roman Jew. He certainly is Jewish in his religious practices and commitments, his reliance on the Israelite scriptures, and his mode of arguing. But Mark makes sure that his Roman identity is equally well-established.

Jesus the Emperor

We are told in the first verse that this is an *evangelion*, the Greek word translated as "gospel," which is normally an imperial proclamation from a Roman emperor that announces information important to the governance of the empire. An *evangelion*, a gospel, is therefore an imperial edict of great importance and interest to the people. Mark made Jesus, the new emperor of a new divine empire, the subject of his imperial edict. In fact, Mark writes an imperial biography of Jesus so that all the necessary information about the Empire of God, drawn from various sources and beliefs about the divine Empire, could be identified with the emperor Jesus's words and deeds. Jesus of Nazareth, then, is of the royal household, indeed a Son of God (1:1).

While Mark proclaims Jesus an emperor, unlike the emperors Caligula or Nero, Jesus is not arbitrary, does not put to death on a whim, and does not marry half the women in the immediate family. Unlike the emperor Claudius, Jesus is not an aged, enfeebled puppet, manipulated by the bureaucrats. In fact, Mark portrays Jesus as a very different kind of emperor and the Empire of God as a very different kind of empire. Jesus from the beginning of the Gospel of Mark has a consistent focus on the sick, the poor, the foreigners, the children. While Jesus has called disciples to be companions on the journey, they control neither Jesus nor his message. Blandishments to assume a "normal" life from Jesus's family and friends are met with disdain: "Get behind me, Satan. You are thinking not as God does, but as human beings do" (8:33). In his virtuous, upright life, Jesus resembled the great Caesar Augustus. Like Caesar Augustus before him, Jesus defends traditional Roman family values, denying the right of remarriage to divorced men and women (10:2–12). There is no mention of a spouse or children, so that the royal line dies with Jesus: there will be no internecine battles for supremacy.

Jesus is a vigorous emperor, walking the countryside of Palestine and southern Syria. There he takes on and defeats "legions of demons" (5:9) who inhabit the country. And like the recent majority of emperors, Jesus ends up being killed by Roman soldiers, who nonetheless acknowledge royalty with the sign on the cross "Jesus of Nazareth, King [Emperor] of the Jews" (15:26).

The Roman and Jewish Jesus

In many of these attitudes and behaviors, Jesus of Nazareth resembles a Stoic sage. Like a good Stoic, Jesus understands the ways of the world well enough to be able to predict a fate of death by assassination. And like a good sage, Jesus went on with life in accordance with that same fate. Jesus's royal powers and stoicism are combined in the story in Mark 4:37–41. Here Mark recounts the story of Jesus's falling asleep in the stern of the boat during a squall so violent that his disciples were compelled to rouse him. Jesus, perhaps annoyed at being awakened, rebuked first nature (the wind and sea) and then his disciples: "Why are you terrified? Do you not yet have faith?" The story is reminiscent of one told of a Stoic sage who showed fear at the onset of a storm, although Stoics should be indifferent to external circumstances. In that story, the sage takes the opportunity to show why this occurs. Our point, however, is that Jesus acts as the perfect Stoic sage, indifferent to the tempestuous seas.

Jesus was also, however, a Roman Jew. From the very beginning of the text, Jesus's history is situated within the prophetic tradition of Israel. At the Transfiguration, Jesus appears with two great prophets and leaders of the nation, Moses and Elijah. Later, when confronted by the high priest to reveal his identity (14:61–62), Jesus quotes from the book of Daniel, and refers to himself as the Son of Man, the one who would come at the end of time to judge the world (Daniel 7:13). Throughout the passion narrative, unquestionably the most carefully constructed section of the gospel, the text refers directly to Jesus fulfilling numerous Messianic prophecies, and has other allusions to prophetic sayings.

Jesus was intimately familiar with the texts of the Israelite scriptures, attended synagogues on the Sabbath and, the reader surmises, faithfully practiced the religion of Israel. According to Mark, Jesus taught about the impending Empire of God, conversion and repentance in lives, the priority of care for the poor, the sick, and the oppressed, and the need to reconcile with sinners.

How does such a portrait jibe with a rhetoric of dissimulation? The audience would hear a story of the most failed political leader imaginable: dead four decades with no land of his own; crucified for treason, claiming to be an emperor; and deserted by followers. The rehearsal of a royal triumph that the Jesus followers saw played out in Jesus's final hours reads on the surface as the typical brutality of the Roman legions. In Jesus's death throes, he cries out the first line of Psalm 22: "My God, my God, why have you forsaken me?" Are the remarks of the centurion ironic (perhaps "THIS was a son of God?") or emphatic ("This WAS a Son of GOD!")? That would depend on the inflection of the speaker. The empty tomb is only attested to by a group of women who themselves, we learn, tell no one out of fear. Perhaps Judeans would be enamored of such a philosopher, for such he well might have been, but his death meant nothing to the glory of the Roman Empire. Mark portrays Jesus, the true emperor of the true

Empire, as a person who on the surface was a complete failure, a marginalized and defeated leader of a group of intimate followers who neither understood him nor stayed with him in his great hour of need.

But surely Mark did not really consider Jesus a failure, a defeated and crucified pretender to imperial power. That is the point of dissimulation: that the true meaning of the gospel is masked under a facade. The more Mark makes Jesus appear like a failure, the more Mark underscores Jesus's success. The disciples who on the surface do not understand Jesus and who abandon him know much better than the demons that Jesus is the Holy One of God, and they know better than the Roman soldiers that Jesus is the Son of God and that Jesus is indeed an emperor not just of the Jews, but of the whole world. Mark embeds this truth, however, in his dissimulation so that the readers and hearers learn the opposite message hidden in the surface of Mark's biography. The readers and hearers must attend to a very different message than the one portrayed on the surface of this biography of Jesus. The community sees how the rhetorical technique of dissimulation can be used to preserve the life of the community and how the same technique points the believer, the insider, to the deeper meanings of scriptures and other texts. Using the Simple style engages the whole of the community and leads the performer away from ostentatious declarations. For Mark's gospel, dissimulation models a way of living in a hostile environment without attracting undue attention or hostility.

Formation and Dissimulation

It is interesting to watch how Colbert trains his audience, his "Nation," in understanding his message. He never strays from the conservative perspective, but through various means he trains his readers to see otherwise. One example is the recurring segment called, "The Word." Here Colbert takes a word that he analyzes with a commentary consistent with his conservative ideology. But the images and words projected into "The Word" frame on the television screen present the opposite message; that is, it undermines the conservative statements with images and phrases that speak in a more truthful or more liberal perspective. The dissonance between Colbert's speaking and the projected images trains the audience to look deeper into the message.

Mark's gospel does the same kind of forming of a community. But how did the gospel form people while dissimulating? Two passages in the early narrative of the Gospel of Mark will illustrate our point about both the formative dynamic of the gospel and the centrality of dissimulation to this formation: the Gerasene demoniac (5:1–20) and Herod's birthday party (6:14–29). These two short stories will be read in the narrative and formational context of a series of healings and the commissioning of the disciples in Mark 4:35–6:44.

The Gerasene Demoniac

The story of the healing of the Gerasene demoniac (5:1–20) stands out from the narrative because of its complexity. It is a simple exorcism, a straightforward healing, but the elaborate descriptions—the demoniac's life among the tombs, the name of the demon, the transferal of the demons to the herd of pigs, and the negative response from the villagers—all point to significance beyond the simple healing toward some broader, perhaps more symbolic, understanding of the story. A person with "an unclean spirit" presented himself "from the tombs" (5:2). This sets up the story as being a healing, until the narrator provides a description of the person:

> He had his dwelling among the tombs, and not even with a chain was anyone ever capable of binding him, on the basis that the same person was bound with shackles and chains, and the chains were torn apart by him, and he shattered the shackles, and no one was capable of subduing him; and throughout the night and day among the tombs and on the mountains he was crying out and cutting himself up with stones (5:3–4, our translation)

Such a dramatic description stops the narrative. It portrays the horror of what this unclean spirit does to the person: living among the dead, needing to be shackled and chained and yet destroying the very instruments of his protection, and mutilating himself while screaming loudly. The description draws the reader-listener into the horror of the person's experience. And when the narrator gives the name of the demon after it has been expelled from the person, the reader-listener begins to understand the import of the description: "and he [Jesus] asked him [the demon], 'What is your name?' He [the demon] replied, 'Legion is my name. There are many of us.'" (5:9). The use of the Roman and Latin term for a military unit, a legion of soldiers, gives political meaning to the story. The unclean spirit that persecutes the person represents the Roman military establishment. The Roman army causes the possession of people and drives them into the tombs, and tortures them, and causes them to mutilate themselves. The Roman army is the source of the demonic.

This is dissimulation at its best. Under the guise of an exorcism, a simple healing, a very dangerous political statement is made about the violence of the Roman army. But more than that, the narrator guides the reader-listener into experiencing the horror of the Roman military oppression. The narrator provides the reader-listener with a description of the experience so that the point that is made is not simply intellectual (i.e., the army causes possession), but experiential (the oppression causes people to live among the dead, and to cry out, and to be bound in terrible places and do terrible things to themselves).

The narrator lightens the seriousness of the situation by describing the fate of the legion—to enter pigs and to drown. That this is humorous does not take away from its significance, because, just as people were being fed to animals in the arenas in Rome, so are the military units sent into the favorite Roman meat—a meat forbidden for Jews to eat—and drowned. It may be funny, but it has a serious point: the Romans deserve to become their own food and die. The army deserved to enter a food despised by Jews and die. Colbert could have made a similar statement and the audience may well have found it hilarious!

Finally, the narrator presents a contrast between the formerly demon-possessed person and the crowds. The narrator presents the previously "demon-ized person" as both "clothed" and "exercising self-control" (our translation)—his clothing signifies that without the demons, the person may be restored to proper social dignity, while his self-control signifies that the person exercises the virtues of the philosophical nobility. But the crowds, who probably signify those people within the community of faith who fear the repercussions of overthrow-ing the enemy, cannot endure to see the restoration of the person, so "Then they began to beg him [Jesus] to leave their district" (5:17). The healed person asks to follow Jesus, and being denied, he begins to preach in the Decapolis, but the crowds go away fearful. There is real danger here, danger enough that the local people fear being rid of the Roman army. The dissimulation has worked: the reader-listener knows the awful horror of the Roman imperium and the ef-fect of the Roman army on human sanity, and the fear it instills in the general populace without ever having to invoke any direct criticism of the emperor or his army. The oblique message remains hidden in the otherwise normal story of the miraculous exorcism of a person with a demon. Under the guise of a simple exorcism, the author of the Gospel of Mark has mapped out the effect of the autocratic authority of the Roman Empire, and at the same time he taught his community how to be honest about the oppression they were experiencing without speaking about it openly.

Herod's Feast

Equally as intrusive into the narrative and dramatic in detail is the narrative of Herod's birthday feast (6:14–29). The narrative consists of three parts. The first section (6:14–17) connects the Herod sequence to the announcement of the success of the mission of the disciples:

> And after they went out, they preached so that they might repent, and they cast out many demons, and they anointed many sick folks with oil and they were healed. And when Herod, the king, heard, for his [presumably Jesus's] name had become known, and he said, "John the baptizer has been raised from the dead." (6:12–13, our translation).

The summary description of the deeds of Jesus and his followers, that they preached and healed, raised the question of Jesus's identity. Herod heard about

Jesus's mission and it makes him wonder. This passage questions who Jesus is, but Herod concluded that "the one whom I decapitated, John, he is the one who has been raised" (6:16, our translation). The story switches abruptly from Jesus to the fate of John the Baptist; the story about John intrudes. The second part of the narrative (6:17) gives the reason for John's arrest and Herod's simultaneous fear and fascination with John as background information. The third section relates the story of the dinner (6:21–29). This three-part flashback story takes over the narrative and forces the reader-listener to confront a difficult situation far removed from the main lines of the developing narrative of the gospel. The readers or performers of the gospel find themselves sifting through dissimulation about the identity and role of Jesus under the cipher of John the Baptist.

Herod is named the king. The Greek word for king is also translated as emperor. It is a striking introduction of the multivalency of the term in the story. It could be quite innocently used as simply a petty client-king of one of the eastern Roman provinces. But it also could be quite more. In fact, in the Roman context, there is no question about who the only and true emperor is; this identity remains solid and true, the questioning of which is dangerous. Having introduced the term, the narrator retreats from the implications of the term into a discussion of Jesus's identity, then the story of John's arrest.

When the narrator finally arrives at the dinner, the imperial, or at least ruling-class, implications return. The occasion was a dinner on the occasion of the king/emperor's birthday. Among the honored guests (6:21) are the magisterial commanders of the Roman army, the grandees of the community, and the first citizens of Galilee. This dinner includes the upper echelons of society, invited by the very highest ruler. What follows is well-known. Herodias's daughter dances and pleases Herod, who grants her a wish. The daughter asks for the head of John the Baptizer on a platter and gets it. The narrative aside of this story, which does not easily fit into the developing narrative of the first part of the gospel, has dramatic impact. At the overt level, it tells of the kind of leadership expected from the Roman officials—they are shifty, untrustworthy, weak, and degenerate, doing things they would rather not, because they are bound by the Roman system of honor and shame. At the covert level, however, we have a snapshot of the Neronian court—bloodthirsty, degenerate, powerful, and fickle—controlled by an emperor himself controlled by women. The dissimulation here speaks of Nero under the guise of Herod and tells the readers-listeners that they do not stand a chance at fighting Roman hegemony and autocratic power even by divine vocation (as witnessed in John the Baptizer's fate). Nero's imperial court could be parodied by talking about a far-away people and circumstances surrounding the beheading of a distant prophet. But the Roman Christians would have understood the true reference of the story and would have seen in it their own lives and circumstances.

Living Dangerously

Both these stories (the Gerasene demoniac and the Herodian dinner party) warn the reader-listener about the experience of living in volatile political times. The demoniac describes in detail the sort of oppressive dominance of the ruling powers and the effect of their dominance on the sanity and health of those dominated, while the Herodian dinner party graphically displays the sport of killing favored by the emperor and enjoyed by the Roman upper classes. Both stories point to the political environment in which the gospel narrative functions. While the narrative world of the gospel describes a more pastoral context, since Jesus and all his followers seem to travel by foot or by boat to various regions in the countryside, these two stories shock the reader-listener into remembering that the pastoral dimension is fictional and unrelated to the political realities of the cities where the gospel is being performed. These stories point the way to the great dissimulation that happens in the gospel, where the message is disguised in order to enter into the good graces of the listeners, while delivering a serious and important concept.

Now we can step back into the narrative flow of the gospel as it is being performed. The lengthy section on parables ends at 4:34, and the narrative immediately begins a series of miracle stories. The miracle of the stilling of the storm (4:35–41) shows how people of faith ride out the storm, just as Jesus does, by not being concerned about its impact on them. Jesus sleeps with his head on a pillow and rebukes those who are worrying as lacking faith. The point for the reader-listener is that when the political and social storms engulf them, then they should rest in faith, stand firm, and the buffeting of the storm will not overwhelm. Then crossing to the other side of the sea safely, the Gerasene demoniac meets Jesus (5:1–20). The reader-listener receives a graphic description of the impact both personal and social of those tumultuous, political times. Then follows the interwoven healings of Jairus's daughter and the hemorrhaging woman (5:21–43). Both these stories center on the message of endurance in the face of difficulties, or trust and faith in the face of disheartening situations, and of release from long-term bondage by bold, faithful, and honest action. The interweaving of these stories creates a response to the previous healing of the demoniac possessed by Legion, and provides assurance. The rejection of Jesus by his own people (6:1–6a) underscores this assurance: it is not his longtime friends who understand and have the access to the power of God, but (by implication) the readers-listeners and those in the story who have been healed. In fact, it is those selected who are commissioned to go out to preach and heal (6:6a–13). When they return successfully after their first mission, the narrative plunges us again into the political realities instantiated in Herod's dinner (6:14–29). But this awful dinner returns to the narration of the success of the disciples' mission, and is followed by a true symposium (a Greek and Roman formal dinner party for intellectual conversation): the feeding of the five thousand (6:30–44)—in a green field, with simple fare that fills the stomach, but more so the mind. This symposium organizes an army of God, but the point of the army (unlike the awful effect of Legion on the demonized person) is to provide richly for the members of the community.

The narrative flow of this little section continuously refers back to itself—Legion and the seating of the people in military formations of fifty and a hundred, the miraculous feeding at a symposium on the green and the destructive dinner party of the rich and powerful, to name the two most important self-references. The narrative thread develops on an overt, and seemingly innocuous, level while carrying a potentially dangerous and rebellious message to those capable of hearing it. This is dissimulation put at the service of community formation.

The Markan Narrative

Mark's dissimulation revolves about the relationship of the narrative foreground (the biography of Jesus) to the narrative background (the depiction of the people with whom Jesus interacted and the circumstances surrounding their individual and corporate reactions to him). The background provides the information for the formation of various groups in the proper manner of living and dying through their engagement with Jesus. The dissimulation shifts attention from the foreground to the background, so that the reader-listener attends to the hidden and opaque clues of the context, rather than the transparent and obvious elements of the biography, because the covert message takes precedence over the overt narrative.

The narrative provides the reader-listener with an early and important clue to this rhetoric of dissimulation. The thorny issue of the text, "to you has been given the secret [or mystery] of the imperium of God" (4:11, our translation) with the harsh statement that "to those who are outside, all things occur in parables [or puzzles]" and the proof-text from Isaiah 6:9 ("so that looking, they will look and not see, and hearing, they will hear and not comprehend, lest they turn and it be forgiven them" [our translations]) becomes a simple statement of the rhetorical strategy. Those outside are those outside the community for whom the narrative was created, who, though they hear the narrative, do not understand it because what they will hear concerns the life and death of Jesus, while the real emphasis in the text, by virtue of its dissimulation, is the training of people properly to live and to die under a most repressive political regime. The key to the mystery, or hidden text, is the dissimulation, the saying of one thing, but really referring to an entirely different message for the audience. Once the reader-listener looks to the background, to the covert and hidden dynamic of the text, the message is clear. The narrative of Jesus is the occasion for the communication of a hidden message that will not make sense to those who do not realize that they are engaged in a rhetoric of dissimulation.

In fact, the theme of secrecy in the gospel makes more sense from the perspective of dissimulation, because the secret operates, as it were, outside the narrative world. It points to the reality that those in the background, the demons and those who are healed, understand what is going on about them: Jesus gives them the clue that there is a covert and secret message that is being communicated. Jesus tells them that the narrative engages in rhetorical dissimulation. If the hearer/reader looks to the overt message, the so-called "Messianic secret" refers to Jesus, but from the perspective of the covert message, the orientation toward keeping the secret points to the fact that the message emerges from a hidden and mysterious dynamic in the performance. Over and over again, the narrative reminds us that there are secret things going on in the gospel narrative and that the hearer/reader needs to remember that the secret is the key to the message.

Reading Scriptures

Another formative practice in Mark's gospel related to the way that he trained his community to find common ground in the interpretation and application of the Israelite scriptures to the life of Jesus. Mark made frequent use of the Israelite scriptures in organizing his text and presenting his conception of the meaning of the ministry, passion, death, and resurrection of Jesus. The use of the Israelite scriptures served at least two purposes. In the first place, like the students of other philosophical schools, the Christians' goal would have been to take on the mind of their Master, to become as much like Jesus of Nazareth as possible. Unlike the followers of other philosophers and masters of schools, however, they had no texts attributable to their Master. By showing how Jesus lived, ministered, and died consonant with the Israelite scriptures, Mark valorized this collection of texts for his community, particularly the prophetic texts and psalms of the Israelite scriptures. Reading Jesus's life through these texts, one begins the process of taking on Jesus's mind.

We can see, as well, that the use of texts foreign to the surrounding Romans provided a kind of code, easily understood by an insider but indecipherable to an outsider. It was not unlike the U.S. Navy's use of native Navajo speakers in World War II as radio operators. These men could communicate openly with each other in Navajo with no fear that enemy intelligence officers could decode their conversations. In the same manner, an intelligent, well-read Roman, hearing the Gospel of Mark for the first time, probably would "get" fifty percent of its content and meaning. That is the fifty percent that resonates with the general Greco-Roman culture. The remaining fifty percent comes from allusions and citations from the Israelite scriptures. As a consequence, the author has constructed an overarching means of dissimulation: the true insider knowing the Israelite scriptures hears the resonances of the gospel of the Son of God, while the Roman neighbor understands only a fraction. Because this technique flows through all sixteen chapters, even a cursory review is impractical. Here, we will discuss how Mark sets up the reader's expectations about the entire gospel, informs two key moments with scripture, and shapes the Markan passion narrative.

The use of scripture begins in Mark's first sentence:

> The beginning of the gospel of Jesus Christ (the Son of God) is as it is written in Isaiah the prophet: "Behold, I am sending my messenger ahead of you; he will prepare your way. A voice of one crying out in the desert 'Prepare the way of the Lord! Make straight in the wasteland a highway for our God!'" (1:1–3, our translation).

The important point is that this reading emphasizes that the whole narrative of Jesus is rooted firmly in the prophetic tradition of Israel. The full implications of this statement are important, so we will take the time to consider carefully these words and the form in which they are placed.

Though the author ascribes the quotation to the prophet Isaiah, in fact, the first half of the quotation is taken from the writings of a different and later prophet, Malachi (3:1) (active in the first half of the fifth century BCE), and the second half is from Isaiah (40:3), writing one hundred years earlier. The vocation of the Hebrew prophet is well-characterized as afflicting the comfortable and comforting the afflicted. Mark's cobbled-together quotation artfully incorporates both aspects of prophecy. The Malachi quotation is excerpted from condemnations of Israel for an impure way of life. For Malachi, the messenger who is coming will judge and purify the nation, definitely one afflicting the comfortable. The quote from Isaiah, on the other hand, tells of the work of the Lord returning the people from fifty years of captivity in Babylon, an instance of "comforting the afflicted."

There is one more point to be made with this text and that is the use by Mark of small sections of a familiar passage to cue the congregation to at least remember and probably recite together the whole of the passage. Production of texts in antiquity was an arduous and expensive process. One technique that Jewish scholars followed was to cite just the first word or two of a verse that then stood in for the whole scripture. It would be as if Colbert's "Nation" heard the words "Dearly beloved, we are gathered here . . ." and remembered the whole of their wedding ceremony. In the case of Mark 1:1–3, we have some evidence that this was the case here as well.

So in these few verses, Mark has begun the process of opening the mind of the Master to the Christians in Rome. Surely they must have been intrigued, for this text calls itself a gospel, a proclamation of a new imperial power, resident in one completely fulfilling the prophetic tradition. How can one person embody both the emperor, the most comfortable of the comfortable, and the prophet, the afflicter of the comfortable? How will Jesus of Nazareth resolve this tension?

The Feeding of the Multitudes

During the description of Jesus's ministry, Mark includes two stories of feeding massive numbers of people, five thousand men in chapter 6 and four thousand in chapter 8. The first is an especially illuminating study of Mark's crafting of a long narrative using both Roman traditions and Israelite scriptures. We will first give a plot synopsis and then analyze the text, going a little deeper as the practice of dissimulation requires us to do. The narrative describes Jesus sending the disciples on a missionary expedition and includes the reports of their success. While they are gone, the narrator tells the story of Herod's beheading of John the Baptist, an event which took place at the start of Jesus's career. When the disciples return, Jesus takes them to "the wilderness" for some rest, but rather than having rest, they are met by a crowd of five thousand men whom Jesus proceeds to feed from five loaves of bread and two fish. The whole narrative concludes with another sea-calming story. The disciples, while sailing back to their previous habitat, are caught in a storm. Jesus appears, calms the sea, and the disciples are astounded.

To Roman ears, the story of the feeding of the five thousand would appear as it appears to many of us: an idyllic, pastoral story. Roman nobility valued their farming life, their simple life close to the earth on their rural estates, and in their letters and literature they expressed this pastoral, country life as the epitome of their longing and desire for the good life. They would note with chagrin its contrast with the despicable behavior of the local royal family, while applauding the generosity of the prophet/philosopher/king who used his powers not for his own profit, but to benefit the multitude. If they only went this far with the text from Mark, however, they would miss the rich layers of meaning to be drawn from references to the Israelite scriptures.

First of all, Mark drew heavily on the Exodus story of the deliverance of the Hebrew people. The great Hebrew prophet Moses led the people across the Red Sea out of slavery in the civilized country of Egypt into the wilderness of the Sinai desert, located between Egypt and Palestine, in the Bible's great story of political liberation. Since that time, perhaps fourteen hundred years before Jesus was born, this event has been celebrated by Jews in the springtime of each year. Mark evokes memories of this event in many ways. He begins with Jesus calling his disciples to go into the "wilderness" to rest. To get to the wilderness, the disciples needed to cross the Sea of Galilee, an inland lake thirteen miles long by eight miles wide, just as Moses led the Israelites across the Red Sea out of Egypt, away from the pursuing armies of Pharaoh, into the safety of the wilderness. In the course of the description of the feeding, Mark tells us that Jesus ordered the crowd to sit "on the green grass," indicating that this is springtime, the only time of year grass would have been green. So the feeding of the five thousand becomes a mini-reenactment of the original Exodus, as Jesus leads a large group of Jews into the wilderness in the springtime.

During the time in the wilderness, after the Israelites complained that they were taken from the fleshpots of Egypt only to starve in the wilderness, the Lord God fed the people miraculously with bread and quail. Not trusting in the miraculous in the Markan narrative, the apostles demand that Jesus dismiss the crowd so that the people can find food on their own. But Jesus continues the parallel with the Exodus by miraculously multiplying five loaves of bread and two fish so that they feed the multitude, with twelve baskets left over.

At the conclusion of the feeding, with the crowd dismissed and the apostles on their way, Jesus goes "off to the mountain to pray" (6:46) alone, reminiscent of the times when, during the journey through the wilderness, Moses went to Mount Sinai to commune with God, by himself. The book of Exodus tells us that the people could not see God face-to-face for if they did so, they would die.

Meanwhile, the disciples start back across the Sea of Galilee but the wind is against them. Jesus approaches the boat and identifies himself with the phrase "I am," one of just three times Mark uses the phrase. As with the other two (13:6 and 14:62), the phrase carries with it the remembrance of the appearance of the Lord, the God who delivered the people from slavery in Egypt, to Moses at the burning bush in Exodus 3:14. Mark now attributes the "I am" reference to Jesus, reinforcing his image of a political liberator. In the Exodus context, the Lord is a warrior God who visits ten plagues on Egypt and then destroys the Egyptian army. When Israel is in a proper relationship with their God, the Lord will destroy the enemy. In the Markan episode, with this proclamation, Mark casts Jesus of Nazareth as this warrior Lord, first revealed in the book of Exodus.

Mark tells us that when Jesus sees the great crowd gathered in the wilderness, he pitied them "for they were like sheep without a shepherd" (6:34). The image of a shepherd with her sheep often evokes images of a person comforting and caring for another. The shepherd, we seem to automatically imagine, is cradling a lost sheep, bringing him back to the flock. To be sure, Mark wants the audience to perceive Israel as needing protection and guidance, but there is a distinctly militaristic sense in which shepherd can be taken. In the history of Israel, King David was the most famous shepherd. Now David was anointed to be king when God had withdrawn the divine support from the reign of King Saul. So just as the people of Israel were losing their duly appointed king, becoming like sheep without a shepherd, God has David, a real shepherd, installed. David went on to be a hugely successful military leader, establishing the kingdom of Israel at its greatest extent.

The Israelite scriptures contain other references to sheep and shepherds in a political-military context. In Numbers 27:17, Moses prays for a leader of the people, "who shall act as their leader in all things, to guide them in all their actions; that the Lord's community may not be like sheep without a shepherd." This leader turns out to be Joshua who leads the people across the Jordan River, into the promised land where, according to the book of Joshua, the Hebrew people conquer those living there. In 1 Kings 22:17 the prophet Micaiah foretells the defeat and death of King Ahab: "So Micaiah said: 'I see all Israel scattered on the mountains, like sheep without a shepherd,' and the Lord saying, 'These have no master! Let each of them go back home in peace.'" A third example is the prophet Ezekiel, who condemns the leaders of Israel, the shepherds, because they did not take proper care of the people of Israel.

> You did not strengthen the weak nor heal the sick nor bind up the injured. You did not bring back the strayed nor seek the lost, but you lorded it over them harshly and brutally. So they were scattered for lack of a shepherd, and became food for all the wild beasts. My sheep were scattered and wandered over all the mountains and high hills; my sheep were scattered over the whole earth, with no one to look after them or to search for them (Ezekiel 34: 4–6).

When Mark used the phrase "sheep without a shepherd," the audience remembered how this phrase referred in their scriptures to the relationship between a king and the people of Israel. Making this reference to Jesus of Nazareth and a crowd of five thousand men could not help but evoke images of royalty, kingship, and dominion.

This line of thinking is supported by a phrase we might pass over without much notice, when Mark tells the audience that Jesus "gave orders to have them sit down in groups on the green grass. The people took their places in rows by hundreds and by fifties" (6:39–40). Notice that the first verse implicitly tells us that the men were standing while Jesus was teaching them: not the usual posture for a student in school, but typical for an army receiving instructions. Then they grouped themselves in rows by hundreds and fifties, not in conversation circles, not randomly, but in the numbers reminiscent of Moses organizing the Israelites into companies of "thousands, of hundreds, of fifties, and of tens" (cf. Exodus 18:25 and Deuteronomy 1:15). In other words, the crowd organizes itself into political and military units.

Now we can see how the story of the feeding of five thousand displays the rhetoric of dissimulation. As heard by a nonbelieving Roman, the story speaks of a wilderness miracle. Certainly this was an impressive miracle, but there is nothing about it that seems to threaten the structure of the Empire. For those steeped in the Israelite scriptures, use of highly evocative symbols and phrases (wilderness, spring, sheep without a shepherd, "I am," hundreds and fifties and tens), it leads to a process of reading below the surface. Especially when performed audibly, the insider sees and hears Jesus of Nazareth proclaiming his divinity and exhibiting his imperial power. In the end, however, Jesus sends away the army that would take him to be a king. While in 69 CE, the Roman army in Palestine declared Vespasian emperor of Rome, Jesus of Nazareth declined the importunings of an army of Israelites.

The Transfiguration

The feeding of the five thousand provides our first example of Mark's instruction of the audience in the way to read Jesus's life in the light of Israelite scriptures. We see, as well, how the use of scriptures unfamiliar to the Romans hides from outsiders the true meaning of Mark's narrative. The audience witnesses another highly dramatic scene a bit later: the Transfiguration of Jesus on a high mountaintop.

In this story, related in Mark 9:2–9, Jesus takes three of his Twelve, Peter, James, and John, to a high mountain. Mark is elusive about what happens next, saying only that Jesus was "transfigured before them, and his clothes became dazzling white, such as no fuller on earth could bleach them." We know that his clothes were really white; but we do not have as good an idea of what Jesus looked like, perhaps because Mark wants his audience to remember other mountaintop experiences, those of Moses and Elijah. When Moses asked to see the face of the Lord on Mount Sinai, the Lord refused to do so because such a sight would destroy Moses. In Exodus the Lord did allow Moses to see the Lord walking away from him. Elijah, after fleeing from Jezebel in Israel to Mount Horeb, another name for the same Mount Sinai, wraps his face in his robe and encounters the Lord in a still small voice (1 Kings 19:11–18). On both occasions, the prophet is unable to look directly on the Lord; with a similar logic, Mark lets his audience imagine for themselves what a transfigured Jesus would look like.

The dramatic high-point of the scene occurs when a cloud covers the actors, and from the cloud comes a voice: "This is my beloved Son. Listen to him" (9:7). The action of the cloud, the description of Jesus as Son of God, and the order to the apostles all have resonances with the histories of Moses and Elijah. In the book of Exodus, a cloud both hides the face but reveals the presence of the Lord. At Exodus 24:15 a cloud covers Mount Sinai and from it a voice beckons Moses to be instructed. In Exodus 34, whenever Moses enters the Tent of Assembly, a cloud marking the presence of the Lord appears at the front door of the tent. During their forty-year journey through the Sinai wilderness, a cloud leads the people by day. Then a cloud fills the Temple (1 Kings 8:10–11) at its dedication, marking the Lord's acceptance of it as a dwelling place.

The reference to the Temple dedication carries overtones of the dedication, or enthronement of the kings of Israel and Judah. Of this event, the psalmist sings "I will tell of the decree of the Lord: He said to me, 'You are my son; today I have begotten you'" (Psalm 2:7). This psalm was composed for the enthronement of the king of Israel, considered the Son of God. In the Transfiguration, Jesus's own enthronement is prefigured by the shining white robes signifying divine beings, as in Daniel 7:13, the witness of Moses and Elijah, and the voice from the cloud, reminiscent of Psalm 2:7, honoring him.

In their mountaintop experience, both Moses and Elijah receive instructions from the Lord: Moses receives the Law that the people of Israel are to follow and Elijah receives orders to anoint Hazael king of Aram (modern-day Syria), Jehu king of Israel, and Elihu prophet to succeed him. In Mark, the apostles receive two instructions, one from the voice in the cloud "Listen to him!" (9:7) and the second from Jesus himself: "Don't tell anyone one of this until the Son of Man has risen from the dead" (9:9, our translation).

It is not that the Transfiguration duplicates any one of these Old Testament scenes, but the people hearing and reflecting on Mark's story could be expected to recognize and respond to these resonances. Their cumulative rhetorical impact is to advance the narrative with a minimum of words on the Transfiguration of Jesus: the divinized image of Jesus is well-established even while the narrative moves on.

The stories of feeding the five thousand and the Transfiguration of Jesus are examples of the way Mark uses Israelite scriptures to frame Jesus's identity. Mark entwines Jesus in the images and history of the Israelite royal tradition and the power of the divine Roman emperor, using his royal prerogative and divine power to feed the masses. A volunteer army appears ready to proclaim him emperor of a limited geographical area, Israel, but Jesus will have none of that. The Empire of God is concerned with healing the sick, feeding the hungry, driving out demons. The proclamations at the baptism and Transfiguration provide divine reassurance that this is the agenda of the Son of God. The Roman Christians see that the acquisition of power may be estimable when the power is used to the proper ends, and in Jesus's ministry, Jesus displays divine power imperially.

Time and the Passion

As Jesus's life draws to a close, Mark displays an abrupt change of style. Before chapter 11 (about two-thirds of the way through the text), when Jesus enters Jerusalem, Mark provides very few indications about the passage of time. There are events that take place at night with a follow-up the next day, but that is about all. Because there is no birth narrative, nothing specifying the year Jesus was born, we do not know how old Mark thinks Jesus was when he died. We cannot tell how long Jesus's public ministry lasted after his entry into Galilee (1:14). But all of this changes when we reach chapter 11. During his last week, time slows down for Mark, and we know what he did each day and then, at the end, what happened each hour.

This change in style is also marked by an equally abrupt increase in the intensity of Mark's references to the Israelite scriptures. To see that best, we step back in the text to Mark 10:45–52, the last healing story in Mark. In it, Bartimaeus calls upon Jesus as the "Son of David" to cure his blindness. The appellation "Son of David" would have had significant political overtones in early first-century Judea, as this was the title to be given to the king of Judea, whether the king be a birth descendant of David or, more probably, one adopted on his enthronement. This would fulfill the royal covenant God made with David as recorded in the book of 2 Samuel when God promised "Your house and your kingdom shall endure forever before me; your throne shall stand firm forever" (2 Samuel 7:16).

Mark records that as Jesus approaches Jerusalem, the end of his long walk from Galilee, he sends two disciples into the town of Bethany, perfectly predicting that there will be a wild colt there and bystanders who will question the disciples taking the colt (11:2–6). With just two miles to go to Jerusalem, the insistence by Mark that Jesus now wants to ride a colt signals its importance. For an audience familiar with Jewish scriptures, the whole event would resonate with Zechariah 9:9, "Rejoice heartily, O daughter Zion, shout for joy, O daughter Jerusalem! See, your king shall come to you; a just savior is he, Meek, and riding on an ass, on a colt, the foal of an ass." As Jesus enters Jerusalem, his disciples and the crowds greet him with "Hosanna! Blessed is he who comes in the name of the Lord! Blessed is the kingdom of our father David that is to come! Hosanna in the highest!" (11:9–10), an explicit quotation of Psalm 118:25–26.

Observers of this demonstration of patriotic fervor might have predicted with great confidence that before Jesus and the crowd got too far into Jerusalem, the Roman guard would haul Jesus off to a short stay in prison before crucifying him for fomenting rebellion against Caesar. They might have been expected to say this even more quickly had they understood that the Zechariah reference occurs in the middle of a prediction that the king's entrance would be preceded by Judeans' successful resistance to the nations surrounding and oppressing them.

After this triumphant arrival in Jerusalem, Mark reports that Jesus spent most of his days in the Temple. On the second day's visit, Jesus drove out

> those selling and buying there. He overturned the tables of the money changers and the seats of those who were selling doves. He did not permit anyone to carry anything through the temple area. Then he taught them saying, "Is it not written: 'My house shall be called a house of prayer for all peoples'? But you have made it a den of thieves" (11:15–17).

The hostility of the religious authorities toward Jesus may be explained as their reaction to this action. More puzzling is why Jesus "overturned the tables of the money changers and the seats of those selling doves." Since both of these groups facilitated the observance of clearly specified requirements for sacrifices by Jews, the incident may be a symbolic representation of Jesus's antipathy to the Temple authorities. In fact, the Israelite scriptures often recount a tension between the charismatic prophet and the more establishment, settled priests. The prophetic books of Isaiah (11:1–15; 66:3), Jeremiah (6:15–25; 7:21–23), and Hosea (8:10–14), for example, all include denunciations of simplistic reliance on the sacrificial system rather than emphasis on care for the poor. In the fifth chapter of the book of Amos, there is a passage in which the prophet contrasts the priests' works of cultic worship with the works of justice, which the prophet claims God wants. Speaking in the name of God, Amos the prophet claims

> I hate, I spurn your feasts, I take no pleasure in your solemnities; Your cereal offerings I will not accept, nor consider your stall-fed peace offerings. Away with your noisy songs! I will not listen to the melodies of your harps. But if you would offer me holocausts, then let justice surge like water, and goodness like an unfailing stream (Amos 5:21–24).

We remember that in the first verses of the text, Mark 1:1–3, Mark situates Jesus in the tradition of the prophets, particularly Malachi and Isaiah. In what will turn out to be the last week of his earthly ministry, Jesus takes on the ultimate challenge for a prophet: demanding a reform of the Temple, for many the bedrock of Jewish identity.

For two more days, Jesus moves freely in the Temple and in Jerusalem. On the third night after eating their Passover meal, Jesus and the disciples proceed to the Mount of Olives, an incident with strong Davidic overtones. There Jesus prays and is captured, but the disciples escape (14:26–49). Mark apparently modeled the action after the most desperate moment of David's life as described in 2 Samuel 15:13–37, 17:23. In that incident, after his trusted friend and advisor Ahithophel had betrayed him to his enemy, David fled Jerusalem with his followers, crossed the Kidron Valley to the Ascent of Olives where he wept and prayed. David arranged for his followers not to suffer his fate but to return to Jerusalem to wait for a future reunion. The unfaithful Ahithophel, meanwhile, on learning that his plan against David was unsuccessful, went home and hanged himself.

Jesus is brought before the religious authorities where under questioning by the high priest, he joins the titles Messiah, Son of God, and Son of Man:

> Again the high priest asked him and said to him, "Are you the Messiah, the son of the Blessed One?" Then Jesus answered, "I am; and 'you will see the Son of Man seated at the right hand of the Power and coming with the clouds of heaven'" (14:61–62).

Messiah means, literally, the "anointed one." While priests and prophets may receive an anointing, it was the anointed king of Judea who was almost always referred to with the title "Messiah." In the anointing, the messiah king became the son of God. The people believed that when the Messiah came, the political autonomy and the historic geographic boundaries established by King David would be restored to Israel. It was, in other words, a very political title.

The Son of Man has two connotations in the Israelite scriptures. The English phrase "son of Man" appears over one hundred times in the Israelite scriptures, of which ninety percent appear in the book of the prophet Ezekiel. In all but a handful of cases, the term refers simply to a mortal human being, one who is an offspring of a human. In that handful of other cases, the term "Son of Man" refers to one seen by the prophet Daniel in a vision concerning the end of the world. That Son of Man will come and rule the world:

> I saw One like a son of man coming, on the clouds of heaven; When he reached the Ancient One [that is, God] and was presented before him, He received dominion, glory, and kingship; nations and peoples of every language serve him. His dominion is an everlasting dominion that shall not be taken away, his kingship shall not be destroyed (Daniel 7:13–14).

Mark makes it clear that it is to this second image of the Son of Man that Jesus refers. The effect is to join, therefore, two powerful political symbols, the liberator of Judea and the one who will rule in the final Empire of God, in the person of Jesus.

When Jesus makes this plain, open statement of a royal and divine identity (in saying "I am" he claims for himself the name of God given to Moses) and it is proclaimed inside the home of the high priest, Jesus's situation is dire: he stands bound, alone, unprotected. A Roman seeing this tableau would see no more than one of scores of failed revolutionaries. This Jesus's lack of armed manpower made him small potatoes indeed compared with the always restive, always militaristic Germanic tribal leaders from the north of Rome. Christians in Rome, however, might thrill at this ringing declaration, the confirmation by Jesus of the testimony at his baptism and the Transfiguration.

As explained earlier, the Romans acknowledge Jesus's royalty in their reenactment of an imperial triumph and in the sign on the cross, "The King [Emperor] of the Jews" (15:16–20, 26). At Jesus's death, the Roman officer directing the soldier-executioners is the sole human in the Gospel of Mark to acknowledge Jesus's identity, when he declares "Truly this was [a] Son of God" (15:39). There is then a fairly uniform arc in the passion narrative in which Jesus's cosmic role unfolds.

As the passion narrative unfolds and achieves its denouement, there is a shift in the citations and allusions, from the prophets to the Psalms, the most prominent being Psalm 22, Jesus's prayer on the Cross (15:34). Parallels between Psalm

22 and Mark's account of Jesus's crucifixion are dramatic. Mark 15:24 reads: "Then they crucified him and divided his garments by casting lots for them to see what each should take," while Psalm 22:19 says "they divide my garments among them; for my clothing they cast lots." Mark 15:29–30 states "Those passing by reviled him, shaking their heads and saying, 'Aha! You who would destroy the temple and rebuild it in three days, save yourself by coming down from the cross,'" connecting to Psalm 22:7–9 "despised by the people . . . they shake their heads at me" and "you relied on the Lord—let him deliver you; if he loves you, let him rescue you." And the most dramatic of course is Jesus's statement from the cross in Mark 15:34: "Jesus cried out in a loud voice, 'Eloi, Eloi, lema sabachthani?', which is translated, 'My God, my God, why have you forsaken me?'" and its origin in Psalm 22:2: "My God, my God, why have you abandoned me?"

While this is a relatively conservative construction of parallel quotations, it is still striking how many of the details of the crucifixion scene are found in Psalm 22. We find it likely that, faced with the need to write a crucifixion scene, the author of Mark used Psalm 22 as a resource or inspiration. As we mentioned earlier in discussing Mark 1:3–4, it is probable that the author expected the congregation to participate in the concluding verses of the quotations from the prophets. That is an even stronger possibility here. Concluding the crucifixion scene with Jesus's proclamation of but one verse, and that a cry of lament for his abandonment, makes as strange an ending to this crucial scene as one might contemplate. Psalm 22 is indeed a psalm of personal lament, and as such is appropriate for the setting. The second half of the psalm, however, expresses the confidence of the psalmist in the Lord, God of Israel. The concluding verses may have been found especially appropriate for a congregation meeting nearly four decades after the crucifixion:

> The poor will eat their fill; those who seek the Lord will offer praise. May your hearts enjoy life forever! All the ends of the earth will worship and turn to the Lord; All the families of nations will bow low before you. For kingship belongs to the Lord, the ruler over the nations. All who sleep in the earth will bow low before God; All who have gone down into the dust will kneel in homage. And I will live for the Lord; my descendants will serve you. The generations to come will be told of the Lord, that they may proclaim to a people yet unborn the deliverance you have brought (Psalm 22:27–32).

These last six verses of Psalm 22 neatly sum up themes we have seen in Mark's use of the Israelite scriptures: the privileged place of the poor and the ultimate dominion of the Lord. We can easily imagine the Christians in Rome praying the psalm as the living witnesses that God honored the loyalty, trust, and confidence of Jesus—in sum, Jesus's faith—and would honor as well their faith that, despite the oppression they faced, there would indeed be future generations to hear their story.

In this section, we focused on how Mark uses Israelite scriptures to understand Jesus. Mark uses Israelite scriptures, in other words, to illuminate the mind of Jesus and the meaning of Jesus's life. The reader of the twenty-first century should realize that Mark also began the process of Christians reading the Israelite scriptures through the lens of the crucified and resurrected Jesus of Nazareth. While Mark invoked the prophetic texts to show that Jesus was in that line, Christians now read Israelite scriptures as foretelling the birth, mission, death, and resurrection of Jesus, even though scholars endlessly document, for example, that the real concerns of the writer known as Deutero-Isaiah were the people in Babylonian captivity. Deutero-Isaiah had enough trouble dealing with that situation and did not worry too much about something that would happen five centuries later.

Community Life

Mark's gospel is really a remarkable and complex book. It does not seem so on the surface, but by searching for the submerged meaning we have found the formative dynamic that makes the gospel such an important starting point for understanding the development of Christianity not only in Rome, but throughout the vast Roman Empire. Mark's tactics of writing a dissimulation biography, of gathering diverse functions in a portrait of Jesus, and of guiding his community in reading the scriptures as a means of making sense of the Empire of God have all had a profound influence on the way all subsequent Christians have understood Jesus and the Empire of God that Jesus announced and inaugurated. Most of the tactics we have explored to this point, however, primarily relate to the relationship of the Christians to the outside world, to Romans and to Roman authorities. These outside relationships were important to Mark, but the gospel tells us much more about the formative life of the community of Roman Christians he united in the biography of the emperor Jesus. The gospel also tells us of the inner workings of the community, and these inner workings were also important to his project of uniting the various factions into a cohesive community, into a church. Mark describes four community practices of importance: the important role of baptism, the central place of the sacred meal of the Christians (the Lord's Supper, or as it was eventually called, the Eucharist), the development of a particular kind of leadership, and the modeling of an open meal that would even gather enemies and dissidents into the community.

Baptism

The Christians in Mark's community clearly practiced baptism. Mark records how John baptized many Judeans and even Jesus himself was baptized with water. In Mark 10, Jesus predicts that James and John will be baptized, but not necessarily in water. We know from references to baptism in a number of Paul's letters that early Christians, particularly non-Jewish or Roman ones, entered the Empire of God through a ritual washing. In his letters, Paul refers to baptism as the entryway into the death and resurrection of Jesus. In Galatians, Paul goes further to argue that the baptized have clothed themselves with Christ so that "There is neither Jew nor Greek, there is neither slave nor free person, there is not male and female; for you are all one in Christ Jesus" (Galatians 3:27–28). Such a characterization of the importance of baptism fit Mark's agenda to unite disparate and divided social and economic groups under the aegis of one, united story about the Empire of God. Baptism served for Mark not only the beginning of the ministry of Jesus, but also the model for the entry into the Empire for all people, both Jewish and Roman. These references in the gospel indicate that baptism was the entry point for all, including Jesus.

Eucharist

Mark also included information about the Eucharist, which was probably an important ritual to his community. The sacred meal seems to have pervaded early Christian practice generally, but Mark gives that practice a location in the life of Jesus. Paul witnesses to the practice in the period prior to the writing of Mark's gospel: on the night before his death, Jesus celebrated the Passover meal with his disciples. Mark probably knew of Paul's account in 1 Corinthians:

> For I received from the Lord what I also handed on to you, that the Lord Jesus, on the night he was handed over, took bread, and, after he had given thanks, broke it and said, "This is my body that is for you. Do this in remembrance of me." In the same way also the cup, after supper, saying, "This cup is the new covenant in my blood. Do this, as often as you drink it, in remembrance of me" (1 Corinthians 11:23–25).

Mark takes Paul's description and puts it into a narrative of the life of Jesus in this way:

> While they were eating, he took bread, said the blessing, broke it, and gave it to them, and said, "Take it; this is my body." Then he took a cup, gave thanks, and gave it to them, and they all drank from it. He said to them, "This is my blood of the covenant, which will be shed for many. Amen, I say to you, I shall not drink again the fruit of the vine until the day when I drink it new in the kingdom of God" (14:22–25).

Mark adds that Jesus and the disciples then sang psalms before leaving the supper, a practice which Paul notes in Corinth as well. We assume that the Romans' Eucharist followed the order in 1 Corinthians and in Mark 14 for sharing a meal, singing psalms, and remembering Jesus the Lord. Thus the Gospel of Mark shows us some of the rituals the community performed to perfect their life together. The Eucharist was a formative practice, one intended to unite the community to the founder and prime teacher of the Empire of God.

The Open Table

An important question for communal living is "Whom do we invite to dinner?" The letters and biographies we have from the first communities of Christians suggest that this question was of great concern. Now we turn to how Mark addresses what has come to be called "table fellowship." In Mark 2:16–17, the religious authorities question the propriety of Jesus eating with tax collectors and sinners. Jesus replies that he "did not come to call the righteous but sinners." Jesus here models table fellowship as a means of reconciling with those distanced from the community, which probably reflects more Mark's Roman community than the time of Jesus. Then in the seventh chapter, Mark records a long debate between Jesus and the religious authorities about both eating rituals and clean and unclean food. With surprising emphasis, Mark records that Jesus "declared all foods clean," what would have been a most surprising teaching in Palestine but not necessarily in Rome where Jews would find it difficult to avoid unclean foods. Mark also records two major feeding stories. We have analyzed the first, the feeding of five thousand found in Mark 6, at some length. The second, a similar story in chapter 8, recounts the feeding of four thousand. The most prominent difference between the two stories is that the feeding of four thousand is set in a non-Jewish geographic area. In neither case does Jesus seem bothered by sharing food with whoever showed up, Judean or Roman. For Mark's community, the table was open to anyone who wanted to participate in the Empire of God.

We think the most dazzling example of table fellowship in the Gospel of Mark occurs at the Last Supper in chapter 14. This is an important place, because it shows how deliberately Mark tries to unify the various groups in his community, even those who betrayed the community. Mark tells us that Jesus has sent two disciples ahead to prepare the Passover meal and "when it was evening he came with the Twelve" (14:17). Jesus then predicts "Amen, I say to you, one of you will betray me, one who is eating with me" (14:17). Jesus goes on to say that it were better for that person to never have been born (14:21) but then, with no indication that anyone has left the room,

> While they were eating, he took bread, said the blessing, broke it, and gave it to them, and said, "Take it; this is my body." Then he took a cup, gave thanks, and gave it to them, and they all drank from it. He said to them, "This is my blood of the covenant, which will be shed for many. Amen, I say to you, I shall not drink

again the fruit of the vine until the day when I drink it new in the kingdom of God" (14:22–25).

We have seen these words before, as the words instituting the Christian ritual of the Eucharist. We emphasize here that Jesus shared this inaugural Eucharist with Judas, the one who had agreed to betray him to the religious authorities. Nowhere in the text of Mark is there any indication that Judas left the table before the sharing of bread and wine. Thus, just as throughout the course of his ministry Jesus ate with tax collectors, sinners, clean and unclean Jews and Gentiles, so now at his ministry's conclusion, Jesus shared a meal with one who would have been better off not born, his own betrayer. This most radical of all Jesus's practices models complete inclusiveness in table fellowship for Mark's community.

This is exactly what Mark tells us Jesus did: he shared his last meal, celebrating the greatest feast in the calendar, with his betrayer. Compared with breaking bread and sharing wine with one's wicked, evil adversary—or even with petty Roman bureaucrats and sinners—the Markan practices of mingling with those of different classes probably seemed easy to Roman Christians. Earlier members of this community were betrayed to Nero by other Christians. The very radical nature of shared table fellowship leads us to surmise that these betrayers were still, in some sense, Christians and part of Mark's Roman community. This community knew what betrayal was all about and how it utterly annihilates bonds between members. Yet each time the Roman community of Jesus's followers enacted the gospel of Mark they embodied the practice of sharing table fellowship with their betrayers. We cannot know Mark's motivation for this portrayal. Perhaps Mark wanted to reconcile the betrayers and the betrayed, and so offered Jesus's own example of open fellowship. Perhaps Mark wanted to valorize those who were already engaged in such reconciliation and tied their practice back to Jesus. In any case, Mark provided an especially hard practice for both the ancient and postmodern worlds. For Mark, the unity of the community even included those sinners and betrayers who put the community at risk during Nero's principate. The Markan table was completely open.

Leadership

These practices of reading scriptures, baptism, and open fellowship at the Eucharist are concerns both for the individual and the community. The Christians would also want to know how Jesus intended the communities to be organized. To the point: who is in charge? The Gospel of Mark offers no obvious blueprints for community organization, but a careful reading provides some insights on the direction the community should follow.

First of all, Mark describes Jesus's ministry within the tradition of itinerant Hebrew prophets, unaffiliated with and possibly disagreeing with both the religious authorities attached to the Temple and political rulers. Mark records only one trip by Jesus to the Temple, and on that occasion Jesus drives out the money changers and sellers of doves. Very early in Jesus's ministry religious leaders in Galilee begin to plot against him, and there are numerous contentious encounters between Jesus and various groups of the establishment religious authorities.

The only time Jesus interacts with the Roman authorities is when he calls Levi the tax collector to join the group of Twelve and then dines at his home. Jesus expects the Twelve to be similarly unencumbered with establishment ties: witness his commission of the Twelve to preach repentance, to cast out demons, and to heal, with expectations that they would be supported by the people to whom they ministered (6:7–13). As itinerants, whether received well or ill, they are not to stop permanently in one place but are to move on to the next town (1:38; 6:11). Thus as Jesus was supported so he expected that his disciples, those sent out to carry on his work, also would be supported.

The pervasive observation throughout Mark's text that the Twelve never really understood Jesus's ministry and that the leaders were called to be itinerant prophets meant Mark's community had an antiauthoritarian bent. The communities did not support any overarching hierarchical structures. On two occasions (9:35 and 10:42–45) Jesus emphasizes that his disciples are called to be servants to each other. In the second instance he compares them with the leaders of other nations:

> Jesus summoned them [the Twelve] and said to them, "You know that those who are recognized as rulers over the Gentiles lord it over them, and their great ones make their authority over them felt. But it shall not be so among you. Rather, whoever wishes to be great among you will be your servant; whoever wishes to be first among you will be the slave of all. For the Son of Man did not come to be served but to serve and to give his life as a ransom for many" (10:42–45).

While this provides no blueprint for the new Christian community, it certainly lets us know what it is not. It is not a community ruled by an autocrat as was the Roman Empire. It is to be a community of servant prophets.

Conclusion

In order to attain the mind of the master, listeners would have learned to study their own Israelite scriptures, particularly the prophetic literature. In these scriptures, and not in any writings of Jesus himself, they would find the roots, the images, the arguments that formed his mind. At the same time, these scriptures helped Mark shape narrative portions of the gospel: as the community became the living embodiment of Jesus of Nazareth, so Jesus was the embodiment of the Israelite scriptures. The scriptures point to Jesus as not only a prophet but also an emperor. Like the Roman emperor, Jesus provided the citizens with food. Unlike the Roman emperor, Jesus renounces all attempts to establish an earthly reign: the army of Jesus literally sits down.

Given the turbulent political climate in Rome and the recent barbaric persecution by Nero, the practice of dissimulation, the perennial refuge of the oppressed, seemed very prudent. For those who are "in," there would be no trouble understanding the message of the text, but for those "outside," the text would appear a bizarre tale of just one more failed Messiah. The Christians are laughable, not dangerous.

The Christians practiced baptism and the Eucharist. Both rituals were meant to reconcile the members of the community to one another. In the few years since Nero's persecution, we believe that those among the Christians who betrayed other community members were still somehow affiliated with the community. Jesus modeled a radical practice of reconciliation through table fellowship, sharing food with Jews and Gentiles, tax collectors and sinners, even the sinner who betrayed him. The prophet who prophesied his betrayal and crucifixion shared his last meal with his betrayer.

Mark's gospel was indeed a brilliant and significant achievement for the Roman churches. By using dissimulation, Mark's gospel trained the Roman Christians to look deeper, to tell their story about the true Empire of God in such a way that they (and probably only they) would see the truth of their lives in these seemingly innocuous and pastoral stories of a failed Jewish Messiah crucified and defeated by the Roman authorities. The hidden meaning in the newly created biography of Jesus, the founder of the Empire of God, encouraged, instructed, and transformed the persecuted church, while providing a structure in a story that would help them endure in the face of persecution. Mark's gospel also gave the community an overarching story in the life of Jesus to put together all the disparate things they knew about the Empire of God—the wisdom, the miracles, the confrontations, the resonance with the Israelite scriptures—and how to hold it all together as a unified, cohesive community. Each person could recognize herself or himself as part of this larger story of the life of Jesus and see her or his perspective on the Empire of God united through Jesus to other perspectives. The gospel united them all under the aegis of Jesus's life and death; the gospel showed them the whole Empire of God as it was woven into the life of Jesus. Mark's gospel also bridged the divide between Jew and Gentile, so prevalent a question in the letters of Paul. Mark's gospel, by portraying Jesus as simultaneously a Roman and a Jew, made it possible to see how such different ways of thinking and living could function harmoniously together in one corporate entity. For Mark, it was possible for a Christian to be at once a Jew and a Roman, just as it was for Jesus. That openness to a comprehensive community is even more evident in the way even enemies were welcomed to the ritual table for the sacred meal in which the Body and Blood of Jesus made Jesus present to them. Mark's achievement was simply brilliant in achieving all these things.

The remarkable production of Mark's gospel had a significant impact on the entire future of the church throughout the world. Produced in Rome, the gospel spread quickly through the Roman Empire and became the founding document for this new religion. Once Mark united all the parts into a story about Jesus, the developing churches throughout the empire could no longer look back to the earlier ways of understanding the Empire of God. Jesus moved to the center, and Christians from then on would understand themselves as those who followed Jesus. The move from the Empire of God to the gospel of Jesus's life and death became the way all future Christians, even until today, understand Christianity. From this perspective, we could say that the Gospel of Mark created the Christianity all subsequent Christians would know. Mark's gospel made the Empire of God into a religion, and his gospel became the formative document for the Christian church through the ages. Granted we no longer read Mark's gospel as dissimulation—none of the other gospel writers read it as dissimulation either—because the story in a sense spoke for itself. So each subsequent gospel writer started with the story of Jesus and moved into their community's formation in different ways. Matthew's gospel, to which we now turn, was the first one to take up the Markan project and to refract it through another community to come to different conclusions and to form a community in a different way.

Questions for Discussion

1. Assuming an acceptance of our thesis that the Gospel of Mark is a text exhibiting *dissimulatio*, how does this reading alter the way you understand the process of reading the gospels? How has such a thesis forced you to read Mark differently? How would you describe that difference to someone else?

2. Taking the opposite perspective: assuming that you do *not* accept the Gospel of Mark as a dissimulation text, how would you explain those characters in the gospel who understand and proclaim who Jesus is (the Roman soldiers and the demons) and those who do not (the disciples)? How would you understand Jesus's injunctions to keep his identity secret?

3. We argue that the pastoral and rural itinerant Jesus was a literary and dissimulatory device selected by the author of the Gospel of Mark to make Jesus seem innocuous. What are the consequences of Mark portraying Jesus as a rural rather than an urban emperor? What implications does this difference have for understanding Christianity today?

Resources for Further Study

"When in doubt, read the text!" This chapter has focused on the text of the Gospel of Mark and has drawn from it a number of illustrative practices advanced by its author for the formation of the community. There are others as well. To really understand how the text works, the student must be prepared to spend time with it: to read it aloud communally, to read it dramatically, to act out—indeed to enflesh in the acting out—these very practices.

On the singular importance of the Gospel of Mark as a foundation document for Christianity, especially in the way Mark's gospel completely transformed and redirected Christianity, see Burton L. Mack, *A Myth of Innocence: Mark and Christian Origins* (Philadelphia: Fortress, 1988). Mack argues persuasively that the story that Mark develops in his gospel created the myth of Christian origins from which all the other gospels, and even all later Christians, developed their understanding of Jesus.

Commentaries are an unusual scholarly work, as their authors are expected to provide a dispassionate survey of the current state of scholarship (with a state-of-the-art bibliography) while nevertheless arguing their own points of view and providing a verse-by-verse analysis of the complete text. Adela Yarbro Collins produced the current standard commentary for the Hermeneia series: *Mark: A Commentary* (Minneapolis: Fortress, 2007). Francis J. Moloney is a fine scholar whose *The Gospel of Mark: A Commentary* (Peabody, Mass.: Hendrickson, 2002) is less extensive than Collins's and less daunting for students. Finally, Vincent Taylor's *The Gospel According to St. Mark: The Greek Text with Introduction, Notes, and Indexes,* second edition (London: Macmillan, 1966) is an older but still insightful reading of Mark. Those students with a facility with Greek will find Taylor a helpful, if conservative, analyst of the text.

Compilations of recent books, essays, and articles on the Gospel of Mark run to many pages. If the student is looking for just one compilation, we recommend William R. Telford's (editor) *The Interpretation of Mark,* second edition, *Studies in New Testament Interpretation* (Edinburgh: T. & T. Clark, 1995). This work is a compilation of the most influential works on the Gospel of Mark up to its publication date.

Our claim that the Gospel of Mark was written in Rome for a Roman audience is not uncontested. Both Collins and Moloney argue that evidence is insufficient to support the traditional setting, basically calling the location indeterminate; Taylor, on the other hand, argues for a Roman provenance. Their commentaries may be consulted for their arguments. John R. Donahue wrote an article in 1992 in which he surveyed the various arguments on this point ("The Quest for the Community of Mark's Gospel" in F. Van Segbroeck, et al., eds. *The Four Gospels 1992,* vol. 2 (Leuven: University Press, 1992), 817–838. A strong, and we find compelling, defense of the traditional location is provided by Martin Hengel in *Studies in the Gospel of Mark*, trans. John Bowden (Philadelphia: Fortress, 1985). Peter Lampe wrote a definitive history of the Christian community in Rome, *From Paul to Valentinus: Christians at Rome in the First Two Centuries*, trans. Michael Steinhauser (Minneapolis: Fortress, 2003).

The reader is also referred to the Resources for Further Study at the end of the portal for references on the literary style of the Gospel of Mark, Roman history, and religious and philosophical schools.

CHAPTER FOUR

Portal to the Gospel of Matthew: School Time in Antiquity

Junia and Gaius watched the children as they waited to see the teacher for their weekly lesson. It was a warm day so they were sitting on a settee in the internal courtyard of the villa in which they all lived and studied. Ten students, seven men and three women, live and study with their teacher, Epaphras, a man who studied philosophy in Berytus (modern Beirut) and whose knowledge made him a hit in the Italian province where he founded his school. Their home, a typical Roman villa, had the common rooms (dining room, library, study, and entrance where guests would come to greet them) on the ground floor in the front of the villa. In the rear of the villa there were sleeping rooms, one for men and one for the women and children. Epaphras had adopted the children of Roman elite people who could not care for them or who had given them over to Epaphras when the parents grew old and were about to die. Epaphras took the children into his school community, provided food and shelter, and, of course, lessons from the great master. The children were an important part of the school's community.

Frequently the lessons took place in the inner courtyard of the villa. There were orange and apple trees there, benches to sit on, a water fountain whose sound of dripping water lulled the students both young and old into a contemplative state. Epaphras's voice was strong and clear when he taught, animated by the subject that they were studying that week and enthused by the engagement of the students as they worked their way through their teacher's thinking. That's what they did in the school. The teacher walked them through the lesson, laying out the arguments, testing the reasoning, exploring what is good and what is bad in the thought, applying the thinking to their way of life, and creating short pithy statements to help the students remember the whole discussion.

But Epaphras was also performing his teacher's thought. Epaphras had studied in the great city of Alexandria in Egypt with Sophronius, a brilliant and famous philosopher.

Whenever Epaphras began to teach, he would bring Sophronius's way of thinking and living to his mind, and he would recite his lessons as though it were Sophronius himself who was the teacher. Epaphras understood himself as passing on an intellectual and social tradition that he had learned, so there was nothing (so Epaphras thought) "new" in his teaching. Epaphras was simply the well-trained medium for a knowledge that was far older than himself. It was fascinating for his students to watch him teach. His voice would get soft and gentle, his eyes closed as he began to remember and recite the lessons he learned from Sophronius, his arguments flowed easily and fluidly from his lips, and he engaged his students in the logic and its application to daily life in the same way he was taught by his teacher. There was an educational succession not only of patterns of thinking, but also of a way of living the good life, the philosophical life, whose origins were found in Sophronius's teachers, and his teacher's teacher, going back generations into the great minds that had transmitted the unchanging and eternal wisdom of the ages to new generations. Wisdom is like that: it is eternal, unchanging, and yet ever adapting to new circumstances in different ages, and passed on from one great teacher to another. So Junia and Gaius actually sat at the feet of many teachers, all embodied in their beloved Epaphras.

The children were getting restless. Epaphras began a conversation with one of their student colleagues, and he was completely enthralled in the conversation. Time meant nothing when Epaphras began to teach. The children were getting hungry, so Junia and Gaius marched them to the dining room to eat some crusty, multigrained bread with a special fish sauce. This would give them energy and sustain them through their lesson. As soon as Epaphras began teaching the children, Junia and Gaius could take their daily walk and begin to recite their lessons in preparation for their own time with the master. As the children were finishing their meal, Epaphras took his honored seat in the courtyard. He was clearly lost in a thought, as he enjoyed the solitude while he waited for the children to gather. One by one, the little ones sat at his feet, silently waiting for their teacher to begin their lessons. They loved him deeply, not only as a father, but as their spiritual guide. Epaphras exuded spiritual and intellectual power. Even the children understood this, so the time they spent with him was the most important time of their day. Even when they did not understand what he was saying, they still memorized his teaching. Every word was sacred to them.

It was the same for Junia and Gaius. Every word that Epaphras spoke they worked hard to memorize exactly. Epaphras was their connection to the divine reason that ruled the universe, that regulated their lives, that inhered in every relationship, and that was to become manifest in their daily living. Epaphras was a holy man whose intellect and way of living modeled for them a life lived in communion with the divine reason.

For the adults Epaphras took up the question of whether forced exile by the emperor aided a person's ability to contemplate. Yesterday they learned that exile to a barren and distant island seemed only in appearance to be evil, but was not actually evil. The apparent evil involved separation from familiar society, reduction of civic benefits like baths and gymnasia, lack of fresh water, and unfamiliar (and somewhat distasteful) food. These were evil only because in their Roman society they were unacceptable, but they were good in that exile provided a change of lifestyle that forced them into a more contemplative life. So Junia and Gaius were thinking about how such changed circumstances might lead to contemplation. On their walk that afternoon, they considered the options. They knew that Epaphras would help them, but they wanted to apply their learning in new circumstances. The wondered about how such persecution in exile could possibly lead to the rest and peace necessary for contemplation. Later, in the class session, Epaphras talked about the way that exile creates a kind of purity of mind because the mind no longer gets caught up in social life in the city, in the dinner parties, in the politics of the Senate, in the court cases pending; now freed from such immersion in the world, the mind could explore the divine principle. The purity of mind emerges from stripping away the peripheral and turning the mind toward the divine. Epaphras summarized the teaching in this way: "Happy are the pure of mind, for they can see God." This is a lesson they would never forget.

After the children's class and their own session with Epaphras, they all gathered around the dinner table. Conversation flowed easily from the requirements of daily living to the heights of contemplation. Epaphras joked with the children, teased the adults, explored implications of their reactions during teaching, and even addressed problems in the community. Their life together in this school encompassed everything. Since learning and philosophy was a way of life, even the meals and leisure time were times of learning and reflection, times of watching the divine principle become manifest in the lives and thinking of the fellow students. Junia and Gaius considered themselves "happy indeed" to be studying and living with so holy and brilliant a teacher as Epaphras in the context of a group of people seeking similar holiness and intelligence for themselves.

This day in the life of a Roman-era school is based on a biography of a famous philosopher, Plotinus, written by his student Porphyry at the beginning of the third century CE. It gives a snapshot of a familiar social institution in antiquity, the philosophical school, which succeeded the scribal schools of even more ancient times. Ancient schools did more than teach people the traditional subjects of rhetoric, music, mathematics, physical education, literature, and astronomy. They taught a way of life based on a way of thinking and reflecting.

Scribal Schools

The origins of education tell an interesting story. In the ancient Near East, every king had a school of scribes who served as the official communicators of the kingdom. Kings needed people who could produce their letters, promulgate their laws, publish their pronouncements, and announce the verdicts the king reached after hearing legal disputes. Scribes did all that work for ancient kings, and the kingdoms depended upon them for official communication. Within the king's household, the scribes formed schools to train young children in the writing arts. Scribes often held a place of honor within the ancient king's court, and they were always present when the king conducted official business.

The scribes' training was an arduous and rigorous process. Learning to write made them an elite class of people, so their training intended to make them a refined member of the king's household. Without the modern conveniences of school supply stores, easily accessible pens, and readily available paper, the scribes had to learn to do everything: make styluses with which to write, prepare the surface of stone, or wax, papyrus, or parchment, and then to produce the communication in the chosen medium. So the scribes learned the mechanics and materials of written works. But the labor did not stop there. The most arduous part of a scribe's education revolved about learning to write letters. This sounds strange, but it is true. To read letters in antiquity was an art because words were not separated on the medium. There were no spaces to indicate where words began or ended, so the scribe first learned the letters of the alphabet in a variety of forms, then they learned how to make syllables by combining vowels and consonants, and then they mastered how to string syllables into words, and words into sentences, and sentences into the various genres of writings they needed to produce (official letter, proclamation, treaty, or household account, for example).

The way scribes learned their craft sounds tedious, and it probably was, but the scribes functioned as important mediums of wisdom. To learn their letters, syllables, sentences, and genres, scribes needed a corpus of material that would keep them engaged in study as well as teach them the morals and values of the court. Early in the scribal schools, that material emerged as what we now call the "wisdom tradition." Scribal education centered on wisdom sayings, short sentences that embodied traditional moral and ethical values. Student scribes learned to write by memorizing and producing in writing the wisdom sayings. The Israelite scripture's book of Proverbs, Wisdom of Solomon, and Ecclesiasticus come from this kind of ancient scribal school. The wisdom tradition provided the lessons for learning the craft of writing, while at the same time providing social and moral formation for the scribes. The connection, then, between writing as scribes and traditional wisdom was very strong.

In the Hellenistic period and the Roman period, these scribal schools turned from traditional wisdom to a more philosophical subject matter. The later schools not only expanded their understanding of wisdom to include philosophical speculation, but they also moved the learning center from the royal household to the household of the teacher and the teacher's financial supporters. The focus of the schools, however, remained remarkably the same: while living in community, a person learned to write and to think by pursuing wisdom.

Philosophical Schools

The schools of the Greco-Roman period succeeded the ancient scribal schools. Schools in the Roman period expanded even further to become live-in communities. Students became a part of a school, wore distinctive clothing, lived together in dormitories, probably shared a particular diet, and often were fiercely dedicated exclusively to their teacher. To learn in an ancient school involved not only training the mind, but also refashioning the body and creating a society in such a way as to reflect the philosophical teaching. Mind, body, and society met in philosophical discourse, and the schools were really workshops for manifesting the school's philosophical principles. To enter a school, then, required a commitment to a new way of living as well as a new way of thinking, and the school communities provided the context for living out that commitment.

The school communities functioned as extended family households. They frequently included men and women who studied together, listeners from outside the community who came to hear lectures by the philosophical teacher, members of the philosopher's own household such as his spouse, children, and slaves, as well as the slaves who provided for the community's needs by maintaining the school environment and providing meals. In the case of Porphyry's community, the school also included orphans from the upper classes. School communities varied greatly from school to school, but they all treated communal living as a primary site for intellectual, spiritual, political, and social transformation.

In the Roman imperial period during which the gospels were written, scribes played an important role. Most people did not write their own treatises, letters, household or business accounts, or lessons themselves. Instead they spoke their teaching, conducted their inventory, or wrote their letters by speaking them aloud before a scribe who transcribed the oral words into writing. The scribe, often a slave in a rich household or a student in a school, kept the records of the wisdom that was to be passed on to the next generation of students or kept the record of business or social engagements. Although the masters and teachers knew how to read and write, their job was primarily to do the thinking, leaving the recording to someone trained as a scribe. And scribes also worked together in various kinds of networks, refining not only their skills as scribes, but transmitting important intellectual, religious, social, political, and business information to a wider public. Performing such a vital function for the community, scribes lived in the communities they served either because they were a student in the school or a readily available resource in a wealthy household. The letters of Paul, for example, often refer to the scribe to whom Paul dictates and bring greetings from the scribe to the sender as part of the letter.

This description of scribes and philosophical schools shows that education in antiquity held a place of high regard. It was not simply classwork, writing essays, taking exams, and studying new material. It also involved learning to live a particular way of life, to engage in community in a different way, and to think through the practical consequences of ways of thinking.

Wisdom Traditions

Wisdom sayings formed the core curriculum of the scribal schools. But where did this wisdom come from? This is another interesting window on the ancient world. Wisdom operates at a number of levels. At its most basic level, wisdom simply refers to the accumulated knowledge that the elders of previous generations have distilled as a guide to subsequent generations. This is worth considering further. Previous generations, the elders of a community, made observations about the proper way of living and relating, doing business, marrying, raising children, social and personal faults or sins, the proper way to grow old and die, the best way for a young man or woman to wend their way through life's crises, and all other regularly occurring circumstances of living. They offer their observations, honed by their inherited wisdom from even earlier generations, to their children and grandchildren as a guide to proper living and dying. Their knowledge, their wisdom about living, becomes a beacon for generations to come. Encapsulated and distilled as proverbs, this wisdom presents a tested and proven pattern for living; it is traditional because it replicates the patterns of previous generations; it is conservative because it preserves previous patterns of living for the next generation. This wisdom is ethical and moral in content.

The next level on which wisdom operates becomes more theological and spiritual in its content. Here the distilled and encapsulated knowledge of previous generations explains the contours of God's plan for creation. If the moral and ethical level asks the question "How should I live my life?" then the theological level answers "According to God's plan that has been revealed in ages past and continues to be revealed to those to whom God discloses it!" Theological wisdom reveals God's intention for creation, the plan God had in mind when God created the world and set the cosmos in order. Theological wisdom reveals the way that God operates with individual seekers after wisdom and with communities who desire to know God better. So theological wisdom guides subsequent generations in the ongoing and unfolding divine presence that helps to explain the created universe and everything that occurs within it: human beings; societies; the stars, sun, moon, and the planets in their courses; the virtuous life that connects the seeker to the mind of God; and the vices that lead the seeker far away from a proper understanding of God's ways. This theological wisdom is often personified: Proverbs describes Wisdom as the person who is there with God at creation (the "us" and "our" in the "Let us make human in our image" of Genesis). And in the gospels of Matthew and John, Jesus is the Wisdom of God incarnate and accessible to their communities. This theological wisdom usually has a mediator, or revealer, whose purpose is to make the divine plan evident to those capable of understanding it. Wisdom in Proverbs and Jesus in Matthew and John serve that purpose, but so do many teachers who have studied the divine ways and come to know Wisdom intimately so that they might teach others.

There is yet a third way to understand wisdom. This third level is more contemplative. Wisdom, according to this way, articulates the divine presence in creation that a seeker or believer may access through contemplation of divine things. Contemplation demands an ascent from more practical ways of living, through climbing upward through ethics and morals to a consideration of the divine plan for all creation, and ends in a direct face-to-face vision of the divine presence. In this context, Wisdom has become God's mind encountered by those capable of leaving aside old ways of thinking and understanding in order to ascend to direct apprehension of God in the world. Wisdom becomes the principle for divine presence in people and events. The guides toward this contemplative Wisdom have a deep connection to God; they seem to manifest and transmit the divine directly to their followers; their writings carry the weight and authority of the divine presence when read in the community. This contemplative Wisdom is mysterious, transformative, compelling, and fascinating, and it always leads to a new way of living and thinking.

Schools in the ancient world understood and valued all three understandings of wisdom, because they understood that ultimately all wisdom, all propriety, all ethics, all contemplation connects the person through elder mediators to the presence of God. So the philosopher-teacher became a hierophant, some-one who interpreted the holy mystery of God's plan and purpose for human existence and made visible the invisible presence of God in teaching and learn-ing. The rabbi, the teacher, the revered elder, the philosopher, the spiritual guide—all these brought the Wisdom of God to their communities in different contexts. And equally, all learning and study ultimately led to a knowledge of God. That is Wisdom's way. That is what school is all about. All three levels of understanding wisdom function in the Gospel of Matthew.

Ritualized Living

The description of the school as community brings into view the concept of ritualized living. By ritualized living we understand a way of living that fol-lowed a particular patterned and religiously signified manner of eating, social relations, religious observance, and study. The way of living in community fol-lows these patterns as ritual performances that bond the community members to each other and the community to God. Every aspect of living falls into the category of ritualized living so that every action, no matter how mundane, bears significance within the community's living. Ritualized living sounds strange to postmodern ears, but we too follow these ritualized patterns, although generally they do not bear religious significance in our minds: we wash our hands after going to the bathroom; we stand in a queue when ordering coffee; we raise our hands when we want to speak in class; and we shake hands with people we meet on the road, to name a few. In antiquity, these kinds of daily ritualized actions carried strong associations of social, political, educational, and religious positioning of people with others and with God.

In philosophical circles in the Roman period, communities shared meals and living space. The students and teachers engaged in ritualized forms of question and answer in their studies. They offered libations to the gods before meals and made sacrifices together to the gods whom they worshipped. They initiated new members through a ritual bathing and vesting in particular clothing. They observed the birthday or death date of famous teachers such as Socrates. They venerated their ancestors in the philosophical life. Ritual pervaded the way they lived, learned, and related.

In early Christian communities we see the same ritualized living. Members of the community called each other "brother" or "sister." Their meals became sacred moments of bonding not only to each other, but through their conversa-tion, to God, making all eating a kind of little eucharistic meal. They engaged in religious ritual: reading scripture and reciting the psalms together every day at set times in the morning, at noonday, and at evening. They celebrated sacraments together: through baptism, a ritual bathing, they incorporated new members into their community; through the Eucharist, they displayed their connection to each other as the Body of Christ and feasted on the bread and wine as a way of uniting with Christ. Through other rituals such as foot washing, confession of faults, use of incense and holy water, fasting, and almsgiving, the Christians lived their daily lives as filled with sacred moments that reminded them of their relationship to God. Ritual pervaded Christian relationships, study, and worship. In order to understand the Gospel of Matthew, we must understand the way ritualized living functioned within both Christian and Roman communities.

Diaspora Judaism

An important religious, philosophical, political, and social phenomenon essential to understanding the gospels, particularly the Gospel of Matthew, is Diaspora Judaism. Starting with the deportation of Jews from Judea to Babylon, the number of Jews living outside Judea grew so large that by the time the Gospel of Matthew was composed, there were more Jews living outside the homeland than within it. It is true that many Jews were first moved forcibly by conquering forces—Persian, Greek, Egyptian, Syrian—but they and their descendants remained in their new locations willingly. Other Jews saw better opportunities in the new cities founded by the Greeks and Romans throughout the Mediterranean, such as Alexandria in Egypt, or Thessalonica and Ephesus in Greece. The Jews in these cities formed associations where they could keep alive their religious practices, continue their cultural traditions, and engage with the wider Greek-speaking world in which they lived. Jewish associations met on the Sabbath for reading scripture, prayer, singing the psalms, and common meals. Their associations taught the scriptures in Greek to their young members and even to Greek and Roman converts to Judaism. They continued to observe Jewish eating patterns, not mixing milk and meat in meals, and generally following a vegetarian diet that was deeply valued by some Roman philosophical schools. These Jews became Greek speakers, translating their scriptural texts into Greek, and generally assimilating their biblical traditions to Greek ways of thinking and living. These Jews were part of the Jewish Diaspora, the spreading out of Jews from their homeland into Hellenistic and later Greco-Roman cultures.

Diaspora Judaism, precisely as a Greek-speaking Judaism, engaged in rigorous religious speculation. Philo Judaeus (20 BCE–50 CE), a Greek-speaking Jew of Alexandria, became an important philosopher of his day, intent on reconciling his Jewish beliefs with the Platonic philosophical system. To do so, Philo read the Jewish scriptures allegorically, adapting a Greek method of reading the events and characters of Homer's epics to his reading of Jewish scriptures. The Greek method was called "allegory," a system of reading where each character and event signified something other than what the narrative suggests on the surface. For Philo, for instance, Abraham's journey from his home in Ur to Canaan was an allegory of the human soul's journey from the mundane to a union with the divine. Writing about the same time, Paul composed a Jewish diasporal allegorical reading in his interpretation of Hagar and Sarah in Galatians 4:22–31, where Hagar signifies slavery and the Mosaic covenant, while Sarah signifies the freedom of the promise of a new covenant in Jesus. Here Paul reads two characters from the Bible story as relating theological information about the relationship of Jews to Christians in his communities. The characters Sarah and Hagar have allegorical significance because they point to something that is imported into the text to give the text new meaning in a new context.

Another important aspect of Diaspora Judaism relates to the way the Jews explained themselves to their Greek, Roman, and Egyptian neighbors. They presented monotheistic Judaism as an ancient religion with philosophical depth: they presented Jewish monotheism as the apex of the philosophical yearning for a unified divine pantheon. The Greek and Roman gods were then considered mere descriptions of the One God who informs them all. Both Greeks and Romans respected this aspect of Jewish monotheism as an ancient religion that demanded respect, but looked askance at Jewish circumcision and the Jewish dietary laws.

The Roman Conflict with the Jews in Jerusalem and Palestine

Practically from the time Pompey conquered Jerusalem in 63 BCE, the Jews living in Palestine challenged Roman rule. Jews considered the Roman appointing of kings and high priests for the Temple an intrusion that defiled their ancient heritage, cultural practices, and religious beliefs. The story in the four books of the Maccabees in the Old Testament Apocrypha (a set of Jewish texts written in Greek and contained in the Roman Catholic and Orthodox Old Testaments) tells of the eagerness and enthusiastic willingness of Jews to resist Roman authority and intrusion by becoming martyrs for the Israelite tradition. The Maccabees' mother looked on as her sons one by one were tortured and killed, refusing to eat the piece of pork (the favorite food of Romans and one forbidden for Jews) they were offered by their Roman rulers. The Maccabean revolt informed generations of Jewish resistance to Roman rule. But there were also Jewish leaders and aristocrats who found Roman ways of living and even the Roman dominance attractive. These aristocrats supported the Romans and adopted their way of life, much to the dismay of the more rigorously religious people like the Maccabees. These Roman supporters found a way of being at once Jewish and Roman, which the religiously rigorous martyrs neither could understand nor accept.

These conflicts came to a head in 66 CE when a serious revolt broke out in Palestine. Rome dispatched the general, soon-to-be emperor, Vespasian to quell the revolt and to bring Palestine into submission to Roman rule. The war was long, bloody, and intense. On his ascendancy to the imperial throne, Vespasian left his son Titus to finish the war. Titus defeated the Jews in 70 CE, destroying the Temple and dispersing the Jewish leaders and upper classes, bringing many of them to Rome as slaves.

The Temple in Jerusalem had been the center of Israelite religion, society, politics, and culture. The Israelite God lived in the Temple, God's house and dwelling place on earth. In the Temple, Jews related immediately to their God who was present there. Outside the holy of holies—the center of the Temple restricted only to priests—Jews would perform the sacrifices of meat, or bread, or incense required by the Torah, the first five books of the Israelite scriptures. Jewish identity, as well as cultural practices and teaching, centered on the Temple. It was the heart of Israelite religion.

Peripheral institutions grew up around the Temple. The Temple treasury served as a central bank, a safe place for people to deposit their wealth. The Temple priests served as political leaders of the Israelite and Palestinian Jewish people, because the Temple also served as the political heart of the Israelite people. The high priest of the Temple, whom the Romans chose to impose on the Jewish people, was the political head of the province as well as the chief religious leader of the Temple. The priests and various officials of the Temple also became the primary teachers of Israelite religion, language, culture, and literature.

When the Temple was destroyed, much more than a building collapsed. In addition to the religious trauma of destroying the Temple, which we will explore later, the entire economic, social, political, cultural, and religious fabric of the Jewish nation collapsed. In raiding the Temple treasury, Titus stole the wealth of the nation and its people. In destroying the Temple, he ripped the heart out of religious and cultural education, decimated the cultural center of the society, dismantled the political structures that held the nation together, and dispersed a people who had lived together for centuries. The Temple's destruction affected the very fabric of the people. It finally brought a chapter in Jewish history to a close. Although the war continued outside Jerusalem for another three years or so, the devastation of 70 thrust Palestine into chaos.

The chief impact of Titus's destruction of the Temple, however, was felt in the religious sphere. How were the people to perform the duties incumbent upon them from their scriptures? Without a Temple, the sacrifices could not be offered, the prayers in the presence of God could not be prayed, the priests of the Temple had no function, and the theology that had developed around Temple life no longer applied. There were a number of responses to this traumatic destruction. Some attempted to build a new Temple in Antioch, where sacrifice could be resumed. Others looked to the synagogue—the meeting halls where study of scripture and teaching took place outside of the Temple—as a place to locate their religious devotion and study. But the most dramatic response came from the Pharisees.

The Pharisees were a Jewish sect whose primary interest after the destruction of the Temple focused on translating Jewish religious observance from the Temple to the home. In other words, the Pharisees began a process of making each Jewish home a place where the prayers and religious practices of the Jews could be located and maintained. They created systems of daily prayer in the morning and at evening that substituted for the incense offering in the Temple. They articulated a dietary regime that protected the household from inadvertently violating scriptural dietary restrictions. The Pharisees created a Jewish lifestyle, a Jewish way of living, that made it possible for Jews to observe their way of life and maintain their identity as Jews without the Temple.

Beginning in 70 CE and continuing until the end of the third century, noted rabbis also began to accommodate Jewish living to the exigencies of a post-Temple Judaism and the dominance of hostile Romans. These rabbis poured over the meaning of scripture to articulate the way of life the scriptures demanded in the absence of a Temple. Since the Law related to the Temple on its surface, the rabbis began to read those scriptural injunctions in new ways that could be observed by all. The rabbis were teachers and holy men, whose disciples memorized their sayings. The various rabbis formed schools where their disciples could live together, study, and teach one another. As with most Greco-Roman schools, the adherents of various famous rabbis debated with each other, compared arguments and conclusions, defended their teacher from misinterpretation, and advocated the truth and sanctity of their teaching. Eventually all these rabbinic teachings were codified into two large collections of rabbinic commentaries on the scriptures. These commentaries, called the Talmud, were codified in two centers of Jewish learning: Jerusalem and Babylon, hence the names the Jerusalem Talmud and the Babylonian Talmud. The Talmuds bring together the often-conflicting teaching of the various rabbis around the text of the Torah upon which they comment, and readers of the Talmud then enter the fractures created by the various rabbis' interpretations to create new meanings and new levels of understanding.

For all its destructiveness to Jewish religion, the destruction of the Temple opened new worlds to the Jews. Rabbinic Judaism as we know it now was birthed from the teaching of the rabbis and the work of the Pharisees and made it possible for the Jewish religion to survive in ancient times and until today. The long struggle for holiness, defined by the Maccabees as resistance to Roman culture, now became possible for Jews in the midst of Roman living and through the centuries for Jews living in many different cultures and among many different languages and peoples. This observation is not intended to diminish the trauma of the destruction of the Temple, but to point to the unexpected consequences it had on the capacity for the surviving Jews to straddle different worlds, while holding on to the center of their lives, the Torah, the scriptures, and their interpretation by famous rabbis. The Gospel of Matthew, we will argue, provides an example of a community holding together disparate worlds: the world of the Torah, the world of the Romans among whom the Jews lived, and the Empire of God proclaimed by Jesus. The community that produced the Gospel of Matthew constitutes yet another response to the trauma of the Jewish wars and the destruction of the Temple.

Apocalyptic Literature

One of the features of Judaism that had an enormous impact on early Christianity was apocalypticism. The word *apocalypse* means an unveiling, an uncovering of something that is hidden. Jewish apocalypses referred to the unveiling of the divine plan, generally through angelic mediators, to restore the world to its proper submission to God. Apocalyptic traditions related to the final destruction of the known world, when the God of Israel would send emissaries to establish a permanent kingdom on earth, destroy the competing Roman and Greek empires, and bring the entire world to judgment. These apocalyptic hopes nourished Judaism, because apocalypses told of the final victory of God over every competing ruler during a time when Jews suffered under the hegemony of foreign rulers and cultures. The book of Daniel contains an apocalyptic revelation of the coming of the Son of Man who would judge the world. Paul, as a Jew who also followed Christ, brought certain apocalyptic expectations into his letters, especially in 1 Thessalonians when he describes the end of the ages. The book of Revelation also shows Jewish apocalyptic traditions now adapted for Christians experiencing persecution.

Transmission of the Texts

Postmodern people have a relatively inflexible understanding of text. We usually see texts set in type, printed in books, and put in forms that mass produce specific writings that many people can read in exactly the same form whenever they are read and wherever they are found. This was never the case in antiquity when texts were far more fluid.

First of all, texts were produced in a *scriptoria* where the reader would read the text and the scribes would write what they heard. Obviously this kind of text production leaves a lot of room for error, mishearing, and miswriting. Even though the reader would go through the text to correct errors, changes in the text were easily introduced by the scribes as they were doing their work. The scriptorial readers and scribes also modified texts according to the way they understood them, or altered them to fit different times, or interpreted them by choosing words and phrases that explained the text in a way they found more acceptable or suitable to the people for whom the text was being produced.

The production of texts was fluid, but so was the use of text. Books were rare and expensive, so people learned texts "outside," that is without access to the written words, by memorization or by paraphrasing. Quoting a text, then, could really mean what we might call a reference to a text. Seldom was the text itself present for direct quotation as we might expect it. So errors crept into the text by virtue of the combining of similar texts. To aid the memory, *florigelia* were produced. *Florigelia* were collections of texts around a similar theme. We believe the sayings of Jesus were gathered into such a *florigelium*. Christians also made *florigelia* of Jewish prophetic texts that they thought predicted things about the life of Christ.

Christians were particularly fluid in the use of the gospel text. The Gospel of Mark was used by Matthew and Luke as a written source for their gospel outlines. But Matthew and Luke felt free to change the text of Mark in ways that suited their own communities and sensibilities. So they adjusted the language of Mark, changed expressions in Mark, omitted parts that seemed inappropriate to them, and otherwise worked the text to their own advantage. Mark was a text they could use, adapt, change, and transform to fit their own purposes. This way of reading and working with texts survived until the invention of the printing press, when the standards for using text could be regularized.

Cultural Interaction of Jews and Romans

What is most interesting and exciting to observe is the complex manner in which the various cultures, religions, and social organizations of diverse peoples interacted in the Roman world, especially in the outlying provinces. The Jewish rabbis adopted the Greco-Roman school with its communal center as the model for their rabbinic schools—the schools would look alike—and yet they also held on to the ancient scriptures that they interpreted, and they continued to forge new ways of remaining faithful to the older traditions in radically different political and social circumstances. Romans, on the other hand, admired the moral teaching and religious devotion of their Jewish neighbors and no doubt the contact with their neighbors spurred them to more religious devotion to the Roman gods. Traditions of incense burning and lighting candles, among others, seemed to have moved from cultural context to cultural context, creating and refracting new meanings, and piling tradition upon tradition.

The Roman Empire seemed to spur such cultural interaction and engagement, and the many different cultures and religions of the time seemed energized by the prospect of creating their own religious and social identity and finding ways to sustain their unique identity in the cultural mix that Greeks created and the

Romans sustained. It was a time of creativity and experimentation, of holding on to the riches of the past, of looking boldly into the future, of old things and new things coming together in surprising and enlivening ways. It was a time when social organizations could flow from community to community so that the Christian communities could look like and be organized like a Roman club or association; a synagogue could use the same titles of leaders as the Roman club, and the live-in school could host Roman, Christian, or Jew. The Gospel of Matthew, to which we now turn, represents a community in that cultural mix that displays an intriguing and exciting energy about old revelations of God in the scripture and new understandings from their chief rabbi, Jesus.

Questions for Discussion

1. The ancient schools fostered a way of living through which knowledge emerged in a fully relational setting. What are the benefits and problems of such an educational model? How does it compare with models of education in which you have participated?

2. In recent years, filmmakers have produced a large variety of apocalyptic films such as *Apocalypse Now*, the *Terminator* series, and *Armageddon*, among many others. What makes these films "apocalyptic"? What characteristics define contemporary apocalypticism? Why do you think these films have been produced at this time? What affect do these films have on the viewer?

3. The closest parallel to the destruction of the Temple in Jerusalem in 70 CE is the destruction of the World Trade Center in New York City on September 11, 2001, when many of the financial, economic, political, and social institutions were destroyed in the name of religion. Using 9/11 as the model, imagine and describe the personal and social impact of the Temple's destruction on people living in Jerusalem in 70 CE. How would a young person respond to that destruction? What impact would it have on families and their relationships? How would residents of Jerusalem respond to the dramatic impact of the event?

Resources for Further Study

The scene of the ancient school at the beginning of this chapter is an imaginative portrayal based upon the school described in Porphyry's "Life of Plotinus and the Order of his Works." To read the original, see "Life of Plotinus," trans. Richard Valantasis, "Porphyry, 'On the Life of Plotinus and the Order of His Books,'" in *Religions of Late Antiquity in Practice*, ed. Richard Valantasis (Princeton, N.J.: Princeton University Press, 2000), 50–61.

On the relation of wisdom to the ancient scribal schools, see John Kloppenborg, *The Formation of Q: Trajectories in Ancient Wisdom Collections* (Philadelphia: Fortress, 1987). For Jewish scribes, see Christine Schams, *Jewish Scribes in the*

Second-Temple Period (Sheffield, UK: Sheffield Academic Press, 1998). For a social scientific perspective, see the work of Anthony J. Saldarini, *Pharisees, Scribes, and Sadducees in Palestinian Society: A Sociological Approach* (Livonia, Mich.: Dove Booksellers, 2001).

For Roman scribes, see Kim Haines-Eitzen, *Guardians of Letters: Literacy, Power, and the Transmitters of Early Christian Literature* (New York: Oxford University Press, 2000). For an interesting account of the way in which books were produced, promulgated, and read, see Harry Y. Gamble, *Books and Readers in the Early Church: A History of Early Christian Texts* (New Haven: Yale University Press, 1995). See also H. Gregory Snyder, *Teachers and Texts in the Ancient World: Philosophers, Jews, and Christians* (New York: Routledge, 2000).

Ancient philosophical schools have been widely studied. The most important book that reflects our approach to formation and education is Pierre Hadot, *Philosophy as a Way of Life: Spiritual Exercises from Socrates to Foucault* (Oxford: Blackwell, 1995), and also his *What Is Ancient Philosophy?* (Cambridge, Mass.: Harvard University Press, 2004).

On the Jewish Diaspora see the important work of John J. Collins, *Between Athens and Jerusalem: Jewish Identity in the Hellenistic Diaspora* (Livonia, Mich.: Dove Booksellers, 2000). See also the collection of essays *Diasporas in Antiquity*, eds. Shaye J. D. Cohen and Ernest S. Frerichs (Atlanta: Scholars Press, 1993). On the question of Jewish identity, see Shaye J. D. Cohen, *The Beginnings of Jewishness: Boundaries, Varieties, Uncertainties* (Berkeley: University of California Press, 2001) and Erich S. Gruen, *Diaspora: Jews amidst Greeks and Romans* (Cambridge, Mass.: Harvard University Press, 2002). Gruen also addresses the question of Jewish Christian relations in the Roman period.

The most helpful articles that explain apocalyptic literature by defining the genre of literature and providing characteristics for its identification are in the *Semeia*, vol. 36 (1986), ed. Adela Yarbro Collins, *Early Christian Apocalypticism, Genre and Setting*. See also John J. Collins, *The Apocalyptic Imagination: An Introduction to Jewish Apocalyptic Literature* (Grand Rapids, Mich.: Eerdmans Publishing, 1998).

CHAPTER FIVE

The Gospel of Matthew:
Learning How to Read

Science fiction fans know The Matrix *trilogy: it's a cult favorite. The film introduces viewers to two worlds operating at the same time. One world is that of illusion named "the matrix," a computer-generated environment intended to keep humans in slavery and to farm human bodies for producing energy by creating the illusory appearance of normal American metropolitan life. The illusory matrix constructs a false reality in the twenty-first century where people go to work for large corporations, watch TV, commute, walk the city streets, eat at restaurants, surf the Internet, and go to nightclubs. The other world, the real world of the machines sometime in the twenty-second century and later, is dark and bleak. These machines, the evolutionary result of humans creating artificial intelligence, have almost completely taken over the world. The machines, using their artificial intelligence and the knowledge they attained, attempted various illusory worlds including one utopian world where there was no war or violence, but they learned quickly that humans, so essential to their functioning, required wars, struggles, and conflicts, and competition to thrive and reproduce, so the world they created was the conflicted and competitive world of the twenty-first century. We say the machines almost took over the world, because there are still some humans who battle the machines. The struggle between the resisters and the machines, which use humans as their primary energy source, dominates the world. The two worlds clash and interrelate, and the relationship of human to machine becomes an intriguing story.*

The movie takes the viewer through the discovery of the dark world and the illusion created by the matrix. The central character Neo has two identities in the illusory world of the matrix. Neo is Mr. Anderson, a run-of-the-mill computer programmer working for a top-notch corporation in the illusory matrix. But his other identity is that of a seeker, someone searching for the truth. He is a computer hacker who spends most of his time surfing the Internet for a man named Morpheus, whom he has heard can teach him the truth. Neo intuits that the reality of his existence in the twenty-first century world does not cohere or make complete sense. Neo intuits that something is terribly wrong, and so is driven to find Morpheus and to find answers. As viewers discover, Neo's perception of his reality as Mr. Anderson, is indeed a false one.

In his search for the truth, Neo discovers the false reality of the matrix through Morpheus, who awakens him from the torpor created by the matrix and who opens his eyes to see the way the machines work on humans. Neo awakens to discover that he lives in a future that is dominated by technology and machines that have evolved from artificial intelligence and who won the war between human and machine in a much earlier age. Neo comes to understand that the machines have won and dominate the world, but there still remains a large population of humans who continue to resist and attempt to take back the world they lost.

Neo sees the dark reality for its awful implications. The human beings living inside the matrix are in reality the energy source for keeping the machine world running and dominating. This human generator is a hybrid of sorts, part human and part machine, that is plugged into the matrix. Neo finds himself to be a hybrid. The world of Neo's identity as Mr. Anderson is simply an enormous computer program in which the hybrids participate in order to feed the machines. Neo also discovers that a remnant of humans who have not been made into hybrids exists, and he learns that the resistance to the matrix depends upon the cooperation of humans and the awakened hybrids to reclaim and restore the original world to human dominance.

As the story of the resistance in The Matrix unfolds, viewers discover that Neo has a very special destiny. Neo is the "One" who will bring balance to the dark and bleak world of humans feeding machines and machines creating the reality of the matrix. The concept of the "One" originates out of prophetic readings from the movie's city of Zion, the refuge city of human and awakened hybrids. Morpheus, a respected and beloved leader of the resistance, sought out Neo because of his strong faith and belief in this prophecy. Neo is for Morpheus a very special student.

Morpheus educates and guides Neo through his awakening to the illusion of the matrix and to the importance of his role in battling the machines. Human resistance to the machine world consists primarily in disrupting the matrix program, and this disruption requires the hybrid's dangerous reentry into the false reality to awaken others. Those who attempt reentry must be well prepared for their efforts, and Morpheus trains Neo to prepare him for his destined work.

Neo's formation through Morpheus involves a series of computer downloads. The hybrids that enter the matrix have gone through a series of computer-generated programs that mimic the matrix as their primary formative practice. They use the same technology as the machines and literally download the hybrids into "training programs." This type of formation occurs at times very quickly, because downloading in the future is even faster than it is now on our present-day PCs. For example, in one scene a hybrid woman disciple of Morpheus downloads in a matter of seconds information on how to fly a specific type of helicopter while she is in the matrix. Although the downloading into the mind of a human hybrid can happen swiftly, many downloads require time for the hybrids to digest and process. As the hybrids are led through specific formative programs for training purposes and begin to excel in learning how to defy gravity, dodge bullets, and fight "agents" (the name given to the antivirus program that detects and destroys the hybrid warriors), they still find themselves perplexed by the false reality of the matrix as they move between the two worlds. Hybrids find the matrix reality so real, so familiar, so normal that their memory of the matrix world makes the movement between worlds both troubling and dangerous. It is simply overwhelming to realize a reality is false which is experienced as so real. The awakened hybrids constantly have to redefine in their minds what is real and what is false. This redefinition is only achieved through the care and attention in the formative practices that Morpheus teaches. Neo experiences all these complexities and computer programs, and the viewers thrill at seeing the interaction of realities.

The Matrix really is a very shocking introduction to the Gospel of Matthew. That is our intention. What is interesting about the film *The Matrix* is that all participants, whether human or machine or hybrid, use knowledge, both old and new, in order to make sense of their lives and to understand the various realities in which they live. Knowledge reigns supreme. Guides and teachers are essential for transmitting that knowledge. Without specific classes of knowledge and understanding and without guidance on how to use them, the known world is doomed to remain asleep and live in an illusion. Formation in *The Matrix* remains crucial to the world's survival and hope. The Gospel of Matthew resonates with *The Matrix* because it too provides a comprehensive formative training program that leads its followers in specific ways of understanding not only the past, but also how to function and live in the present.

The Matthean Community in History

Historical context is essential for understanding the Gospel of Matthew. Matthew's gospel was written after the destruction of the Temple in Jerusalem in 70 CE and a number of years after the publication of the Gospel of Mark, dating it to sometime around 80 CE.

In the Portal to Matthew, we described the consequences of the outcome of the Jewish conflict and the destruction of the Temple and we maintained that creative energy was released through this religious, social, economic, and political trauma. The trauma forced new ways of thinking and living in order for Jews to continue to live faithfully to their scriptures in new times and under new circumstances. The Gospel of Matthew, as a document written in this context, testifies to that creative energy set loose in a community at once trying to be faithful to the traditional religion of Israel, holding on to Jesus as the inaugurator of a new era, engaging vigorously with Gentile Christians from other parts of the Roman Empire, and working diligently to create a kind of Jewish Christianity that would guide and form their lives. This was a daunting task and one that demanded creativity to forge new directions both for Jews and for Christians, while holding on to the riches of the past. Matthew's community had several years after the destruction of the Temple and the publication of the Gospel of Mark to creatively experiment. The written gospel attests to this creative endeavor.

So what happened in Matthew's community that created the Matthean school? What was their motivating task? How did they hold everything together? We envision a community living in the flow of cultures, religions, and society created by Roman domination of the province. The gospel was produced in a city like Antioch in Asia Minor where adherents of the Jesus movement were first called Christians; where many Jews moved after the Jewish War, with some even thinking of building a new Temple there; where the Roman social institutions like schools and clubs thrived; where close proximity forced various religious movements to interact; where some tried to convert others to their way of life; and where we know there were large numbers of Jewish, Christian, and Roman religious practitioners. It was a cultural mix that Roman domination created and held together. It was a heady place full of religious, social, cultural, economic and political energy—energy to forge new directions, explore new identities, create new institutions, and explore different ways of thinking.

Matthew's community entered that cultural mix with vigor and enthusiasm, and often with a great deal of passion. The members of this community started off as a Jewish community responding to the trauma of the destruction of the Temple in Jerusalem. Sometime in the following decade or so, they came in contact with those who believed in Jesus as the person announcing a new Empire of God in their own day. The community experienced the continuity of Jesus's teaching and life with what they had known as Temple-worshipping and scripture-believing Jews. In a sense, Matthew's community continued what James, John, and Peter, the Pillars of Jerusalem, strove to achieve: an authentically Jewish form of Christianity that valued deeply the connection of Jesus to Israelite traditions, that took seriously Jesus's instruction, and that lived authentically in a Roman intellectual, social, and political context.

The School of Matthew

Matthew's community organized themselves as a school. This would not have been unusual for either Jews, Greeks, Syrians, or Romans. During the Roman period, schools were live-in communities organized around a talented teacher, gathering disciples who not only studied but lived together so as to live out their philosophy and provide a center for intellectual and spiritual formation. The Jewish rabbis, after the destruction of the Temple, had also turned to schools, which the synagogues of Diaspora Judaism, following the Greek and Roman models, had used for years for teaching and training in Judaism outside Palestine. In the Roman period, schools formed around a succession of teachers, that is, the students reached back through their teacher to the many teachers under whom their teacher studied, so that there was a sense of connecting current knowledge and study with the knowledge and study of the past. In a modern example, Bleyle and Haugh, two of the coauthors of this book, studied with Valantasis, another coauthor, who studied with Dieter Georgi at Harvard, who had been one of Rudolph Bultmann's students; this establishes a succession: Bultmann to Georgi to Valantasis to Bleyle and Haugh, and links the systems of knowledge and formation back to the founder. The succession of teachers meant that the former teachers remained a vital and present force in later schools. We know, for example, that the Platonists looked back to the

founding spirits of the Academy, Plato and Socrates, as ground for their arguments. It is important to note that because Plato's writings are often ambiguous
and open-ended, later Platonists did not feel constrained by the formulations
of prior generations, but instead appropriated their teachings for the needs of
their community. In this way, Socrates, Plato, Aristotle, Epicurus, and the Stoic
masters taught new generations long after their deaths. Matthew's community
did the same thing, but with a very different succession of teachers and knowledge. Matthew's community seemed naturally drawn to the school as the place
where they could creatively forge a new way of living around courses of study
that connected them to the Israelite scriptures, to the teaching of Jesus, and to
the Roman context in which they lived. It was the cultural mix of a place like
Antioch that made this possible for them.

The Gospel of Matthew was written at the same time that rabbinic Jews,
adopting a Roman style of education, formed their schools to enable Jews to live
faithful lives without the Temple as the center of their sacrifice rituals. These
Jewish rabbinic schools organized themselves around the teaching and sayings of
important teachers, or rabbis, whose sayings provided a context and practices that
made Jewish life possible in a Roman context. Matthew's school in many respects
resembles the kind of school the rabbis created. In fact, Matthew's gospel provides
an important window on what was going on in these Jewish rabbinic schools, since
we have no similar description of the schools from an exclusively Jewish context.
In Matthew's school, however, Jesus was the rabbi who connected the community
to the Torah, the Israelite scriptures, and offered practices for living a life faithful to
the Torah in a new age, after the destruction of the Temple. But Matthew's school
operated in a complex Roman culture, which meant that the participants were not
just interacting with Christians and Jews, but also with their Roman neighbors.

Matthew's school had four courses of study that formed the core of their
teaching. The first was a course in Jesus that reframed the way Jesus was understood by the Matthean community's Gentile and Roman neighbors. The second
was a course in the Torah, the Israelite scriptures. The third was a course in
the Gospel of Mark and that course adapted the Roman gospel for a decidedly
Jewish Christian context. The fourth course taught a community life that encapsulated their way of life in particular practices. These courses of study show
the creative energy of the Matthean community. Without careful attention to
the context and the way the community studied and formed their students, we
miss the vigor and enthusiasm of the Matthean community's production.

The Course in Jesus Reframed

As Jews who came to believe in Jesus, the Matthean school had to attend to
the way they understood their originating teacher. Jesus's sayings and deeds pro-

vided the major link between their school's teachers and the past. We could say that the succession of teachers depended upon Jesus as the link back to Israelite traditions and forward to the life of these Jewish Christians in the future. The school of Matthew, then, was a school organized around the teaching of Jesus, the Messiah. This reframing of Jesus took a number of different forms, reaching back into Israelite traditions.

Moses and the Torah

Moses was an important figure in the Israelite tradition, not only because he guided the Israelites out of the bondage in Egypt into the promised land, but also because Moses was believed to have written the Torah, the center of Israelite scriptures, and given it to the Israelites to guide and direct their lives. Moses communicated directly and intimately with God and provided the Israelites with the substance of that communication and relationship with God. Through Moses the Israelites communicated, as Moses did, with their God, the God who gave Moses both the oral and written Law—the Torah—to guide and structure their relationship to God. The Matthean Christians imaged Jesus as providing similarly for them: Jesus, also a leader in intimate and direct communion with God, not only led them into the new Empire of God, but Jesus's teaching also provided direction and guidance for the conduct of their lives. For the rabbis of the Matthean school, Jesus, as a new Moses, taught a new Torah in his teachings.

The Israelite Torah given by Moses consists of five books: Genesis, Exodus, Leviticus, Numbers, and Deuteronomy. Each of these books provides very different ways of knowing how God relates to Israel, ranging from narratives of the patriarchs to lists of laws to be practiced by the people in the Temple. Matthew's rabbis took their collection of the sayings of Jesus and organized them into five long speeches, or sermons, that provide five different ways of systematizing Jesus's teaching in ways that the students of the school could easily memorize. These five sermons have long been understood as the creation of a Christian Torah, the refracting of the Jewish tradition into a Christian frame. The first sermon, the Sermon on the Mount (chapters 5 to 7) provides the core teaching of the school of Matthew. Here the moral teaching, which we will discuss later, takes its form so that the teachers of the community provide a systematized and consistent pattern for living for their students. The second sermon (9:35–10:42) presents instruction to the disciples for their missionary work, and here the teachers instruct their students about ways to gather new people not only into their school, but also into the Empire of God. The third sermon (13:1–52) presents the students of the school with parables to be interpreted and digested in order to know how to learn properly in the new Empire. These parables, long understood by teachers in all ancient schools to be mind twisters that challenged traditional ways of learning and knowing, gave the Matthean school material upon which people could ruminate to discover their unique way of living and thinking. The fourth sermon (17:24–18:35) instructs the community on the way they should live and the proper relationships within the community. The Matthean school taught a different way for its members to relate to one another, especially in resolving conflicts within the school and the church at large. The fifth sermon (chapters 23 through 25) explains the apocalyptic time in which the school of Matthew teaches. These apocalyptic sayings, reflecting the effect of the Jewish wars, forge new ways of understanding the import of the efforts to study and learn in a troubled time.

These five sermons of Jesus do not displace the five books of Moses in the Torah, but seem to set up a supplement to them that reflects the Matthean school's commitment both to the past and to their present reality. It is a bold move. It maintains the Law given by Moses, while at the same time looking far beyond it to new arenas for study and learning in the students' own context and with his or her own commitments to Jesus. We might say that the five books of Moses have been symbolically refracted through the five sermons of Jesus. Or better, that for the Matthean school, Jesus was the new Moses to lead the Israelites into a new Empire, a new age, a time after the Temple, a symbolic new promised land. The Matthean school presented Jesus as creating a new Torah for the new age. The Matthean school reframed the understanding of Torah through their reframing of Jesus as a new Moses.

Jesus as Wisdom

Another bold move by the Matthean community occurred in the framing of Jesus as Wisdom. The rabbis of the Matthean school thought much more of Jesus than a messenger of God, as was Moses. They understood Jesus not only to teach the Wisdom of God, but he himself to *be* the Wisdom of God.

In our Portal to Matthew we discussed the scribal schools and their connection to the transmission of wisdom. Sages in antiquity taught through sayings, short, often pithy encapsulations of advice and direction for living a moral and spiritual life. Sayings, in fact, defined the sage. In the Roman philosophical context, these sayings summarized patterns of thinking and learning that could be easily brought forth in new circumstances. Many Roman philosophers were not only known through their sayings, but through the collections of sayings their students compiled and published. In the Jewish context, the scribal schools also promulgated collections of wisdom sayings for their own social and religious formation. In fact, the Jewish wisdom tradition was a very comprehensive one. We have many collections of Jewish wisdom, reaching from Israel's interaction with Egypt and its other Near Eastern cultures to Hellenistic times through the Roman period. Books like The Wisdom of Solomon, Proverbs, Ecclesiasticus (or in the Greek Old Testament, the Wisdom of Jesus ben Sira), the Testament of the Twelve Patriarchs of Israel, among many others, testify to this rich Jewish wisdom tradition. And all these books consist of sayings of the wise. So for both Romans and Jews, the presence of sayings in a corpus of literature by a teacher signified that the teacher was a sage, a bearer of wisdom.

These collections of sayings, both for Romans and for Jews, provided a means of social and religious formation. Wisdom had a function: to train people in the proper way of living. The Jewish wisdom tradition defined this way of living primarily through the development of virtues culled from the scriptures. The Jewish wisdom tradition, that is, aimed to train students in a way of living consistent with their religious revelation. The Roman tradition did likewise. The Stoics, for example, held the creation of a sage to be the culmination of philosophical study through the philosophical investigation of a way of life attuned to reason, the divine principle inherent in the universe. Roman philosophy, as we have said, was a way of life. So, too, was Jewish wisdom.

Jesus's wisdom was encapsulated in sayings. The source Q, which Matthew used to construct his five sermons, consisted primarily of sayings. Jesus, therefore, could easily be portrayed as a wise sage in such a way that both Romans and Jews would appreciate what he was doing. Jesus's wisdom laid out a particular way of living, and his sayings provided a guide to that way of living. Matthew's community, living in a Roman context and holding on to Jewish traditions, understood Jesus precisely as a bearer of wisdom and a teacher of a new way of life based on the Torah.

For Matthew's school, Jesus could lead and teach as a new Torah, because Jesus is portrayed as Wisdom, as the mind of God leading and teaching the people in a very traumatic time in their history. According to the wisdom tradition, this is precisely how the God of Israel works, by sending a new messenger to the people to awaken them from their delusion, to guide them in right understanding, and to show a new way of living. The five sermons, reorganizing the sayings of Jesus in a way students could master, became the central focus of wisdom for Matthew's school. These sermons create a corpus, a body of literature, summarizing the wisdom Jesus provides for the awakening and forming of the students. More than anything else, the mere existence of these five sermons establishes that the Matthean school understood Jesus as Wisdom.

But Matthew was even more creative than that. Like the miraculous events around Moses's birth—his rescue from infanticide and his unusual adoption by an Egyptian family—Jesus also had miraculous events surrounding his birth and early years. Matthew creates a highly symbolic infancy narrative to relate the birth of Jesus to wisdom. Matthew's infancy narrative (1:18–2:23), portrays Jesus as the center of wisdom by piling images of wisdom around Jesus. In the infancy narrative, Magi—wise men from the East, the seat of great wisdom—visit Jesus and present him with gifts (2:1–12). We are to understand Jesus as the wisdom that even foreigners desire and follow. Then Joseph takes Jesus for a sojourn in Egypt

(2:13–15), another country famous in antiquity as a source of wisdom. Here not only is Egypt a source of wisdom, but the flight into Egypt recalls Moses's sojourn in Egypt as a prerequisite to the giving of the Law on Mount Sinai. Several times in the Matthean birth narrative, dreams—sources of wisdom both in antiquity and in contemporary psychoanalysis—provide a clue to how to save Jesus's life. The events of Jesus's birth point to wisdom, and specifically to the wisdom of God on the mount of God presented to Israel after a sojourn in Egypt.

Connecting Jesus to Tradition

Matthew's imaging of Jesus as both a new Moses and Wisdom is simply stunning. The way that Matthew combines old traditions and new, the history of Israel, the giving of the Law, the sayings of Jesus organized into sermons, and the birth narrative, reconstitutes and refracts everything through the person of Jesus as Wisdom so that students see both the new and the old in a new light. This imaging of Jesus creates a sense of security: everything that held the Israelites together throughout their history, even through the destruction of the Temple, has been preserved in a new form in the teaching of the sage Jesus, a sage whose wisdom would make sense both to Jews and to Romans.

That linking of Jesus to the past Israelite tradition, however, finds even more concrete expression in the gospel. Clearly these connections to the past were important for the Matthean school, and they do not tire of making the connections. For them, Jesus was the last link to the entire history of God's unique relationship to Israel. The genealogy with which the Gospel of Matthew begins makes this connection. The gospel begins: "The book of the genealogy of Jesus Christ, the son of David, the son of Abraham" (1:1). From there the genealogy progresses down through the ages until Joseph and Mary have Jesus as their son. These generations are the first download, and the genealogy makes the point very dramatically. Just as David founded the first kingdom for the Jews, so has Jesus founded the first Empire of the Jews. The times had changed from an era of kingdoms to an era of empires, and Jesus founded the empire that was to replicate the work of David in Jesus's own day. The Christian rabbi makes this succession a vital part of the story of how Jesus fulfills the Israelite yearning for a nation of their own by connecting the story of Israel to the story of Jesus: "Thus the total number of generations from Abraham to David is fourteen generations; from David to the Babylonian exile, fourteen generations; from the Babylonian exile to the Messiah, fourteen generations" (1:17). Jesus and Israel are connected in such a way that his teaching refracts all of the traditions of the scripture.

Jesus as Fulfillment

There is a remarkable sense in which this school of Matthew holds on to the realities of their lives, realities that on the surface do not make immediate sense.

They seem to be connecting the dots of their lives in a particularly creative way, relating elements to each other in such a way that new understandings become apparent. They connect Moses to Jesus, Jesus to the tradition of the sages, sages to wisdom, wisdom to the history of Israel. They hold on to all of their past in Judaism and to their current experience through Jesus without in any way deflecting from the task of forging a new way of life. But there was more going on with them than merely connecting old with new. They realized, it seems, that the past and the present were even more intimately connected—a connection that went far beyond symbolic correlations between past and present. In fact, they describe the relationship of past to present as a process of fulfillment. Jesus did much more than recapitulate the past symbolically. Jesus fulfilled it; that is, Jesus brought the past to the brink of new associations and a new significance that created new meanings of past events and opened new possibilities for the future. The Law and the prophets acquired a different meaning as they were read through Jesus.

Jesus's role as rabbi and his teaching were far superior to that of just another teacher. His teaching completes what the Torah enjoins. Matthew often speaks of events in Jesus's life as fulfilling of the word of God. These fulfillment statements take the form "this was to fulfill" the word spoken by God, or through the prophets, or through the scriptures. At Matthew 1:22, for example, the gospel states: "All this took place to fulfill what the Lord had said through the prophet." And at Matthew 26:56, the gospel further states: "But all this has come to pass that the writings of the prophets may be fulfilled." For these Christian Jews, Jesus was not someone new doing something different, but the one who completed and continued the work of God among God's people.

This sense of fulfillment is most evident when the teachers in Matthew's community present the Law from the Torah and the teaching of Jesus that expands that Law for a new era and a new Empire. The Sermon on the Mount aligns Jesus's teaching and the revelation of the Law to Moses: "When he saw the crowds, he went up the mountain, and after he had sat down, his disciples came to him. He began to teach them" (5:1–2). Jesus, like Moses, goes up on the mountain to engage the Law. The first part of the sermon is called "the beatitudes," which we will take up later, but the second part, called "the antitheses" (the responses) is the section that holds the Law and Jesus's teaching together by portraying the continuing place of the Torah of Moses and Israel for Matthew's community. This second section opens with a very strong statement of the Torah's continuing relevance:

> Do not think that I have come to abolish the law or the prophets. I have come not to abolish but to fulfill. Amen, I say to you, until heaven and earth pass away, not the smallest letter or the smallest part of a letter will pass from the law, until all things have taken place. Therefore, whoever breaks one of the least of these

commandments and teaches others to do so will be called least in the kingdom of heaven. But whoever obeys and teaches these commandments will be called greatest in the kingdom of heaven (5:17–19).

This is a direct endorsement of the Law put in the mouth of Jesus. The school of Matthew sees no disjunction between the teaching of Jesus and the Law as they received it. Then Jesus begins to extend the Law for his Empire. He says:

> You have heard that it was said to your ancestors, "You shall not kill; and whoever kills will be liable to judgment." But I say to you, whoever is angry with his brother will be liable to judgment, and whoever says to his brother, "Raqa," will be answerable to the Sanhedrin, and whoever says, "You fool," will be liable to fiery Gehenna (5:21–22).

Each of the sayings is preceded by the formulaic "You have heard that it was said to your ancestors" with a repetition or paraphrase of a commandment. Jesus's practice was well-accepted in the first century. It was, in fact, the practice of the Pharisees to interpret the provisions of the Law so that it would not be abridged by the people. For instance, three times the Torah commands "You shall not boil a kid in its mother's milk" (Exodus 23:19, 34:26 and Deuteronomy 14:21). Neither in the time of Jesus nor now is this a completely lucid commandment. As the prohibition appears three times in the Torah, however, it was considered to be especially important, despite its opacity. Does the prohibition really mean that one has to worry only about the preparation of the meat of a young goat or does it extend to other kinds of meat as well? Teachers in Israel, including the Pharisees, began the process of interpreting this law and from that process came the prohibition of eating dairy and meat products at the same meal. The entire process is sometimes referred to as "putting a fence around the Torah," as the added provisions make it more certain that the participant will not inadvertently break a prohibition.

We can see that Jesus is following in this same tradition. Rather than denying the continuing validity of the Torah, Jesus is putting a fence around it. Not only must Christians not kill, they must not even become angry with others. The implication is that anger could lead to killing.

Another example of Jesus's extension of the Law for his own era relates to the question of adultery: "You have heard it said, 'You shall not commit adultery.' But I say to you, everyone who looks at a woman with lust has already committed adultery with her in his heart" (5:27–28). Again we find the Law affirmed ("you have heard it said"), but extended by a teaching about lust. Jesus teaches the Law, but sets up parameters that protect a person from even inadvertent transgression. The rabbis who taught in this school experienced no disjunction between the Law and Jesus's teaching: Jesus fulfilled the Law by setting a different standard for its observance.

These fulfillment statements both about Jesus and about Jesus's extending the Law provide an interesting window into the way the Matthean school is connecting the dots of the past to the present. There is energy here that is interesting to explore. The fulfillment and extension passages of the gospel play with time. The past, described as the Law as it was given to their ancestors, takes on new meaning through Jesus's teaching. At the same time, Jesus's teaching is projected into the past, bringing his teaching to the past as a way of articulating what the fullness of the Law truly meant. The fulfillment and extension passages collapse time in this way, making the past something new in the present and making the present revelation of Jesus something that was known in the past. Not only do these passages play with time, they also play with confirmation. The Law, as Moses gave it to the Israelites, forms the basis for confirming that what Jesus teaches is truly of God, because, after all, he simply extends the Law. At the same time, however, the extension of the Law confirms Jesus as the one who continues to develop and present the Law in a new context. By articulating the relationship between Jesus and the Law as fulfillment, the gospel confirms the authoritative status of both. This affirmation of the authoritative status of both Jesus and the Law creates a sense of hope. The Matthean community, conjoining as they do two religious systems, can see the promise of the future more clearly. It is not that the Christian system has replaced the Jewish system, or vice versa, but that both together can grow into something fulfilling and promising in the future. This gives hope that the teaching and study, and even the new way of living, will be cohesive and harmonious despite the differences. Fulfillment makes this hope possible. The sense of completion, of bringing everything full circle, results from this hope. The fulfillment and the extension passages of the gospel bring this all to completion: what has been spoken in the past has been completed in the present; what is happening in the present completes what was begun in the past. The school has achieved a kind of harmony that enables the community to live at once in two worlds and to experience not disjunction and hostility, but cohesiveness and completion. That is a stunning way of reframing Jesus, the Law, and the past, while forging vigorously into the future.

These are examples of Matthew forming new wisdom sayings by combining Matthew's unique material, the Torah of Moses, and the teachings of Greco-Roman philosophers. Where the Torah places almost exclusive emphasis on deeds, Jesus expands the teaching to include control of one's interior life as well. The Stoics, in particular, understood that with imperfect knowledge it is often difficult to judge the correct path. They argued, then, that it was the *intention* of the person acting that controlled the value of the judgment. One who goes through life with the attitude of doing everything in accordance with the will of God acts correctly. The Stoics extended this to control over one's emotions to avoid lust, or greed, or vengeful feelings, just as Matthew has done. By this practice of combining Torah and Roman philosophy, Jesus gives Matthew's community permission actively to incorporate the best teachings of the world into their own, basically Jewish, practices.

The same sense of playing with time, of confirmation, of hope, and of completion occur throughout the reframing of Jesus by this community. Moses is present in Jesus, and Jesus in Moses. The history of Israel's liberation from the Egyptians plays out in Jesus's infancy. Jesus speaks wisdom in sayings, a universal language of the ancient sage and of the contemporary philosopher. In a sense, the fulfillment of the scriptures in Jesus brings to a close an era that at the time of Matthew was conflicted between Judaism and the emerging Christian church. But it brings it to an end, not by denial and denigration, but by a very hopeful posture of fulfillment and completion. These reframing techniques gather together all the disparate and disjointed elements and somehow weave them almost seamlessly into a new story, one full of hope and promise.

The Course in the Torah and the Sayings of Jesus

In *The Matrix*, Neo agrees to be awakened by Morpheus to understand the reality of the matrix. The first program downloaded into Neo's mind begins with a conversation with Morpheus in a white room with only a television set and a chair. This is a very shocking conversation for Neo because he was forced to come to grips with the fact that the world as he knew it was not the real world in which he lived. The conversation presents the fragmentary paths that were necessary to understand the sequence of events that led to the rule of the matrix and the subjugation of humans. Morpheus gives Neo the history, as best he can relate it, about when the matrix took over command of the universe sometime in the twenty-first century. Neither Morpheus nor Neo know what year it is, only that they are many years, possibly centuries, away from the time in the twenty-first century when the matrix coalesced to rule. The first download for Neo, and for all the hybrids who struggle to free humanity, requires this history and the received wisdom from the underground to help locate them in time.

The same happens in Matthew's school, but here the download is the knowledge of the Israelite scriptures. We are given a glimpse into Matthew's scribal world when Jesus says, "then every scribe who has been instructed in the kingdom of heaven is like the head of a household who brings from his storeroom both the new and the old" (13:52). Matthew's community brought the new Jesus to bear on the old Torah in order to create something hybrid, something mixed of the two elements that would help these Christian Jews to live faithfully at once to Torah and to Jesus. This hybrid consisted of the Torah and the collection of the sayings of Jesus.

The collection sayings of Jesus (commonly designated as Q) is an important source for Matthew's school. The sayings of Jesus, like the proverbs and sayings in the wisdom literature, comprise a collection of the sayings of a wise man. The first of Jesus's five sermons in Matthew, the Sermon on the Mount, extends for slightly over one hundred verses from the opening of chapter 5 to the close of chapter 7. We believe that Matthew produced it for his community as an epitome, a summary, of the wisdom teachings of Jesus.

Recall that wisdom in antiquity was not viewed as an end in itself, but as a means of achieving the goal of human life. Wisdom, because it related to the mind of God, was the same everywhere, so Greeks, Romans, and Jews alike pursued wisdom. The Platonists taught that the goal of life was to join the individual human soul to the divine. Upon death, the human being could take on the mind of the divine. The Gospel of Matthew, and the Sermon on the Mount in particular, are pointed to helping the student of the school achieve something like this goal. Matthew's Christian Jews dedicate themselves to the process of taking on the mind of Jesus, who is the Wisdom of God. Matthew marshals all of the resources at his disposal to assist the student, as we will see.

The Example of the Beatitudes

The way the Christian-Jewish rabbis work is fascinating, weaving together fragments from many places in the Torah and blending them with new suggestions in Jesus's context. The Sermon on the Mount opens with Jesus proclaiming nine Beatitudes:

> Blessed are the poor in spirit, for theirs is the kingdom of heaven.
> Blessed are they who mourn, for they will be comforted.
> Blessed are the meek, for they will inherit the land.
> Blessed are they who hunger and thirst for righteousness, for they will be satisfied.
> Blessed are the merciful, for they will be shown mercy.
> Blessed are the clean of heart, for they will see God.
> Blessed are the peacemakers, for they will be called children of God.
> Blessed are they who are persecuted for the sake of righteousness, for theirs is the kingdom of heaven.
> Blessed are you when they insult you and persecute you and utter every kind of evil against you (falsely) because of me. Rejoice and be glad, for your reward will be great in heaven. Thus they persecuted the prophets who were before you (5:3–12).

The Beatitudes, in some form or other, are familiar (at least in hearsay within the popular culture) in the postmodern world. So familiar, in fact, that just as the word *gospel* has lost its imperial, revolutionary connotations, so the word *blessed* has lost its depth of meaning. The Greek word normally translated into English as "blessed" is *makarioi*. While blessed has a religious, pious kind of sense in contemporary usage, the Greek original is plainly rooted in the here and now. One who was *makarios* was completely fulfilled: physically, emotionally, financially, and spiritually. The beatitudes, then, tell the participant what Jesus believes is needed to achieve this goal of complete fulfillment. In this, Jesus, and his scribe Matthew, are following in the traditions of other philosophical schools, all of whom argued that their traditions of wisdom practices and texts provided the proper route to achieving this state. So Matthew supplies from the collection of the sayings of Jesus a short summary of the teachings on happiness.

Let's try to replicate the process that the Christian Jews of Matthew's community might have used to make meaning of these wisdom sayings. It is easiest to start with Matthew's known sources. The Israelite scriptures include various approximations of the beatitudes. Though Matthew does not explicitly cite the Israelite scriptures in the beatitudes, they all have deep resonances with the Israelite scriptures. This Christian-Jewish rabbinic school knew their scriptures! The book of Numbers in the Torah contains one of the earliest blessings, when God instructs Moses and his brother Aaron on the proper way to bless the people: "The Lord bless you and keep you! The Lord let his face shine upon you, and be gracious to you! The Lord look upon you kindly and give you peace!" (Numbers 6:24–25). As did Moses and Aaron, Jesus assures the people that God will care for them and bring them to fulfillment. The people will be blessed and should expect blessing. This beatitude on the lips of Jesus invokes Moses's and Aaron's blessing, but does not quote it directly. The perceptive student would hear the similar language and make the connection.

Another source for this beatitude, taken from the collection of the sayings of Jesus, relays this beatitude in this way: "Blessed are the poor, because the Empire of God is yours." Matthew's community has expanded the saying adding "in spirit" as a qualifier of "the poor." Matthew expands the number of those who can be fulfilled because it is not just the financially poor, who were many, that are blessed, but anyone who is "poor in spirit" regardless of financial status. Those who are "poor in spirit" truly enter the Empire of God as Jesus commands.

For the wealthy in Matthew's community, the sigh of relief may have been short-lived as they reflected on the qualifier: "the poor *in spirit*." Matthew's major source, the Israelite scriptures, provides some clues on the meaning of this phrase. One way to understand "poor in spirit" is as one who has faced the challenges of life, particularly maintaining a life in covenant with God, and experiences a poverty of spirit even, as Saint John of the Cross calls it, a "dark night of the soul." The book of the prophet Isaiah describes God's commitment to those who struggle, often without obvious success, for the benefit of the people of Israel:

You were wearied with the length of your way, but you did not say, "It is hope-less"; you found new life for your strength, and so you were not faint. . . . For thus says he who is high and exalted, living eternally, whose name is the Holy One: *On high I dwell, and in holiness, and with the crushed and dejected in spirit, To revive the spirits of the dejected, to revive the hearts of the crushed.* . . . The spirit of the Lord God is upon me, because the Lord has anointed me; he has sent me to bring glad tidings to the lowly, to heal the brokenhearted" (57:10, 15; 61:1, RSV, *emphasis added*).

Matthew appropriates the promises of the Isaiah passages for his community: The Lord, the God of Israel, stands with and fortifies those building the nation of Israel, though their spirits may be downcast.

Yet another persuasive case can be made that the "poor in spirit" are those enumerated in the rest of the beatitudes: those who mourn; who are meek; who hunger and thirst for righteousness; who are merciful, clean in heart, and are peacemakers; those who are persecuted for righteousness's sake; and those who are reviled and persecuted and defamed for Jesus's sake. We suspect that all of these interpretations and others would have been discussed, defined, and redefined in Matthew's community. In a moment of challenge, the recitation of these short sayings could prompt recall of the whole panoply of arguments.

There are no known parallels in the collections of Jesus's sayings for the sec-ond (mourners), third (meek), fifth (merciful), sixth (clean of heart), seventh (peacemakers), and eighth (persecuted for righteousness's sake). As an example of marshaling all resources, consider the fifth beatitude, "Blessed are the mer-ciful, for they shall obtain mercy." The rabbis found ample material for this beatitude in the Israelite scriptures. In Psalms, in prophetic sayings, and in nar-ratives, God's mercy is extolled throughout the Israelite scriptures. Mercy is also a human virtue whose absence is condemned and whose exercise is praised. For instance, in the book of Proverbs, a collection of wisdom sayings, one proverb covers both: "He who mocks the poor insults the one who made him; he who rejoices in calamity will not go unpunished; but the one having compassion will receive mercy" (Proverbs 17:5, LXX). The last phrase clearly could have been a forerunner to Matthew's own beatitude.

The fourth and eighth beatitudes may reflect two sides of a discussion. The fourth, "Blessed are those who hunger and thirst for righteousness, for they shall be satisfied" (5:6), provides a promise while the eighth, "Blessed are they who are persecuted for the sake of righteousness, for theirs is the kingdom of heaven" (5:10), serves to temper the promise. Common to both beatitudes is the notion of righteousness, a term with a range of meanings in the Israelite scriptures and among Greco-Roman philosophers. The notion of "righteousness" commonly includes the idea of justice, but as here, it goes beyond legalities to embrace the concept of the right ordering of relationships among God, the individual, society, and the natural world. The expectation of the Empire of God surely would incorporate this broader concept. The eighth beatitude, however, gives fair warning of persecution for those who attempt to do so. Here Matthew provides a foreshadowing of the fate of Jesus: the one who sought righteousness experienced the ultimate persecution.

By placing the beatitude among school sayings like this, Matthew would also prepare the audience to view Jesus's death within the entire tradition of the philosopher. In the Greco-Roman world, the Greek philosopher Socrates was known as the classic example of one unjustly executed by the political authorities in his native Athens. Philosophical schools looked to him as one who chose to endure an unjust death rather than be untrue to his own self. During the turbulent Roman history, prominent philosopher/politicians such as Seneca followed Socrates's example and committed suicide rather than be exiled or face disgrace. In this beatitude, Jesus takes a stand in the same tradition: persecution, even death, is the expected consequence for the one who seeks right relationships.

The Example of the Lord's Prayer

We can see another way that the Jewish Christian rabbinic teachers in Matthew's community employed other honored Jewish traditions when we read how Matthew's community transformed the prayer that Jesus gave his followers. In many ways, Matthew's version of the Lord's Prayer stresses continuity with the Jewish tradition. The initial verses of the Lord's Prayer bear a strong resemblance to the Jewish prayer, the *Kaddish*, which was probably written shortly before the fall of the Temple in 70 CE: "Magnified and sanctified may his great name be in the world that he created, as he wills." Jesus's prayer mirrors that prayer: "Our father in heaven, hallowed be your name; your kingdom come, your will be done, on earth as in heaven," but goes much further: "Give us today our daily bread; and forgive us our debts, as we forgive our debtors; and do not subject us to the final test, but deliver us from the evil one" (6: 9b–13).

If composed two decades earlier than Matthew's text for Temple liturgies, the *Kaddish* would have been a prayer familiar to those Christians, like the Matthean community, still participating in the life of the synagogue. By proposing a new prayer, Jesus was not denying the continuing validity of the *Kaddish* or synagogue liturgies, but was using them as an opportunity for reflection and expansion. The old and the new have been brought together by the scribes of the school working with Jesus's sayings.

The parallels in these verses are striking, as they call for the sanctifying of the holy name and the will of God to be done on the earth that God created. Both prayers ask God to magnify the divine name, to make it universal and powerful throughout the world. In the modern world, a sense of one's name being powerful has largely been lost. Some of that aura around a divine name is captured in scenes from movies set in medieval times. We see royal messengers demanding "Open in the name of the King!" The king's name and the official with authority to act in the king's name carry all of the imperial power of the king himself. Matthew is calling on God, the father of Jesus, to establish the divine name and divine imperial rule as the source of power throughout creation.

Now we begin to realize that praying these petitions was a political act—indeed a treasonable act. When the believers ask "thy kingdom" or, as Matthew's community would have heard it, "thy empire come," they set the Empire of heaven in opposition to the Roman Empire. In the first-century Mediterranean world, there was one and only one empire, the Roman Empire, and one and only one ruler, the Roman emperor. For many decades the Roman Senate had proclaimed living, ruling emperors to be divine. To be sure, the Romans welcomed other gods into their empire, but only one god, and he a Roman emperor, would ever have a name that would open doors.

The rest of the Lord's Prayer describes in language that bridges the old with the new how the community will experience this divine Empire. Just as the beatitudes describe the individual's life in the Empire of God, here Jesus describes how the sovereign God will reign over the community. God is asked to supply "daily bread," suggesting a limited, one-day supply of food for the community, just as the Roman emperors traditionally provided the common people with a daily supply of bread. The community will rely on the same gracious God who fed the Israelite people in the desert with one-day's ration of manna at a time. The community will not countenance storing and hoarding food or other trappings of wealth.

The community will honor the Torah's three-fold prohibition of charging interest on loans (Exodus 22:24; Leviticus 25:36–37; Deuteronomy 23:20–21). As we commented earlier with regards to boiling a kid in its mother's milk, a thrice-repeated Torah injunction was to be closely followed. The Matthean community acknowledges this when they tie God's forgiveness of the debts to God incurred by the community to the way that the community itself responds to the loans it makes: "Forgive us our debts, as we forgive our debtors" (6:12). There will be a one-to-one correspondence between the generosity of the community and the generosity of God!

The next petition, "do not subject us to the test," is ambiguous, vague, and altogether similar to the elliptical aphorisms of a fine Greco-Roman philosopher. What test could the petitioners be thinking about? In fact, there are many tests that the community may be anxious to avoid. The same Greek word used here for "test," *peirasmon*, appears prominently in Genesis 22:1, "God tested Abraham," the beginning of the story of the sacrifice of Isaac by Abraham, the paradigmatic "test" of the faithful one. The community may, then, be praying not to be asked to sacrifice their own children, the future of their community, as God asked Abraham to do. In this test, there are echoes of the test of the parents of the infant boys in Bethlehem, killed by the representative of Caesar at the birth of Jesus (2:16–18). When Jesus goes to pray in the garden of Gethsemane in preparation for his trial and execution, he tells his disciples to pray that "you may not undergo the *peirasmon*," the test (26:41). Hence, the disciple praying the Lord's Prayer may remember this incident and associate the "test" with Jesus's own trial and death.

The Example of Ministering to Jesus
The expansive reading of Israelite scriptures and traditions found in the Lord's Prayer reaches deep into the Christian traditions about Jesus. The school of Matthew was not interested simply in presenting tradition but, by connecting to ancient tradition, in forging new understandings of the ways of God. This is evident in another implication of the petition in the Lord's Prayer "do not bring us to the test." A final "test" is also described by Matthew in chapter 25 when he describes the judgment of the nations by the Son of Man (a figure from the end times mentioned in the book of Daniel, 7:13). This brings us to the second major wisdom text on which we wish to reflect:

> When the Son of Man comes in his glory, and all the angels with him, he will sit upon his glorious throne, and all the nations will be assembled before him. And he will separate them one from another, as a shepherd separates the sheep from the goats. He will place the sheep on his right and the goats on his left. Then the king will say to those on his right, "Come, you who are blessed by my Father. Inherit the kingdom prepared for you from the foundation of the world. For I was hungry and you gave me food, I was thirsty and you gave me drink, a stranger and you welcomed me, naked and you clothed me, ill and you cared for me, in prison and you visited me." Then the righteous will answer him and say, "Lord, when did we see you hungry and feed you, or thirsty and give you drink? When did we see you a stranger and welcome you, or naked and clothe you? When did we see you ill or in prison, and visit you?" And the king will say to them in reply, "Amen, I say to you, whatever you did for one of these least brothers of mine, you did for me." Then he will say to those on his left, "Depart from me, you accursed, into the eternal fire prepared for the devil and his angels. For I was hungry and you gave me no food, I was thirsty and you gave me no drink, a stranger and you gave me no welcome, naked and you gave me no clothing, ill and in prison, and you did not care for me." Then they will answer and say, "Lord, when did we see you hungry or thirsty or a stranger or naked or ill or in prison, and not minister to your needs?" He will answer them, "Amen, I say to you, what you did not do for one of these least ones, you did not do for me." And these will go off to eternal punishment, but the righteous to eternal life (25:31–46).

Coming at the conclusion of the last of Matthew's five sermons, Jesus's discourse inscribes the bedrock values of the Matthean community. In the first place, Matthew once again emphasizes that the righteous person builds a right relationship both with others and with God. Feeding the hungry, giving drink to the thirsty, welcoming the stranger, clothing the naked, and caring for the ill are deeds recited in Jewish and other non-Christian texts as worth emulation. The teaching here, however, goes beyond that to claim that caring for one of the least brothers is identical to caring for Jesus himself, the Master. This is the surprising punch line of the story: Jesus is the least of the brothers, those in desperate need.

Matthew's community doubtless identified themselves with those undergoing the test of the judgment, among all the nations of the earth. And they would ask themselves, who are the least among us to whom Jesus refers? Earlier in Matthew (12:49–50) Jesus distinguishes between his birth family and calls those who "do the heavenly will of my father" his sisters, brothers, and parents. This would say that the primary focus for the Matthean community would be Christians, those whom Christians themselves addressed as "sister" and "brother." This interpretation helps account for the unusual practice of caring for prisoners who may be identified with Christians, especially Christian missionaries, imprisoned for preaching their Gospel.

The educational process in Matthew's community, however, has three different focuses: the Israelite scriptures, the sayings of Jesus, and the Roman philosophical tradition. So we should not be surprised that the identification of "brothers" with other Christians is not the only way the text can be read. Indeed, we have seen how Matthew will take a traditional Jewish or Christian statement and add a twist from the Greco-Roman philosophers. In the case of this discourse, Matthew's disciples would have also had occasion to reflect on the doctrine from the Stoics who envisioned the whole world as a single home in which all peoples are brothers and sisters. It was these same Stoics whose ideals influenced many of the revelatory sayings in the Sermon on the Mount, Matthew's summary of Jesus's teaching. So, it is not simply probable but most likely that the statement of "brothers" was deliberately ambiguous, left open-ended by Matthew to provide an opening for reflection on theory and practice by the disciples in the school.

Due regard to the possible debates within Matthew's school on "who is my brother" should not deflect our attention from the amazing statement Matthew records, that Jesus is identical to the poorest. This treatment is without precedent in the Israelite scriptures, where the Lord, the God of the Israelites, required such works by the people that they might "be holy as I am holy." The popular religions of antiquity also missed this identification of a god with a group of even prosperous, happy humans, much less the most abject. The Greek gods, for instance, might take on the form of humans for romps through the world, but there was no identification of them with humans. Jesus claims here that rather than humans taking on his mind, he resides in the life and mind of the poorest in the world. Stoic philosophers, who portray all humans as brothers and sisters, also saw the divine *logos*, or reason, imbuing all the world. For them, care for anyone would be care for the divine spark in everyone.

Matthew's teaching that care for the least is care for Christ may have had a genesis in earlier and contemporaneous Christian literature. Paul, in his first letter to the Corinthians, goes beyond the impersonal *logos* of the Stoics to reimagine the Christian community as forming the Body of Christ (1Corinthians 12:12). This formation occurs through the Eucharist, when all Christians share the cup and the bread (1 Corinthians 10:16) and through participation in the death of Christ (Romans 7:4). The letter to the Ephesians, composed after the Gospel of Matthew, emphasized again the image of the Body of Christ (Ephesians 4:10–14). These letters stress the role of the Christian in building up the Body of Christ. Matthew has introduced a new way to reflect on the mystery of the Body of Christ, as Christ sharing, acting through, and sustaining the least of the world.

We noted that in the first beatitude, Matthew modified the tradition received from Q ("Blessed are you poor, for yours is the kingdom of God") to move beyond concern for those financially poor to those poor in spirit—those building the Empire of heaven despite the toll this commitment exacts. Matthew is consistent in his approach from the first beatitude to the Last Judgment. In the latter he defines building the Empire of heaven as care for the hungry, the thirsty, the stranger, the naked, the sick, and the imprisoned. Those who perform these deeds enact and inherit the Empire of heaven.

The depiction of the Last Judgment (25:31–46) is the conclusion of the last sermon recounted by Matthew before Jesus's Passion, death, and resurrection. It is, then, Jesus's last word on attaining wisdom and happiness. It grounds the Matthean community in practicable works of righteousness on behalf of others, Christian and non-Christian alike. As with the Sermon on the Mount, the summary of the wisdom of Jesus, the Last Judgment combines authentic Jewish wisdom, traditions from the life of Jesus, and the teachings of the traditional Greco-Roman philosophers. For this community, wisdom is to be sought in the traditions of inherited religions and in the teachings of the world. They are to lead to practices of righteousness, of enacting a proper relationship among God, the self, the community, and the world.

Parables

Bringing together different traditions is a tricky business. It is not easy to find a spiritual place where Israelite traditions may live comfortably with traditions of Jesus and Roman philosophy. But ancient schools reveled in the problem of bringing disparate traditions of wisdom to bear on their lives. Every ancient school did this and found the challenge compelling. One of the ways that ancient teachers presented material was through ambiguity and conflation, particularly as it played out in the favorite literary genre for teaching, the parable. Parables present narratives in seemingly real-life situations as a place to bring wisdom to bear in daily living. Because it is a story with multiple perspectives open to the reader or hearer, it becomes a kind of intellectual puzzle, something to think about and explore. The multiple perspectives of the parable foster ambiguity and the story line always allows for this ambiguity and conflation; the exploration of the parable's ambiguity allows for the convergence of various traditions.

For example, Matthew uses a short saying in 13:33: "He spoke to them another parable. 'The kingdom of heaven is like yeast that a woman took and mixed with three measures of wheat flour until the whole batch was leavened.'" The notion of relating the Empire of heaven to yeast in three measures of flour must have seemed bizarre to many listeners. Three measures of flour, first of all, was an enormous amount of flour, nearly 40 liters worth, enough for 110 pounds of bread. Furthermore, it is rare in the Hebrew or Christian scriptures that yeast is not thought of as a corrupting influence. At Passover, for instance, any amount of yeast left in a house will defile the house. But here, a bit of yeast in an enormous amount of flour is elevated to a major symbol found in the gospels, the Empire of heaven.

It is a picture that may be interpreted in many ways and illustrates a feature of Matthew's wisdom material: it is deliberately ambiguous, inviting the reader to explore the mystery of the Empire of God. We described at length Mark's use of the rhetorical strategy of *dissimulatio*, how that strategy, among other things, helped deflect unwanted attention from Roman authorities on the Christian community. Ambiguity works in exactly the opposite way, as it piques the imagination and provokes the interest of the reader to explore the saying further. In this case, Matthew deliberately juxtaposes the contrasting images of yeast, a corrupting influence, and the Empire of heaven, the goal of the Christian and something utterly pure. The ambiguity of the statement, the fact that Jesus does not explain how the statement should be understood, encourages the reader to think about how these might be related.

This use of ambiguity is an especially appropriate way to encourage reflection on a "mystery." By mystery, we do not mean a puzzle that is difficult to solve, like a murder mystery. Rather by mystery we mean a reality that the wise person can begin to understand, unfold, and enact in her life, but a reality that is so immense that a lifetime of reflection cannot exhaust its meaning. Throughout Matthew's text, the Empire of heaven serves as the primary mystery that the gospel writer wishes to present to and explore with readers. For instance, we can think of at least one way that the Empire of heaven can be likened to yeast. Matthew might have wanted to describe the Empire of heaven as corrupting, disrupting the old order and its systems. Once the Empire of heaven has been introduced into the world, it enlivens, moves, transforms even the largest, most inert masses into nourishment for the multitudes. Are there other ways to interpret the saying? Doubtless there are. The disciples of Matthew who memorized the saying would bring to mind not only the ways that it might be interpreted but also the discussion and teachings on the aphorism.

The school of Matthew worked with energy as the traditions swirled around them. We can understand how they began their work by thinking again about *The Matrix*. Neo is taken back into the matrix to consult the oracle. As Neo travels with Morpheus and Trinity (Neo's romantic interest in the story), he finds that he must reorient himself to a new world, realizing that what he thought was real in his twenty-first-century life was really an illusion. Neo must come to terms with his new context, and he does that by listening to Morpheus piece together the history that explains how the machines took over the world after the humans had taught them to think for themselves. It is a confusing history that can only be pieced together from fragments. Neo's shock at the history forces him to learn a new way of living and experiencing. So he begins with downloading the programs that enable him to function in the machine world in relationship to the illusory world: he learns to fly, to defy gravity, to dodge bullets, and to escape into phone lines. These new skills come to him from learning where the world really functioned after the catastrophe that the machines visited on humanity. The Matthean community, also experiencing a catastrophe, begins to piece together traditions in order to make sense of their world. They reached back into their ancient history to understand how Jesus related to their past traditions. They reached around them to the Roman philosophers to speak in a language current for their situation in the Roman Empire. And, of course, they reached into the teachings of Jesus to help them bring all these things together into something that would enable them to be God's people in a disastrously new context. Their oracle, however, was a book already written, the Gospel of Mark. In *The Matrix*, the oracle brought clarity to the life situation of humans; in the Gospel of Matthew, the Gospel of Mark also brings a clarity and cohesion to their own life and story.

The Course in Mark

To understand the role of the Gospel of Mark in Matthew we return again to *The Matrix*. Neo needed to know the context that Morpheus provided in order to be prepared to download the knowledge and begin to contest the matrix that had taken over the world. That context, the story of piecing together the chronology and order of events that led to the matrix's supremacy, organized Neo's training, thinking, and responses, and it gave direction to his life's project from that point onward in the film series. The community that produced the Gospel of Matthew had the same tool in the Gospel of Mark. They used the previously written gospel as the organizing context for their training, thinking, and responses, and the gospel gave direction to their life's project. The Gospel of Mark provided the contours of the story of Jesus's life that would organize and direct the school's teaching.

By the time the Gospel of Matthew was written, the Gospel of Mark had been circulating among Christian communities across the Roman Empire for over a dozen years. Once Mark created a biographical form for the life and teachings of Jesus, it became the standard way of imaging and understanding Jesus's church. Mark's gospel became the standard for all the other written gospels, as the literary relationship between the gospels that we discussed in the introduction to this book makes clear. Matthew's community read Mark's gospel as a major source for their study; Mark's gospel gave the contours of the mission into which Matthew's community could insert their own teaching. Mark's gospel became a primary textbook for the Matthean school.

We use the term "course in Mark" to identify how Matthew used the Gospel of Mark as part of an instruction manual for the Matthean community. Matthew made extraordinarily extensive use of the Gospel of Mark: about ninety percent of the verses in Mark are also found in the Gospel of Matthew. More important than the words, Matthew also took on board the basic narrative structure of Jesus's biography in Mark: Jesus's relationship with John the Baptist; his ministry of teaching and healing centered in Galilee; opposition to him from the religious and political establishment; his recruiting and training of disciples, particularly twelve charged with the task of nurturing the fledgling community; and concluding with his Passion, death, and the announcement of his resurrection in Jerusalem. The Gospel of Mark was an important text for Matthew's community, one for which Matthew had to account in his own teaching. But like all textbooks, the teaching in the school went beyond merely quoting and organizing the way Mark did. Matthew's community made significant changes to Mark.

Adapting Mark to New Circumstances

The first change one sees is in the very first verse. We noted in the discussion of Mark the political and prophetic tone which the opening verses take: the use of the term "gospel" (*evangelion*), the title "Son of God," and the quotes from the prophets. These, we saw, offer a challenge to the political and religious establishment(s). How does Matthew start? With a carefully crafted genealogy, tracing Jesus's ancestry back to Abraham. There are many messages that the genealogy does provide, including the message that Jesus is an heir to God's promises to Abraham and Sarah; that Jesus is a descendant from King David, hence a possible heir to the throne of the kingdom; and that Jesus is in fact worthy of a genealogy. One cannot produce a similar genealogy for most Judeans born at the time of Jesus: their lives were not deemed worthy of such chronicling. In both Roman and Jewish schools like Matthew's, however, genealogies served another purpose: to create a specific line of teachers. The Roman Stoic schools used genealogy to trace a lineage of teachers beginning with their own and going back to Zeno of Citium, the founder of the Stoa and of Stoicism. In antiquity, with written documents at a premium, students relied on the pedigree of their teachers to assure themselves of the authenticity of the teaching. By tracing Jesus's lineage back to Abraham, Matthew tells his community that Jesus shared the mind of Abraham and they could look forward to sharing Jesus's mind as well. Jesus stood in a long line of teachers who revealed the ways of God to Israel. For those who know the Gospel of Mark, the Gospel of Matthew, from the very first words, indicates that the community made changes to their Markan textbook.

But there were other changes as well. While Matthew reproduced about ninety percent of Mark in his gospel, the material he omitted shows a consistent editorial hand. One of the directions of the alterations is to emphasize Jesus's role as the master of the school of Jesus's followers. As a consequence, other characters are downplayed or discounted. Another change is that Matthew's gospel is a text for a philosophical school and so the biography becomes a written text to be read, studied, and memorized. In the process, Matthew's school excised raw emotions; clarified ambiguities in Mark's narrative—perhaps part of Mark's *dissimulatio*—and fashioned the disciples and the immediate teachers of Matthew and his colleagues as proper inheritors of Jesus's teachings. We note too that the teaching is out of the closet and in the street. While our locating the Gospel of Matthew's production in Antioch may be debated, it is abundantly clear that the time and place were amenable to the Christians who were comfortable openly proclaiming their gospel.

Subordinating John the Baptist

The characterization of John the Baptist in the Gospel of Matthew illustrates how Matthew downplays other characters and also dispels ambiguities about them. The Gospel of Mark left open the question of the relationship between Jesus and John the Baptist. We commented on the significance of the first three verses of Mark. There Mark recalls the prophecy of "one crying in the desert, 'Prepare the way of the Lord.'" While the traditional exegesis of these verses claims that they refer to the mission of John the Baptist, the structure of the sentence in Greek supports a reading that they refer to Jesus and to his mission, his gospel as described in the first verse. In this reading, Jesus is a prophet of the coming of God's Empire, and John is not the prophet of Jesus. Potentially more dangerous than a slight degradation of John's mission is the fact that Jesus was baptized by John. Was this to be understood as an initiation rite for Jesus into the school of John the Baptist? Was Jesus in fact a disciple of John's? Matthew wants to make sure that his students do not have any misunderstanding about the relative status of the two.

In chapter 3, he begins the process of clearly subordinating John to Jesus. The prophetic utterance discussed above appears after the introduction of John and, most pointedly, it is introduced by the phrase "It was of him that the prophet Isaiah had spoken when he said . . . ." There then follows an account of John's ministry. Then, in verse 13, Jesus appears seeking John's baptism. Now John confesses his own inferior status, saying, "'I need to be baptized by you, and yet you are coming to me?'" (3:14b).

Matthew largely reproduces Mark 2:18–22 at Matthew 9:14–17, a dialogue between Jesus and disciples of John, in which Jesus implicitly claims superior status to John as the bridegroom during whose life his disciples need not fast. Then in chapter 11, Matthew adds another dialogue and monologue (also found in Luke) concerning John. In Matthew 11:11, Matthew really administers a *coup de grace* to any question of John's status, when Jesus affirms that "among those born of women there has been none greater than John the Baptist; yet the least in the kingdom of heaven is greater than he." The teaching is clear: the least among Jesus's own disciples have a status superior to that of John the Baptist, no matter how exalted some may consider him.

Mark's gospel undergoes significant modification at the hands of Matthew. In the case of John the Baptist, we see Matthew dealing decisively with the thorny issue of Jesus's relationship to him. Matthew moves material to clarify any ambiguity, modifies Mark's text to show John's sense of inferiority, and takes on other traditions that clarify the preeminence of Jesus with respect to John the Baptist. The textbook is being rewritten.

Other Changes

Just as Matthew modifies characters' roles in Mark, he also adjusts the way characters operate in the gospel even when he uses Mark's gospel as a guide. Although Matthew changes characters throughout his gospel, we look at two chapters (8 and 9) to explore how he does it. At Matthew 8:14–15 we see how Matthew removes various characters from Mark's story. Matthew relates the story of the healing of Peter's mother-in-law that appears also in Mark 1:29–31. In Mark's recounting, we learn that Jesus entered the house of Simon and Andrew, accompanied by them as well as by James and John. They inform him of the woman's illness and he then cures her. At that, she rises from her bed to serve them. Matthew writes the apostles out of the text so that Jesus enters alone, sees that she is ill, touches her, and she arises to serve. Matthew uses the Greek word *diakonein*, which means to serve as deacon, or to wait at table, the work of a deacon. Alone among the synoptic gospels (Mark, Matthew, and Luke), Matthew records that she serves Jesus, not all the people present in her home. Matthew's version is thirty words compared with Mark's forty-three words. This reduction and the subtle modifications move the reader more quickly to a revised point: the cured are to rise and serve Jesus. As we saw in the discussion of Matthew's Last Judgment, one serves Jesus in serving the most oppressed, even such as an aging and sick woman living with her son-in-law. Matthew created this meaning by eliminating the other disciples from Mark's story.

Another technique the school of Matthew used to adapt the Gospel of Mark to their own circumstances involved toning down the emotional language they found in Mark. In one of Jesus's nature miracles, the calming of the storm in Matthew 8:18, 23–27, Matthew's simplified story blanches the emotional color out of the story. Matthew reduces Mark's description of the storm and of Jesus's stoic attitude ("A violent squall came up and waves were breaking over the boat, so that it was already filling up. Jesus was in the stern, asleep on a cushion" [Mark 4:37–38]) to a spare minimum: "Suddenly a violent storm came up on the sea, so that the boat was being swamped by waves; but he was asleep" (Matthew 8:24). Similarly, Matthew changes the apostles' speech when they wakened Jesus. In Matthew, even *before* Jesus stills the storm, Jesus takes a moment to chastise their lack of faith. Mark, perhaps the more seasoned sailor, remembers Jesus calming the storm and the sea first. Jesus's words to the disciples are practically identical in the two narratives but arranged somewhat differently. When these two versions are read aloud, the Markan text works better. Almost as if it were a play, the reader is given ample direction on how the scene will be played out: the boat is awash in water, we know where Jesus is located when the disciples go to look for him, and we even know to give him a cushion on which to rest. Matthew gives us none of these stage directions. They are unnecessary if we are studying a text, a hard enough task to produce and to read without adding superfluous verbiage: there was a big storm; Jesus was asleep; panicked disciples woke Jesus; Jesus rebuked disciples; Jesus calmed storm. End of story. One can imagine Matthew and his disciples then taking apart the story in the same way we did earlier. But in such an intellectualized discussion, whether Jesus lay on a wooden plank or on a cushion is of little or no consequence. What matters is the teaching about faith, accomplished literarily by simplifying and toning down the emotional content in Mark.

Matthew streamlined other stories in Mark as well. In some cases this streamlining seems drastic as in the story of the healing of the Gadarene demoniacs (or the single "Gerasene demoniac" in Mark). Mark composed a story that a ham actor relishes. The demoniac breaks bonds, roars obscenities, knocks himself unconscious with stones, but then gets cleaned up and wears nice clothes: a cameo role made for Dwayne "The Rock" Johnson, a professional wrestler and actor! All of these telling features are gone from Matthew, who reduces the description of the demoniacs to half of one verse: "They were so savage that no one could travel by that road" (Matthew 8:28b). Mark's version of the story is politically charged, with the demons naming themselves for the Roman army, being cast into the most unclean of animals, swine, and thence into the sea. By omitting the naming of the demons as Legion, Matthew's narrative also misses part of the rationale for the reaction of neighbors who want Jesus, the troublemaker, out of their district quickly. Mark's account concludes with the poignant vignette of the cured man begging to accompany Jesus but, in the end, accepting his mission to preach Jesus's healing deeds. If we imagine this account as a play, with this last scene our attention is drawn to the one who understands what it means to follow Jesus. Matthew does not want to distract attention from Jesus. The man is cured and is never heard from again. Through all of these parings, Matthew reduces the story from Mark's twenty verses to just seven. When one considers that in total Matthew is about fifty percent longer than Mark, a two-thirds reduction here is remarkable.

Right through this section, Matthew edits details, as in the very next story of the healing of the paralytic (Matthew 9:1–8 vs. Mark 2:1–12). Cutting to the bottom line: Matthew has reduced the text by one-third. Notices about the size of the crowd in the home are excised and a detail much beloved by preachers through the ages—the report that because of the crowd the friends of the paralytic cut a hole in the roof to lower him into the room below—has been deleted.

Analysis of these stories in chapters 8 and 9 in Matthew demonstrates how Matthew consistently edits out and reduces the agency of the often colorful minor characters in Mark's gospel. By doing this, Matthew intensifies the focus of the text on Jesus, his wisdom, and power. We now move further into the Gospel of Matthew to see other ways in which Matthew changes the textbook to accommodate the fact that his community is living in different circumstances and in a different part of the world. We will look at three important moments in the gospel tradition: the feeding of the five thousand; Jesus's announcement of his impending arrest, torture, and execution; and then the passion narrative itself.

The Example of the Feeding of the Five Thousand

The feeding of the five thousand in Matthew illustrates how Matthew excises the political connotations in Mark's text. In the discussion of the Gospel of Mark, we described Mark's positioning and construction of the story of the feeding of the five thousand, emphasizing the subtext of revolutionary politics in the story. Having seen Matthew's action on other narratives, we should not be surprised that this story too undergoes subtle but significant editing, omitting key features of the Markan text as it appears in Matthew 14:13–21. The first excision occurs when Matthew drops the reference to the "People were coming and going in great numbers, and they [Jesus and the disciples] had no opportunity even to eat" (Mark 6:31b). Later, Matthew omits the reference to the fact that the people were "like sheep without a shepherd" (Mark 6:34) and that they were grouped as in battle array "by hundreds and by fifties" (Mark 6:40). Not only do these changes shorten the narrative, they also excise politically charged material that Matthew and his community must have found objectionable. Even though in the story as we understand it Jesus renounces all the usual political positions, Matthew wants no part of politics. "Keep politics out of religion" seems to be his motto.

The Announcement about the Necessary Death ❜

Jesus's announcement of the need to suffer and die in Matthew illustrates how Matthew rejects Mark's negative conception of the disciples. Both Mark and Matthew recount Jesus telling his disciples three times of his Passion and death in Jerusalem (Matthew 16:21–23 and Mark 8:31–33; Matthew 17:22–23 and Mark 9:30–32; Matthew 20:17–19 and Mark 10:32–34). In Mark's version of these revelations, Jesus's prediction is followed each time by an unnervingly insensitive response on the part of one (Peter), all, or some (James and John), of the apostles. After the first prediction, Matthew follows Mark in having Peter rebuke Jesus, followed by Jesus rebuking Peter. Matthew makes two subtle changes in this dialogue. The first is to actually let Peter talk for himself: "God forbid, Lord! No such thing shall ever happen to you" (16:22) and, rather than making it clear that Peter receives a public rebuke as in Mark (Mark 8:33 "At this he [Jesus] turned around and, looking at his disciples, rebuked Peter.") Matthew leads the reader to assume that the whole dialogue occurs in private, away from the other disciples, thus avoiding the undermining of Peter's status.

After the second pronouncement, while keeping an important teaching of Jesus, Matthew defuses the overreaching ambition Mark attributes to the disciples. In Mark 9, the pronouncement by Jesus is met by bafflement: "they did not understand the saying and they were afraid to question him" (Mark 9:32). Thereupon the narrative moves immediately to the inside of the house at Capernaum where Jesus upbraids the apostles for arguing over who was the greatest (Mark 9:33–35). How does Matthew improve the image of the apostles? First of all, Matthew reports not that the apostles didn't understand Jesus's saying but rather that they were "overwhelmed with grief" (Matthew 17:23). Then Matthew inserts a uniquely Matthean selection about whether Jesus is obligated to pay the Temple tax (Matthew 17:24–27). After this is disposed of, now well away from the pronouncement of Jesus's impending Passion, the disciples *come to Jesus* with the question of who will be the greatest in the Empire of heaven (Matthew 18:1). Perhaps they recall Jesus's teaching that the least in the Empire will outrank John the Baptist (Matthew 11:11). In any event, it surely is not an untoward question on the part of the student to seek to find out what it takes to be the greatest. So rather than being castigated as in Mark, Jesus is affirming. But Matthew drops Mark's teaching that "If anyone would be first, he must be last of all and servant of all" (Mark 9:35) and expands the teaching about becoming as a child (Matthew 18:2–4). With a deft pen, Matthew has deflected castigation of the apostles by Jesus and, for that matter, by later Jesus followers, and removed one of the teachings that the apostles are to be table waiters (literally, from *diakonein* as in Peter's mother-in-law) of all.

Mark follows the third prediction with an untoward request by James and John, who are after Peter the most often named disciples in the New Testament and apparently major figures in the earliest community. According to Mark, hardly had Jesus finished predicting that the Gentiles (for which everyone would hear Romans) "will mock him, spit upon him, scourge him, and put him to death, but after three days he will rise" (Mark 10:34 and Matthew 20:19), than James and John come to request that they sit at his right and left hand when he enters his glory (Mark 10:37). Matthew turns the embarrassing moment into a moment of near comic relief. Matthew introduces for the first and only time in the gospels the mother of James and John, who makes the exact same request of Jesus that Mark believes her sons made (Matthew 20:20–21). Both evangelists then turn this into a teachable moment about the mortal dangers of discipleship: "You do not know what you are asking. Are you able to drink the cup that I am to drink?" (Mark 10:38 and Matthew 20:22). For our purposes, the important editing has been accomplished: the disciples' mother now bears the onus for being overly ambitious, not the disciples themselves.

With this artful editing, Matthew has been able to reduce the embarrassment associated with the disciples' behavior considerably. It is probable that in addition to simply burnishing the history of the origins of the Christian movement, Matthew wanted to avoid tarnishing the image of Jesus's disciples. Consider that both Paul's letter to the Galatians and Luke's Acts of the Apostles tie the apostle Peter closely to the city of Antioch. Now just as the authors of this present book trace their intellectual genealogy back to preeminent scholars of the New Testament, so in antiquity the unbroken line of teachers reaching back to the original master philosopher was crucial for establishing the authority of a teacher. Teachers, masters in their own right, who traced their genealogy to the original disciples (perhaps Peter, in this case), would lose authority if the image of Jesus's disciples were tarnished. We will discuss some of the implications of this move on the part of Matthew in the last section on community life.

The Passion Narrative

In Matthew's editing of the passion narrative in Mark, we see the steady move within the entire gospel tradition to excuse the Roman authorities in the death of Jesus. In his rewrite of Mark's passion narrative, Matthew worked counter to his usual practice. Rather than reducing the number and role of subordinate characters, Matthew adds to the roles of Judas Iscariot and the Roman governor Pontius Pilate and introduces Pilate's wife, with her dream about Jesus's innocence. In none of the canonical gospels does Judas Iscariot play any individual role before the passion narrative. Matthew adds telling details to Mark's story at three places. In his first solo appearance, Matthew makes a point of the fact that Judas received thirty pieces of silver for the betrayal of Jesus. Then at their last supper together, Judas presses Jesus as to whether he will betray Jesus and Jesus confirms this (26:25). Finally, Matthew adds an account of the despair and suicide of Judas and the purchase of the burial site for foreigners with the silver pieces (27:3–10).

The addition of the material on Judas complements the additional material describing the trial of Jesus before Pilate. Here, Matthew adds a new character, Pilate's wife, who counsels against condemning Jesus. Matthew also ritualizes Pilate's literal washing of hands of responsibility for Jesus's death with a ritual hand washing. The last major insertion into Mark are the words used by anti-Jews through the centuries, when the crowd answers Pilate with the cry "His blood be upon us and upon our children" (27:24–25). A misunderstanding of Matthew's context and intent in all of this has been used to justify two thousand years of Christian persecution of the Jews, and contributed to the death of, literally, millions of innocent people.

For the main purpose of this book, however, our goal is to highlight the practices that flow from the text: what would Matthew want to transmit from the course in Mark? First of all, the student would understand that the basic narrative frame that Mark provides is critically important. Mark's gospel, their prime textbook for their course of study, provided the basic points and structure of Jesus's life, death, and resurrection. But Jesus or, perhaps more precisely, the Jesus story, is shown to be malleable. Texts produced within Mark's framework are not authoritative in and of themselves. They may be expanded, or reduced, words with different nuances may be introduced, or recontextualized.

Mark's portrait of the twelve apostles has also been sufficiently modified that there will be a need to reassess their position in the Matthean community. With the editing out of most of Mark's negative comments about the apostles, Matthew's rehabilitation of the twelve proceeds to provide them a much broader scope than one would expect.

Matthew's school reached back into their roots in Israelite scriptures and searched out their origins as a basis for understanding themselves and the contours of their lives after the destruction of the Temple in Jerusalem. Their first formative practice, then, involved going back to the sources of their lives that in previous generations had sustained and nurtured them. But their circumstances had changed dramatically, and they needed to explain their origins and their future by reference to Jesus, whom they experienced and understood as a significant change to themselves and to their religion of origin. Jesus became the center of their school, the master whose mind their rabbinic teachers had brought to bear on new teaching and new understanding. They used the only textbook then available, the Gospel of Mark, to help them reorder their lives. Working with their textbook, they transformed it to make sense for their community and their school. But school work and community life demand more than just study. Their lives had to reflect their teaching. The ancient Roman and Jewish worlds alike insisted on the linking of theory and practice, of religious precept and daily living. The practices of the community expressed their theology.

The Course in Community Life

After Neo learned from Morpheus about the history and context of the development of the matrix, Neo had to learn a different way of living. He downloaded programs to help him perform the new reality in a false world that looked like the world of the twenty-first century, but that was in fact an illusion created by the matrix. So defying gravity and dodging bullets became for him the performances, the practices, of a new identity for himself—an identity that others in the community of humans and hybrids fighting the matrix also mastered. These practices, in fact, formed an important point of connection among those humans and hybrids in their contest against the matrix. It was an important connection, because Morpheus (a version of John the Baptist) had identified Neo as "the One" (a version of Jesus) who would liberate the humans and hybrids from the matrix. In the latter two movies of *The Matrix* trilogy, Neo becomes a model for others to imitate, even though the other hybrids and humans could not accomplish all that Neo became. Other hybrids and humans began to believe that they could alter the matrix through imitation of his life as a means of experiencing liberation for themselves, even while the matrix was still being contested. But that liberation could only come when the world of concepts and theories could be practiced in the daily lives of the humans and hybrids as they struggled. Practices gave body to the mind of those struggling. The same dynamic operates in the Gospel of Matthew. The school of Matthew set up the practices that regulated their lives so that they could live together in harmony, study together with clarity, and accomplish their mission with unanimity.

The precepts and teaching of the school, the result of the various curricula of the school, needed to be made concrete and manifest in specific practices within the Matthean community. The Gospel of Matthew specifies six sets of practices to encapsulate and concretize their beliefs: to preserve the Law through a kind of double vision (the Law and Jesus); to promote itinerant missionary work with miraculous deeds in order to recruit more students; to perform sacraments; to practice hospitality; to redefine social relationships, especially the primary family relationship; and to create a lasting model of leadership for the school and the church. These practices made the teaching something livable by the students and the members of the church by giving specific instruction on how to live according to the precepts taught by the Christian Jewish rabbinic teachers in their Roman context. How to live in relationship within a community itself requires attention, care, and instruction. Matthew was very concerned that the community enact right relationships.

Double Vision: the Law and Jesus

The first and most crucial practice of the Matthean school is to preserve obedience and faithfulness to the Law given to Israel by Moses in the Torah. In a typical Matthean articulation, Jesus announces to those Jewish Christians traumatized by the destruction of the Temple: "Do not think that I have come to abolish the law or the prophets. I have come not to abolish but to fulfill. Amen, I say to you, until heaven and earth pass away, not the smallest letter or the smallest part of a letter from the law will pass from the law, until all things have taken place" (Matthew 5:17–18). And just before his trial and crucifixion, Jesus announces "Heaven and earth will pass away, but my words will not pass away" (24:35). The Matthean school learned through practice of a kind of double vision. One eye is set firmly on the Law and the prophets that will never be discounted; the other eye is set firmly on the words of Jesus. The Matthean community practices this double vision by reading the Law through Jesus and Jesus through the Law.

The context for this double vision, however, remains constant: the Roman world in which the school functioned. We have noted places where Matthew modifies both Torah and Jesus sayings with material akin to the general consensus of the Greco-Roman philosophical schools of Matthew's day. Matthew so modified the original sayings tradition of the beatitudes to change the reference points for them from, for example, the absolute priority of poverty ("Blessed are the poor.") to the sense of humility and general care for the world ("Blessed are the poor in spirit."). In a similar manner, when speaking of the Torah, Matthew appends to the commandments an insistence on control of those emotions and desires that might lead one to transgress the Torah commandments. In these cases, we see Matthew taking material coming from his double-visioned religious tradition, Israelite scriptures and Jesus sayings, and finding the right relationship with the best Greco-Roman philosophical traditions. In this way, Matthew and the Matthean community modeled a process of development of religious doctrine in which doctrines and mysteries are explored in new ways using current philosophical and scientific tools. When done well, both the tradition and the latest teachings receive their due.

A by-product of this double-visioning process results in an embrace of ambiguity as a practice. As part of being amenable to a dialogue between the religious tradition and secular thinking, the community shows a high tolerance for ambiguity. In this, the community followed the intellectual tradition of both the Israelite scriptures and many of the Jewish teachers. The Israelite scriptures are quite content, for instance, to have two essentially contradictory stories of creation sitting side by side in the book of Genesis. In the first, Genesis 1:1–2:4, God's process of creation is to speak a word as if from afar, and the world is created. The creation of the first female and male humans is the last step in the creation process. The second story, Genesis 2:5–24, portrays God as walking on the earth as a farmer might walk his acres. God creates the human being before creating animals and fish, who are created so that the human will not be alone. After this first experiment does not work out well, God forms from the rib of the human a second human who will become the mother of the human race. The two stories are, in their settings and terms, contradictory and mutually exclusive. They have, however, remained in the book of Genesis for each generation to discover how each story contributes to understanding the human relationship with God, and with all of God's creation. So neither the Israelite scriptures nor the Gospel of Matthew provides a field manual on how to respond to every test, in every generation. But Matthew provides words, phrases, and images to which the disciple can refer to recall the gamut of the discussion and the many arguments that are encapsulated in the sayings of Jesus. From the arguments and discussions, the disciple can then choose the best remark for the current situation.

Itinerant Missionaries

The second practice in the Matthean school and community involved becoming an itinerant miracle-working missionary. This probably became part of the practice for honing the skills of advanced students in the school and leaders in the community. The goal of all the schools in the Roman period involved gathering new students, spreading the message, and trying to lead others into health and salvation through the teaching of their masters. And part of the mystique of these itinerant missionaries was their ability to perform miraculous deeds. We find this manifestation of divine wisdom in miraculous deeds in Roman as well as Jewish literature. Matthew's school was no different. Jesus was the model for this itinerant missionary work. The gospels are unanimous in their depiction of Jesus as an itinerant teacher, even though Mark's gospel may have had the Cynic itinerant missionaries in mind when he described Jesus as a wandering teacher in Galilee. So Matthew's community takes seriously Jesus's instruction to the disciples in Matthew 10:1, 5–14:

> Then he summoned his twelve disciples and gave them authority over unclean spirits to drive them out and to cure every disease and every illness. . . . Jesus sent out these twelve after instructing them thus, "Do not go into pagan territory or enter a Samaritan town. Go rather to the lost sheep of the house of Israel. As you go, make this proclamation: 'The kingdom of heaven is at hand.' Cure the sick, raise the dead, cleanse lepers, drive out demons. Without cost you have received; without cost you are to give. Do not take gold or silver or copper for your belts, no sack for the journey, or a second tunic, or sandals, or walking stick. The laborer deserves his keep. Whatever town or village you enter, look for a worthy person in it, and stay there until you leave. As you enter a house, wish it peace. If the

house is worthy, let your peace come upon it; if not, let your peace return to you. Whoever will not receive you or listen to your words—go outside that house or town and shake the dust from your feet."

For the itinerant missionaries, the miraculous healing of the sick and raising of the dead and healing of lepers and exorcism of demons constituted a sign of the divine presence in their teaching. Those who received these actions or witnessed them were drawn to the teaching and approached the health and salvation that the advanced students proclaimed. These missionaries were dependent upon hospitality and positive reception from their audience. To reinforce the message, Matthew records Jesus's response to a scribe asking to be one of his followers: "Foxes have dens and birds of the sky have nests, but the Son of Man has nowhere to rest his head" (8:20). This saying also predicts the disciples' lives as those of itinerant ministry, a prediction that would have been understood immediately by both Romans and Jews. Advanced students honed their skills as itinerant missionaries.

But such missionary fervor was incumbent upon the whole school. Matthew also records the missionary charge to the disciples at the conclusion of the gospel: "All power in heaven and on earth has been given to me. Go, therefore, and make disciples of all nations, baptizing them in the name of the Father, and of the Son, and of the holy Spirit, teaching them to observe all that I have commanded you. And behold, I am with you always, until the end of the age" (28:18–20). Here Jesus commands and legitimates the geographic and ethnic expansion that had occurred by the time the Gospel of Matthew was produced. The school of Matthew existed to create more students, to train more people, and to gather an ever-larger community.

Sacraments

Matthew's school also had a rich ritual life, which formed an essential part of the community's practice. Again, the community practiced double vision, attending both to the Jewish and the specifically Christian rituals. In accordance with Jesus's teaching that the teachings of Torah are to be honored, Matthew's community continued to observe the Jewish rituals and feasts. They would honor the Sabbath, celebrate Passover, and fast when directed. In accordance with specifically Christian rituals, Matthew tells us they knew and practiced the rites of baptism and Eucharist. Both rituals are narrated in the text, in passages strongly reminiscent of Mark's recounting.

As the school grew into a church community, other ritual acts needed to be developed. Matthew is the first gospel to use the word *church* as a description of the larger community that came into being around the school. Paul used the word *church* to describe the communities he formed, and Matthew designates the larger community with the same word. Once the school environment ceded to the church community, the potential for disagreement arose. This potential for disagreement led to a ritualized process of reconciliation:

> "If your brother sins (against you), go and tell him his fault between you and him alone. If he listens to you, you have won over your brother. If he does not listen, take one or two others along with you, so that 'every fact may be established on the testimony of two or three witnesses.' If he refuses to listen to them, tell the church [*ekklesia*]. If he refuses to listen even to the church, then treat him as you would a Gentile or a tax collector. Amen, I say to you, whatever you bind on earth shall be bound in heaven, and whatever you loose on earth shall be loosed in heaven. Again, (amen,) I say to you, if two of you agree on earth about anything for which they are to pray, it shall be granted to them by my heavenly Father. For where two or three are gathered together in my name, there am I in the midst of them." Then Peter approaching asked him, "Lord, if my brother sins against me, how often must I forgive him? As many as seven times?" Jesus answered, "I say to you, not seven times but seventy-seven times" (18:15–21).

The ritual includes three steps: a personal, one-on-one dialogue; a meeting with others from the community; and finally a request for assistance from the entire community. Whether such rituals were ever followed, we do not know. Nevertheless they, and the following dialogue between Peter and Jesus (18:21–35), speak to the community's concern for reconciliation and the maintenance of right relationships among the disciples.

As we have seen, a great deal of Matthew's wisdom teaching describes the attitudes and practices for the individual to acquire wisdom and to attain and maintain a right relationship with God. The rites outlined above highlight the importance of similar relationships within the community. Matthew's community was also concerned to maintain right relationships with the outside world, first with fellow Christians but also with those outside the larger Christian community.

We have argued that Matthew's community was stable but, at the same time, the community acknowledged Jesus's directives to engage in a worldwide missionary activity. Jesus's directives in chapter 10, quoted above, are directed to the disciples (carry no money, keep only one tunic but no staff, and so forth) and indirectly to the people in the towns the disciples visited: to be a worthy household, to receive the disciples hospitably, and to listen to their words. While the other evangelists include similar orders for the towns, only Matthew records such dire consequences for a town or household ignoring these commands: "Amen, I say to you, it will be more tolerable for the land of Sodom and Gomorrah on the day of judgment than for that town" (10:15), and this fate is in addition to losing the presence and healing powers of the disciple. In this way, Jesus links hospitality to the reception of teaching and healing from the disciples.

Redefining Social Relationships and Hospitality

Another practice of the Matthean school and community relates to a redefinition of social relationships, particularly the understanding of the family and the way family members became responsible for one another. This redefinition is reinforced in Jesus's description of the Last Judgment, Matthew 25, when the recipients of the good deeds of the nations are called the king's "least brothers." While their identity is ambiguous—does the king refer only to other Christians or to anyone so afflicted?—it is clear that at least fellow Christians are included in the term "brothers." In chapter 12, when his mother and birth brothers come for a visit, Jesus takes the opportunity to teach: "'Who is my mother? Who are my brothers?' And stretching out his hand toward his disciples, he said, 'Here are my mother and my brothers. For whoever does the will of my heavenly Father is my brother, and sister, and mother'" (12:48–50). For Matthew's disciples, steeped in the Israelite scriptures, Jesus's identification of brothers with those who follow the Father's will makes each of them mothers, sisters, and brothers of Jesus, part of his family and therefore mothers, sisters, and brothers of each other. They might then reflect on their responsibilities to each other, expressed first in the negative in the querulous response of Cain to the Lord's interrogation about the murder of his birth brother Abel, "Am I my brother's keeper?" (Genesis 4:9). As the Lord held Cain responsible for the health and well-being of his brother Abel, so will God hold Matthew's community responsible for the health and well-being of other Christians. The addition of prisoners to the typical list in Israelite scriptures of those meriting the careful attention of the community—the widow, the orphan, and the alien—reflects the situation of Christians, especially Christian preachers, whom the political authorities might imprison for sedition or instigating treason, and points to the necessity of care for the wandering preacher.

We can see, then, how Matthew expects the community to form right relationships with other Christians. The community includes all who see themselves as brothers in Jesus. Beyond that, Jesus twice commands that disciples proclaim the gospel and go about curing diseases and exorcising devils as part of the missionary project. As these efforts successfully draw into the community new Christians, reforming unbelievers into believing brothers and sisters, then unbelievers too must be regarded as potential mothers, sisters, and brothers, and deserving the careful attention of Matthew's community. Therefore, a consequence of the missionary command is care for the whole of humanity.

These portraits of life drawn from Matthew's text, depict an intellectually mature, geographically stable community who recognize their responsibilities to Christians and non-Christians throughout the world. Matthew's emphasis on righteousness is enfleshed in right relationships among texts and scriptures; in the rituals that reconcile community members to each other; and in the care provided for Christians and non-Christians alike. As a stable, growing community, Matthew's disciples also saw the need for organized leadership. This is marked in that Matthew is the only one among the gospel writers who uses the term *church*. The use of the term is significant because Paul also uses it in reference to the local churches he founded in Greece and Asia Minor. The latter were geographically settled communities that welcomed Paul's instructions and had tenuous ties with other churches.

We have seen how Matthew's characterization of Jesus's disciples generally improves their image from the one that Mark constructs. For example, Matthew edits presumption out of Mark's depiction of the disciples who "had argued among themselves as to who was greatest" (Mark 9:34) to the more philosophical, less personal direct question to Jesus "Who is the greatest in the kingdom of heaven?" (Matthew 18:1). The disciples are transformed from power-grasping individuals to those seeking wisdom, presumably asking "whom should we emulate?" This and other instances discussed earlier display Matthew's interest in rehabilitating the disciples so that they become more like the disciples and teachers of the traditional Greco-Roman schools: learning at the feet of the Master and preparing to hand this knowledge down to their own disciples, including the leaders in the community of Matthew.

Leadership

The final practice of the Matthean school relates to the structure of leadership. The Matthean community had a leadership structure descending from Jesus's disciples specifically related to the role of Peter as the first among the disciples. Matthew's Peter holds a special position, most forcefully found in Jesus's words after Peter has affirmed that Jesus is the Anointed One, the Son of the living God:

> Blessed are you, Simon son of Jonah! For flesh and blood has not revealed this to you, but my Father in heaven. And I tell you, you are Peter, and on this rock I will build my church, and the gates of Hades will not prevail against it. I will give you the keys of the kingdom of heaven, and whatever you bind on earth will be bound in heaven, and whatever you loose on earth will be loosed in heaven (16:17–19).

Simon, always mentioned first in lists of the Twelve (Mark) or the apostles (Matthew), receives in Matthew's gospel, and only in Matthew's gospel, a preeminent place in Jesus's church. As we mentioned, this Greek term *ekklesia* is ordinarily applied by Matthew and Paul to the local assembly of Christians. Paul tells the Galatians about his confrontation with Peter in Antioch, the probable location of the Matthean community. There is every indication that Paul lost whatever power he had enjoyed in Antioch as a consequence of the conflict. The scriptural texts, therefore, seem to portray a community comfortable with the leadership of Jesus's disciples, probably under the direction of Peter and his successors. This model would also fit a Greco-Roman school in which the original master would designate a successor to carry on the tradition. Thus Peter becomes the successor of the Master, Jesus, and Peter would name his successor, perhaps the leader of the community when the Gospel of Matthew developed. The impetus to such a model of leadership was clearly present two decades later in the writings of Ignatius, bishop of Antioch. In his writings, the church is present in the bishop and Christians only celebrate rituals validly when they are in union with the bishop.

This leadership style is markedly different from that we deduced in Rome from Mark's gospel. But it is a style consonant with the way that we have depicted the Matthean community as a school dedicated to taking on the mind of the master. It is also consistent with Matthew's emphasis on righteousness as "right relations": individual Christians are to establish and maintain a right relationship with the wise scribe who produced the Gospel of Matthew and, if that person is not the leader of the community, with the person who does lead the community and speak for it. In the writings of Ignatius, this relationship became a Christian way to access the divine.

Conclusion •

The formative practices of the school of Matthew and the community that formed around the school show how teaching and living combined to create a new response to the traumatic events that led to the school's instruction. Using a technique that we call double vision, Matthew's gospel guided its students and community in ways at once to preserve the Law and prophets and to live out the sayings of Jesus. The school sent out advanced students as missionaries, gathering new students to the school and new members to the community. The school lived a vital, vibrant religious life, observing the traditional Jewish Sabbath, feasts, fasts, and holidays while celebrating the rites associated with Jesus (baptism and Eucharist) and developing new rites for the reconciliation of their members. The school and community practiced hospitality, recognizing that the missionaries were dependent upon hospitality for the success of their efforts and the community was dependent upon one another's hospitality for their graceful development. Matthew's community also redefined social relationships by making everyone connected to the school a brother or sister, and by directing attention of its membership to care for the needs of others. And they developed a particular kind of leadership, setting up a pattern and model for leadership in the story about Peter. Like Neo learning to dodge bullets and defy gravity, the Matthean community learned to live out its understanding of itself, God, Jesus, and the Law in particular and specific actions that showed who they were and what their mission meant. The Matthean community was learning to combat their own form of matrix, their own story of tragedy and renewal as they lived into the new age.

The trip through the Gospel of Matthew can sometimes seem as strange as Neo moving through the illusion created by the matrix, but like Neo, we find a new life through the engagement. It is an infinitely fascinating world that Matthew creates, embodying a kind of formation that carries us back and forth between traditions to find a home for ourselves. Matthew formed his community and subsequent readers of the gospel, by taking us deep into the Israelite scriptures, the Law, and the prophets, to establish faith and practice. The community lived that faith in-between worlds at a time when the world they knew, and the religious life they had valued for centuries, was destroyed by Titus when he razed the Temple in Jerusalem. The community's world had collapsed. Their religion had collapsed. And yet they were faithful to the written and oral traditions and to a way of learning that brought both to bear on daily living. So as painful as it might be, they established a school for studying the Law and the prophets through the lens of Jesus, whom they understood as the key to the future. With a strict formation in the Law and prophets, they embraced Jesus, the Wisdom of God come down to save them in their time of trauma. They established a school with a curriculum that would help them sort things out: one curriculum reframed Jesus through a number of explicitly Jewish lenses; another retained the Law and the prophets as inviolable and unalterable; yet another embraced the sayings and wisdom of Jesus as a new Law and prophet, as a fulfillment of the Law and prophets of old; and the last laid provisions for community living. The school adopted a textbook, the Gospel of Mark, to help them bring the two worlds together, changing and adapting Mark's gospel to their own circumstances and needs. And they began to live the gospel, to practice their faith, to make their learning into a way of life. What a remarkable group of people! A church organized around a school! In the end they got it all together.

The Matrix series is a trilogy. It takes three different movies to begin to lay out the implications of Neo's discovery that he is the One who is to save the people. The Gospel of Matthew is also a trilogy: it takes the Jewish tradition, the Jesus tradition, and the church to make sense of it all, especially since the community lives in a foreign world dominated by the Romans. It is no wonder that Matthew has become the favorite gospel for the church. It is as fascinating as science fiction!

Questions for Discussion

1. There are special times in world history when political and social circumstances seem to coalesce with various religious and philosophical movements to produce a creative time of change. We think in particular of such nodal events as the papacy of John XXIII and the Second Vatican

Council, the Camelot period of John F. Kennedy's presidency, Lyndon B. Johnson's "Great Society," the Age of Aquarius later in the 1960s, and the election of Barack Obama, the first African-American president of the United States. How do social, political, and religious institutions at these nodal points maintain tradition while at the same time changing them to suit new times? How do you understand Matthew's community to have done this?

2. Using the Gospel of Matthew as your source, write a description of a typical day in the school of Matthew. What would their classes look like? What would they be studying? What kinds of assignments would the teacher give?

3. Compare the typical day from Matthew (question 2 above) with your typical day. What values, ethics, and religious convictions do each suggest? How do practices, yours and theirs, compare to the values, ethics, and religious convictions?

Resources for Further Study

Again and again: "When in doubt, read the text." Students should be familiar with the whole arc of the narrative but, more than is the case with the Gospel of Mark, the Gospel of Matthew warrants study in large, discrete blocks. Students may study each of the five individual sermons identified in the text in relation to the entire narrative, to each other, and in their relation to the surrounding culture.

There are many excellent commentaries on the Gospel of Matthew. As in the case of the Gospel of Mark, the *Hermeneia Series* provides a highly scholarly, three-volume, work: Ulrich Luz, *Matthew: A Commentary*, vols. 1, 2, and 3, *Hermenia Series* (Minneapolis: Fortress, 2005–2007). Daniel Harrington is one of the foremost American Matthean scholars. His *The Gospel of Matthew*, *Sacra Pagina Series* (Collegeville, Minn.:, Liturgical Press, 1991) provides a shorter, more accessible commentary. *The New Q* is a commentary by one of the authors of this book (Valantasis) on the sayings source, emphasizing the ascetical function of the sayings of Jesus for the original Christian communities (New York: T. &T. Clark, 2005).

For primary and secondary sources on Greco-Roman wisdom literature, the student is referred to Resources for Further Study at the end of chapter 2.

Jewish writers produced a rich and diverse wisdom literature, extending over a period of at least half a millennium. Richard J. Clifford has written a concise, readable introduction to this literature, *The Wisdom Literature*, *Interpreting Bible Texts* (Nashville, Tenn.: Abingdon, 1998). John J. Collins's work *Jewish Wisdom in the Hellenistic Age*, *Old Testament Library* (Louisville, Ky.: Westminster John Knox, 1997) addresses wisdom literature produced both in Palestine and in the Jewish Diaspora during the Hellenistic period and concludes with a chapter on the tensions the authors faced in reconciling Biblical revelation with Greco-Roman philosophical constructs.

Two works on Jesus's parables are also helpful. John R. Donahue's *The Gospel in Parable: Metaphor, Narrative, and Theology in the Synoptic Gospels* (Philadelphia: Fortress, 1988) provides a good introduction to the study of the parables. Brad H. Young produced a book showing the close parallels between the parables of Jesus and those of the early rabbis: *The Parables: Jewish Tradition and Christian Interpretation* (Peabody, Mass.: Hendrickson, 1998).

CHAPTER SIX

Portal to the Gospel of Luke and Acts of the Apostles: Getting Your Book Published in Antiquity

Dear Publius,

If you are well, my brother, I am well. It has been a difficult trip. Many ships wrecked on the shores of the Greek islands, but the gods spared ours and we arrived battered but alive and safe. The weather prevented a timely departure from Cyprus and the seas raged on every route and at each stop all the way to Corinth, from where I, Lucius, your friend and elderly teacher, greet you. Philebus, the scribe that you sent with me, has had a difficult time in the travel, but he returns now to the production of the book. So rest assured, the books that you commissioned me to write are with me and safe. I shall dispatch them to you by imperial courier, my benefactor and patron, as soon as I arrive at Puteoli. I, a man of little writing style and poor intellect, still am honored that you requested these volumes on the history of our people in provincial lands. Even in my humble acquiescence to your request and my undeserved support from you, I find joy in assembling the notes and traveling to speak with the descendants of those first provincial leaders.

It is sad to report to you the fate of our countrymen in distant lands. Some were seized by pirates and sold as slaves to distant regions. Those who live in the countryside near the seashore were particularly vulnerable, and we lost both young men and young girls. I shudder to think of their fate with their foreign masters. May the gods protect them. Others have begun to follow new and strange gods, joining the peculiar names of these foreign gods to our well-beloved and renowned Roman gods. The eastern provinces are filled with soothsayers and miracle workers. I witnessed some of these myself. Tobias, one of your clansmen and our countryman, has become famous as a wonderworking healer. Tobias sees demons that inhibit the health and sanity of those around him and expels them by waving the end of his tunic over their heads. Tobias also has been known, as the local people were eager to tell me, to raise the dead as well as to heal the sick. The god Aesclepius seems to be his familiar spirit and strengthens him to do his wonders. Many other of our countrymen take part in the local rituals and liturgies of the people in their foreign lands as a way of finding solidarity with those with whom they live, even though at times these dramatic liturgies offend our Roman values of dignity and solemnity. Some of your clansmen have even been thrown in jail and some condemned to fight beasts in the circus because of their unsightly and stubborn adherence to foreign gods. These dissident relatives seem to have corrupted our Roman ways and refuse to honor our gods and to pray for the genius of the emperor. Their atheism and superstition has made them the scorn of the Romans in the province, but the heroes of their sect.

In every place, however, whenever and wherever I presented your letter of recommendation, my dearest Publius, I was greeted warmly and provided richly with accommodations and hospitality. Your clan remembers well their roots in Rome and fondly acknowledge you as the elder and leader. They eagerly awaited news of your well-being and thanked the gods for your generosity toward them, not only in sending me to do the research for your books, but in sending your warm greetings and being present to them in my person.

My soul seems bereft, being so far from your presence, my dearest Publius. The philosopher Plato describes friendship as two souls separated before birth seeking reunion and union. So is my heart and yearning to be reunited to you, my beloved patron and friend. The companionship with your clan has only shown the greatness of that friendly love that holds us together. It is good that the gods have joined us in the work of producing these books, so that the good fortune visited by the gods upon your household would spread not only to me, your humble and obedient client, but also to your entire clan living in far off places.

I will see you soon; as soon as I arrive in Italy, I shall dispense Fidelius, my slave, to you with word of our safe arrival. I am concerned, however, because an evil portent has been announced here by the priests. A black falcon has devoured the mother swine, leaving her piglets. This bodes ill for the Corinthians, and I must make haste to leave them before the evil deeds that have been predicted occur. Be strong and be well, dearest Publius, and may the gods protect us all. Lucius, your devoted servant.

I, Philebus, the scribe, who has written this letter for Lucius, also send you my greetings, dearest master. May the gods remember you always in your gracious deeds and thoughts.

Although we fabricated this letter, it reflects a good deal about the Greco-Roman context in which the two-volume work that we call the Gospel of Luke (volume 1) and the Acts of the Apostles (volume 2) was produced. In antiquity imitating ancient literature was an important part of developing the skills of an orator and writer, often revealing a great deal about the values, social attitudes, religious sentiments, political positions, social interactions and stratification, and piety of the writer. But it is always like listening to only one side of a telephone conversation and trying to piece together the whole conversation. Understanding comes obliquely through the analysis of the rhetoric, the metaphors, the references to other literature or events, and the style of language used to convey the message. The gospels are no different. So what do you need to know about this two-volume work in order to understand it?

Let us begin with this imaginary letter. It refers to a number of historical circumstances, like movement of people throughout the Roman empire, the spread of non-Roman religious traditions into the Roman frame of mind, and the troublesome relationship of Roman officials to those deemed either atheist or superstitious. Atheists were those people who did not honor the Roman gods, not people, as in our day, who do not recognize any god. As the gods of Rome were believed to protect the city and its citizens, "atheism" was akin to treason. Superstitious people were those who engaged in worship and honor of foreign gods not recognized by the Roman people. The Romans usually were willing to incorporate foreign gods into their theology, but only those gods most like those in the Roman pantheon. These references to atheism and superstition reflect the expansive religious environment of the vast Roman empire. They are important aspects of Roman social and religious history. So, first of all, we need to explore the way ancient history is written.

Ancient Historiography

We modern folks think of history in terms of *facts*: what really happened in a particular time and place with specific characters and people. Ancient people did not think that way. They were interested in what it might have been like to be present at an historical event. One of the purposes of creating histories was to provide the reader-listener with models of how one should act in the great moments of life. They wanted to know what an historical figure like a famous general might have said in his victory speech, or what an important teacher could have said upon his deathbed, or what a religious figure would have taught on a particular occasion. Not facts, but impressions and creative, imaginative constructions. Ancient history was more evocative, suggestive, and entertaining rather than a series of indisputable facts that described an event in history.

Ancient historians worked through the development of characters. They strove to define the way greatness became manifest in the person. They studied physiognomy, the way the bones and skin of the face and body were put together, in order to understand the biological basis for character formation. They also studied psychology, the way the important person responded emotionally to the situation. And they studied health, the way the body reacted under stress to important circumstances. All these studies focused on the question of how a great person became great and how that person manifested greatness in an important event.

Historians gathered all this information in speeches, classified as "speech in character." These were fully developed and lengthy speeches that reflect, not what a person actually said at an historical event, but what a person might have said given his character and response to the situation he confronted. These made-up speeches showed the character, the strength, the values, and the intellectual acuity of the person speaking so that the reader and hearer might understand the complexity of the person speaking and marvel at the person's abilities. In fact, readers and hearers were called not simply to admire but to imitate the actions and speech patterns of the great leaders in order to function similarly in their own contexts. What made the "speech in character" true was not the facts behind it, but the listener's ability to confirm that the speech made sense of the character of the speaker. Granted there were such things as chronologies, lists of events compiled by priests, notebooks written by philosophers or emperors, and certainly inscriptions on walls and other materials that preserved important information. But when an ancient historian sat down to write, he generally gathered the materials and began to write a story, a narrative, that would capture the true identity of the person or the situation.

Finally, ancient historical writing, much like historical writing today, always had a purpose and a motive. The information was always presented in such a way as to argue a point important to the writer or speaker, to valorize or praise a person or situation, to convince people of some particular perspective, or to please people so as to win their approval and favor. This was part of the rhetorical structure of writing and school children learned these techniques from their earliest education. Rhetoric demanded that writing and speech move toward a specific goal or end, and the successful writer or speaker did this in an artful way that masked the skill within it.

Ancient Biography

Ancient biographers also had the same goals as ancient historians. Ancient biographies were more focused on the character of a person. Biographies began as funeral orations, a recitation of the valorized deeds and characteristics of a dead member of a family. These ancestral rites and recitations became part of the daily

recounting of a family's history: every day a member of the family would offer incense and prayers to the ancestors and in doing so would recount their mythic ges-
tures and characteristics that founded a family's identity. The ancestors, though
dead, remained a part of the living family structure, and succeeding generations
memorialized their character, their genius, and their intellectual presence as a way
of defining themselves and differentiating themselves from others.

Ancient biographies turned these kinds of funeral and daily recitations into
story. The important thing for a biography was to evoke the character and describe the life circumstances with particular attention to the birth, apex of life,
and death of the character. These were often stylized, not reflecting the facts of
a person's life, but the values and virtuous characteristics that those reading or
listening could affirm really evoked the true character of the person. If the community could not recognize the validity or confirm the veracity of a biographer's
description, the biography would be deemed a false one. The rhetoric of writing
biographies required that the community assent in some way to the writer or
speaker's evocation of character.

Our letter from Lucius to Publius also provides information about their social
location. Publius is Lucius's literary patron who has commissioned Lucius to write
books on a subject of his choice, the history of his clansmen in the provinces. The
clan must be a large one, and they seem to have settled in various areas on the
outskirts of the provinces. Publius has financial resources and wealth sufficient to
support a research team of three (Lucius, Philebus, and Fidelius) in their travel
to collect material for the books. One way to describe Lucius's relationship to
Publius is that of client to patron, and that opens the way to understand how
identity is constructed in antiquity. This is the second point of what we need to
understand in Luke/Acts. When a person tells an historical or biographical story,
the listener can learn as much about the storyteller as about the plot. Stories, narratives, construct identities. We learn about systems of social relationship such as
client and patron, religious beliefs such as the importance of praying to the gods
and honoring the genius of the emperor, prejudices such as the Roman abhor-
rence of emotional expression and frenzy, and customs like condemning criminals
to fight beasts or gladiators in the arena. The writer of the book, then, sets out to
construct a particular identity for the characters, communities, and circumstances
through the weaving together of a narrative that documents those identities.

Ancient Rhetoric

Our fictional letter also reflects the importance of rhetoric in the Roman world.
In the ancient world, style of communication was as important as the content.
Rhetoric, the art of persuasion, formed a part of advanced learning for noble
people who played an important role in public life, especially making speeches

in the civic arenas such as the Senate or public courts. The skilled orator was an important person in the Roman Empire. To speak well in public provided the opportunity to display a person's good education, clear thinking, and ability to sway the audience to the speaker's perspective.

Two very popular rhetorical handbooks were written in the Roman period: the *Rhetorica ad Herennium*, an anonymous work attributed to Cicero that provides an outline of rhetorical strategies, and Quintilian's, *Institutio Oratoria* published about 95 CE that provides a complete program for the formation of the Roman gentleman-orator. Every form of communication reflected the pervasive interest in training: letters, legal arguments, philosophical treatises, oral teaching in schools, Jewish or Christian sermons, advertising in the marketplace, official imperial proclamations—in short all communication displays the interest in rhetoric. Rhetoric was the thread woven into every aspect of Roman civic, religious, social, and political life.

Ancient Novels

Imagination was not foreign to ancient Greek and Roman society. In fact, it was during this period that the novel as a genre of literature began. Novels are the third point we need to understand. We do not know where the novels came from. They could have been fantastic interpretations of historical writing or imaginative extensions of interest in biography and character development or they may even have emerged from religious cults as a means of dramatizing the new life these new religions offered. Or, perhaps more simply, novels provided rich entertainment and a delightful way to learn about far-off peoples and events, much like travel narratives about Italy or Greece do today.

The novels all had very interesting characters. The stock characters included star-crossed lovers, pirates, local officials, priests, sailors, farmers, foreign kings and queens, and a host of unsavory minor characters such as gravediggers, magicians, witches, or soothsayers. The star-crossed lovers faced shipwrecks (a favorite theme in the novels), capture by pirates, long sea voyages, engagement with foreign powers and leaders, encounters with strange social customs and religious rites, and peculiar practices that would titillate the Roman mind and imagination. Always there were speeches of welcome, grief, reunion, separation, recognition, threats, cultural explanation, and, of course, homecoming to the community that wondered at the dire circumstances of the two lovers. These were fantastic stories whose impossibility was masked by the sheer wonder of the deeds, experiences, and circumstances of the fated lovers. Fortunately, in the end, the lovers got back to their home city and lived happily ever after, just as so many novels have ended since antiquity.

Christians also had novels, called the "apocryphal acts of the apostles." These novels, like their Roman and Greek counterparts, were equally fantastic in their imaginative narratives. These narratives of the works of the apostles and their mission to the entire world relate the acts, miracles, deeds, and speeches of Andrew, John, Peter, Paul and his female apostolic companion Thecla, and Thomas. They, too, visit far-off and exotic places to document the spread of Christianity from Jerusalem to the ends of the earth: Paul and Thecla to Asia Minor, Peter to Rome, Thomas to India, and the rest to equally exotic places. The story, rather than relating the fate of two star-crossed lovers, narrates the exploits of very ascetic apostles preaching an ascetic gospel. These novels preach virginity, abstinence from meat and wine, and a lifestyle of vigorous self-denial in order to be worthy of the gospel.

The Acts of Paul, for example, portrays Paul as giving a version of the Sermon on the Mount with such sayings as: "Blessed are the ones who have preserved their flesh pure, for they will certainly become a temple of God. Blessed are the (sexually) self-controlled, for God will speak to them." Thomas is credited with going to the wedding of a king's daughter on his way to India and convincing the couple in the marriage bed to renounce sexual activity, remain pure, and enter into a spiritual marriage with Jesus. The apostles heal the sick, raise the dead, celebrate the Eucharist in graves, kill villains and raise the unjustly killed from the dead, work fantastic feats of magic, fly in the air, and make animals speak the word of God to the recalcitrant characters in the stories. The Christian novels make wonderful reading and stimulate the imagination about the way earliest Christianity fantasized about how to live the Christian life and to move through the ancient world.

Ancient Travel and Tourism

After the emperor Augustus secured the breadth of the Roman Empire, travel and tourism became a major preoccupation for wealthy Romans. The roads were well-paved and accessible, being maintained by the Empire; Pompey had cleaned up the pirates in the Mediterranean basin and made travel safer; inns and places for refreshment grew up along the travel routes. Wealthy Romans, enjoying the newly formed tourist business, traveled to distant and exotic places to enjoy the riches of their vast empire. And, of course, writers began to write about their exploits.

Much like our letter of Lucius to Publius, Strabo in the first century BCE produced the first detailed travelogue and geography of the eastern Empire for the education and entertainment of the Roman elite. Two centuries later, Pausanias wrote about his travels to Greece, Asia Minor, and Egypt and described topography, architecture, countryside, cities, and all the wonders before him that spurred his imagination. Egeria, a fourth-century CE noble Roman woman from Spain, traveled throughout Egypt, Palestine, Jerusalem, Syria, and Mesopotamia, and wrote valuable descriptions of monks, monasteries, rituals and liturgies, and holy places. Her household in Spain learned from first-hand experience about the wonders of the Christian world. As interest in other cultures, religions, ways of living, and languages developed, people learned more and more in their home settings about places far away. The Greek, Roman, and Christian novels also fed this interest in distant places. We also benefit because these travelogues still provide scholars with important information about ancient architecture, art, topography, and travel arrangements.

It seems that the Roman world was hungry for information about the peculiar and fascinating multiple cultures that came under Roman rule. Their hunger for knowledge and information about different ways of living spawned important industries: literary productions, tourist agencies, hotels and food establishments, and educational institutions to teach the Romans about cultural and religious difference. It was an eagerly curious and actively fascinated time for Romans to explore their own identity in light of the foreign identities now incorporated into the dominant Roman Empire.

Ancient Conversions

Sometimes this interest in other religions and philosophies in the Empire led to conversions. Lucius's letter to Publius about his family spread out in the Empire refers to some of his family members' conversion to local religions. The ancient writer Apuleius (ca. 123–165 CE) in fact wrote a long novel in Latin describing the exploits of Lucius, a man who was too fascinated by negative magic and was inadvertently turned into an ass. Apuleius's work, entitled *The Metamorphoses, or the Golden Ass*, sets Lucius on a long path of self-discovery by experiencing many strange and peculiar things, by enduring incredible tests of his character and strength, and by witnessing many wonderful and exotic things as he traveled the boundaries of the Roman Empire. In the end, witnessing the procession of the Egyptian goddess Isis, Lucius is transformed from an ass back into a human being and becomes a devoted adherent to the cult of Isis. The story ends with Lucius being initiated into the cult of Isis by fasting, prayer, a baptism in water, and a clothing in white garments, and he enters the sanctuary as a fully transformed person. The metamorphosis signifies that Lucius finally became a fully articulated person only through his conversion to the new cult in the Roman Empire. His transformation, signified in his change from a human being to an ass and back to a human being again, plays out the role of conversion possible in Roman life.

Conversion in the Roman Empire, however, generally meant something different than it means today. We assume today that a converted person leaves behind all other beliefs and adopts a new set of beliefs exclusively. But such exclusive worship of gods did not hold in ancient Rome. Most people converted to new religious or philosophical systems simply by adjusting their worldview and their understanding in order to incorporate new beliefs, new deities, or new ways of living into the familiar and common pattern. Apuleius's character Lucius converted to the Isis cult, but he also remained faithful and prayed regularly to the Roman gods that supported the emperor, the Empire, and the Roman way of living. Conversion was not exclusive adherence to one religious path, but the inclusion of other religious beliefs and practices into the dominant religious context. Such a religious combination, called "syncretism," functioned throughout the Roman Empire.

Some religions, such as Christianity and Judaism, differentiated themselves from such syncretism. Their understanding of conversion differed from the dominant Roman practice and this got the Christians into some trouble when they refused to honor the Roman gods. That is why the Christians were called atheists: their God, the Father of Jesus Christ made manifest in the holy Spirit, was the only true God and they refused to recognize the Roman gods as gods at all. In fact, most Christians describe the Roman gods as demons, or lesser divine beings who rule the universe but were subordinate to the higher gods or to the true God of the Christians. Before the destruction of the Temple in Jerusalem, Jews (and probably Christians) were permitted by Rome to honor their own God provided that they made daily offerings on behalf of the emperor and the Roman Empire. After the destruction of the Temple in 70 CE by the Roman general Titus, the Jews and Christians faced the same problem of needing to honor only the one, true God and to relegate the Roman gods to demonic status. Conversion for Christians and Jews was more exclusive than the Roman syncretistic practice would allow. But Jews and Christians, bonded together by a common set of scriptures, stood outside the Roman norm and had to create for themselves a legitimate way of living in the Roman Empire.

Roman Philosophical Schools

The philosophical schools offered the most vibrant site for conversion. The leading Stoic philosophers of the day, like Musonius Rufus and his student Epictetus, both came from the eastern regions of the Empire, and took up important positions in the heart of the Empire in Rome. Their teachings, together with those of the Roman nobleman Seneca, himself from Spain at the western edge of the Empire, created a rich religious environment for the formation of a truly noble Roman identity. Remember that the Roman world did not distinguish religion from politics and other social systems, because everything in the end had religious meaning. So philosophy functioned both as a way of life and as a religious system in the Roman world, and people recognized the philosophers as religious and spiritual leaders as well as intellectuals.

The philosophical schools of the Roman Empire probably looked more like modern-day monasteries than universities. The students and teachers lived together, ate together, had close ties to one another, wore distinctive clothing to identify themselves with a particular philosophical way of living, and were initiated into the community through religious rites. The members of a school made offerings to the gods, engaged in divinization, honored their ancestors, prayed to the familiar spirits that guarded and protected their teachers, and poured libations to the gods before their meals. Philosophical schools carried heavy religious meanings. A student of the philosopher Plotinus (205–269 CE) describes the community that Plotinus developed around him. Plotinus's school consisted of resident students both male and female, the orphaned children of Roman nobles, doctors, health consultants, and a full complement of slaves who helped maintain the household. Since philosophy was a way of life, the entire household, including the slaves, held to the philosophical ideals that the teacher Plotinus taught. The philosophy encompassed every aspect of living, down to the financial arrangements made by parents for their children orphaned by their deaths. Everything had sacred meaning.

The philosophical schools, then, really engaged in spiritual formation. They were places where the students and the wider community engaged in practices promoted by the philosophical teacher to develop moral, ethical, religious, and social character for their students. The philosophers were really spiritual directors guiding their students and their communities into living an authentically religious life. Musonius Rufus taught a system that helped his students cope with the odd vicissitudes of Roman elite living. He argued that the students should learn to distinguish what is truly good from what is only apparently good, what is truly evil from what seems on the surface to be evil. These distinctions, he argued, improve the capacity for a person to endure both hardship and happiness with deep understanding and with a satisfaction in whatever life brought, whether good or ill. The process was a simple one. In class, the students argued about what was truly or only apparently good or evil. The students honed these arguments carefully, crafting sophisticated responses to them so that they fully explored the situation. Then they would create a short maxim, a ready-to-hand statement that would summarize their whole argument. As they lived their lives and encountered similar situations, the short maxim could be invoked to bring the whole argument back into their minds and thus help them cope with life's challenges.

Maxims and Sayings

Let us give an example. Often Roman emperors exiled Roman nobles whom the emperor deemed a threat, or offensive, or troublesome. The places to which they were exiled were often secluded, waterless places with few trees. It was a hard life. Musonius, however, theorized that exile provided the person an opportunity for uninterrupted contemplation and thought without the constant pressure to attend and give dinner parties, the drain of governing the Empire, or even the difficulties of running a household in the city. Far away from all the social and political demands on a person, the exiled one could turn the mind to philosophy and prayer. Musonius also argued that the absence of water and good food made the exiled person stronger, more capable of living through the rough times that the god Fortune might bring. So thirst and hunger strengthened the soul to endure. So Musonius argued that exile was only an apparent evil, since so much good could come from it. The maxim, then, might be: "exile fosters growth." When a student was exiled, the student could recite that maxim, recall all the arguments it summarized, and begin to construct an alternative understanding of exile that took advantage of the time not as a punishment but as a time of renewed intellectual and spiritual growth.

During the first few centuries many philosophers' sayings were collected and published. We have the sayings of Musonius Rufus, Epictetus, and Jesus, among many others. Yes, Jesus looked very much like a philosophical teacher because he taught through maxims or sayings. Consider these: "Do to others as you would have others do to you." "Do not attempt to take the twig out of someone else's eye until you have taken the log out of your own." "Love your enemy and pray for those who persecute you." "Pick up your cross and come follow me." Jesus's sayings, like those of Musonius Rufus, summarize a new way of thinking and living, and Jesus's followers used them as a means of connecting with Jesus's teaching as they lived in circumstances different from those that Jesus encountered.

Parables
In addition to the maxims, Jesus's use of parables also identified him as a kind of philosophical teacher. Parables were ancient mind-teasers. Parables demanded that the hearer use the imagination to discover the meaning that often seemed to move and fluctuate according to the way the reader or hearer put the elements together. For example, the parable of the lost sheep, the one-out-of-a-hundred. The meaning shifts whether the hearer identifies with the shepherd who risks all to save the one, or with the sheep for whom everything was risked, or with the ninety-nine sheep who felt abandoned or at least unworthy of attention while their shepherd left them.

This teasing of the mind with interesting ways of responding to circumstances of living formed part of the philosophical school's way of teaching and constituted a way of spiritual formation for people identified with a particular philosophy. Jesus, the teacher, was a prime example of a philosophical school teacher, and his teaching spread more rapidly and more aggressively through the Roman Empire than most other teachers. But like the other philosophical teachers and schools, the Jesus school taught a way of living, a set of rehearsed responses to the exigencies of living, and a set of teachings intended to help the adherents of the Jesus movements to cope with daily living in complex and conflicted communities.

Ancient Book Production

When Lucius wrote to Publius, his benefactor, he provided a report on the status of the production of the books that Publius had commissioned from him. This was not an uncommon circumstance in the Roman period. Wealthy people, interested in a particular religious, philosophical, social, or political subject, approached scholars to produce books for them. Often the writer acknowledges this request and commission at the beginning of the book. Writers often use a familiar commonplace: "I, so and so, who is unworthy to write anything and I who am not a very clear thinker, have honored you, most honorable patron, with the weakness of my writing and thought, out of love and affection and wishing to honor your request to write." Of course, the writer knew a great deal and was in fact quite competent to write the work requested (otherwise the patron would not have asked), but for humility's sake the writer eschewed praise and honor in order to promote the honor and praise of the patron.

Part of the reason for this humble fiction resides in the fact that producing books in antiquity was an expensive proposition. The patron paid not only for the work of the writer by supplying the physical support of the writer and his household, but also for the scribe who actually produced the book, and the scribes who copied the book again, and often provided other slave support to attend to the writer so that the writer could attend to the production of the work. Writers composed orally, that is, they spoke what they wanted to write and the scribe recorded the words in a kind of shorthand as the writer spoke.

At this time both reading and writing were performed "out loud," that is to say, with the voice. (Reading silently only became common in the Middle Ages.) Since writers had received sophisticated rhetorical training in their youth and practiced rhetorical speaking frequently in their classrooms and in the public arena, speaking fully articulated arguments came naturally. Long books could be produced with a minimum of outlining and preparation, because the speakers/writers had become accustomed to articulating complex thoughts in sophisticated and pleasing ways. So long books required many hours of speaking, note-taking by a scribe, and production of a text by a scribal school: when dictation was completed the scribe would read the text aloud to other scribes who would produce the finished manuscript. After the subordinate scribes wrote down what they heard, the head scribe would correct each page according to the text from which he had read. Both the original page and its corrections became part of the final version of the text as it was produced. After two copies of the text had been completed (one for the patron, one for the teacher to keep in the archives), the better text was sent to the patron and the lesser text filed in the teacher's library. Book production was labor-intensive, expensive, time-consuming, and difficult work for all. Patrons paid well for the books they desired, and writers worked tediously to produce the books requested of them.

Questions for Discussion
1. Analyze a famous speech, like Lincoln's "Gettysburg Address" or Martin Luther King's "I Have a Dream" or Sojourner Truth's "And Ain't I a Woman?" What techniques does the speaker employ to convince you of his or her perspective? What emotions does the speaker create in you? How are you guided to come to the same conclusion as the speaker?
2. Write a two-page spiritual biography of someone you love. What incidents from his or her life do you find critical for understanding them? What were your criteria for choosing those incidents over others? How do you characterize the interior or spiritual dimensions of the person's life? What is the message about the person that you want to convey and how do you do that?
3. History always has a perspective. Watch a news account of some important current event. What are the "facts" that are presented? Where do you find evidence of the reporter's perspective and assumptions about the event? What are other perspectives not addressed by the reporter? How can you relate the event using other perspectives and assumptions?

Resources for Further Study
Our fictitious letter attempts to follow the form of ancient letters. For a more thorough explanation of ancient letter writing, especially as it applies to the New Testament, see Hans-Josef Klauck and Daniel P. Bailey, *Ancient Letters and the New Testament: A Guide to Context and Exegesis* (Waco, Tx.: Baylor University Press, 2006). See also Stanley K. Stowers, *Letter Writing in Greco-Roman Antiquity* (Philadelphia: Westminster Press, 1986).

On Roman rhetoric, read the ancient Roman handbooks: the *Rhetorica ad Herrenium, Loeb Classical Library* (Cambridge, Mass.: Harvard University Press, 1954); and Quintilian's *Institutio Oratoria, Loeb Classical Library* (Cambridge, Mass.: Harvard University Press, 2002). On the history of ancient rhetoric, see George A. Kennedy, *A New History of Ancient Rhetoric* (Princeton, N.J.: Princeton University Press, 1994). On the influence of classical rhetoric on Christian communication, see George A. Kennedy, *Classical Rhetoric and Its Christian and Secular Tradition from Ancient to Modern Times,* second edition (Chapel Hill: University of North Carolina Press, 1999). On ancient oratorical formation and education, see Stanley F. Bonner, *Education in Ancient Rome: From the Elder Cato to the Younger Pliny* (Berkeley: University of California Press, 1977).

An important resource for understanding conversion in antiquity is Arthur Darby Nock, *Conversion: the Old and the New in Religion from Alexander the Great to Augustine of Hippo* (New York: Oxford University Press, 1933). For a more recent study of conversion a little later than the time of the writing of the gospels, see Ramsay MacMullen, *Christianizing the Roman Empire (A.D. 100–400)* (New Haven: Yale University Press, 1984).

For the particular kind of ancient history we take as the model for our understanding of ancient history writing, see G. W. Bowersock, *Fiction as History: Nero to Julian* (Berkeley: University of California Press, 1994). See also Gregory E. Sterling, *Historiography and Self-definition: Josephos, Luke-Acts, and Apologetic Historiography* (New York: E. J. Brill, 1992). More recently, see *Ancient Fiction: the Matrix of Early Christian and Jewish Narrative*, eds. Jo-Ann A. Brant, Charles W. Hedrick, and Chris Shea (Atlanta: Society of Biblical Literature, 2005).

On ancient biography, see the collection of essays *Greek Biography and Panegyric in Late Antiquity*, ed. Tomas Hagg and Philip Rousseau (Berkeley: University of California Press, 2000). See also Patricia Cox, *Biography in Late Antiquity: A Quest for the Holy Man* (Berkeley: University of California Press, 1983). Both of these works take up biography in a later period, but the rhetorical principles remained constant through the Roman period.

The ancient novels are a fascinating subject. For Jewish novels, see Lawrence M. Wills, *The Jewish Novel in the Ancient World* (Ithaca, N.Y.: Cornell University Press, 1995). For Christian novels, see Christine M. Thomas, *The Acts of Peter, Gospel Literature, and the Ancient Novel: Rewriting the Past* (New York: Oxford University Press, 2003).

On the difficulties and ease of ancient travel, see Lionel Casson, *Travel in the Ancient World* (Baltimore: Johns Hopkins University Press, 1994).

The best survey of ancient philosophical schools is embedded in a dissertation by R. Alan Culpepper, *The Johannine School: An Evaluation of the Johannine-School Hypothesis Based on an Investigation of the Nature of Ancient Schools* (Missoula, Mont.: Scholars Press, 1975). Culpepper describes the various Greek, Roman, and Jewish schools from Pythagoras through Stoicism, Hillel, and Philo.

CHAPTER SEVEN

The Gospel of Luke and Acts of the Apostles: A Nobleman's Biography

The television series Queer Eye for the Straight Guy *caught the imagination of many people when it first aired a few years ago.* Queer Eye for the Straight Guy *is in the genre of the radical makeover cable-television series, but instead of radically making over a house, or an automobile, or a kitchen, these five gay guys help make over a straight guy who lacks style, class, and culture. The program aims to show the "before and after" of a social and stylistic klutz now transformed into a suave and debonair man capable of entertaining his girlfriend in stylish clothes, in a totally fashionably renovated apartment, with sophisticated food and wine at a well-set table. The queer guys specialize in five categories for reconstruction: one of them addresses the straight guy's grooming, another the design of his living quarters, yet another the guy's cultural ambience, still another his wardrobe and fashion, and finally one takes care of food and wine. Their work together constitutes a complete makeover of the straight guy, who functions not only as a straight guy in relationship to the gay guys, but also as the "straight man" to their wit and humor. While laughing at the interaction between the straight guy and the queer eyes, the audience begins to develop its own sense of style and culture and appreciates the transformation that takes place before their eyes. The transformation, in that sense, also becomes a means of educating a wider viewing audience in the graces and style of the fashion and culture gurus.*

Each episode follows a typical pattern. The gay guys select some slob of a guy, a real fashion klutz. They enter his house and usually find it a mess: clothes all over the place, dirty dishes in the sink, unmatched furniture in the living room and bedroom, drab colors on the wall, a closet full of tacky clothes, and furnishings that look like they were all bought at yard sales. The gay guys look on the mess with both disgust and enthusiasm at the potential the mess presents. And then the gay guys set to their tasks.

The first to get working is the one who will remake the house. This gay guy goes through the house making sarcastic and witty remarks about the present state of the house, but begins to envision what he can do to make the apartment look classy and sophisticated: he chooses a color scheme, envisions how he can dress up the walls with artwork and other creative wall hangings, arrange furniture, organize the kitchen and supply it with appropriate china and cutlery, and generally transform the entire living space to speak of elegance and sophistication.

The next gay guy to get to work is the wardrobe master. He takes the straight guy on a shopping spree. They begin to put together a wardrobe that is fashionable. Each element of the wardrobe receives specific attention to make the straight guy look stylish—from his underwear all the way to his shirts, jackets, ties, sweaters, pants, socks, and shoes. His closet is emptied of the old clothes, and his new wardrobe is placed neatly in the closet.

When the shopping spree ends, the straight guy and the wardrobe master enter the apartment, and they wonder at all the activity. The other guys are painting walls, making wall art, and moving in new furniture. The culture master begins his work of teaching the straight guy how to be suave and debonair in his relationships, especially with his girlfriend. All the time the teaching and work unfold, the gay guys make disparaging remarks about the old straight guy while at the same time teaching him to be someone different. As the program comes closer to the end, the gay chef begins to put together an elegant dinner with which the transformed straight guy will dazzle his girlfriend. They teach the straight guy how to put together a fabulous and impressive meal. The culture master sets the table with the new china and glassware, linens, and flowers. He instructs the straight guy about the proper wine to serve with the dinner and the proper way to serve it to his guest.

By the end of the program, the straight guy and his apartment have been completely transformed. He showers and dresses in his new clothes. He puts the finishing touches on the dinner and opens the wine to be prepared for the arrival of his girlfriend. The gay guys put the finishing touches on their straight-guy project with last minute instructions, final tweaking of the clothing, and they step out of the apartment to a room where they can watch via a television camera the girlfriend's response to the transformation. The doorbell rings, the girlfriend enters, and all watch as she expresses her amazement and delight at the transformation of her boyfriend. In the room where they watch, the gay guys revel in the delight of their transformed straight guy, huddled on a couch and commenting on every aspect of their work. When the transformation is complete, the gay guys' work has been completed, and they begin anticipating their next transformed straight guy.

Queer Eye highlights the way something offensive and uncultured can become something cultured, beautiful, and valued. We think of *Queer Eye* in relationship to the author of the two-volume work in the New Testament: the Gospel of Luke and the Acts of the Apostles. The transformation of people became necessary in the time of Luke because of the way that Jesus was condemned and died. Roman authorities used crucifixion as a degrading way of killing people the Roman Empire considered expendable, especially political enemies among subjugated peoples. There was nothing at all glorious or noble about the founder of a religion dying as a Roman criminal by crucifixion. To the Roman eye, the crucified Jesus was not someone the Romans could respect or follow. After all, the Roman general Titus (son of the emperor Vespasian and himself Vespasian's successor) destroyed the Temple of Jerusalem and brought the spoils from the Temple and many slaves to Rome in a triumphal procession that showed the complete subjugation and pillaging of Jewish Jerusalem. Jesus was from a people and province that the Romans decimated: How could he be the founder of a religion Romans would cherish and respect? If Roman citizens were to join the Jesus movement and enter the church, they would need a story more compelling to their sensibilities and intellectual tradition. The Romans needed a Roman Jesus. We described earlier the portrayal by Mark of Jesus as a "Roman Jew." Why couldn't Luke use Mark for his portrayal of a Roman? That's because Luke wanted Jesus to be a completely Roman gentleman. While Luke admits Jesus's ethnicity, his life is lived as a Roman gentleman's would be. The story of Jesus needed to be transformed, so that those who might hear it would be able to relate to it fully. That's exactly what the author of the two-volume work we call Luke/Acts did: he was the queer guy for the straight history of the church. The author took the story of a crucified criminal and transformed it into a glorious story that explained the origins and history of Jesus and his earliest followers for a Roman audience.

Four Strategies for Making a Roman Jesus

The author of these two volumes transformed the story through four specific strategies, as specific in their motives as the queer guys'. These strategies make the achievement of these volumes very compelling because what seems so evident from the other gospels has been completely transformed. First, the author created an ideal origin for Christianity as an ancient religion. Romans (and most ancient people) did not like new things. Something new was always considered strange, threatening, and somehow illicit. Old things, traditional things, had the validity given them through long and established practice and belief. Old things could be trusted. So the author of Luke/Acts could not present Christianity as a new religion; Christianity needed an old pedigree. And that pedigree was the religion of Israel. Even though the Romans destroyed the Temple and enforced Roman rule in Palestine, the Israelite religion was still an ancient and privileged religion to the Romans, who respected its antiquity and the clarity of its moral teaching. So Luke/Acts makes it very clear that this new religion grew out of the old religion.

Second, the author of Luke/Acts made Jesus into a wandering Roman noble- man, a kind of wise man who lived a noble and upright life, teaching others wisdom, and dying a noble death. The noble death, Jesus's crucifixion, presents him like the ancient Greek philosopher Socrates, unjustly suffering but ap- proaching his death with dignity, honor, and religious propriety. Socrates's death, in fact, became a model for many Roman nobles whom the emperor killed unjustly or forced to commit suicide. Jesus resembled the best of the Ro- man male tradition of sobriety, strength, honor, and fortitude in the face of an unjust and politically motivated sentence of death.

Third, the author of Luke/Acts portrays Jesus as a philosopher in the tradi- tion of Roman philosophers. Techniques that Greek and Roman philosophers employed in their schools included memorizing and meditating on short, pithy maxims that encapsulated the main point of the lesson or the curriculum of the school and the construction of narrative brain-teasers, or parables. Jesus teaches a particular philosophy through maxims, or short sayings that could be easily memorized or repeated in life situations that recalled the need for the philosophical and religious truth. Luke recounts a number of Jesus's masterful parables recorded nowhere else. Luke/Acts uses the sayings and parables of Jesus to summarize his teaching to his disciples. In fact, the second volume, Acts, shows how the disciples formed a philosophical school that replicated the teachings and deeds of their founder, Jesus. Such a school appealed to Roman noble people and gave Christianity an aura of respectability.

And finally, the author of Luke/Acts wrote in elegant Greek. The other gos- pels are written in a more humble, sometimes even crude Greek, but the author of Luke/Acts writes an elegant, graceful, stylistically pleasing, and sophisticated language that clearly would delight his educated and sophisticated audience.

These four strategies worked. The characterization of the founder of the movement and the creation of a history that reached back to ancient traditions and forward into new arenas transformed the story so that sophisticated Romans could hear and appreciate it. The author of Luke/Acts was the queer eye for the straight Christianity.

A Two-volume Work

You are probably wondering why we refer to this writing as a two-volume work that encompasses both the Gospel of Luke and the New Testament book Acts of the Apostles. We do this because the books themselves are linked by their author. Unlike the other books we call gospels, Luke's gospel really is the first volume of an intended two-volume work, the first one of which deals with Jesus and his life until his ascension, and the second volume which begins with the ascension in order to show the development of the church through the ministry of the apostles, primarily Peter and Paul. Christian tradition named the first volume a gospel because it seemed to parallel the other gospels (Mark, Matthew, and John) in writing that seems to be a biographical account of the life of Jesus. We do not really know the name of the author of Luke/Acts, but the early church attributed the first volume to a certain Luke and called it The Gospel according to Luke. The second volume, Acts of the Apostles, was not linked in the same way to one named Luke, but clearly the author connects the two works. Acts of the Apostles was included in the canon of the New Testament as a separate book that describes the early history of the church in the apostolic age. The church has read them as separate texts ever since. But the author links the two books as one large research project, and so they should be read together. In this chapter we will connect the two books and read them together as intended by their author.

Volume One: The Gospel of Luke

Let's begin with the introduction to the first volume, the one we commonly call the gospel. The prologue to volume one, written in very high literary style and with impressive rhetorical flourishes, reads:

> Since many have undertaken to compile a narrative of the events that have been fulfilled among us, just as those who were eyewitnesses from the beginning and ministers of the word have handed them down to us, I too have decided, after investigating everything accurately anew, to write it down in an orderly sequence for you, most excellent Theophilus, so that you may realize the certainty of the teachings you have received (Luke 1:1–4).

Starting at the end of this prologue, the author tells us that his purpose in writing was to help his patron Theophilus, the person who sponsored and paid for the project, to "realize the certainty of the teachings you have received." The author wrote in order to instruct Theophilus and to confirm as true what he has been taught. The intention is not simply instruction, but verification of the truth of the received instruction for an important person. The book therefore has an educative function, but not by way of introduction to new material, but rather as a reorganization of material that will deepen Theophilus's understanding.

This educational program of the prologue presents a scenario typical of a school environment: the author tells us that he has done his research before writing his book—research that included reading other writings and listening to people who have information beyond what has been written. The author of these two volumes, aware of other writings and oral communication, tells the reader that he bases his work on the work of his predecessors. New Testament scholars, in fact, have long recognized the literary relationships among the gospels. In the Introduction, we discussed at some length the most widely accepted explanation, known as the two-source hypothesis, which maintains that Matthew and Luke used a version of the Gospel of Mark, supplemented by a second source, a collection of sayings of Jesus commonly called Q (for the German word *Quelle*, which means "source"). These two sources, in addition to material peculiar to Luke and other material peculiar to Matthew, display that the later writers, in this instance the author of Luke/Acts, used earlier sources in order to produce their writings. The author of Luke/Acts acknowledges that he has used other sources and most scholars recognize those sources as Mark, Q, and traditions and stories peculiar to the Luke/Acts author, traditions known only to this author and the community that supported this author. These other traditions or narratives come to this author as eyewitness accounts and traditions handed down by those who had early contact with Jesus or with those who had contact with Jesus's early followers.

Typical also of a professor in a school, the author of Luke/Acts has produced his own work based on his own research and ordering of the material. The prologue states clearly that this author researched and evaluated other people's writings, and then put them into a different order, an orderly narrative, for the enlightenment and formation of his patron. The author does not claim to be presenting the material in a historically accurate chronology, nor does he claim to be writing an historically accurate portrait of Jesus and the church. The author may be doing this, but that is not his stated intent. His purpose rather is to create a different sequence of deeds and sayings of Jesus, to write an expanded narrative of events and teaching that makes sense for his patron's education and formation. The material has all been rearranged and ordered for the confirmation of information for his patron. So the author writes not to be historically accurate, but to assist his patron in continuing his life of faith and to understand the basis of his faith.

These four beginning verses of the first volume, the one we call the gospel, certainly provide us with a great deal of information. It is a precious insight into the workings of an early Christian author who writes clearly and articulately about his intentions as a writer and as a leader of the faithful.

Volume Two: Acts of the Apostles

Although the second volume does not acknowledge the same kind of sources as the first volume, the author does tell us that this is the second part of his work. Acts 1:1–2 continues the story of Luke 1:1–4 and continues the work commissioned by his patron Theophilus: "In the first book, Theophilus, I dealt with all that Jesus did and taught until the day he was taken up, after giving instructions through the holy

Spirit to the apostles whom he had chosen." This, too, tells us much. The image of Jesus as an instructor, a teacher, a philosopher continues. These first verses in Acts tell us that Jesus's primary postresurrection function was to teach through the holy Spirit those whom Jesus had selected to be his emissaries. The instruction is given to his closest students, the apostles, the ones who were sent to continue Jesus's mission in the world. Not only were these followers students of the philosopher/teacher Jesus, but they were also his elect, his chosen ones. The introduction here of the Holy Spirit as part of Jesus's teaching introduces the readers to the Spirit who will be a primary character in the second volume.

The complete project as it is articulated in these two introductory sections of the two volumes indicates a story that begins with Jesus, but that continues through Peter and Paul and other apostles until the mission culminates in the imperial capital city, Rome. The author writes his narrative in two sections, the first dealing with Jesus until his ascension, the second taking up the time after the ascension and following the apostolic missions as the apostles move from Jerusalem to Rome. Jesus functions as the guide in the first section, while the Holy Spirit guides in the second. Both Jesus and the Holy Spirit influence and guide the development of the church in its earliest days. It is important to remember, however, that for the author of these two volumes the story of Jesus did not stand alone. Jesus's story was not sufficient to explain the development of the church from the time of Jesus until its arrival in Rome. Jesus's teaching alone was not sufficient narrative to explain Christian faith and practice; the apostles' ministry, which certainly imitated the ministry of Jesus, played a central role in explaining and articulating the life of the Christian church in its earliest days.

In order for the author to transform the story of Jesus and the church for his Roman audience, that is, for the author to be the queer eyes for the narrative, he had to do some serious research and writing. The story as he inherited it did not work for his audience. Something more was necessary. The story needed to be bigger, more dramatic, more Roman, more aristocratic than his sources. So the story expanded from Jesus and his origins to include the work of the now very Roman-looking apostles who continued his mission right into the center of the Roman Empire, the city of Rome.

This expanded story created a space for the author to articulate a different understanding of the Jesus movement and of the church, a story not oriented solely to the origins of Christianity in the life, teaching, and shameful crucifixion of its founder, but now one oriented toward the historical development of the church through a missionary effort guided by the Holy Spirit. It is the church and its work that made the story of Jesus complete, and so it is the church and its spirit-filled life that worked to transform the story into one a noble Roman could read, understand, and enter. Since the older narrative of the life of Jesus and the origins of the church in Jesus's teaching and death no longer spoke eloquently, it needed to be updated, revised, contextualized to fit a new audience. To put it more positively, the history needed to be created in order to establish the Holy Spirit's church, and the Jesus movement that founded it, as a legitimate religion in the Roman Empire—a Roman Christianity for a noble Roman faith. This tells us that the times have changed for Christianity. Now the Roman nobility and educated class want to enter the church, but they need the way paved for their entrance with systems and teachings they recognize and appreciate.

Comparing the Accounts of Jesus's Ascension in Each Volume

So what other clues might we have that this assessment of the transformation of the story is what actually happens in these two books? This is what makes reading Luke/Acts fascinating. Let's compare the end of the first volume and the beginning of the second. They both tell the story of Jesus's ascent into heaven, but they tell the story differently. The difference shows that the author of these two volumes adjusts his story to accommodate his shifting agenda. The story shifts and changes as he writes it, and this did not apparently trouble the author or the early readers of the gospel. It shows us that the ultimate concern for both author and readers was something other than accuracy of detail, consistency of description, or even consistency of historical information. Something else was happening. So let's try to figure it out.

The first volume ends with the story of Jesus's ascension on the day of the resurrection after appearing to the disciples on the road to Emmaus and coming into the disciples' presence in Jerusalem. After eating to prove that he was not a ghost, he says to the disciples:

> "These are my words that I spoke to you while I was still with you, that everything written about me in the law of Moses and in the prophets and psalms must be fulfilled." Then he opened their minds to understand the scriptures. And he said to them, "Thus it is written that the Messiah would suffer and rise from the dead on the third day and that repentance, for the forgiveness of sins, would be preached in his name to all the nations, beginning from Jerusalem. You are witnesses of these things. And behold I am sending the promise of my Father upon you; but stay in the city until you are clothed with power from on high." Then he led them out as far as Bethany, raised his hands, and blessed them. As he blessed them he parted from them and was taken up to heaven. They did him homage and then returned to Jerusalem with great joy, and they were continually in the temple praising God (Luke 24:44–53).

This account of the ascension of Jesus takes place on the day of the resurrection and it is related to the fulfillment of scripture in Jesus's words and deeds, especially his suffering, death, and resurrection. In fact, Jesus opens their minds to comprehend the way that he fulfilled these scriptures—it was not obvious to them, so they needed Jesus's assistance to understand. The ascension, then, connects to a singular event of enlightenment for the disciples that founds their mission to witness to his death and resurrection "to all the nations." Jesus informs these newly enlightened disciples that he will empower them with the Father's promise, but they must wait for this in Jerusalem.

Now let's compare this to the story of the ascension at the beginning of the second volume, the Acts of the Apostles. This story is much more elaborate and provides richer detail for the reader and for the author's patron, Theophilus:

> In the first book, Theophilus, I dealt with all that Jesus did and taught until the day he was taken up, after giving instructions through the holy Spirit to the apostles whom he had chosen. He presented himself alive to them by many proofs after he had suffered, appearing to them during forty days and speaking about the kingdom of God. While meeting with them, he enjoined them not to depart from Jerusalem, but to wait for the "promise of the Father about which you have heard me speak; for John baptized with water, but in a few days you will be baptized with the Holy Spirit." When they had gathered together they asked him, "Lord, are you at this time going to restore the kingdom to Israel?" He answered them, "It is not for you to know the times or seasons that the Father has established by his own authority. But you will receive power when the Holy Spirit comes upon you, and you will be my witnesses in Jerusalem, throughout Judea and Samaria, and to the ends of the earth." When he had said this, as they were looking on, he was lifted up, and a cloud took him from their sight. While they were looking intently at the sky as he was going, suddenly two men dressed in white garments stood beside them. They said, "Men of Galilee, why are you standing there looking at the sky? This Jesus who has been taken up from you into heaven will return in the same way as you have seen him going into heaven." Then they returned to Jerusalem from the mount called Olivet, which is near Jerusalem, a sabbath day's journey away (Acts 1:1–12).

The details of this account are much more elaborated. Jesus teaches the disciples for forty days, suggesting a more prolonged and sustained training and formation of the disciples in the proofs of his suffering and resurrection. For forty days, Jesus continued to prove to them that he was alive and preparing a mission. As in the end of the first volume, Jesus tells the disciples to stay in Jerusalem, but now Jesus gives a specific reason: they will be baptized in the Holy Spirit, just as John baptized with water. In response to the disciples' question about restoring the kingdom to Israel, Jesus responds that the disciples have limited access to full knowledge. Some things they cannot know, but what they do need to know is that they will be empowered to become Jesus's witnesses from Jerusalem to Rome and beyond. Then Jesus ascends, and the disciples need angelic figures to interpret what they saw. The angelic figures say that Jesus will return in the same way that he ascended, and the disciples return rejoicing, to Jerusalem.

The new details added in the account of the ascension in Acts shift the emphasis from a kind of miraculous enlightenment in the first volume to a sustained (and yet somehow still limited) instruction over forty days when the disciples could interrogate Jesus about the unfolding and meaning of his mission. The work of the disciples also shifts: in the first volume Jesus instructs the disciples to preach repentance and the forgiveness of sins, but in the second volume the disciples have become empowered, spirit-filled witnesses about Jesus's proven and verified death and resurrection. The author shifts from an orientation toward the sayings and teachings of Jesus in volume one to setting up an apostolic mission to preach Jesus in volume two. The story has developed from a story about Jesus alone to the story of the church and that demanded that the author expand and adjust his description of the ascension in the second volume.

In reading these two accounts together we see clearly that the author constructs the story of Jesus and the church so that his reader (and patron) understands the events in multiple ways. The meaning of an event shifts as the needs of the instruction, as the needs of the readers, and as the plot of the story, demands. The author, that is, continually transforms the story according to the immediate educational and formational needs of his audience and according to the changes that have taken place in the life of the church. This is not *one* story, but a transforming story, a queer eye for the straight guy.

It is now easier to understand some of the specifics of the writing of these two volumes. Luke/Acts was written after the Gospel of Mark and other early Christian writings (the Gospel of Matthew and perhaps even the *Didache*, a late first-century or early second-century document that gives instruction on ordering the church and its sacraments). If Mark was composed around 68 in Rome, and had been found unsuitable for a Roman-Christian audience, then the first volume by Luke was probably written around 90 CE (roughly twenty years later) and the second volume sometime between 90 and 100 CE. These two volumes were produced somewhere in the Roman Empire where wealthy nobles, retired generals, and successful merchants lived in sufficient numbers to support research and writing, and at a time when the upper classes of Rome (witness Theophilus) found the political situation such that they could explore Christianity without fear of reprisal. This could be Rome, but it also could be any of the larger Roman provinces such as those in Italy, Greece, or southern France. Clearly these volumes reflect a more stable and receptive environment for the promulgation of Christian living and for forming the powerful among the elite in a new way of life. So the dating of these volumes is between 90 and 110 CE, the audience is the Roman elite, and the place of composition is somewhere in the large Roman provinces in Europe. Like the queer guys on the TV show, the author has composed books that will reflect this new environment and this different audience in such a way that they too, like Theophilus, will find their faith deepened and their understanding expanded.

To rewrite the story of Jesus and the church to suit this audience took great skill and creativity. The author uses Greek and Roman historical, biographical, and literary themes to shape and mold a new way of understanding where Christianity originated, who founded it, and how that foundation grew and developed from its origins in Palestine to its arrival in Rome. It is these Greek and Roman themes that make these volumes interesting: the way the author rewrites the story to make Jesus part of an imperial history, the creativity with which he portrays Jesus as a hero, the kind of social and religious identity he develops for his upper-class audience, and the way he describes the teaching of Jesus and the life of the early church as a utopia. All of these—imperial history, heroic Jesus, narrative identity, and utopian vision—aim to train his audience in the proper way to live the Christian life in their own times. So by exploring these themes in this chapter, we open the book on the formative practice of these early Christians and look into their world. We watch as the author, like the queer guys, makes a new person, in a proper environment, live out a different way of living as a Roman Christian.

Luke/Acts as Imperial History and Legend

The *Queer Eye* programs always start with a person whose ways, although rough and unsophisticated, show potential for remaking. The social klutz is never so much a klutz that there is no hope for change. Without hope for transformation, the program falls flat. The author of Luke/Acts knows that reality well. Starting with rough documents written in poorer Greek (the Gospel of Mark) and in peculiar Greek (the Gospel of Matthew and perhaps the *Didache*), the author of these volumes begins to work his magic. The story line, the rough edges of the originals, need to be made into something more dramatic, something with flair, something that will amaze the readers. So he decides to make Jesus a Roman emperor. This Roman imperial Jesus would certainly please his audience and enable them to learn the right way to live as a Christian. This Roman imperial Jesus would have real class.

An imperial history would do the trick. Rewriting the history with a Jesus who acts like a Roman emperor and speaks and relates like a Roman nobleman would tell the story in a way that would resonate with his Roman audience and in language and actions that would speak to Romans in a dramatic way. So the author rewrote the story in such a way as to make Jesus a legendary imperial leader, an intellectual and religious actor in categories and patterns of thought that the educated and elite Romans would readily understand. This imperial history invoked Roman traditions in important ways: the author uses portents to signify a new imperial beginning, and he reorganizes time to reflect the work of a true Roman emperor. When we understand how the author uses portents and writes an imperial history, we begin to understand how he reshaped the story to suit his audience.

Portents

So now let's look more closely at how Luke/Acts presents this story. The author uses a number of different lenses to portray Jesus and the movement he founded. Probably the most exciting to Romans revolved about the divine portents surrounding Jesus's birth and early ministry. A divine portent indicates that something really important, or inspired by God, is about to happen. Portents function as omens of future events, as prophetic statements about amazing and wonderful events that are about to unfold. Romans loved to divine the future through portents, which particularly announced the presence and work of emperors. Part of the regular Roman formation of a noble man involved various priesthoods in Rome, and the process of progressing through these priesthoods was called the *cursus honorum*, the sequence or ladder of honors and offices that a Roman undertook in order to assume various levels of public service. In fact, the regular course of social and political progress (the *cursus honorum*) included being augurs, priests who read the portents before every important event in Roman history. So portents speak loudly and clearly to the Roman mind.

The first two chapters of the first volume present a storm of portents that announce a new imperium, a new empire, a new emperor, and a new era. The first two chapters, in fact, are so full of portents that we readers have difficulty knowing who the main characters will be: is this a book about John the Baptist, or Jesus, or Jesus's family, or the Temple in Jerusalem? The many portents simply point to an auspicious and important new era. Even without knowing *who* the prime character in the story is, the portents tell the readers that something auspicious, important, and cosmic unfolds in their lives.

The very first story, of the announcement in the Temple of the birth of John to the elder Zachariah and the long-barren Elizabeth, opens the book. This story is reminiscent of many such stories in the Israelite scriptures when God intervenes to raise up important figures from barren women and men. The story is a simple one: Zachariah, serving his appointed priestly time in the Temple in Jerusalem, has a vision brought to him by the angel Gabriel that his wife will bear a son who should be named John. Zachariah questions the angel, and so is made mute until the portent should be realized. After the birth of John, Zachariah signs to those around him to name the child John, recovers his speech, and sings a lovely hymn, much to the astonishment of his neighbors. Romans would understand visions given to someone who was serving a period of priesthood in a temple, the *cursus honorum*. Romans would have understood exactly what Zachariah was doing in the Temple and why he received a vision: Zachariah was doing his Roman-style duties when he received a vision proper to his service.

Zachariah's vision involved a child, John, who would show divine favor. The angel Gabriel "who stand(s) before God" reveals the renewing program that the child will inaugurate: "for he will be great in the sight of the Lord. He will drink neither wine nor strong drink. He will be filled with the Holy Spirit even from his mother's womb, and he will turn many of the children of Israel to the Lord their God. He will go before him in the spirit and power of Elijah to turn the hearts of fathers toward children and the disobedient to the understanding of the righteous, to prepare a people fit for the Lord" (Luke 1:15–17). To Roman eyes, John will be a strange person because he will not drink wine, but his mission of renewal of the people would sound very much like the work of the emperor Augustus, who prided himself on the renewal of ancient Roman custom in his own day. John will herald the coming of the new era, the new imperial structure. His moral reformation and his personal discipline will ensure that the new thing God is doing will be holy. John, we will learn a little later in the story, announces the new regime and sets the stage for its unfolding. This inaugural portent in the gospel thus lays the foundation for the entire two-volume history. A Roman reader would have understood this.

Things get more interesting when the portents relate to Jesus. Portents also surround the announcement of Jesus's conception and birth (1:26–38). Again, it is the angel Gabriel who announces to Mary that she will conceive a child by being overshadowed by God and that she must name the child Jesus. Mary questions how this can be, and the angel Gabriel assures her of the validity of the proposition. Romans understood that the emperor who would be pronounced a god upon his death should have a story of a portentous birth. The portent regarding Jesus bears all the marks of the proclamation of a new emperor with divine favor: Gabriel says: "He will be great and will be called Son of the Most High, and the Lord God will give him the throne of David his father, and he will rule over the house of Jacob forever, and of his kingdom there will be no end" (1:32–33). This announces the new imperium, the new Empire, under a new emperor born of a famous line of Davidic emperors. Jesus is also, like all the Roman emperors, a "son of God." Emperors not only had divine power by virtue of their office and position in Roman society, but the gods always favored them and their actions above those of all others. And Roman emperors adopted favored politicians as their sons so that their sons could succeed them in office by becoming emperors themselves. In this way emperors, "sons of god," always had imperial and divine ancestors. This applies to Jesus as well: Son of the God, who overshadowed Mary, and son of David, the king of Judea. This portent, then, establishes the story of the two volumes as definitely that of Jesus, the new emperor, and of Jesus's work, the establishment of a new empire. Roman readers readily understood this narrative portent and its significance.

But the author also takes liberty with the tradition of portents. He uses these portents about John and Jesus to set up a hierarchy of revelation about them. Normally portents might reveal who would win a battle, or at least who had the favor of the gods going into battle, but the author takes that tradition a little further in the next set of portents. That John prepares the way for the new emperor Jesus becomes clear in the meeting of Mary and Elizabeth (Luke 1:39–56). When the two women who have miraculously conceived their male children meet, Elizabeth's child John leaps at Mary's greeting. Elizabeth understands this as a portent of Jesus's superiority, saying "For at the moment the sound of your greeting reached my ears, the infant in my womb leaped for joy. Blessed are you who believed that what was spoken to you by the Lord would be fulfilled" (1:44–45). Then Mary sings her famous hymn, the Magnificat: "My soul proclaims the greatness of the Lord; my spirit rejoices in God my savior." (The full hymn can be found in Luke 1:46–55.) These signs—the hymn as well as the baby greeting his master in the womb—point to something auspicious and powerful about to happen among God's people. Roman readers would understand: there is a hierarchy of authority that divine forces set in place.

The author also mixes themes. Around the time of the emperor Augustus, Roman poets wrote poems about how the natural world reflected the energy and power of the new emperor in poems we call "pastoral poems," because they describe country people, the countryside, and the farmland. These poets describe the pastoral life, the farming life so dear to Roman noblemen and so necessary to their wealth (and thus their political success), as being renewed by the birth and life of the new emperor. The author of Luke/Acts combines this pastoral theme with a portent. Luke 2:8–20 shows angels announcing the birth of Jesus to shepherds. This pastoral scene invokes the Roman pastoral traditions about the emperor Augustus written in Virgil's *Aeneid* as well as works by other Latin Silver poets. The Roman pastoral tradition made the birth of the emperor a cosmic event, an event that not only influenced politics, but also had its effect in the physical world. In addition to the pastoral portent, we find the portents about Jesus made by Simeon and Anna in the Temple (2:22–40), who both attest to the particular vocation and divine favor the child Jesus holds. And there is the portent of the very young Jesus in the Temple (2:41–52), when he instructs his elders about the meaning of religious texts, and the portent of God speaking at Jesus's baptism "You are my beloved Son; with you I am well pleased" (3:22). These portents point the way to a new emperor, a new regime, and a new era. Even the demons recognize the propitiousness of these events and recognize Jesus's divine status: Luke 4:34 reports the speech of the demons of the man with the unclean spirit in the synagogue: "Ha! What have you to do with us, Jesus of Nazareth? Have you come to destroy us? I know who you are—the Holy One of God!" The demons themselves attest to the divine favor and identity of Jesus. The author summarizes these demonic portents in this way: "And demons also came out from many, shouting, 'You are the Son of God.' But he rebuked them and did not allow them to speak because they knew that he was the Messiah" (4:41). These revelations of Jesus's identity pack a powerful punch. The author seems to be piling portent upon prophesy upon revelation to make his point: "Listen, Roman friends. This Jesus really is the emperor to best all other emperors!" Like the final product of *Queer Eye*, the new person has had a complete makeover of what he eats, what he wears, and where he lives.

These portents set the stage for the unveiling of the new emperor and the new imperial order. They relate the divine favor, the unlimited cosmic powers, the miraculous events surrounding the conception and birth of the new emperor, and the enormous power that the new emperor will wield over humans, demons, and physical events. The Roman audience could read these portents and immediately understand that the new emperor Jesus was just like the other emperors they knew, and they understood that they could follow him as emperor into a new era. The author begins his story by simply portraying the portents that point to Jesus as emperor. These portents play an important role in characterizing the birth of Jesus as a cosmic, imperial, and historically significant event. The infancy gospel at the beginning of volume one of Luke/Acts organizes these characterizations into an interesting and fascinating story of the auspicious birth of a new emperor. The cosmic revelations to prophets in the Temple, in the sky to shepherds, to the mothers of Jesus and John the Baptist, to demons terrorizing the people, and to Simeon and Anna in the Temple, all emphasize that a new age has begun. The author then develops a genealogy of Jesus (3:23–38) that takes him back to Adam, God's son, the first human, so that the new age inaugurated in Jesus's birth connects with the entire history of the human community. The stage is set.

Historical Periodization
Portents set the stage announcing that something important is happening or is about to happen and they create eager anticipation of the new things the divine energies set in place. The author of Luke/Acts uses that anticipatory expectation to write the new story of Jesus. Since Jesus inaugurates a new divine-imperial reign and since God has pointed to the importance of this reign, the story of history must change. History cannot be understood in the same way. Things are different. Times have changed permanently. So as a good imperial interpreter, the author rewrites history to accommodate the new era.

In fact, almost every new emperor had an historian to document the successes and victories of his rule. For the author of these two volumes, that historical record was important to building the case for an imperial history and legend. As the portents announced, time itself has taken on new meaning under Jesus, the emperor, so chronology and the sequence of events point to the new age and the new way of living in the new age. Although scholars break up the two volumes into large categories (Jesus's ministry, procession to Jerusalem, the trial and death of Jesus, the resurrection accounts, the ascension, and the work of the apostles), the author of Luke/Acts has a more sophisticated set of chronological categories that make his periodization more suggestive and telling. The way the author breaks up time in Jesus's reign makes an important statement not only about Jesus, but about the whole Christian movement and its growth as a community, as a church.

The first period covers all the material that we have already talked about in the infancy narrative, the time of portents. This early history, with its deep ties to the Temple and to the ancient revelations to Israel, establishes the origins of the movement. Time begins with Adam, the first human and the son of God, whom Luke has documented as Jesus's ancestor, and progresses through various revelations in the Temple, culminating in the birth of John the Baptist and Jesus. This period signifies that the new emperor follows in a long and noble tradition and connects Jesus and his imperium to the line of the Israelite king David. The origins establish Jesus's pedigree.

The inspiration for this new imperial reign of Jesus comes from yet another source, the divine energy called the Holy Spirit. The author of Luke/Acts organizes his history around the Spirit and the Spirit's antagonist, Satan. The next periodization revolves about Satan and the Holy Spirit. Satan operates in the first volume as bookends to the work of Jesus. Satan's time, contrasted with the time of the Holy Spirit, creates a very dramatic chronology in the beginning of the first volume that ends with the time of the Holy Spirit in the second volume. This is an interesting series that can be missed if readers separate the two volumes. In the first volume, Satan tempts Jesus in the desert (4:1–13) with food, power, and authority, but Jesus resists. As a character, Satan plays an inaugural role in establishing Jesus's authority and power but, as the author tells us, "When the devil had finished every test, he departed from him until an opportune time" (4:13). Satan plays a role at the beginning of Jesus's ministry and departs until another time in his ministry. The period of Satan begins early and ends later.

Satan's reentry into the chronology is as dramatic as his first appearance. Satan returns to the scene at the Passover plot to kill Jesus, during the Last Supper, and Jesus's instruction to the disciples before his arrest (22:1–71). Satan inaugurates these dramatic actions:

> Now the feast of Unleavened Bread, called the Passover, was drawing near, and the chief priests and the scribes were seeking a way to put him to death, for they were afraid of the people. Then Satan entered into Judas, the one surnamed Is-

cariot, who was counted among the Twelve, and he went to the chief priests and temple guards to discuss a plan for handing him over to them. They were pleased and agreed to pay him money. He accepted their offer and sought a favorable opportunity to hand him over to them in the absence of a crowd (22:1–6).

Satan's return, filling Judas with evil as the Holy Spirit will fill the apostles with good, sets into motion the final actions of Jesus and his detractors before the crucifixion. What happens to Jesus in his crucifixion and death (and ultimately with his resurrection) occurs because of the time of Satan. Through Judas, Satan instigates the process of salvation.

The time between these Satanic bookends defines another period, the time of Jesus's free teaching and performance of miraculous deeds. This periodization between the Satanic bookends signifies a time of Jesus's uncontested supernatural powers and his free teaching of disciples and other followers. It is an important part of the way history was understood: there is a time of temptation that inaugurates Jesus's ministry, a time of Jesus as uncontested victor, and finally a time of Satan's capacity to test Jesus in a death that will ultimately lead to Jesus's victory.

But this periodization does not end there; it is succeeded and balanced by a time of a Holy Spirit, who will take the place of the cosmic evil forces. This Holy Spirit comes into the narrative in the early chapters of the second volume. Jesus tells his disciples at the end of the first volume to await their empowerment and in the second volume to await a baptism in the Spirit. The reign of the Holy Spirit, undoing the reign of Satan and fulfilling the reign of Jesus, carries time forward into the church through the activities of the apostles whom Jesus sends out on mission. The new empire operates in a time of the Spirit. Though tempted as every emperor always is by opposing forces, both exterior to and within his court among his closest allies, the new emperor Jesus operates during his life as a victorious emperor; simultaneously he inaugurates an imperial line through the agency of the Holy Spirit. The positive chronology describes a victorious time of Jesus ultimately unthwarted by opposition and a victorious time showing the Holy Spirit guiding Jesus's successors in their work in the world. The period of the Holy Spirit fulfills the period of Jesus's life. This is a new imperial history written into time, a new way of understanding the history of the world as directed by the emperor Jesus.

The author further breaks down the chronology of the time during Jesus's life between Satan's departure and his later entry into Judas. Jesus has a ministry in Galilee in the first part of the gospel (5:1–9:50). The author presents Jesus as moving about the province teaching, healing, giving speeches, and engaging with both friends and foes. Then, quite dramatically, the author has Jesus do something unexpected: he turns his face toward Jerusalem. This creates yet another periodization technique used by the author: the time of Jesus's teaching from the moment he turns his face toward Jerusalem until his triumphal entry into Jerusalem (9:51–19:28). The author clearly demarcates this time as a special time of teaching when his followers go ahead to prepare for Jesus:

> When the days for his being taken up were fulfilled, he resolutely determined to journey to Jerusalem, and he sent messengers ahead of him. On the way they entered a Samaritan village to prepare for his reception there, but they would not welcome him because the destination of his journey was Jerusalem. When the disciples James and John saw this they asked, "Lord, do you want us to call down fire from heaven to consume them?" Jesus turned and rebuked them, and they journeyed to another village (9:51–56).

What an amazing story! The author emphasizes that this turn toward Jerusalem has historical import: "when the days for his being taken up were fulfilled." The early part of Jesus's work has been completed. The past now lies in the past, and a future event calls Jesus forward to Jerusalem.

In the story line, before this turning of his face to Jerusalem and his ascent into heaven, the disciples (in this instance, the Twelve, the women who were healed and financed his mission, and others) attend to Jesus. After this point, Jesus sends out the seventy missioners. The future event, the day of his ascension, calls forth new missionary and ministerial strategies. This time of the preparation for his ascent involves teaching and the expansion of the mission. Although Jesus has been portrayed to this point as a kind of Roman, wonder-working philosopher, it is at this point in the story of the first volume that the author shows Jesus conveying the rich content of that teaching.

The heart of Jesus's philosophical teachings in this long section of the first volume resides in his sayings, parables, and teaching on the road to Jerusalem. Roman philosophers such as Musonius Rufus and Epictetus were well-known for their teaching through short maxims. Their students collected them, published them, and used them as the basis for their teaching of their own students. It was the way philosophers taught in Roman times.

On Jesus's journey to Jerusalem, to the time of his ascent, the author inserts most of his source of the collected sayings of Jesus (including the Sayings Source Q). These maxims are to today's Christians some of the most familiar teachings of Jesus. They include the Lord's Prayer (11:1–4), familiar parables like the Good Samaritan (10:29–37), the story of Martha's kitchen work and Mary's contemplative relationship to Jesus (10:38–42), as well as sections such as these:

> He said to [his] disciples, "Therefore I tell you, do not worry about your life and what you will eat, or about your body and what you will wear. For life is more

than food and the body more than clothing. Notice the ravens: they do not sow or reap; they have neither storehouse nor barn, yet God feeds them. How much more important are you than birds! Can any of you by worrying add a moment to your life span? If even the smallest things are beyond your control, why are you anxious about the rest? Notice how the flowers grow. They do not toil or spin. But I tell you, not even Solomon in all his splendor was dressed like one of them. If God so clothes the grass in the field that grows today and is thrown into the oven tomorrow, will he not much more provide for you, O you of little faith? As for you, do not seek what you are to eat and what you are to drink, and do not worry anymore. All the nations of the world seek for these things, and your Father knows that you need them. Instead, seek his kingdom, and these other things will be given to you besides. Do not be afraid any longer, little flock, for your Father is pleased to give you the kingdom. Sell your belongings and give alms. Provide money bags for yourselves that do not wear out, and inexhaustible treasure in heaven that no thief can reach nor moth destroy. For where your treasure is, there also will your heart be" (12:22–34).

The journey to Jerusalem is peppered with such philosophical and moral speeches, as well as parables and dialogues between Jesus and his opponents. His teaching centers on questions of the proper moral life: attitudes toward food and clothing, wealth, and desire. Jesus's movement toward his ascent involves a travel time of intense teaching and of increased conflict with religious leaders. The periodization, then, becomes the times of preparation, his ascent into heaven (in both Luke and Acts) and the time of the Spirit, which Jesus's ascent makes possible.

Geographical Location

Geographical location emerges as an important indicator of the status of Jesus's ministry. As we have seen, Jesus's ministry begins in Galilee. When he turns his face to Jerusalem, the journey itself provides the backdrop for his teaching. Then we have the events of his betrayal, trial, death, and resurrection in Jerusalem. But this geographical organization goes even further when we look at both volumes together. In the second volume, the story picks up in Jerusalem and progresses through a series of journeys and adventures to Rome. Thus, in the broadest strokes, Luke/Acts organizes itself around the progression from Jesus's ministry in Galilee to Paul's proclamation of the gospel in Rome (Acts 28:11–31). Each geographical area involves a different period of the mission of the church. These geographical progressions constitute a kind of historical sketch of the expansion of Jesus's empire from its humble beginnings in Galilee to its arrival at the heart of the Roman Empire. The progression—Galilee, Jerusalem, Judea and Samaria, Greece, Rome—shows the gospel's historical development across the Roman Empire.

The imperial history that the author creates, then, is a rich assembly of ways of understanding the importance of the work that Jesus performs. It is not simply that Jesus inaugurates a new reign of God on the earth, which supervenes the Roman imperial structure, but it is also that Jesus's life and teaching have shifted the very way history is to be understood. Time has been turned around, redefined, reformulated in order to show graphically the way that the world has changed. The new history makes the work of Jesus and of the Holy Spirit a permanent fixture. No longer do Romans or Christians divide time by the emperor and the dating of his officials alone, now time is divided by the geographical location within the history of Jesus and the church and by the time marked by the activity of Satan and the Holy Spirit. This is a dramatic reworking of time, place, and history, one worthy of a story of a Roman imperial Jesus inaugurating a new kind of imperial rule of God on earth.

These two volumes develop an imperial history and legend for Jesus in very dramatic images. Divine portents point to the imperial authority, the cosmic power that brings the new emperor into view. That new emperor inaugurates a new understanding of time and history, which the author demonstrates in a variety of ways. And that new emperor functions as a different kind of emperor, one bridging the philosophical world well-known to the Roman elite and the Israelite prophetic tradition that the Romans would have found more confusing. These literary modes characterizing Jesus as an emperor inaugurating a new empire, however, are not the last statement. The author of Luke/Acts makes an even bolder move as he dresses up Christianity for the long haul, as we will explain in the next section.

Jesus as Valorized Hero

In *Queer Eye*, the guy who is remade becomes a hero of sorts. His friends, associates, and his family, especially his girlfriend, look on him with awed surprise at his transformation. The *Queer Eye* hero has gained new power and authority as a person through the transformative work of the queer guys.

An imperial history also needed its emperor-hero. The poet Virgil, for example, made the emperor Augustus a hero in his epic poem, *The Aeneid*. Virgil makes Augustus a god-like figure performing important deeds and engaging in spectacular feats of valor. An imperial history demanded that the emperor be valorized and made a hero in epic proportions. A hero was a real or imaginary figure who was worshipped as a god. In literary productions, the hero became a kind of divine figure who commanded temporal, cosmic, spiritual, and political authority.

The author of Luke/Acts certainly portrays Jesus as the hero who founded the dynasty that was continued in the work of his successors, the apostles, under the guidance of Jesus's divine inspiration, the Holy Spirit. Later in this chapter we will also see how the apostles Peter and Paul, especially, were also portrayed as heroes who succeeded the hero-Jesus in the narrative. But for immediate purposes, let us describe the way that the author made Jesus the hero of volume one of his two-part work.

The Hero in the Synagogue

The easiest way to understand how the author portrayed Jesus as a hero is to explore the portrayal of an early event in Jesus's life: his inaugural teaching in Galilee (cf. Luke 4:1–30). Since Galilee geographically demarcated the first historical phase of Jesus's mission, the author provides a summary statement that sets the tone for Jesus's opening ministry in the synagogue of his hometown, Nazareth: "Jesus returned to Galilee in the power of the Spirit, and news of him spread throughout the whole region. He taught in their synagogues and was praised by all" (4:14–15). Such a summary would warm the heart of a Roman nobleman: it is replete with power, with good report, and with praise. This is what made Roman noblemen proud. Jesus would make them proud.

But that pride was short-lived. When Jesus went back to his old synagogue in Nazareth, he both claimed his authority as a leader and at the same time incurred the praise and blame of his village. Praise and recognition by one's peers formed an important part of the Roman ideology of manhood. Jesus was no exception. After being honored by the attendant of his boyhood synagogue with the privilege of reading the appointed scripture, Jesus reads the following from the prophet Isaiah:

> The Spirit of the Lord is upon me, because he has anointed me to bring glad tidings to the poor. He has sent me to proclaim liberty to captives and recovery of sight to the blind, to let the oppressed go free, and to proclaim a year acceptable to the Lord (4:18–19).

This reading presents a potent picture of God's powerful activity among the people. Jesus claims the authority of the passage and makes it clear that the Isaiah passage articulates his mission, his authority, and his power among the people:

> Rolling up the scroll, he handed it back to the attendant and sat down, and the eyes of all in the synagogue looked intently at him. He said to them, "Today this scripture passage is fulfilled in your hearing." And all spoke highly of him and were amazed at the gracious words that came from his mouth (4: 20–22).

Such valorization, public acclaim, comment on rhetorical ability, and respect portray Jesus in the most positive light, reflecting Roman virtues appropriate to a Roman gentleman. Jesus, like the well-educated and sophisticated Roman senator, took his proper place in the religious arena where power, rhetoric, status, and authority were put on display.

Although things turned sour for Jesus when others in the community took offense at him and were jealous of his achievement, Jesus continued to show the Stoic philosophical detachment that Roman noblemen admired: "They rose up, drove him out of the town, and led him to the brow of the hill on which their town had been built, to hurl him down headlong. But he passed through the midst of them and went away" (4:29–30). Jesus was unmoved by their rage; he remained self-composed and poised in the face of opposition. The author of Luke/Acts portrays Jesus as an heroic figure who embodies the Roman Stoic virtue of passionlessness (*apatheia*) and displays it in his thoughts and relationships.

In addition to portraying Jesus as an heroic Roman nobleman, Luke/Acts also portrays him heroically as a healer, a wonder-worker, a divine man, a suffering prophet, as a noble philosopher at his death, and as a mystagogue. In every way, Jesus displays heroic virtue and elevated social and religious status. These varied characterizations of Jesus underscore his power and authority as a person and make his life even more noble and representative of a person under divine authority and with divine power.

Hero as Healer and Wonder-worker

Jesus performs many healing miracles in the gospel. The narrator summarizes such events and connects them to the good opinion of the people in this way: "The report about him spread all the more, and great crowds assembled to listen to him and to be cured of their ailments, but he would withdraw to deserted places to pray" (5:15). Another summary statement emphasizes the power given to Jesus:

> And he came down with them and stood on a stretch of level ground. A great crowd of his disciples and a large number of the people from all Judea and Jerusalem and the coastal region of Tyre and Sidon came to hear him and to be healed of their diseases; and even those who were tormented by unclean spirits were cured. Everyone in the crowd sought to touch him because power came forth from him and healed them (6:17–19).

Jesus commanded authority and displayed it for the benefit of the people who gathered around him. Generally, Luke cleans up the healing stories from his Markan source: he does not like the roughness, crude and dramatic emotionality, and apparently magical way that Mark portrays Jesus's healing miracles, but rather makes Jesus perform his healing miracles with dignity, grace, equanimity, and direct power. Jesus is a proper Roman gentleman-healer.

The author also portrays the hero, Jesus, as a wonder-worker and a divine figure. Romans understood their emperors as "sons of God," divinely inspired and generated leaders, who had divine power at their disposal. The ability to heal and to perform wonders reflects that imperial power. For the author of Luke/Acts, Jesus is no different. The wonder-working Jesus stills the storm that scares the disciples on their boat at sea. After calming the sea and giving them assistance, the disciples respond in this way: "But they were filled with awe and amaze[ment] and said to one another, 'Who then is this, who commands even the winds and the sea, and they obey him?'" (8:25). Jesus commands this power and authority not only because of the power to perform miraculous deeds [like the feeding of five thousand people with five loaves of bread and two fish miraculously multiplied to satisfy a huge crowd (9:10–17)] but because he is a divine man, a divine figure whose "face changed in appearance and his clothing became dazzling white" when he was transfigured on the mountain and spoke with Moses and Elijah (9:28–36). The resurrection stories of Jesus's rising from the dead and appearing to the disciples also confirm his divine status (24:1–49). Jesus displays divine power over and over again in the gospel. He is no regular human being, but one through whom divinity shines brightly.

Such manifestations of divine presence, divine power, and divine authority present a picture of Jesus as a person so imbued with divinity that his life does not follow the course of just any person, but only the course of an extremely important person, a hero like the emperor. These heroic two volumes revel in creating an exciting and intriguing portrait of divine agents who operate in the mundane world, transforming the world in much the same way the Roman Empire transformed the world—and with the same power and authority.

Hero as King and Messiah

In the research materials that the author used, however, Jesus's imperial authority came from a Jewish source: Jesus was a Jewish man in the imperial line of David, and his life and ministry were set by Luke/Acts's sources in Jewish traditions. The author, then, combines and bridges Roman sensibilities with Jewish social and religious traditions. His problem is that this Jewish Messiah suffered in a way that Roman emperors did not. Jesus, then, is a decidedly different kind of emperor. While drawing on Roman imperial traditions, the author has to make the new-style emperor understandable to his Roman audience.

It is important to the author that the audience understand Jesus not only from a Roman perspective, but also from within the Jewish tradition. The author portrays this Jesus, as indicated in the chronology that located the announcement of the birth of Jesus in and around the Temple in Jerusalem, through the eyes of the prophets, those who were understood retroactively to predict that the Messiah needed to suffer and die in order to redeem Israel. Jesus, acting as his own prophet (reflecting the author's interpretation of the Israelite prophets), predicts his own suffering and death. After Peter confesses Jesus as the Christ of God, the Messiah, Jesus proclaims his role in this way: "The Son of Man must suffer greatly and be rejected by the elders, the chief priests, and the scribes, and be killed and on the third day be raised" (9:22). Again after his transfiguration on the mountain when he spoke to Moses and Elijah in the presence of his chief disciples, Jesus attempts to explain his prophetic role to the disciples, whom the author portrays as lacking proper understanding:

> While they were all amazed at his every deed, he said to his disciples, "pay attention to what I am telling you. The Son of Man is to be handed over to men." But they did not understand this saying; its meaning was hidden from them so that they should not understand it, and they were afraid to ask him about this saying (9:43b–45).

Probably just like the audience, the disciples did not understand the necessity of the emperor's betrayal and death. The "meaning was hidden from them"; it was not something familiar to the disciples. It was even more foreign to Greek and Roman readers, who could identify with the reaction of the disciples' confusion.

That understanding, both for the disciples and for the Roman audience, emerges later. The coming of the Holy Spirit at Pentecost, described in the second volume, shows that under the guidance of the Spirit, the disciples finally understood Jesus's prophecy. Peter's first speech on the day of Pentecost displays how the author empowers the disciples' understanding and their capacity to incorporate the prophetic dimension of Jesus's life into their ministry:

> You who are Israelites, hear these words, Jesus the Nazorean was a man commended to you by God with mighty deeds, wonders, and signs, which God worked through him in your midst, as you yourselves know. This man, delivered up by the set plan and foreknowledge of God, you killed, using lawless men to crucify him. But God raised him up, releasing him from the throes of death, because it was impossible for him to be held by it (Acts 2:22–24).

Here the full story of Jesus as hero comes together: mighty acts, wonders, signs, suffering, death, betrayal, and resurrection show Jesus as a divine figure whom death cannot contain because God has foreordained him to do a mighty work among God's people. Roman expressions of power and authority merge with Jewish messianic expectations about the suffering Messiah. The traditions blend almost seamlessly into a new story of the now simultaneously Jewish and Roman Jesus. This is the heroic emperor portrayed by one of his followers as the one whom divine energy enables to do miraculous deeds defying human limitations—patterns of thinking that would appeal to both Romans and Jews.

Hero as Mystagogue

An important way that the author portrays Jesus and his remarkably heroic deeds and teaching is as a mystagogue, a revealer of the hidden mysteries of God. The Roman road to senatorial preferment led through various priesthoods and cultic activities including augury, the ability to reveal the divine plan through reading signs in the sacrificed bodies of animals or in the natural universe. Romans believed in revelation of the hidden mysteries of the gods through physical means. Jews also believed that God revealed God's plan through prophets and priests who attended to the signs God sent to the people. Both Romans and Jews, then, had mystagogues, revealers of the divine plan.

The author of Luke/Acts achieves the characterization of Jesus as a mystagogue in two ways. First, he portrays Jesus's death in the literary tradition of the noble death of the holy and innocent philosopher unjustly put to death. The divine presence in Jesus, as in lives of Roman and Greek philosophers, was read in their manner of death. The story of a person's death, like Socrates's, showed the power and dignity of the philosophical revelation written into the momentous event of a forced death. Both Pontius Pilate and the centurion at the cross attest that Jesus is innocent. Pilate states boldly: "'I find this man not guilty" (Luke 23:4), but he succumbs to the desires of the Jewish authorities to have Jesus killed. And the centurion at the foot of the cross proclaims: "This man was innocent beyond doubt" (23:47). The author may be looking to spare Roman officials the opprobrium of killing Jesus; in that way the Roman readers would not bear the guilt now transferred to the Jewish authorities whom the Romans had conquered by the time Luke/Acts was written. But the author also seems to suggest that this philosophical teacher, this wonder-working mystagogue, suffered injustice nobly and went to his death with serenity and dignity, as any proper Roman philosopher should. Luke/Acts does not portray Jesus as mocked by the soldiers or denigrated in any way, but as a hero completely in command of his own person: at his death "Jesus cried out in a loud voice, 'Father, into your hands I commend my spirit'; and when he had said this he breathed his last" (23:46). This is indeed a description of a noble death by one who controlled his own fate, given him by God, and who retains his authority over himself, his strength, and fortitude, to the very end, when he himself releases his spirit to God without compulsion and without any external interference.

The second way that the author characterizes Jesus as a mystagogue, a revealer of divine mysteries, comes out in the resurrection appearances. Jesus walks with two disciples on the road to Emmaus. They did not recognize him, but poured out their hearts to him about their dejection at the death of Jesus and their confusion about the report of his resurrection. Jesus responds to them with postresurrection instruction:

And [Jesus] said to them: "Oh, how foolish you are! How slow of heart to believe all that the prophets spoke! Was it not necessary that the Messiah should suffer these things and enter into his glory?" Then beginning with Moses and all the prophets, he interpreted to them what referred to him in all the scriptures (24:25–28).

After his resurrection, Jesus becomes a revealer of divine mysteries. The second volume also emphasizes Jesus's role as revealer. Here the author summarizes Jesus's postresurrection life:

> In the first book, Theophilus, I dealt with all that Jesus did and taught until the day he was taken up, after giving instruction through the holy Spirit to the apostles whom he had chosen. He presented himself alive to them by many proofs after he had suffered, appearing to them during forty days and speaking about the kingdom of God (Acts 1:1–3).

The author portrays the resurrected Jesus primarily as a revealer, a mystagogue, and teacher, whose instruction relates not simply to the scriptures and how they referred to Jesus, but also to the reality of his physical and bodily resurrection and to information about the Empire of God. His teaching in Galilee also focused on the teaching about the Empire of God, but now the revelation is one that empowers the apostles to be Jesus's "witnesses in Jerusalem, throughout Judea and Samaria, and to the ends of the earth" (Acts 1:9).

Romans as well as Jews had concepts of the resurrection of the dead, and so these appearances would not have surprised them. After Nero's death, there was an expectation that Nero would return. This is the tradition of Nero *redivivus*, Nero living again, because Nero disappeared and was presumed dead, but no one was really sure. So Romans wrote about the way Nero would return to reestablish his rule once again. In addition to Nero, however, Romans also believed that the ancestors of a household remained part of the household even after death. They were present in the household sanctuaries, the small altars set up in the house where the family would regularly pray. So it would not surprise Romans to hear of a divine figure, a person portrayed as an emperor, returning to life after death to continue his work among his family and friends.

Likewise some Jews also believed in the resurrection of the dead. In Acts, the author reports: "For the Sadducees say that there is no resurrection, or angels or spirits, while the Pharisees acknowledge all three" (23:8). Resurrected bodies and people were part of Jewish tradition, even though some may have doubted it. Some Jews would easily have understood Jesus as a resurrected Jewish mystagogue and also understood the divine power associated with resurrection as part of the revelation of God. The author of Luke/Acts blended the Roman and the Jewish concepts in such a way that Jesus's revelatory power shines, clearly resonating with both traditions and forging new ground for understanding the unique imperial authority of Jesus.

The author of Luke/Acts presents a very sophisticated and complex characterization of Jesus as an imperial hero. He connects Jesus to a long tradition of Israelite leaders, but through the prophetic tradition that describes a suffering and resurrected Messiah. And he describes that suffering Messiah as a powerful, self-controlled, miracle-working philosopher whose noble death attests to the veracity of his teaching and to the integrity of his being. It is a characterization that modeled for his Roman audience the proper way to live as a Roman Christian—dignified, articulate, self-sacrificing, heroically doing the divine work that God has ordained, but always with nobility and strength, with the virtues held dear by the Roman philosophers and the educated Roman public.

Luke/Acts tells a story about Jesus the hero in such a way that different ways of understanding become fused into something new and different. That seems to be the point of these two books: present a history of a new emperor, a new kind of community, a new way of understanding how God operates in the world, and a new way of understanding Roman culture, Jewish religion, and Christian history all at once. That storytelling, however, did more than just describe what happened in the time of Jesus translated now into a Roman context; it also described how the readers then and now need to understand themselves in relationship to that story. In other words, the story is also about the identity of the Christian believer. To that story we now turn.

Narrative Identity: Christianity as a School for Noble Folks

Queer Eye for the Straight Guy fits into a genre of television stories of transformation: rebuilding houses, refurbishing *This Old House*, *The Biggest Loser* on NBC about weight loss, planting gardens, and emptying closets in preparation for a new wardrobe—all these fit into the same genre. These programs all look to transforming people and their life circumstances. One way to understand the transformation is to look at the way a person's identity changes in the program, to listen for the story or narrative that defines what is new and exciting in the life of the person. The genre of programs tells the story of a transformation of a person or a house. The author of Luke/Acts does the same thing, but for a community rather than for individuals. His narrative, starting from the Temple and ending with Paul's preaching in Rome, tells a story about the identity of the Christian people. The author creates a narrative identity for his readers. This is in support of his heuristic purpose in writing.

About Narrative

By narrative identity we mean simply the story, or the narrative, that makes it possible for hearers or readers to understand who they are. As this involves the individual in his or her social context, this is a complex process. It provides answers to the most basic questions: how the community came to be, how it models a way to live in the world, how systems of communal authority connect participants with each other and with their past, and how information is transmitted to future generations. That is, the story that describes the community's current identity, remembers its formation, and insures its future.

Greeks (in Homer's *Iliad* and *Odyssey*), Romans (in such works as Livy's *History* or Vergil's *The Aeneid*), and Jews (in their Torah) were accustomed to using narratives for understanding their communal identity. Moreover, just as some in early twenty-first century America look back to the mid-twentieth century as an ideal time, so in antiquity many lamented the erosion of the "old time, family values." Luke's account of Jesus's philosophical school forming a community of noble men and women enacting a new empire effectively drew on both of these traditions.

The Model of the School

In order to create that narrative of identity, the author needed to look for exemplars, for correlative systems, to explain Christian identity. Readers need to relate to known examples in order to understand something new, something unknown. For these two volumes, the narrative identity creates a Christianity that looks like a philosophical school for noble Romans. The readers would understand philosophical schools, and so that was the starting point for explaining both how Christianity resembled a philosophical school and how it differed from what they knew of these schools. The author portrays Jesus as founding a school with a specific program of preparation, a curriculum of study, and with a succession of teachers. This school exists for the moral and ethical formation of the Roman middle and upper classes.

To understand Jesus's school and its succession in the work of his apostles demands an appreciation for the context in which the author sets the educational mission. The two volumes differ in their subject matter: the first volume focuses on the founding of the school in the teaching and deeds of Jesus in his ministry in Galilee, in his travel to Jerusalem where he will ascend, and in the account of his trial, crucifixion, resurrection, and ascension; the second volume picks up with the apostolic successors of their founder's work and portrays the development and expansion of that school's message to ever-widening audiences in ever-expanding cultural and religious contexts. The progression, then, begins in the story of the origins of the teaching in the life and deeds of Jesus and ends with the preaching by his successors of their founder's resurrection as fulfilling the scriptures, about which Jesus had instructed them.

Jesus's message relates to the explanation of the Empire of God, while the apostles' teaching relates to the living out of an Empire focused on the resurrected Jesus. After their minds were opened by Jesus, at the ascension (Luke) or during the forty days before the ascension (Acts), the apostles teach by opening the scriptures and pointing the way toward understanding the scriptures as directing adherents to a faith in Jesus, who fulfills the scriptures. The apostles succeed Jesus not only as successors to his teaching but also as those continuing to do the miraculous deeds that Jesus performed—by healing the sick, raising the dead, restoring the limbs of the crippled, and exorcising demons. Each of the stories of the apostles' work in Acts seems to follow this pattern of teaching and miracle-working so that the readers and hearers understand that the same power and energy that Jesus had in his lifetime were made manifest by the power of the holy Spirit in his successors.

The School's Curriculum

Luke/Acts presents the educational program in three phases. The educational program consists of a period of preparation, the proclamation of the Empire in word and deed, and the expansion of the program to include all the people of the Roman Empire. John the Baptist's work and teaching constitute the preparatory school. Jesus, as founder of the school, represents the second phase, while the work of the apostles in Acts describes the expansive third phase.

John the Baptist provides the preparation for entry into Jesus's imperial school. The infancy narrative of the beginning of the gospel clearly lays out the important connection between John's and Jesus's births. The narrative interweaves their lives and yokes them in their work. When the author of Luke/Acts presents John's message before Jesus began his public ministry, he describes John's message as one of repentance and the establishment of social justice:

> He said to the crowds who came out to be baptized by him, "You brood of vipers! Who warned you to flee from the coming wrath? Produce good fruits as evidence of your repentance; and do not begin to say to yourselves, 'We have Abraham as our father,' for I tell you, God can raise up children to Abraham from these stones. Even now the ax lies at the root of the trees. Therefore every tree that does not produce good fruit will be cut down and thrown into the fire" (3:7–9).

The repentance, which means literally the modes for changing a person's life, must be evident in transformed living, the bearing of good fruit under the threat of destruction and judgment. Moral reformation of life is the foundation for participation in Jesus's school. This moral reformation is supplemented and made manifest in a person's commitment to social justice. John exhorts:

> And the crowds asked him, "What then should we do?" He said to them in reply, "Whoever has two cloaks should share with the person who has none. And whoever has food should do likewise." Even tax collectors came to be baptized and they said to him, "Teacher, what should we do?" He answered them, "Stop collecting more than what is prescribed." Soldiers also asked him, "And what is it that we should do?" He told them, "Do not practice extortion, do not falsely accuse anyone, and be satisfied with your wages" (3:10–14).

Justice extends to everyone who has any financial resources for clothing and food, and even to tax collectors and soldiers. Justice, fair play, and living a just life in relationship with others prepares the seeker to find and to understand Jesus's message about his Empire. Moral reformation expressed in social justice prepares the student for study in Jesus's school.

Luke makes clear that John functions as preparation and not as the full teaching. When those who had come to be baptized by John ask him if he is the Messiah, the Christ, he answers definitely that he is not. John points to Jesus; the good news, the gospel that John preaches directs attention not to himself but to Jesus:

> Now the people were filled with expectation, and all were asking in their hearts whether John might be the Messiah. John answered them all saying, "I am baptizing you with water, but one mightier than I is coming. I am not worthy to loosen the thongs of his sandals. He will baptize you with the Holy Spirit and fire. His winnowing fan is in his hand to clear his threshing floor and to gather the wheat into his barn, but the chaff he will burn with unquenchable fire." Exhorting them in many other ways, he preached good news to the people (3:15–18).

All these agricultural images (good fruit, bearing fruit, cutting down trees, separating wheat from chaff) refer to the educational process. John, the preschool teacher, points the way toward an education in which the person will bear good fruit through learning, will separate bad learning from good, and be nurtured with the good while the bad is destroyed. The center of the teaching will come through Jesus. John's work is simply to point the way to the true teacher through moral reformation and the commitment to social justice.

After John's preparatory phase, Jesus presents the basic curriculum of the philosophical school he founds. As a transition between the infancy stories and the preparatory ministry of John the Baptist, the author tells a story about the precocious Jesus leaving his parents, who had traveled to Jerusalem for a festival, and engaging with the teachers and elders of the Temple: "After three days [Jesus's parents] found him in the temple, sitting in the midst of the teachers, listening to them and asking questions, and all who heard him were astounded at his understanding and his answers" (2:46–47). Even as a child, Jesus showed his wisdom and intellectual acuity in relationship to elder teachers. By the time he stepped out into his own ministry, the author shows him to be a fully articulate teacher.

Jesus presents a stunning curriculum in the Sermon on the Plain (6:20–49), which clearly establishes the moral and spiritual teaching of Jesus's school. The teaching revolves around a different way of living, just as Roman moral philosophy of the day taught a different way of living through different ways of thinking:

> Blessed are you who are poor, for the kingdom of God is yours. Blessed are you who are now hungry, for you will be satisfied. Blessed are you who are now weep-

ing, for you will laugh. Blessed are you when people hate you, and when they exclude and insult you, and denounce your name as evil on account of the Son of Man. Rejoice and leap for joy on that day! Because your reward will be great in heaven. For their ancestors treated the prophets in the same way (6:20b–23).

This sermon describes the content of the educational program. The program valorizes the poor, the hungry, and the sorrowful while embracing those who are excluded, reviled, and defamed. The Roman virtues of self-sufficiency, entitlement, a good household, good reputation, and public recognition of being a good person would have been the norm, so valorizing the poor and hungry and embracing outcasts would not sound very appetizing to a Roman nobleman. Yet Jesus teaches a new set of values.

Jesus's curriculum comes at a high cost to his audience, and the author makes sure that the audience hears the cost clearly:

But woe to you who are rich, for you have received your consolation. But woe to you who are filled now, for you will be hungry. Woe to you who laugh now, for you will grieve and weep. Woe to you when all speak well of you, for their ancestors treated the false prophets in this way (6:24–26).

The curriculum of Jesus's school demands a high commitment. The author continues to describe Jesus's curriculum in dramatic terms: love enemies (6:27–28); accept being struck by opponents by offering your other cheek for striking or your clothes if they demand them (6:29); treat others as you would be treated (6:31–33); do not expect to be repaid for loans of money that you give (6:34), stop judging other people (6:37–42); for by these the student will be known to be bearing good fruit and constructing a house on rock instead of sand (6:43–49). Jesus's curriculum demands nothing short of a complete change in the understanding of the world and ways of relating to self and others. John the Baptist's preparation in repentance and social justice provides a strong foundation for this complete makeover of traditional Roman virtues inverted.

The author of Luke/Acts presents Jesus as a wandering teacher and wonder-worker, teaching as he goes about his work of healing. All the while that Jesus teaches, he also gathers a community: his companions, his students, including the twelve disciples as well as women whom Jesus had healed and who supported his ministry:

Afterward he journeyed from one town and village to another, preaching and proclaiming the good news [euangelion] of the kingdom of God. Accompanying him were the Twelve and some women who had been cured of evil spirits and infirmities, Mary, called Magdalene, from whom seven demons had gone out, Joanna, the wife of Herod's steward Chuza, Susanna, and many others who provided for them out of their resources (8:1–3).

Jesus walks along the way, heals the sick, teaches through parables and sayings, and then moves to another city. Jesus is a wandering teacher, gathering students and teaching as he travels. The Roman audience would have understood this well. It was a familiar pattern for philosophers trained in the eastern Roman Empire to come to Rome to gather students and to teach. The message, the curriculum, however, would have initially been foreign to a Roman audience.

Methods of Teaching

Jesus frequently uses parables to teach his philosophy. We now hear the parables as familiar stories whose meaning has been honed over many years of interpretation, and they sound flat to us. But parabolic teaching is meant to challenge listeners to think differently, to reflect creatively, to engage with new ways of understanding and experiencing self and world. Many of these parables have parallels in other Roman literature, because teachers often used them as a means of general instruction in the Roman context. Jesus was no different. He used parables to challenge his students and to make them think.

The author of Luke/Acts presents a Jesus who was a master of parable. As Jesus moves toward his ascension in Jerusalem, the author presents him as telling a long string of parables. Chapter 15 in Luke, for example, has a collection of distinctive parables: the lost sheep, the lost coin, the profligate brother; while chapter 16 has the dishonest manager, and the rich man and Lazarus. The author links these parables only lightly with narrative connections between them so that the hearer and reader experience a string of parables for their instruction and reflection. Just a little later in chapter 18, Jesus tells the parables of the widow and the unjust judge, and the Pharisee and the tax collector. The new Empire, the new way of living, demands a new way of thinking and acting. These parables lay out the mind-twisters intended to help people enter the new world.

Also like the teachers of his day, Jesus teaches through maxims, short pithy sayings that encapsulate a moral or spiritual truth. These, too, sound familiar to us today because they have long been taught as the heart of Christian ethical and theological truth: "And I tell you, ask and you will receive; seek and you will find; knock and the door will be opened to you. For everyone who asks, receives; and the one who seeks, finds; and to the one who knocks, the door will be opened" (11:9–10). Many of these maxims come from a collection of sayings of Jesus that were well-known in his day, because Jesus's sayings were collected in the same way that Jews collected the sayings of the rabbis and Romans collected the sayings of wise philosophers. These sayings or maxims defined Jesus's thought and encapsulated his teaching. Sometimes these maxims have been embedded into narrative stories like the accusation that Jesus casts out demons by Beelzebul. Jesus answers with the saying: "Every kingdom divided against itself will be laid waste and house will fall against house. And if Satan is divided against himself, how will his kingdom stand?" (11:17–18). The parables and the maxims together create a complete curriculum for Jesus's school. The curriculum challenges the students to live and think and relate in ways quite different from the traditional ways of Roman living.

In fact, the school of Jesus has become a new kind of household. This is an important point. Jesus's students and followers are not related to each other by blood, but by commitment to the teaching and mission of the school. Jesus metaphorizes this commitment as taking up the cross and following him (11:17–18). His students must hate father, mother, sisters, and life itself (14:25–27), carry the cross and follow Jesus (14:27), taking stock of the cost of that service like a person taking stock of the cost of building a tower (14:28–30) or like a fighter taking stock of what is necessary to fight an enemy in a war (14:31–32). But in all, as in the curriculum, the student must give up all possessions in order to learn what Jesus has to teach (14:33). The student household differs significantly from every other kind of household that Roman citizens might have known.

Sometimes the author shows us precisely how Jesus taught. Jesus's method of teaching was interactive. The story of the dialogue around the parable of the good Samaritan (10:25–37) provides a good example of this teaching method. The teaching begins with instruction to someone who should know better, "a scholar of the law who stood up to test him" by asking about what he should do to inherit eternal life. (10:25–26). Jesus responds with a summary of the Torah combining Deuteronomy 6:5 and Leviticus 19:18: "You shall love the Lord, your God, with all your heart, with all your being, with all your strength, and with all your mind, and your neighbor as yourself" (10:27). But then the scholar "because he wished to justify himself, he said to Jesus, 'And who is my neighbor?'" (10:29). Jesus answers the scholar by telling a parable (10:30–35). This parable describes a victim of a robbery who lands wounded on the side of the road. Three people pass him: two are recognized and respected religious practitioners (the priest and the Levite) and the third represents a person from a despised and rejected branch of the Jewish family (a Samaritan). The two respected people pass by the victim but the Samaritan makes provision for him. Jesus then addresses the scholar who wished to justify himself with this question: "'Which of these three, in your opinion, was neighbor to the robbers' victim?' He answered, 'The one who treated him with mercy'" (10:36–37a). The lesson uses the parable as a means of changing the perspective of the budding student. But it does not end with simply learning a new way of thinking, rather Jesus's lesson demands a change in a way of living. Jesus commands the scholar: "Go and do likewise" (10:37b). This command moves the curriculum from the mind to the body, from intellectual understanding to a way of living. Jesus's method of engagement with others models a way of teaching that moves the student into new understanding that in turn leads to a new way of living.

The Teacher's Successors

The apostles succeed Jesus as the primary teachers in Jesus's school for Romans. All of the philosophical schools of Jesus's day concerned themselves with proper succession, because the authenticity and purity of teaching needed to be grounded in the transfer of knowledge and ways of living from the founder to those the founder empowered to become teachers. The apostles, then, not only continued the teaching, but assured future generations of connection with the person and teaching of the founder, Jesus. The succession of teachers guaranteed a direct connection through them to the source of the teaching in Jesus's words and deeds. The first volume describes how Jesus selected his students who would become his successors. After an evening of prayer, he chooses them:

> In those days he departed to the mountain to pray, and he spent the night in prayer to God. When day came, he called his disciples [students] to himself, and from them he chose Twelve, whom he also called apostles: Simon, whom he named Peter, and his brother Andrew, James, John, Philip, Bartholomew, Matthew, Thomas, James the son of Alphaeus, Simon who was called a Zealot, and Judas son of James, and Judas Iscariot, who became a traitor (6:12–16).

After selecting these twelve in particular to be his closest students and his successors as apostles of the mission, Jesus immediately begins to lay out the curriculum in the Sermon on the Plain (6:17–49), which we discussed above. The successors must know the heart of the inverted Roman virtues that constitute participation in Jesus's school. Jesus's appointment of these twelve to ministry signified their empowerment to be his successors because they were to do exactly the things Jesus did: "He summoned the Twelve and gave them power and authority over all demons and to cure diseases, and he sent them to proclaim the kingdom of God and to heal the sick" (9:1–2).

The Twelve were selected as successors to Jesus as teachers. The Twelve were not, however, the only followers of Jesus empowered to do missionary work. Jesus prepares a group of people, called in the first volume "the seventy-two," for ministry when he turns his face toward Jerusalem and moves toward his ascension:

> After this the Lord appointed seventy-two others whom he sent ahead of him in pairs to every town and place he intended to visit. He said to them, "The harvest is abundant but the laborers are few; so ask the master of the harvest to send out laborers for his harvest. Go on your way; behold, I am sending you like lambs among wolves" (10:1–3).

The instructions to these itinerant missionaries include not making provision for themselves by carrying money, extra clothing, and shoes. They must depend upon the hospitality of those to whom they minister, eating whatever is put in front of them and simply ignoring those who will not receive them. But their mission is clear: "Whatever town you enter and they welcome you, eat what is set before you, cure the sick in it and say to them, 'The kingdom of God is at hand for you'" (10:8–9). The Twelve have similar missionary instructions, but Jesus also appoints them to be his successors, not simply to prepare the way for his teaching by miraculous deeds and the proclamation of the Empire of God.

The author displays the special role of the apostles as successors in the second volume of the work, after Pentecost, the day when the Holy Spirit fell upon them and empowered them for their teaching. The successors have the right to appoint people as successors of Jesus. This is the point of the description of the replacement of Judas, the one of the Twelve who betrayed Jesus, by another disciple, Matthias (Acts 1:15–26). In this story Peter takes the lead in deciding that Judas must be replaced and names the process for succeeding as casting lots. Peter also stipulates the criteria for selection:

> Therefore, it is necessary that one of the men who accompanied us the whole time the Lord Jesus came and went among us, beginning from the baptism of John until the day on which he was taken up from us, become with us a witness to his resurrection (Acts 1:21–22).

The function of the successor involved witnessing to the resurrection as one who had physically accompanied Jesus throughout his life from his baptism until his ascension. Succession in the school of Jesus depends upon specific criteria of accompanying Jesus and witnessing to the resurrection, even though these successors had not received the instruction given to the other successors during the forty days of instruction that the second volume describes.

Like Jesus, the successors not only name new apostles, but they also appoint people for ministry. The story of the appointment of deacons to assist in the ministry, so that the successors might attend solely to their teaching, attests to this:

> So the Twelve called together the community of the disciples and said, "It is not right for us to neglect the word of God to serve at table. Brothers, select from among you seven reputable men, filled with the Spirit and wisdom, whom we shall appoint to this task, whereas we shall devote ourselves to prayer and to the ministry of the word." The proposal was acceptable to the whole community, so they chose Stephen, a man filled with faith and the Holy Spirit, and also Philip, Prochorus, Nicanor, Timon, Parmenas, and Nicholas of Antioch, a convert to Judaism (Acts 6:2–5).

The successors oriented their work to prayer and proclamation, liturgy and teaching, while the new deacons served the needs of the community when they gathered. The restriction of their function to teaching further underscores their empowerment to be teachers in Jesus's school: the Word was their domain, while the deacons provided table service. At the same time, the establishment of the office of deacon suggests the emergence of a Christian *cursus honorum* for the community. Apostle/successors are to attend to the more refined occupations, while the deacons proceed with the day-to-day work of the community.

The author of Luke/Acts presents a compelling story of a philosophical school founded by Jesus and extending into subsequent generations through the apostolic successors who replicated the teaching and deeds of Jesus. Luke/Acts presents not only the basis for preparation to receive instruction in John the Baptist's baptism of repentance and social justice, but also the full flowering of Jesus's teaching—in his ministry in Galilee and during his travel to his ascent in Jerusalem. And this teaching is enacted in the work of his successors in the years following his ascent. The author develops a full educational program for the Roman middle and upper classes, while providing a rich history of that curriculum from its deepest origins in Judaism to its transformation of the Roman Empire by arriving at its capital, Rome.

It is precisely as teachers for Roman nobles that the educational program develops. Jesus and his successors become moral and religious teachers to the Roman nobles and model in word, deed, and story the way that noble Christians should live. The modeling provides instruction on how to attend and provide banquets, to provide hospitality, to trust visions of God that direct human actions, to establish a Christian household, to produce theology based on specific local requirements, and how to make an apology (an explanation) of a Christian's way of life. This modeling completes the school program for the author of Luke/Acts in that it provides specific patterns of behavior and relating for the audience that manifest the transformed religious and moral living of Christian people.

Modeling Behavior: Banquets and Hospitality

In the first volume Jesus models the Christian banquet in a variety of settings. Jesus seems consistently to dine with other people, although some support while others criticize and denigrate his teaching. And yet Jesus continually eats with everyone. The story of Levi (Luke 5:27–32) provides a good example. Levi was a detested tax collector serving a foreign occupier intent on capturing all the wealth of a society. Nevertheless, Jesus calls Levi to follow him. Levi responds fully, leaving everything to follow Jesus. And the story continues:

> Then Levi gave a great banquet for him in his house, and a large crowd of tax collectors and others were at table with them. The Pharisees and their scribes complained to his disciples, saying, "Why do you eat and drink with tax collectors and sinners?" Jesus said to them in reply, "Those who are healthy do not need a

physician, but the sick do. I have not come to call the righteous to repentance but sinners" (5:29–32).

This model establishes that the tables of those who eat with Jesus are opened to anyone who wishes to attend, despite their place in society or the social perception of their value. Both sinners and tax collectors gather at a dinner given by a person called by Jesus to new life. So Levi models the hospitality of a new convert and the inclusive nature of the community.

The banquet model does even more. At a dinner party given for Jesus by a Pharisee (7:36–50), a sinful woman washes Jesus's feet with her tears and anoints them with expensive oil. The presence of this sinful woman causes a stir among the guests who criticize Jesus for allowing her to do this shameful act in their presence. Jesus justifies his acceptance of her salacious action by telling the parable of two debtors, one of whom owed five-hundred Greek coins; the other owed only fifty. The creditor forgave both debts with the greatest thanks given by the person who owed the most. Like ancient Greek and Roman philosophical banquets, the story contains an educational moment upon which Jesus expounds an important part of his teaching. He castigates the host for not washing his feet, anointing them, or showing him the kind of hospitality the woman provided, and he forgave the woman all her sins in order to restore her to dignity in the community. The banquet models such things as eating with enemies, honoring all people, receiving the sinful into the banquet, and teaching in the context of a meal.

Jesus acts similarly at a dinner party given for him by a Pharisee (11:37–41) who takes exception to the fact that Jesus did not wash before eating. This time Jesus responds with a brief instruction about cleanliness: "Oh, you Pharisees! Although you cleanse the outside of the cup and the dish, inside you are filled with plunder and evil. You fools! Did not the maker of the outside also make the inside?" (11:39–40) Such banquet scenes provide models to others about what should be the central point of eating together: to show hospitality, to gather community, and to emphasize the value of the inner person over the apparent person.

Zacchaeus (19:1–10), another tax collector and a rich man, shows the relationship of hospitality to provision for the poor. Jesus invites himself to Zacchaeus's house for dinner where he is criticized again for eating with a sinner, but here Zacchaeus models restitution for past bad behavior by giving away half his possessions and repaying money to those whom he defrauded. Again, the author presents a model of proper behavior for others to imitate in their hospitality and in their effort to manifest just relationships in the world.

Chapter 14 of Luke actually reads like a manual of proper behavior and attitudes at a dinner party. The author leads the chapter with a healing of a man with a withered hand at a dinner party on the Sabbath (14:1–7). Jesus confronts those who criticize him for healing, but he justifies his action with a maxim. Again, eating, healing, and teaching combine in the proper actions for a dinner party. Then Jesus instructs Christians on how to behave at dinner parties. The guests were claiming the better seats and hoping for the better food, so Jesus provides the Christian social etiquette:

> When you are invited by someone to a wedding banquet, do not recline at table in the place of honor. A more distinguished guest than you may have been invited by him, and the host who invited both of you may•approach you and say "Give your place to this man," and then you would proceed with embarrassment to take the lowest place. Rather, when you are invited, go and take the lowest place so that when the host comes to you he may say, "My friend, move up to a higher position." Then you will enjoy the esteem of your companions at the table. For everyone who exalts himself will be humbled, but the one who humbles himself will be exalted (14:7–11).

The question of honor and shame, so important to Roman codes of conduct, becomes the centerpiece for Christian banquet etiquette. The final maxim about being humbled and exalted puts that teaching into a very specific social context in a way that could easily be remembered by hearers. That is the way maxims work, and in this case, the maxim describes social etiquette.

But Jesus also gives instruction in this chapter about who should be invited to dinner parties. This, too, models behavior. Jesus instructs:

> When you hold a lunch or a dinner, do not invite your friends or your brothers or your relatives or your wealthy neighbors, in case they may invite you back and you have repayment. Rather, when you hold a banquet, invite the poor, the crippled, the lame, the blind; blessed indeed will you be because of their inability to repay you. For you will be repaid at the resurrection of the righteous (14:12–14).

These instructions about who constitutes proper dinner guests, together with the expectation that one should not invite in order to receive invitations from others, provide the Christians reading this gospel with important information about how they should live their lives.

The story of Lydia (Acts 16:14–15) models this hospitality and extends it even further with specific details. After hearing Paul preach, she and her household were baptized, and "she offered [Paul and his companions] an invitation: 'If you consider me a believer in the Lord, come and stay at my home,' and she prevailed upon [them]" (Acts 16:15). Not only were they invited to dinner, but they were also invited fully into the household of believers. The community provides not only for the poor, but for the itinerant missionaries and teachers of the faith.

The modeling in Luke/Acts extends further than banquets and hospitality. Acts consistently instructs the readers to trust their visions of God and to act on their direction. Saul's conversion (Acts 9:1–19) provides an important model. "Saul, still breathing murderous threats against the disciples of the Lord," (Acts 9:1) gets official approval (so the writer of Acts would have us believe) to persecute the Christians. While he does this he is struck down and hears Jesus's voice confront him and give him instructions in a vision. Saul obeys the vision. Ananias also has a vision involving Saul. He, too, obeys despite the fact that Ananias has heard about Saul's persecution. He obeys and goes and baptizes Saul who then becomes an apostle of Jesus. The story emphasizes that visions of God, even when they seem incomprehensibly troubling, must be obeyed. The same applied to Peter at Cornelius's household (Acts 10:1–40). Peter has a vision of eating unclean foods, which God pronounces clean. Cornelius has a vision of inviting Peter to his home to teach. Both follow their visions and eventually Peter, despite his observance of the Law and his question about the Gentiles becoming part of the church, baptizes Cornelius's household. Visions are trustworthy, even if they seem difficult to fathom. These stories model people trusting their visions.

Modeling Behavior: Giving an Apology

Finally, the formation of the Roman community also includes modeling of how to give an apology for one's Christian life. An apology for one's life included the important details that explained how a person came to live and think in a particular way. They were common stories in the Roman period and the rhetorical handbooks helped people understand how to put a convincing apology together. In the second volume Paul models how to give an apology (Acts 22:1–21). Paul announces the apology in this way: "My brothers and fathers, listen to what I am about to say to you in my defense." Paul is speaking to the Jewish leaders in Jerusalem to explain his life. His story begins with his own identity as a Jew, a student of Gamaliel, and a man who persecuted the Christians (22:3–5); then he recounts his experience of the light and the voice of Jesus calling him to follow him (22:6–11); the work of Ananias who both healed him of his temporary blindness and baptized him; the story of his return to Jerusalem to testify to his new life, which would not have been easily accepted because of Paul's complicity in the martyrdom of Stephen, the deacon (22:17–21). Paul's apology gets him in trouble with the Jerusalem authorities, who immediately arrest him. This begins the process that will lead to his being taken to Rome as a prisoner to be tried as a Roman citizen for his religious crimes (Acts 22:22–30). So this modeling for giving an apology also models the kind of response a good nobleman should give to the religious persecution that might follow upon living as a Christian in a hostile environment. The manner of giving an account of one's self becomes even more poignant in such a context, so the model carries extra significance and weight in the context of persecution.

The school of Jesus that the author of Luke/Acts develops in his two volumes presents a very sophisticated system for preparation through repentance and the establishment of justice. Luke/Acts also develops a very complex and challenging curriculum for the school—one that is at once taught by Jesus, encapsulated in his miraculous deeds, and portrayed through his actions and words. The curriculum revolves about the memorization of maxims and the exploration of the meaning of parables in order to bring followers to new ways of thinking and living. But the school did not end with Jesus's ascension, because Jesus empowered his closest followers as apostles and successors of the school's teaching. The curriculum, now lived out and expanded by the apostles who replicate Jesus's teaching and his miraculous deeds, models for future generations the way noble Christians should live. It provides the model for the new Christian empire. It provides guidelines for hospitality, for church organization and church offices, for attending and holding banquets, for testing visions, and for giving an account of one's self before persecuting authorities. This is a very sophisticated curriculum indeed, one meant to nourish church life for many generations to come in the Roman Empire, which was seen as the place for Christian expansion and growth. Like the stories of the transformation of the straight guy, the author tells the story of transformation by describing the education and formation necessary to be a follower of Jesus.

The Christian Story as Utopia for the Training of Romans

When we watch *Queer Eye* we know that the transformation applies only to the straight guy who becomes an elegant person through the efforts of the queer guides. But somehow in the process, the viewers gain insight into themselves. The story of the straight guy's transformation becomes a story about the potential for any person to live an elegant life. The transformation has a kind of universal appeal or a general application that describes the possibilities for anyone to achieve that elegant stature. The *Queer Eye* show presents a utopian picture of social transformation. The utopian vision of transformation comes through a specific teaching moment, which functions as a kind of heuristic device that reveals the possibilities for any of us viewers.

We have emphasized the heuristic thrust of these two volumes in the New Testament: they clearly intend to develop a different way of understanding and teaching about Jesus and the church. The two volumes instruct about Jesus's origins, ministry, deeds, and teaching, and they place Jesus in the context of an explanation of the history of apostolic Christianity as it was lived out in the earliest years. The author tells the recipient of these volumes, Theophilus (literally, "Friend of God"), that he has written the books in order to confirm what he has been already taught. The heuristic purpose of the volumes stands out.

Another way of treating this heuristic emphasis is to look at how the author tells the Christian story by presenting it as a utopia. A utopia is an idealized and imaginary place or state, a kind of vision imagining the way things ought to be. Utopias generally do not describe how things actually exist, but how they *ought* to exist in an ideal world. At a number of points in these two volumes, the author presents a highly idealized perspective on the school of Jesus and the work of the successors in the church. That idealization certainly applies to the modeling that takes place in the stories and teaching of Jesus and the apostles, and it is consistent with the aims to portray a full history of the movement. But those portrayals of people and actions have a utopian quality to them, and these two volumes cannot be fully understood apart from understanding their utopian orientation. It is to that utopia that we now turn our attention.

Perhaps the first place to start to analyze the utopian quality of Jesus's message emerges from a different sort of reading of the Sermon on the Plain (Luke 6:17–49). We have already dealt with this sermon as a foundation for the curriculum of Jesus's school. It is an important part of that foundation. As you recall, the Sermon on the Plain valorizes the poor, the sorrowful, the hungry and persecuted, promotes love of neighbor, and the treating of others as one would want to be treated by them. Earlier, we emphasized that these values seem to undercut traditional Roman values of self-sufficiency, praise by colleagues, honor, and entitlement. With so stark a contrast with Roman values, the Sermon on the Plain presents an idealized view of Christian virtue. What makes it an idealized presentation, a utopia, is the way it is gathered into one place, presented as a full speech by Jesus. The conglomeration of teaching makes the entire speech sound too good to be true, too demanding to be readily implemented, and too difficult for the average person. That is what the author wants to portray. This ethical system is the ideal to which Christians aspire, even if they do not actually live it out yet day by day. It is a utopian view.

The utopian agenda becomes even clearer in the second volume, Acts of the Apostles. The description of the day of Pentecost (Acts 2:37–47) resonates with idealized responses. Peter, acting like a classically trained noble, delivers an oration in which he defends the Spirit-filled Jesus-people not as people who are drunk with alcohol "for it is only nine o'clock in the morning," but as people upon whom God has sent the Spirit as the prophet Joel predicted God would do one day (2:16–21). Like a good lawyer, Peter cites as evidence the prophecies of such a phenomenon (2:18–21). Then Peter proclaims the resurrection of Jesus from the dead whom "God raised . . . up, releasing him from the throes of death, because it was impossible for him to be held by it" (2:22–24), which Peter argues even the patriarch David foresaw (2:25–35). Peter concludes his sermon with this: "Therefore let the whole house of Israel know for certain that God has made him both Lord and Messiah, this Jesus whom you crucified" (2:36). Peter's oration upbraids the Israelites for killing Jesus—not exactly the best way to win them over to a new faith. The accusation, reaching back into Israelite traditions, presents an apology for the authority of the newly empowered successors of Jesus.

The utopian quality of the story continues with the responses from the crowd. Rather than being angry at Peter's condemnation and accusation, they respond positively with a unified voice and want to join Peter and his religious confreres:

> Now when they heard this [sermon], they were cut to the heart, and they asked Peter and the other apostles: "What are we to do, my brothers?" Peter [said] to them, "Repent and be baptized, every one of you, in the name of Jesus Christ for the forgiveness of your sins; and you will receive the gift of the Holy Spirit. For the promise is made to you and to your children and to all those far off, whomever the Lord our God will call." He testified with many other arguments, and was exhorting them, "Save yourselves from this corrupt generation" (2:37–40).

Peter presents them with the preliminary instruction given by John the Baptist: repent, be baptized, change the way you live, and the Holy Spirit will be given to you through Jesus. The response is simply spectacular: "Those who accepted his message were baptized, and about three thousand persons were added that day" (2:41). That is a remarkably successful oration, a response that any politician or preacher then or now would really cherish. To convert three thousand with one accusatory speech overdramatizes the success of the speech. The story is idealized and portrays responses that only happen in a utopian context.

That utopian context continues in the response of those baptized that day: "They devoted themselves to the teaching of the apostles and to the communal life, to the breaking of the bread and to the prayers" (2:42). These early believers, these new converts, immediately respond by four actions: attention to the teaching of the apostles; entering intensely into a kind of communal living that results immediately from conversion; the celebration of the Eucharist, although they have not yet heard about it in the story; and a practice of prayer. The dramatic response to the sermon leads to an even more dramatic reformation of lifestyle for these new converts, as the utopian vision is even further spelled out:

> Awe came upon everyone, and many wonders and signs were done through the apostles. All who believed were together and had all things in common; they would sell their property and possessions and divide them among all according to each one's need. Every day they devoted themselves to meeting together in the temple area and to breaking bread in their homes. They ate their meals with exultation and sincerity of heart, praising God and enjoying favor with all the people. And every day the Lord added to their number those who were being saved (2:42–47).

Now the utopian agenda has been fully articulated. The community became the center of each one's financial life by sharing goods according to need and not according to status or wealth as one would expect in the Roman context. Their Christian commune, founded upon the sale of all their possessions and the adoption of a common life, centered upon prayer, eating meals together, celebrating the Eucharist ("the breaking of bread") and adding new members. Although there may have been pockets of early followers of Jesus who lived this way, certainly not everyone did. The author of Luke/Acts sets this utopia as an ideal, a goal toward which the followers of Jesus were to aspire.

The author fills out that utopia when he describes the life of the first converts to the faith:

> The community of believers was of one heart and mind, and no one claimed that any of his possessions was his own, but they had everything in common. With great power the apostles bore witness to the resurrection of the Lord Jesus, and great favor was accorded them all. There was no needy person among them, for those who owned property or houses would sell them, bring the proceeds of the sale, and put them at the feet of the apostles, and they were distributed to each according to need (4:32–35).

This utopia brings forward all the best of the Roman philosophical tradition. The early Christians live the Stoic virtue of harmony, being of one mind and heart as a corporate entity. They live and eat together like the Epicurean philosophical communities, living a communal life enabled by the sharing of resources. Like Cynics, these followers sell their houses to support the community; they become homeless like the earliest itinerant followers of Jesus. These kinds of details make the Christian community the ideal philosophical community for Romans. But it is indeed an idealized picture, one found only in these two volumes.

Again, the point of the utopian vision is to create an ideal that others can follow. It creates a community for imitation. The utopia models behavior in the same way that Jesus modeled various behaviors and in the way that the apostles modeled themselves on Jesus. The utopia, thus, serves the educational modality of these two volumes: it instructs in concrete and specific ways about how Christians ought to live. This is like the queer guys in *Queer Eye*, who also create an idealized and utopian situation in which a dorky straight guy suddenly becomes a suave and savvy sophisticate.

Conclusion: Training a Roman Nobility

The two-volume work, the Gospel of Luke and Acts of the Apostles, presents itself as a long work intended to train Romans in the proper way to live the Christian life. These volumes describe a life under a new emperor, Jesus, living in a new empire called the Empire of God. The new Empire succeeds the Roman Empire, if it does not take it over with its redefinition of communal living. The educational agenda of these volumes is clear: it presents a clearly articulated, if idealized, curriculum for those who will live in this Empire; it models how that curriculum should be lived out; and it shows how the school can progress into the future. The training these volumes provide leads Romans through an examination of their familiar way of living and thinking to a new life that inverts the familiar and leads them to another Empire: where the poor are fed, where honor is not related to wealth or status, where shame is embraced and valued, where property is held in common by all, where all opinions and thoughts are united within the community. Gradually through story after story in these two long volumes, the details of this new life emerge very graphically and it is articulately portrayed in language, image, and concept that Romans would immediately understand, even if it confounded them. Like *Queer Eye for the Straight Guy*, the author of Luke/Acts has so thoroughly transformed the story that what started as a religion organized around the death of a Roman criminal became instead a story of a new Roman Empire founded by a new emperor. Now that's a real transformation!

Questions for Discussion

1. Watch the musical "Fiddler on the Roof" and write a one-page summary of the plot, but translate it into some other culture or religion as the frame. What problems did you encounter in translating from one religious culture to another? What elements were simply too embedded in a religious environment to translate? What were the problems you encountered? Why were they problems?

2. Write a two-page utopian vision of your religious community. What makes your description utopian? How does the utopian description differ from the reality of your religious community's day-to-day living? What realities about living in your religious community needed to be suppressed to create the utopian description?

3. Consider the context of a modern college student. What training does a student need to be successful as a student? What formative practices do modern colleges or universities teach their students? How do the formative practices differ from class to class (history, philosophy, religion, mathematics, biology, zoology, etc.)?

Resources for Further Study

It is a relatively recent phenomenon to study the Gospel of Luke and Acts of the Apostles together as a single work in two volumes. Most scholars write commentaries on either the gospel or on the apostolic acts. Among those few writing about the full two-volume work, see Clare K. Rothschild, *Luke-Acts and the*

Rhetoric of History: An Investigation of Early Christian Historiography (Tubingen: Mohr Siebeck, 2004), and Donald Juel, *Luke-Acts: the Promise of History* (Atlanta: John Knox Press, 1983), as well as the essays collected in *Luke-Acts: New Perspectives from the Society of Biblical Literature Seminar*, ed. Charles H. Talbert (New York: Crossroad, 1984). On the specific question of the use of the Israelite scriptures in Luke/Acts, see Craig A. Evans and James A. Sanders, *Luke and Scripture: the Function of Sacred Tradition in Luke-Acts* (Minneapolis: Fortress, 1993). On the narrative in Luke/Acts, see Todd C. Penner and Carolie Vander Stichele, *Contextualizing Acts: Lukan Narrative and Greco-Roman Discourse* (Atlanta: Society for Biblical Literature, 2003). A classic 1929 study of Luke/Acts has recently been reprinted: Henry Cadbury, *The Making of Luke-Acts* (Peabody, Mass.: Hendrickson, 1999).

Commentaries on each of the volumes abound. On Luke, consult Francois Bovon, *Luke 1: A Commentary on the Gospel of Luke 1:1-9:50, Hermeneia Series* (Minneapolis: Fortress, 2002); David Tiede, *Luke* (Minneapolis: Augsburg, 1988); Luke Timothy Johnson, *Luke, Sacra Pagina Series* (Collegeville, Minn.: Liturgical Press, 1991); and Judith Lieu, *The Gospel of Luke* (London: Epworth, 1997). Each of these provides a very different perspective on the gospel.

For Acts of the Apostles, consult Hans Conzelmann, *Acts of the Apostles: A Commentary on Acts of the Apostles, Hermeneia Series* (Philadelphia: Fortress, 1977); Richard Pervo, *Acts of the Apostles, Hermeneia Series* (Minneapolis: Fortress, 2009); and Luke Timothy Johnson, *Acts of the Apostles, Sacra Pagina Series* (Collegeville, Minn.: Liturgical Press, 2006).

CHAPTER EIGHT

Portal to the Gospel of John: Wandering Prophets and Homebody Bishops

Early one Sunday as the light of the sun began to dissipate the brightness of the morning star, a scruffy short woman dressed in a dirty tunic and very worn sandals suddenly entered. The people of Delphia gazed intently at her. Lydia, their leader, reminded the community that "Everyone who comes in the name of the Lord should be welcomed." They greeted the stranger as one of their own: "Blessed is she who comes in the name of the Lord." The woman stood and silently looked into each of their faces. Her gentle voice broke the silence and with great clarity she spoke: "Let the children come to me, for they hear the voice and gain entrance into the empire." Immediately they recognized the words of the Lord and embraced her as a holy woman. They washed her feet, and continued chanting their morning prayers.

As they prepared the thanksgiving meal, the holy woman abruptly spoke: "Children, have you not already been fed?" The preparations immediately ceased. Lydia responded, "Lord, we have fasted as our tradition demands, but we have not given thanks in the holy meal." The holy woman responded, "The true bread of God is the bread that comes down from heaven, and gives life to the world. This has already descended on the table. It is not the manna of your ancestors for they have all died." Another person protested, "Lord, must we now forget our ancestors? Are we not adopted children of Adam, Abraham, Moses, and all the prophets?" The holy woman said: "I am the true vine, and my Father is the vinedresser. Every branch of mine that bears no fruit, he takes away, and every branch that does bear fruit he prunes, that it may bear more fruit." And yet another cried out, "In your words I hear the voice of the Lord."

Recognizing this holy woman as the voice of the Lord, many among them spoke at once, "Lord, we are the branches of the holy vine of David made known to us in Jesus your child!" Several of them immediately rose and obeyed the community rule: "Every true prophet deserves the first portion of the produce from the wine vat and the threshing floor, and the first portion of cattle and sheep, for the true prophets are your high priests." They laid them at her feet.

A controversy arose among them. One of the elders of the community protested, "Children, the prophet has only recently arrived. Why are you so quick to be offering?" Another well-respected elder said, "We should elect for ourselves deacons and bishops who are worthy of the Lord to carry out the ministry of these prophets." Many were disturbed by these suggestions. Another elder suggested, "We should take these first portions and sell them so the money can be distributed among the poor." The holy woman said, "The poor you always have with you, but you do not always have me."

The next day several of them, eager to engage with the bearer of the Lord's words, asked the holy woman, "Lord, according to our custom, you can offer a thanksgiving meal whenever you please. Will you feed us today?" Another brought forth a revelation holy in their community, "We do not labor for the food that perishes. We seek the food that endures to eternal life." Another recalled what another prophet had told them, "Our fathers and mothers ate the manna in the wilderness as it is written, and we know that it was not Moses who gave us the bread, but our Father in heaven." The holy woman responded, "I am the bread of life; those who come to me shall not hunger, and those believing in me shall not thirst." They all spoke, "Lord, give us this bread always!" The holy woman said, "All who see and hear the messenger of God and believe shall have eternal life; and I will raise them up at the last day."

Seeing their faith, the holy woman poured water in a basin. She girded herself with a towel and washed their feet saying to each one, "Out of his heart shall flow rivers of living water. For the sheep hear my voice, and I will call each of my sheep by name and lead them. For the sheep know my voice and do not know the voice of strangers."

The holy woman then tightened her tunic, fastened her sandals, and began to walk the road out of Delphia. They wanted to know her name. One of them asked boldly, "Lord, if we do not know your name, how will your words abide with us? How will we remain in them?" The holy woman kept on walking silently and then said, "You may call me Phoebe, voice of the Lord. You may call me other things, 'Way,' 'Light,' 'Good Shepherd,' 'The Gate,' but my name is Phoebe." She walked upon the road that led to the neighboring town, Philadelphia, the holy woman's original destination.

This imaginary portrayal from the *Didache* (*The Teaching of the Twelve Apostles*, probably written sometime around 90 CE) describes a community's response to the arrival of a wandering, itinerant prophet who carries the words of the Lord to Christian communities as she travels. The story poses some interesting questions for us to consider for our reading of the Gospel of John—questions about the way community structures developed, the systems for spreading the oracles or sayings of the Lord, the challenges and conflicts around the structuring of authority (with bishops and deacons taking on the function of wandering prophets and teachers), and the diverse liturgical and sacramental practices of the earliest Christians.

It is important to understand power and authority. Power and authority created tension and conflict in the early Christian communities. The community of John discerned the issues of power and authority by listening to the prophets who were revealers of the presence of the Lord and who brought Jesus's voice to bear upon their community's conflict and tension, as they tried to live as children of God.

The Dilemma of the Bishops and the Gospels

In our other portals, we emphasized the Roman and Jewish context of the various gospels, but to understand the Gospel of John we must turn to the state of gospel literature at the end of the second century. It was then that the bishops of the church turned their attention to the canon of the New Testament, to establish which texts were to be authorized and acceptable books for Christian teaching and for Christian believers to read. The state of the gospels reflects the conflicts and divisions that our imaginative portrayal of the *Didache* displays: the gospels were caught in the crossfire of continuing revelation and the teaching of the bishops who were understood by some to have replaced these charismatic, wandering revealers of the words of Jesus. For the bishops of the later second century, continuing revelation of a resurrected Jesus speaking directly to a community marked the believers as Gnostics, those Christians who relied upon *gnosis* or secret and esoterically revealed knowledge to found their faith. The conflict between revelation and church authority became the central problem of defining orthodoxy, the correct and approved teaching of the bishops of the church.

The background to that conflict is important. From our perspective two gospels stand out as the most creative and significant achievements in the history of gospel literature: the Gospel of Mark and the Gospel of John. In their times, these two gospels broke new ground and set a new path for the entire church. Mark and John were seismic shifts in Christian life. The Gospel of Mark, as we have said, created the biography of Jesus that permanently moved the orientation of Christianity away from the Empire of God that Jesus preached to the person of Jesus himself. Even though Mark's gospel dissimulates, the story of Jesus, the rural, itinerant, Jewish preacher who went to Jerusalem and was crucified as Emperor of the Jews remained the primary lens through which Jesus would be seen from then on. Matthew and Luke extend that story into different contexts. They, too, were creative in their extension of the gospel, but they did not in the end change the story nor the way the church lived its life. Mark wrote the story; Matthew and Luke/Acts wrote the sequels.

When John's gospel comes on the scene, we see the other seismic shift in gospel literature. John knows the Markan story, but chose not to follow it exactly. John knows the way Matthew and Luke used the sayings of Jesus, but does not believe that the collections of sayings exhausted the reality of Jesus. In other words, John's gospel presents a Jesus who is alive, resurrected, continuing to speak to the church in revelation discourses, and fully present to later generations of Christians. To many bishops, John's gospel sounded Gnostic. In fact the first commentators on the Gospel of John were second-century Gnostic Christians who found the revelation discourses in the gospel consistent with their understanding of the continuing revelation of Jesus. John's gospel stopped the trajectory that Mark initiated for the church, the trajectory that marks the sequence of authority promulgated by the bishops: Jesus, to the disciples, to the apostles, and ending in the authority of bishops. The bishops took advantage of the fluid meaning and referent of such terms as "disciple" and "apostle" in the gospel literature to frame this trajectory to substantiate their role and authority in the church. This trajectory was the one based upon the central role of Peter as the founder of the sequence. Matthew remembers Jesus's bold statement: "You are Peter, and upon this rock I will build my church" (Matthew 16:18). John's gospel insisted upon the reality of a living Jesus in the midst of a community eager to engage with a living God. So Mark as the first canonical gospel and John as the last propelled the church into new and creative directions.

The problem for the bishops, however, was that the theology of the Gospel of John formed the glue to orthodox belief, while at the same time presenting some troubling concepts. This was a dilemma. The bishops needed John's direct statement that Jesus was the Word and God: "In the beginning was the Word, and the Word was with God, and the Word was God" (John 1:1), as well as the strong affirmation of the incarnation, the fact that Jesus "became flesh and dwelled among us" (John 1:14). They also needed the eucharistic theology of the Bread of Life discourse (John 6) to explain the sacrament of the Body and Blood of Christ as it was made available to the church under the direction of the bishops. John's gospel provided the theological frame through which all the other gospels were read and interpreted, and without it the theological structure of emerging orthodox belief and teaching could not stand. At the same time that the bishops needed John to develop emerging orthodoxy, they were troubled by John's disavowal of ecclesiastical authority, by John's opening of revelation to simple believers, by the sense that God had other communities to which God spoke, and by the pervasive voice of Jesus that all may hear without mediation. This was the dilemma: the bishops needed John for orthodox theology, but John's gospel sounded dangerously Gnostic and was thus a threat to their authority.

The solution to the dilemma was first addressed by Irenaeus, Bishop of Lyons. Around 180 CE, Irenaeus wrote *The Refutation and Overthrow of Knowledge Falsely So Called* (known also by its Latin title, *Adversus Haereses*, "Against Heresies"); it was an extensive treatise to combat Gnosticism in the church, a Gnosticism that was at once very popular and very well developed theologically. Irenaeus saw in fully developed Gnosticism the effect of the Johannine theology of continuing revelation, but at the same time he needed the doctrines of the divinity of Jesus, the incarnation, and the transformation of the flesh into God that the discourse on the Bread of Life made possible in order to create a theological frame for orthodox interpretation of scripture, orthodox practice and sacraments, as well as orthodox belief about Jesus.

Irenaeus's solution to the dilemma is a particularly interesting one. He circumvented all the theological and ecclesiastical problems and argued for the inclusion of John's gospel in the canon of the New Testament on the basis of the significance of the number four. If it sounds strange, it is. Listen to Irenaeus:

> It is not possible that the Gospels can be either more or fewer in number than they are. For, since there are four zones of the world in which we live, and four principal winds, while the Church is scattered throughout all the world, and the "pillar and ground" of the Church is the Gospel and the spirit of life; it is fitting that she should have four pillars, breathing out immortality on every side, and vivifying men afresh. From which fact, it is evident that the Word, the Artificer of all, He that sitteth upon the cherubim, and contains all things, He who was manifested to men, has given us the Gospel under four aspects, but bound together by one Spirit (*Adv. Haer.*, III.11.8).

Irenaeus clung to John's theology of Jesus, the Word who created all things, and justified the inclusion of this gospel among the others on the peculiar basis of the significance of the number four. The dilemma is solved. From that point forward, the church could use and read the Gospel of John as the frame to the story that Mark created, and that combination became the foundation of emerging orthodoxy. John's gospel indeed had seismic effects upon the church.

The Story of Early Christian Communities

Irenaeus's dilemma about the Gospel of John and the construction of a frame for orthodox theology was also based on the construction of a story about Christian origins. Early Christian communities with their distinctive understandings of the life and ministry of Jesus organized themselves in many diverse ways. Sociologists tell us that at the beginning of many religious movements, communities gather around charismatic leaders who have power and authority to speak on behalf of God. Jesus was certainly one such charismatic figure, but so were Paul, other apostles, and many prophets. In a short time later, we also find communities gathering around hierarchal leaders. Here we include bishops, presbyters, and the later apostolic leaders who claim lineage going back to Jesus and from whom they gain their power and authority. The *Didache*, a document presenting church teachings about sacraments and church leadership written around the beginning of the second century, seems to fall in the middle of this spectrum of charismatic leaders on one side and hierarchal leaders on the other. It includes both charismatic itinerants and bishops. It is important to think about this spectrum of community organization because the Gospel of John works with it in a very interesting way.

Early Christianity was both complex and diverse. Most of us have heard a story of the way the church grew from Jesus, through the disciples at Pentecost when the Holy Spirit empowered them to mission, and into structures of the church with the same kind of bishops and deacons we see in some churches today. But that story was written later, when bishops and presbyters (priests) held the greatest power. There is much more to the story than this. Christian leadership came in many forms. Paul speaks of prophets, apostles, teachers, speakers in tongues, and interpreters. The gospels themselves describe faithful women followers of Jesus, disciples, the Twelve, and the seventy-two who were sent out on mission by Jesus. Even among apostles there were distinctions. Some apostles, like Peter or James, knew Jesus in his lifetime. Most apostles, like Paul and the other apostles in his communities, were empowered and authorized by revelation or by a vision of Jesus. In the earliest days there were probably more leaders like Paul—charismatic, prophetic, and itinerant—who gathered new Christian communities around them. In later days there were probably more leaders like Peter and James—hierarchal, authoritative, and stable—who gave a coherent structure to Christian communities.

The community structure developed in our imaginary scenario with the wandering prophet and the communal body led by Lydia is an attempt to piece together a picture of communal living from the tidbits of evidence left by one of our earliest sources. Texts like the *Didache*, Paul's letters, the gospels, the Acts of the Apostles, official letters from both Christians and devotees of Roman religion, describe a very diverse set of community organizations and theologies. When all these sources are taken together, we find that earliest Christianity is very diverse in social organization, religious practice and beliefs, systems of connection with other Christians, and awareness of other forms of Christianity.

So where did all this diversity come from? Let's start at the very beginning. The gospels portray Jesus as a seriously multitasking, divinely multitalented person: a healer, a gifted rhetorician, a philosopher, a master storyteller, a creator of parables, a naturalist, a miracle worker, a wandering poet, a disciplined person of prayer, and a trusted companion. What a complex person Jesus was! But he thrived on connecting with people, and this is his most influential trait: gathering community at meals, prayer, discourse, theological debate, religious feasts, and celebrations, to witness to and participate in healing, and to prepare for mission. The Acts of the Apostles and other Christian literature suggest that these religious works did not stop with Jesus. Jesus empowered his followers to create the Empire as he did. The followers (both those who knew Jesus directly as well as those who knew him through various revelations) healed, proclaimed the good news of the Empire that Jesus proclaimed, gathered community, observed feasts and celebrations, engaged in divine discourse, and did many other things that Jesus did because Jesus gave them the power to do these things.

Wandering Prophets and Local Communities

In looking at the early Jesus movements, something very interesting emerges. All of the things Jesus and his followers did had two important sets of players: a wandering revealer of God's ways who carried the message to others and a stable community that provided hospitality and received the revealer. The story of Lydia, the children, the elders, and the wandering prophet shows how this mission to communities continues the style of ministry from Jesus's own time. Christianity grew out of these wandering missionaries and soon spread into large, organically connected networks of communities. These stable communities developed various roles of authority reflecting their theology, values, organization, and practices. Some stable communities remained charismatic, as evident in Paul's letters. Some communities began to elect from among their own members bishops and deacons to perform the ministry previously done by the wandering teacher or prophet; this allowed the community to partake of certain rituals or healings on a more regular basis. Still other stable communities seem to have developed as communities of prophets. Some communities organized themselves around ritual purity, others around practices, others as schools of learning, and still others around specific books like gospels. But the wandering prophets continued to perform their ministry among all of these various kinds of communities.

The work of the wandering prophet was simply to generate a word from the Lord for a community and to carry the words of the Lord generated in one community to another. From the time of Jesus onward, prophets produced and transmitted the words of the Lord as revealers who gave audible voice to God's words to local communities wherever they went. God used their voices to reveal God's plan for a new Empire. In fact the only way God's voice could be known was through the voice of the wandering prophet. And the stable communities paid attention to them. All the canonical gospels describe the ministry or mission of Jesus and the early church as beginning with itinerancy. This element carried over into much of early Christian literature which often resembles travelogues of mission and provide descriptions both of Jesus, a wandering prophetic voice proclaiming the Empire of God, as well as the others Jesus sends out on mission. This story of Christian origins helps to explain how stable communities grew out of the missions of itinerant prophets.

Community Organization: *Koinonia*

How these communities chose to organize themselves is another interesting question. Relationship founds every kind of social engagement, and the Greek word that designates a wide assortment of relationships is *koinonia*, which signifies intimate social connection. Lydia and her community exemplified the concept of *koinonia*. Their hospitality demanded that they accept into their community all outside wanderers as potential teachers and that they urge the wanderers to participate in their fellowship. That full participation in their own thanksgiving meal was at once a communion with God and with each other, a mutual inscribing of the community upon God and God upon the community as intimate partners.

Koinonia in a general sense refers to a variety of social relationships between individuals and communities in the ancient world. In the commercial world, *koinonia* denoted a sharing, a holding of common interests, and a participation in a variety of business relationships. On a personal level, the relationships were described as companion, partner, and friend, but with an emphasis on being extremely intimate, because the word also denotes sexual union between people as well as intimate communion with divine beings. And so *koinonia* connoted even more complex social relationships. A *koinonia* community signified a strong solidarity and agreement between all the participants, both human and divine. This suggested that the members maintain strong intimate connections among themselves, with their divinities, and with other communities. A reciprocal and supportive relationship sustains the community and maintains a high degree of honor toward all the participants. For Christians the apostle Paul's mission to found and connect communities best exemplifies *koinonia*.

Paul understood the church as the Body of Christ, so that each person participates in this body according to the gifts given the person by the holy Spirit (1 Corinthians 12:11–13). This complex participation defines *koinonia* for Paul as a wonderfully articulated set of relationships that seek unity both within the local community and between communities of believers. Paul frequently refers in his letters to his collection for the poor in Jerusalem and in Romans 15:26 writes that he is taking a contribution from the churches in Achaia and Macedonia to assist the saints in Jerusalem. For Paul, a significant way to connect with others, to share in their lives, to have *koinonia*, required physical and monetary support for members of the community in poverty or need. Paul envisioned communities forming one body by this kind of supportive connection. But Paul also indicates that through the practice of *diakonia*, or table service to the community at their gatherings as well as ministration to the poor, one may experience participation or *koinonia* (2 Corinthians 8:4). *Diakonia* creates *koinonia* closer to home; the support does not need to be at a distance or only monetary: it can also consist of direct service and table ministration to the poor at home and to other members of the local Body of Christ. One dimension of *koinonia*, then, relates to physical support and nurture.

For Paul, however, *koinonia* means much more. *Koinonia* is not just among humans, but also includes God. For Paul, *koinonia* includes participation with God through Jesus and the holy Spirit. In 1 Corinthians 1:9, Paul calls the people into full participation in the life of Christ. The supreme act of participation in God is the receiving of communion: "the cup of blessing we bless, is it not a participation in the blood of Christ; the bread we break, is it not a participation in the body of Christ?" (1 Corinthians 10:16). Another way for Paul to have people participate in the life of Christ is through sharing in the sufferings of Jesus: "to know him and the power of his resurrection and the sharing of his sufferings by being conformed to his death" (Philippians 3:10). A Pauline believer also participates in God through the holy Spirit, and the evidence for that participation in God is unity and harmony: "If there is any encouragement in Christ, any solace in love, any participation in the Spirit, any compassion and mercy, complete my joy by being of the same mind with the same love, united in heart, thinking one thing" (Philippians 2:1–2). And in 2 Corinthians 13:13, Paul, in a final blessing to the community, honors their fellowship with the holy Spirit: "The grace of the Lord Jesus Christ and the love of God and the fellowship of the holy Spirit be with all of you." Human beings connect with God by sacraments, by suffering with Jesus, and by participating in the Holy Spirit that knits together the community in unity and harmony. Human beings and God meet in the *koinonia* for support, life, and personal as well as corporate transformation.

Koinonia, however, has its darker side as well. Participation also restricts engagement. In 2 Corinthians 6:14–18 Paul strongly cautions his community not to associate with people outside their community of faith. He urges them to withdraw and separate from having any relationships or partnerships with those outside the immediate community. *Koinonia* here defines the acceptable and unacceptable connections for members of the community.

Another New Testament writing closely allied to the Gospel of John, 1 John 1:3 gives the clear directions upon which *koinonia* may exist: "what we have seen and heard we proclaim now to you, so that you too may have fellowship [*koinonia*] with us; for our fellowship [*koinonia*] is with the Father and with his

Son, Jesus Christ." The author continues in 2 John 1:7–9 to show agreement about the interpretation and understanding of the person and work of Jesus:

> Many deceivers have gone out into the world, those who do not acknowledge Jesus Christ as coming in the flesh; such is the deceitful one and the antichrist. Look to yourselves that you do not lose what we worked for but may receive a full recompense. Anyone who is so "progressive" as not to remain in the teaching of the Christ does not have God; whoever remains in the teaching has the Father and the Son.

This letter warns readers to restrict relationships and associations to only those who are found worthy or believe the same things. *Koinonia* in the ancient world is serious. With whom one associates communicates both solidarity and hostility between communities. One finds community depending on the *koinonia* that they share.

Koinonia can also be simply something practical, because it refers also to basic business relationships. Business affairs of the church have a long history and are not a recent phenomenon. Operating expenses, balancing budgets, collections, donations, mission activities, and all the other important aspects of a contemporary church's ministry in the world need solid business associations. For example, Paul has his business associate Barnabas's ministry recognized by Peter and the Pillars in Jerusalem (Galatians 2:9). Paul and Barnabas had formed a business partnership to accomplish their missionary goals. Paul even considers communities to be his business partners: he acknowledges the Philippians as his community partners (Philippians 1:5) and he is indebted to them for their generous financial support to his ministry (4:15). Perhaps the Philippians had provided him with the kind of *diakonia* and *koinonia* that Paul expected from the communities he founded. And as with sharing in Jesus's sufferings, communities also shared the sufferings of the apostle: Paul acknowledges that the Corinthian community shared in the pains of the ministry (2 Corinthians 1:7). The church as a business requires committed partners, a *koinonia*, in order to survive and thrive. For Paul and the early Church, *koinonia* describes the ways of connection, relationship, and support between individuals and communities. This *koinonia* extended from business and financial support to the sacraments of baptism and communion.

Community Organization: Prophets, Apostles, and Local Communities

Sometimes these community structures and relationships came into contact with one another and forced a process of discernment about how a community should organize itself in order to honor its theology and values. Most of the time we postmodern people think that early Christian communities organized around an image of Jesus. That is what the Gospel of Mark created. But maybe a community's discernment related not so much to an image of Jesus, but to the way their community received their revelation concerning Jesus. A community needed to focus its discernment upon the life and teaching of its leaders. The contact between kinds of leadership often came with some strife that forced the question of discernment. The *Didache* cautions: "Let every apostle who comes to you be welcomed as the Lord, but he should not remain more than a day. If he must, he may stay one more. But if he stays three days, he is a false prophet" (*Didache* 11:4–5). The *Didache*'s community, as a stable community, honored and received the prophets, but the functions and titles seem to be fluid: apostle, prophet, teacher, bishop, and deacon take on the others' roles in community simply by community decision. The conflict and, for the *Didache*, the solution rested in local leadership: "And so, elect for yourselves bishops and deacons who are worthy of the Lord, gentle men who are not fond of money, who are true and approved. For these also conduct the ministry of the prophets and teachers among you" (*Didache*, 15:1).

This contact and shift from one structure to another demanded discernment. We begin to see early Christian communities discerning carefully among themselves those who represent the voice or the one who "speaks the word of God to you; honor him as the Lord" (*Didache* 4:1). Leadership and authority start to become critical issues in stable communities receiving prophets. The apostle Paul's ministry represents this tension as well: his charismatic leadership among his partnerships (*koinonia*) carries these similar tensions. Paul also is an example of the kind of wanderer who interacted with stable communities to proclaim the gospel. Paul is primarily known to us as a writer, but he traveled extensively to interact directly with stable communities and attempted to form partnerships with them. Many of these stable communities find themselves conflicted by Paul's message, or his methods, or his ideas. He is a wandering change agent. His focus is on connecting people through the working of the Spirit, not through social or religious agreement. Most likely Paul was not a social or religious reformer; he simply wanted the Gentile community to function intimately with God through Christ and the Holy Spirit. The changes to these social and religious structures that confronted Paul did not stop his mission or ministry to create intimate communities of God. He was a man putting voice to his mission from God.

The wandering prophet sometimes founded a local stable community. Paul was not known for this. Paul is credited with establishing numerous churches throughout the Greco-Roman world: in the cities of Corinth, Thessalonika, and Philippi, and throughout the regions of Macedonia, Achaia, and Galatia, to name a few that we know. But this did not stop him from attempting to connect to other churches that he did not found, like the one in Rome, and so he put pen to paper to write to them as well. Even while founding communities, Paul's ministry remained itinerant and he relied extensively on the hospitality of his host communities for the success of his missions. As Paul's ministry began to grow and develop, it soon had to expand, thus creating a need to have fellow apostles and missionaries carry out their duties: Timothy and Barnabas are the most well-known of the Pauline disciples whose ministries extended Paul's own. Paul empowered them as well, just as Jesus had empowered his followers earlier. Paul's ministry, and that of his missionary partners, provide a good example of a wandering voice of God who became a crucial voice sought out, both by his coworkers and by stable local communities that honored his guidance and counsel. The interaction of stable community and itinerant prophet produced interesting relationships to respond to a wide variety of community needs.

Community and Vocation

So how was one of these itinerant prophets, these voices of God, appointed? How did someone receive a commission to do this kind of work? What kind of problems did these prophets create around themselves? Paul, again, suggests an answer. Paul's authority rests on his divine message as an apostle "to preach the gospel" (1 Corinthians 1:17). Paul is a master rhetorician and well educated to perform this task. Paul insists that his apostleship is directly from God: "For I did not receive [the gospel] from a human being, nor was I taught it, but it came through a revelation of Jesus Christ" (Galatians 1:12). Paul acknowledges forcefully that he had not studied with any of the living followers directly associated with Jesus's ministry (Peter, James, and John who were the Pillars of Jerusalem). When he did relate to Peter, James, John, and the Pillars of Jerusalem, it resulted in a confrontation that led to an agreement that they would operate in separate mission fields, separate *koinoniai* (Galatians 2:6–10). That agreement did not solve the tension because Paul rebuked Peter in Antioch (Galatians 2:11). Paul's authority came from revelation and not association with Jesus's disciples.

Peter and Paul's confrontation in Antioch about table fellowship between Jews and Gentiles shows the degree of tension in communities over discerning true apostles from false: whose gospel would the community adopt? This tension did not stop Paul as he continued his work focused on revelation for his mission to the Gentiles. Even these itinerant prophets, then, often found themselves at odds with one another. Paul claims to be an apostle to the communities he founded, but these communities still receive other apostles, and this creates conflict and tension within the community (2 Corinthians 10:14; 11:5). Paul even finds himself being opposed by other apostles: "And what I do I will continue to do, in order to end this pretext of those who seek a pretext for being regarded as we are in the mission of which they boast. For such people are false apostles, deceitful workers, who masquerade as apostles of Christ" (2 Corinthians 11:12–13). These are strong words. Paul's opponents used a variety of means to convince Paul's communities to follow a different gospel: they charismatically and mystically interpreted the Israelite scriptures, and they performed miraculous deeds like the Roman-style wonder-workers whom Paul called "super-apostles" (2 Corinthians 11:5). The tension of numerous apostles preaching to the same community resonates with the story about Lydia's community. How easy it would have been to receive conflicting messages! Imagine the tension and conflict. Life in community always seems to have some tensions and conflicts.

Paul's itinerant ministry to stable communities is an intriguing example of community formation in early Christianity. This network embodies *koinonia*, and also shows the intense interconnection between itinerant prophet and stable community. Paul stands at the center of a developing network among early Christian communities. In Romans 16, for example, there is a long list of titles and functions given to Paul's fellow workers: Phoebe, the deacon; Prisca and Aquila, the heads of a local church; Andronicus and Junia, noted apostles; Urbanus, a coworker and evangelist; and many individuals who constitute the local Roman church. It is remarkable that Paul knew of these people even though he did not found the Roman church. The Christian network was indeed a well-connected one. Throughout his letters, Paul acknowledges that emissaries are sent from community to community to carry the messages from Paul. In one letter Paul hears about conflict through a member of Chloe's household (1 Corinthians 1:11) and in another Paul praises the Thessalonians for their faithfulness on the basis of verbal reports (1 Thessalonians 1:8–10). Although an itinerant leader, Paul seems to know everything about the communities that he founded and that interested him. Paul's itinerancy did not in any way inhibit his ability to exercise his authority in local community.

Community Organization: Bishops and Deacons

Some early Christians, however, clearly had difficulty with an itinerant leadership. The *Didache*'s community began to discern the need for bishops and deacons. The bishops and deacons inherit the power and authority of the wandering prophets and teachers. Who holds authority and power are critical issues in any community, both ancient and modern. The *Didache*'s community was on the cusp of shifting authority over to someone internal, an insider in this community, and a well-respected person who would be readily available to serve the community on a regular basis. Its discernment on shifting the power and authority still does not take away the importance of the wandering prophet, even though the communities needed to discern false prophets.

Christian communities adopted and adapted models of community from the Roman environment to their own purposes. When we come to the role of bishops and deacons, we are presented with an intriguing corollary. The title bishop is not specific to Christian church structures in antiquity. The bishop is frequently the financial officer, or the primary overseer and supervisor of a Roman organization called a "club," which we will explain more fully shortly. In fact, some early Roman authors suggest that Christians formed clubs in order to associate legally in the Empire. This may even have been the case with Jewish synagogues, perhaps organized as Roman clubs for efficiency of work and recognition.

Clubs developed primarily as small groups of people, most likely all men, to provide social support, entertainment, and professional training. Clubs served artists, bakers, woodworkers, merchants, leatherworkers, smiths, and every other kind of association of like-minded people. These clubs served a wide variety of social needs across the Roman Empire. Clubs point to some crucial elements. The clubs are diverse; they hold together people in widely differing professional, social, and political contexts. And more importantly, the clubs are not secular, but religious associations. They may take on the name of a deity or god; their meals included invocations of the gods and perhaps libations; and they provided proper burial rites for their members. The clubs certainly could have formed a network with other clubs in other communities in the Empire. The small membership characteristic of clubs would enhance their ability to be supportive communities. The clubs gathered around a meal provided as an essential part of the gathering. Although we have no evidence for it, the Pauline churches certainly could have been organized as clubs: these qualities of the clubs resonate with the way Paul refers to their internal organization.

The correlation of bishops in a club and bishops in the church holds some interesting possibilities. The functions in both church and club seem to be the same: supervision of community life and oversight of the organization's finances. It was an important function for a community. The *Didache* insisted that the bishops must be "gentle men who are not fond of money" (*Didache* 15:1). The clubs, because of their meals, also had roles for waiters, called deacons. They served the meals and attended to the internal banquets and provisions of the club. A deacon, playing a religious role as the server at a meal, replicates the attendants serving in a temple. Again in Lydia's community, the wandering prophet could offer a thanksgiving meal at any time, and so there was always need for a resident deacon, according to some of the elders of her community. In the end, Lydia's community probably settled for a resident bishop and deacon to replace the itinerant prophets and teachers, and over the years this became the norm for Christian communities.

Ignatius and Peter: Creating the Monarchial Episcopate

In the Christian tradition, the development of the central role for the bishop is closely identified with two key figures: the apostle Peter, whose legends take him to Rome, where he became its first bishop, and Ignatius (ca. 35–110), bishop of Antioch. The way Ignatius built his theology upon the legend of Peter is an intriguing story that articulates the central role of the bishop in the life of every church in the Roman Empire. So it is an important story to pursue. John's gospel, probably written during Ignatius's lifetime, becomes a player in this story, but that will be taken up in the next chapter. For the moment, let's simply enjoy the story. We start with Ignatius's life and theology.

Ignatius became the bishop of Antioch in Asia Minor during the transitional time between wandering prophets, apostles, and the establishment of permanent, local leadership. In his corpus of letters *To the Ephesians, Magnesians, Trallians, Romans, Philadelphians, Smyrnaeans,* and *Polycarp* he advocated strongly for the bishop to be the primary focal point for unity within the church in order to supplant other forms of community structure and leadership. His letters bear strong testimony to his drive to create what is called the "monarchial episcopate," the rule of one bishop in every city who had authority over all Christian activities in a location. We do not know why, but eventually Ignatius was condemned to death and became a martyr, a witness to Christ. He was sent to Rome, probably because he was a Roman citizen of some note, but we cannot be sure. He became, then, a kind of wandering martyr, like the wandering prophets, writing letters to communities in order to convince them to adopt his church organization based on the rule of bishops who appointed presbyters (priests) and deacons.

Ignatius's church structure centers upon three key roles: bishops, presbyters, and deacons. The role of the bishop represents a point of unity for all the members of a church. In a sense, the bishop is the only one who represents the community, and in the bishop the community finds its identity. In fact, Ignatius, in his letter to the Ephesians, views the bishop as the sole representative of the entire congregation: "Since, therefore, I have received in God's name your whole congregation in the person of Onesimus, a man of inexpressible love who is also your earthly bishop, I pray that you will love him in accordance with the standard set by Jesus Christ and that all of you will be like him" (*Letter to the Ephesians*, 1). The bishop constitutes the church by recapitulating the members in the person of the bishop and by putting forth the bishop as the model or ideal person to emulate. This is a significant change in understanding of Christian community and a far cry from the language of Paul about the Body of Christ consisting of many members filled with the Spirit. For Ignatius, the head, the bishop, is the one who really counts the most.

The bishop is so important that it is through the bishop alone that the people of the church find their sanctification and salvation. Holiness and sanctification now depend not upon a direct relationship with Christ, but with a relationship mediated through the primacy of the bishop and the presbyters the bishop appoints. "It is proper, therefore, in every way to glorify Jesus Christ, who has glorified you, so that you, joined together in a united obedience and subject to the bishop and the presbytery, may be sanctified in every respect" (*Letter to the Ephesians*, 2). The bishop as well as other clerical offices have become the mediators of sanctification for the community. The clerics bridge the world of God to the human world. This kind of thinking has shifted the energy of the community from the constituent members of the Body of Christ to the head alone. The life of the community depends entirely on the bishop.

For Ignatius this dependence upon the bishop rests on the simple fact that it is the bishops alone who are able to present the mind of Christ, the mind of God. The role of the bishop has indeed taken over the function of the wandering prophets and teachers. The bishops in Ignatius's community represent the mind of Christ, who in turn represents the mind of the Father. Ignatius exhorts: "I have therefore taken the initiative to encourage you, so that you may run together in harmony with the mind of God. For Jesus Christ, our inseparable life, is the mind of the Father, just as the bishops appointed throughout the world are in the mind of Christ" (*Letter to the Ephesians*, 3). The bishops in community become the direct line to God, and harmony in community depends upon people having the mind of Christ, which they can only find in the person of the bishop. The bishop and Christ are inseparable, fully united, one function within community, so that the bishops present the only superior authority within the church and the only knowledge of God available to the membership. These elite bishops become the only rule and authority for understanding the divine mind. Their role destroys the possibility of direct access of individuals in community to God. A significant shift of authority now rests in the discernment of a few; there is no longer discernment of the presence or voice of God by the entire community. The voice of God now only rests in the one who bears the title of bishop.

Ignatius's understanding of the bishop's office also has an impact on the understanding of the sacraments, particularly the Eucharist. In the *Didache* the prophet could celebrate the thanksgiving meal with any gifts available, at any time, in any place, and whenever the prophet wanted. Ignatius completely eliminates this function from his community. Ignatius's focus on the unity of the church and knowledge of God located only in the person of the bishop demands that he understand the Eucharist, the thanksgiving, to be tied specifically to the presence of the bishop. Eucharists can only occur at altars at which the bishop presides: "Take care, therefore, to participate in one Eucharist (for there is one flesh of our Lord Jesus Christ, and one cup which leads to unity through his blood; there is one altar, just as there is one bishop, together with the presbytery and the deacons, my fellow servants), in order that whatever you do, you do in accordance with God" (*Letter to the Philadelphians*, 4). The bishops, presbyters, and deacons alone make the sacraments valid and effective. Without them, nothing can happen. This is in stark contrast to the *Didache*, where the Eucharist continues to take place on the Lord's day, but it does not stipulate who can preside or lead the prayers. Ignatius attempts to restrict sacramental acts by others in the communities by connecting the presence of God only to places where the bishop, presbyters, and deacons function.

In the end, for Ignatius, the only real church is the one founded on bishops, presbyters, and deacons: "Similarly, let everyone respect the deacons as Jesus Christ, just as they should respect the bishop, who is a model of the Father, and the presbyters as God's council and as the band of the apostles. Without these no group can be called a church" (*Letter to the Trallians*, 3). This passage connects the orders of the church and the divine order: the deacons serve as Christ served, the bishop represents Christ's Father, and the presbyters do the work of the apostles. Ignatius collapses the divine order on the ordained orders of the church. This collapse of identity solidifies the divine function of the ordained clergy and underscores their determinative role in the creation and founding of the church. The contrast between the communities, the *Didache*'s and Ignatius's, demonstrates the early church's diversity and the subsequent tensions and conflicts arising in roles of leadership and authority. For the *Didache*'s community there appears to be an attempt to hold the diversity of roles together between bishops and deacons with prophets and apostles. Ignatius's focus on the three main offices limits the scope of the church. And this brings us to the Petrine tradition, the tradition that grew out of the legend of Peter as the first bishop of Rome, with which the Johannine community had some difficulties.

The Petrine Tradition and the Role of Bishops

Peter's place in the gospels of Mark, Matthew, and Luke is an ambiguous one: he is heralded as the leader of the group of Twelve in Jesus's immediate circle, but he is also the one who denied him three times during Jesus's trial. Jesus rebukes Peter for not understanding his role as the Christ, and Peter confesses his confusion at Jesus's transfiguration on the mount. Yet, Matthew still reports that Jesus said, "You are Peter, and upon this rock I will build my church, and the gates of the netherworld shall not prevail against it. I will give you the keys to the Kingdom of Heaven. Whatever you bind on earth shall be bound in heaven; and whatever you loose on earth shall be loosed in heaven" (Matthew 16:18–19). That is a strong endorsement for someone whose reputation is so mixed. But that is the primary lens through which Peter has been understood. He is the rock of the church, the founder. He has the keys of the Empire, and he has power both in heaven and on earth. It is no wonder that this passage became identified with the power of the bishops as Ignatius described them. Here Jesus gives to Peter all the authority that Ignatius would eventually give to bishops. So, Peter must have been a bishop! Probably based upon the confrontation between Paul and Peter at Antioch, Eusebius of Caesarea, a fourth-century church historian, describes Peter as the first bishop of Antioch and Ignatius as the second. How convenient. The identification is complete. For Eusebius and all the historians and bishops since then, once bishops had the kind of authority and power that Ignatius describes, then this passage could be read as an endorsement not only of Peter, but of every other bishop as well. Peter becomes the archetype of this kind of church organization, authority, theology of sacraments, and mediated access to God. John's community will have much to say about him and this structure of the church!

But how did Peter become associated with Rome when there is no historical evidence that he went there? This is how legends work. In Galatians, Peter is shown to be one of the Pillars in Jerusalem, holding court in the Temple and seemingly waiting for the establishment of an Empire on earth focused on the Temple and Jerusalem. But the emperor Titus thwarted that design in 70 CE by destroying the Temple and rendering Jerusalem an irrelevant place among Roman cities. So the legends of Peter found in the apocryphal acts, the Christian novels, describe his journey to Rome, where a proper "rock of the church" should be, at the center of the most important empire of the world. As the founder of the church, the apostle needed to be in Rome, where the emperor lived and where all imperial authority resided. Since Peter was obviously a bishop (at least to later writers), Peter became the first bishop of Rome and founded Roman Christianity. The primacy of the bishop of Rome, as first among all the bishops, rests on the joining of Peter to the imperial city and has been sustained by the history of the church throughout the ages. This is a strong testimonial to the power of Peter's legend and to the commissioning of Peter in Matthew's gospel, a testimonial sustained as central throughout the history of Christianity.

This union of Peter's story of prominence with Ignatius's theology of the episcopate became the founding story of Christianity as it was developed by Irenaeus and other bishops. All bishops, following in Peter's footsteps, assumed the same level of authority within their dioceses. Without bishops, especially after the emperor Constantine made the church an official arm of imperial authority, there could be no orthodox church. Every church that deviated from this structure, and every bishop who deviated from the council of these imperially sanctioned bishops, became marked as heretics and ejected from the church. With this union of Ignatian and Petrine traditions, the power of the church in the world was consolidated for generations to come.

The movement, the energy of the church seemed to move relentlessly toward a centralized authority and that authority rested on every bishop who succeeded the apostle Peter and who inherited Peter's authority as the founder of the church. That is the story most told in history books. But there were exceptions, major exceptions, to that story. The Gospel of John is the most significant exception. John's gospel seems to go back to earlier, more charismatic, styles of ministry and revelation to create an image of church and of Jesus that harkens back to less hierarchical and more participatory times in the Jesus movement. This is what we will take up in the next chapter. To understand John's place, however, requires that we understand the full spectrum. Only then does John's genius shine forth.

Questions for Discussion

1. Reread the quotation we provided from Irenaeus (*Adv. Haer.*, III.11.8) about the necessity for four gospels (Mark, Matthew, Luke, and John). What parts of this quotation make sense to you? Why? How would you make an argument for including these four gospels in the canon of the New Testament? What arguments could you envision for including other gospels?

2. This portal raises the question of church authority. Why is the problem of church authority important for understanding the gospels? What difference does it make for the reading of the gospels to adopt one of the other models of church authority? Why do other models of authority make a difference?

3. From your reading of the New Testament, including the letters of Paul, construct a story that explains the origins of Christianity. Why have you chosen the elements you have for this construction? What have you left out and why have you left it out? What have you included and why?

Resources for Further Study

The *Didache* has fascinated scholars for a long time. The *Didache* provides a very interesting window into a diverse community's way of life. We suggest, as always, that you read the primary text first; see *The Apostolic Fathers*, Loeb Classical Library, trans. Bart D. Ehrman (Cambridge, Mass.: Harvard University Press, 2003). Those interested in the wandering prophets and the conflict with apostles, priests, and bishops see Jonathan A. Draper, "Weber, Theissen, and 'Wandering Charismatics' in the *Didache*," *Journal of Early Christian Studies* 6 (1998), 541–576. For those interested in theology and the life of the community that produced the *Didache*, see Clayton N. Jefford, *The Didache in Context: Essays on its Text, History, and Transmission* (New York: E. J. Brill, 1995). For those seeking a collection of essays covering various topics (Eucharist, synoptic tradition, Judeo-Christian ethics) see Jonathan A. Draper, *The Didache in Modern Research* (New York: E. J. Brill, 1996).

The letters of Ignatius provide a window into the early Christian movement in the second century. Again, reading the primary text is highly recommended: see Bart D. Ehrman 's translation in *The Apostolic Fathers*. Those seeking more on Ignatius should see Christine Trevett's *A Study of Ignatius of Antioch in Syria and Asia* (New York: Edwin Mellen Press, 1992) and William R. Schoedel's

Ignatius of Antioch: A Commentary on the Letters of Ignatius of Antioch, Hermeneia Series (Minneapolis: Fortress, 1985).

The Petrine tradition has wide implications found both within academia and the church. The monumental work of Oscar Cullmann, *Peter: Disciple, Apostle, Martyr: A Historical and Theological Study*, trans. Floyd V. Filson (Philadelphia: Westminster Press, 1953) provides the development of the Petrine tradition and has become the one book that all recent work must address. Those interested in a very detailed and expansive work on the Petrine tradition that filters both into the academy and the church with ecumenical issues, see Raymond E. Brown, Karl P. Donfried, and John Reumann, eds., *Peter in the New Testament: A Collaborative Assessment by Protestant and Roman Catholic Scholars* (Minneapolis: Augsburg, 1973). For those seeking a great overview of the Petrine tradition, see Pheme Perkins's *Peter: Apostle for the Whole Church* (Columbia: University of South Carolina Press, 1994).

For those interested in reading more on Irenaeus, see volume 1 of *Ante-Nicene Fathers* eds. Alexander Roberts, James Donaldson, Philip Shaff, and Henry Wace (Peabody, Mass.: Hendricksons, 1997). Irenaeus's work can be sifted through with two helpful books: Mary Ann Donovan's *One Right Reading: A Guide to Irenaeus* (Collegeville, Minn.: Liturgical Press, 1997) and Eric Osborn's *Irenaeus of Lyons* (Cambridge: Cambridge University Press, 2001).

The collection of essays found in the book *Voluntary Associations in the Graeco-Roman World*, eds. John S. Kloppenborg and Stephen G. Wilson (New York: Routledge, 1996) provides a good entry into defining and understanding diverse community formation in antiquity, including clubs.

CHAPTER NINE

The Gospel of John:
Abiding in the Word

Almost Famous *is a film about rock and roll. Actually it is a film that reveals the inner essence of rock and roll in a time of great transition from the first days of the great rock and roll bands of the 1960s to the revised and renewed rock and roll bands of the 1970s. The film explores this transition of the heart and essence of rock and roll through the eyes of William Miller, a young, eager, and devoted disciple of rock and roll from the new generation.*

The film opens with a window into a 1970s family, in many ways clinging to the 1960s. The family's single mother aggressively promotes her alternative lifestyle. She is an avid vegetarian. She resists the dominant commercial culture by celebrating Christmas in June. As a college professor, she values the life of the mind and education as the means for a person to pursue freedom and creativity as well as to make significant changes in the world. William and his sister Anita, however, experience their mother's lifestyle as stultifying.

Anita rebels by listening to rock and roll, dating, staying out all night with her boyfriend, and eventually by simply walking out of the family to live with her boyfriend. Ultimately she becomes a stewardess and travels the world. Before she leaves, however, she hides her collection of rock and roll records under her brother's bed, telling him "Look under your bed. It will set you free." With her stash of records she leaves a note to her brother saying, "Listen to 'Tommy' with a candle burning, and you will see your entire future." Anita becomes the first revealer of rock and roll to this eager younger disciple.

William Miller takes his sister's advice. He pulls the collection of rock and roll records out from under his bed, lights the candle, and listens to "Tommy." His life is changed. He's hooked on rock and roll, and he pursues rock and roll with a passion that his mother simply cannot understand, but which she reluctantly accepts. He writes numerous articles about rock and roll and articulates the way the new generation experiences the music.

William Miller sends his reports and writings to a critic, Lester Bangs, who acts as the story's second revealer, and tells William Miller that rock and roll is dead and his criticism is wasting his time. For Lester Bangs the heart and soul of rock and roll has died because it has sold out to the commercial world of popular, recorded music, the very world William Miller's mother has rejected. But as an aficionado of the earlier rock and roll, Lester Bangs introduces William Miller to the insider world of rock and roll despite his misgivings about where rock and roll is heading.

Lester Bangs does recognize William Miller's giftedness and commissions a review of the rock band Black Sabbath. The assignment propels William Miller into seeing and experiencing firsthand the world of rock and roll. He is no longer a mere fan. As a gifted writer, he begins his quest for the inner essence and energy of the rock and roll movement. And he develops as a perceptive, young writer about rock and roll bands and music.

William Miller goes to the Black Sabbath concert and finds that he cannot enter backstage because the guard says, "Your name is not on the list." In the world of rock and roll, to be invited backstage is to be marked as an insider, a close companion of the band. Persevering and remaining faithful to his mission and assignment, he connects with the girls who follow the band, the "Band Aids," led by Penny Lane, a sophisticated and experienced band groupie who has "retired" from her promiscuous following of the band and become a kind of elder to the other girls. Penny Lane tries to get him backstage, but fails.

Then Stillwater, the opening band for Black Sabbath, arrives and William Miller begins to engage with them. He talks to them about their songs and their manner of performing and displays his knowledge and sensitive perception about Stillwater's art. At first the band experiences him as a critic-enemy, but William Miller's sophisticated knowledge of the band and their music impresses them, and they take him backstage. Now William Miller has entered the inner sanctum of rock and roll, and his heart and mind soar.

An editor of Rolling Stone magazine notices William Miller's talent and, assuming that he is much older than his actual sixteen years, offers him an assignment to write a major feature article about the up-and-coming rock band Stillwater. This begins William Miller's adventure in experiencing rock and roll more intimately.

Stillwater represents the change in generation from the earlier rock and roll bands of the 1960s, such bands and artists as The Who, Led Zeppelin, David Bowie, and Lou Reed, who formed the heart of the rock and roll tradition. This older tradition of rock and roll had created a musical movement that enabled an older generation to articulate their identity and understanding of the world. Stillwater wanted to refract that older tradition in new ways to speak to another generation, and yet they were not yet the medium recognized by the new generation. Stillwater was still almost famous.

William Miller begins his quest to write the article for Rolling Stone *by seeking an interview with the lead guitarist, Russell, who, finding William Miller confusing, keeps postponing the time for the interview, but invites him to join them on tour. William Miller is young and eager to know the inside, which Russell finds intriguing, but William Miller is writing for a magazine that represents the enemy to Stillwater's artistic love. In that sense William Miller represents "the enemy" of rock and roll. At once William Miller is an insider, being invited into the inner circle of Stillwater's life, and yet at the same time he cannot be trusted because he has the power to destroy the band by his article for the most important rock and roll journal.*

Stillwater recognizes that they are playing a style of rock and roll that has already had a long and apparently tired history, and yet they have found life in the music and lifestyle. They love the old way, but they live in a new era. They produce a different sound with new energy. William Miller's devotion to rock and roll at once aligns him with Stillwater's dream of a rock and roll renewal, and makes him an ambiguous agent both of Stillwater's fame and the transformation of rock and roll for a new generation. William Miller understands that he stands at the threshold, the bridge between the exotic past and the dangerous present. Stillwater understands this as well. Along with the Band Aids, they are all both insiders and outsiders.

William Miller witnesses the drugs, angst, and promiscuity of the Band Aids, and the emotional roller coaster these girls experience in their intense relationships with the artists. As an adopted member of the Band Aids, William Miller stays in their rooms, becomes their close friend, and remains faithful to them in their devotion to rock and roll. They become a community of Stillwater followers.

William Miller attempts to bridge the older and the emerging tradition of rock and roll through his reporting on Stillwater, and yet his role remains ambiguous. He is both fan and critic, both bridge and audience for Stillwater's emerging art. William Miller stands at a crossroads in rock and roll history, and he is aware of the possibilities the new rock and roll presents as well as the dangers and seductions that accompany the emerging movement.

William Miller's article for Rolling Stone *symbolizes both the possibilities and the dangers of Stillwater's project. The critical article in a significant magazine holds open the possibility of fame and fortune for this group, a fame and fortune that could at once change their lives for financial success, make them a prominent agent in the history of rock and roll (any band featured in* Rolling Stone *achieves notoriety), but also at the same time might destroy the artistic vitality that characterizes their performances. William Miller could make them famous, but as a fan, he wants not to make them famous but to reveal the truth about rock and roll for his own generation, a truth that would help his generation articulate their identity and values.*

In the end, William Miller succeeds in his quest. While following Stillwater's tour, William Miller discovers who he is and what he values. While writing the article, William Miller articulates the depth and vision of the new generation of rock and roll, even though in the end the band abandons and rejects his writing. In engaging with the Band Aids, William Miller finds the abiding relationships that make life worth living, even though he ultimately remains an outsider to them. And in the end, in the rejection, he gets the elusive interview with the lead guitarist Russell, who reveals the inner workings of Stillwater's art and values. In the end, William Miller reveals all of this in an article in Rolling Stone, *which propels Stillwater on yet another tour that portrays the successful transmission of the older tradition to another generation in a medium at once consistent with it, and yet very, very different. And William Miller, the insider who reveals and bridges the traditions of rock and roll, has found himself as well, just as his sister had predicted he would.*

The church at the beginning of the second century had come to a crossroads, very much like the crossroads that William Miller and Stillwater faced. The church was passing from one generation to the next. The older generation had two competing focuses. One focus was the Pauline tradition of the authentic letters of Paul where there was little interest in the details of Jesus's life; the primary interest revolved about the way Jesus's death and resurrection remade the life of believer and the church. The second focus was the synoptic tradition in which the life of the communities committed to following Jesus was refracted through a made-up biography of Jesus and depended upon the hierarchical and central role of Jesus's twelve disciples. In fact, the Acts of the Apostles followed the development and the growth of the church through the remarkable lives of the leading disciples as they became the central focus for the transmission of the power and authority of the resurrected Jesus from Jerusalem to Rome. The synoptic tradition of Mark, Matthew, and Luke/Acts had become the norm for the church up to the beginning of the second century and became the support for the change from a charismatic leader in the early Jesus movement to the support of the church offices of bishop and deacon.

The new generation of the second century refracted the older Pauline tradition, but in startling ways to make it authentic and vital for new times and new circumstances. In the Pauline tradition, we find Paul's students producing letters in Paul's name, letters that update Paul for a later time. For example, in Colossians and Ephesians we find a very different reading of what Paul preached, but one more appropriate to the realities of the church at the turn of the second century. This bringing of the mind of Paul to bear on new times and circumstances continued through the early second century with the production of the letters to Titus and Timothy and their support of the emerging hierarchy of the church in the roles of bishops and deacons. Ignatius of Antioch inherited the benefits of this updating of the charismatic Paul to become the charismatic martyr-bishop.

The gospel tradition was more complex. The culmination of the synoptic tradition in the hierarchical and central role of the apostles in Acts had set a course for the gospels and the church that would make it dependent upon the succession of the apostles and their teaching rather than any kind of charismatic leadership and revelation. But there were communities of followers of Jesus who resisted this hierarchical direction of the church. The Gospel of Thomas, for example, which reached back to the older sayings traditions like Q, also was published at the beginning of the second century. Thomas has no such interest in hierarchy, but rather promulgates a direct relationship with the living Jesus whose words are recorded in the gospel. In the Gospel of Thomas, each person must engage with the living words of the living Jesus to find eternal life. Other gospels like the Gospel of Mary and the Gospel of Phillip took a similar path to the Gospel of Thomas. And this tradition of a direct, unmediated gospel revelation continued in the Gnostic movement that emerged in the second century.

The Gospel of John takes a similar attitude toward the relationship between the members of the community and their living Lord, but enters much more into the fray of the transition from one generation to another. Unlike the Gospel of Thomas and other second-century gospels, the Gospel of John retains some of the narratives known from the synoptic gospels (such as the healing of the paralytic at the pool, the healing of the blind man, and the feeding of the five thousand), and yet these familiar narratives have been reworked and reformulated to answer different questions and to address other issues that concerned their community at the beginning of the second century. Times had changed. The way of understanding Jesus and the succession of the apostles seemed now to lack the authority and authenticity of the original Jesus movement.

So John's community stood at a crossroads. One road led to the establishment of bishops and deacons and other authorities of the church who mediated the power and salvation handed over to them by Jesus. Ignatius stands there at the crossroads, undergirded by and undergirding the trajectory of authority laid out in the synoptic gospels and the updated Paul. Another road led to the Gospel of Thomas. Here there is only a living Jesus, recorded in words, upon which the believer could meditate and find eternal life. This community, or these believers, had an unmediated and direct relationship to a Jesus living immediately in their presence.

Yet another road was that of the *Didache*, holding on to the ancient traditions of the wandering prophets who brought the living words of the Lord to their life circumstances, while also struggling with the appointment of bishops and deacons to replace them. The community of the Gospel of John stood at the center of these sometimes competing Jesus traditions because of its recognition of a diversity of continuing sources of divine revelation.

The community, probably living in Ephesus of Asia Minor in close proximity to these other churches at the crossroads, accepted the validity of the revelation provided by the overarching narrative of the life of Jesus presented in the synoptic tradition: that Jesus preached and healed in Galilee, went to Jerusalem, and there was crucified and resurrected. The Johannine community also accepted the validity of direct, unmediated revelation as did the Gospel of Thomas. And as with the *Didache*, the Johannine community honored the revelation of itinerant prophets. Unlike many religious communities, the Johannine community was willing to acknowledge the value of contesting sources of revelation. The community believed they could recapture the spirit of the older tradition, of the origins of the Jesus movement, without the mediation of bishops and deacons. The old rock and roll of Jesus's time could be recaptured in the new rock and roll of John's community. The correlation between the film *Almost Famous* and the Gospel of John could not be more dramatic: both reach into the past to make the vitality of an old movement live in new times and new circumstances.

For both, revelation is the key. Like William Miller, the Johannine community seeks to reveal the inner workings of the movement in which they stood as the new generation. Their gospel reveals the living and present Jesus in their midst, even though, like William Miller's mother, the people around them neither understand the revelation they seek nor support the effort to make the revelation accessible to others.

The brilliance of the Gospel of John is this revelation at the crossroads of generations and traditions. Our thesis about this gospel attempts to capture this genius and energy. The community that produced the Gospel of John formed itself around the reception and honoring of revelation. The revelation in the community came from a sense of the living Jesus in their midst, mediated by members of the community who functioned as prophets, the voices of the Lord to new circumstances. These mediating prophets were understood as the intimate followers of the Lord signified by the gospel character of the Beloved Disciple.

The gospel aims to produce more prophets, more revealers of the words of the Lord, more intimate associations with Jesus by recognizing Jesus's voice in the many, often disparate and conflicting voices of those who gathered in the community. Their goal was that the community itself would, over time, consist entirely of intimate associates listening for the voice of the Lord in the midst of their community. The community gathered the disparate revelations from the prophets, valued as the voice of Jesus in their community, as long discourses introduced into the narrative framework of the gospel. The discourses display two kinds of revelation, which we will discuss more fully later: (1) revelations that emerge from the interaction of diverse members of the community, which we call "interactive revelation"; and (2) revelations that emerge from a direct communication, which we call "prophetic revelation."

The revelatory quality of the Johannine community constituted a criticism of the hierarchical trajectory that was becoming dominant in the church and functioned as a renewal movement to return to what they understood as the earliest and most profound engagement with the living Jesus—the one who inaugurated the movement that led to the foundation of the church. The Jesus whom the prophets made present in the community's struggles was the resurrected Jesus, the Jesus who functioned in the church continually as a living agent and force for renewal, revelation, and salvation to eternal life.

The formative practice of the community revolved about a process of remaining, of standing firm, of staying engaged with the living voice of Jesus through personal and communal challenges from the Lord. The Greek word often translated as "remain" or "abide" is used more in John's gospel than any other gospel, and is used throughout the gospel as a touchstone of the community's life. The prophets, the intimate associates of Jesus, were those who remained, who persevered, who stood steadfast in the community through all of their struggles with

ears acutely attuned to the voice of Jesus. The community redefined their practices, their ritual life, to reflect this revelatory dynamic. The formative practice
of the Gospel of John is a process that perceives and hears the revelation in
those presenting the voice of Jesus in the present moment and abides or remains
steadfast in the face of new revelation. This is important to understand.

We get a glimpse of the way it works from *Almost Famous*. William Miller
finds himself projected into the presence of the band Stillwater, and with the
Band Aids who accompany the band. He discovers the power and richness of
rock and roll from inside, from experiencing and observing immediately as the
band and the Band Aids live out their lives together on a cross-country concert
tour. He is not looking to the past, although he knows the past, but rather he
looks to the immediacy of the experience of Stillwater's refracting rock and roll.
And he sticks with the band and lives it.

The Gospel of John also lives in the present. Yes, they know the past, the way
others see and understand Jesus as an historical figure who founded the movement
that eventually became the church. They have before them some narrative gospel, probably the Gospel of Mark, and they understand that these narratives about
Jesus are important to remember. But they recoiled at the way Mark was used to
support a hierarchical institution: their Jesus is not a past historical figure whose
designated leaders define and control the message Jesus presented, but rather their
Jesus is someone *present*. One way of thinking about this is that they are responding to what Luke/Acts presents. Recall that Luke/Acts establishes a sequence of
Jesus, who is left behind in the first volume, and the major apostles who replicate
the activity of Jesus in their ministries as the church grows more and more universal under the guidance of the Holy Spirit. The emphasis in Luke/Acts has shifted
from a present Jesus to apostles who, through the Holy Spirit, perform the same
deeds Jesus did as they proclaim the Empire of God. The Johannine community,
however, experiences the ministry and work of Jesus as a reality in the present
moment, as something real, living, transformative, and immediate. They do not
leave Jesus behind in a narrative, but have immediate access to him through
those intimate followers, those beloved disciples, who hear his voice, know his
presence, and communicate Jesus to those around them. For the community that
produced this gospel, revelation continues to occur in their midst in the voice of
Jesus, who is still present among them and guiding them along.

Countering Apostolic Mediation

The Gospel of John, using apostolic tradition while countering it, introduces
the community to the unmediated voice of Jesus. In focusing on the living Jesus,
the gospel moves away from apostolic mediation of the divine presence in two
ways. First, it redefines the authoritative role of Peter as it is found in the syn-

optic gospels and in the early church tradition, which centers the development of the church on Peter. And second, it develops a particular relationship with the living Jesus through the voice of his revealers.

The Role of Peter

The Johannine community thinks that the Petrine tradition of the church has left Jesus's presence behind in favor of other apostolic mediators of divine presence. The Johannine community experiences the Petrine tradition as having abandoned the real heart of the encounter with Jesus, the engagement with a living God made flesh among them (John 1:14). Their revelation and experience of Jesus continues in their lives. It is not something of a past era, but an experience they have in the present, and they even develop new stories about Jesus (the raising of Lazarus from the dead and the encounter with the Samaritan woman at the well, for example) to serve their needs for occasions for ongoing revelation. The revelation continues, as does the narrative of how Jesus interacts with his followers. That is why the Gospel of John is so very different from the other Gospels. The story for John continues to unfold in their midst, and the gospel's work is simply to record and preserve it as continuing revelation for the health and salvation of Jesus's followers.

It is not that the Johannine community thinks that Jesus does not operate in the Petrine tradition, but that the Petrine tradition does not suffice for them. The tradition does not bear new and engaging revelation, and it is that continuing unfolding revelation that matters to the members of this community. The gospel makes this clear in the description of the relationship of the Beloved Disciple to Peter:

> Peter turned and saw the disciple following whom Jesus loved. . . . When Peter saw him, he said to Jesus, "Lord, what about him?" Jesus said to him, "What if I want him to remain until I come? What concern is it of yours? You follow me." So the word spread among the brothers that the disciple would not die (John 21:20–23a).

Here we find Jesus affirming the living revelations that come through the Beloved Disciple, a revelation that would continue until Jesus returns, and we find Jesus rebuking Peter for being concerned about the Beloved Disciple's presence. The gospel ends with the affirmation that these revelations of Jesus were so numerous that they could not possibly all be written down:

> It is this disciple who testifies to these things and has written them, and we know that his testimony is true. There are also many other things that Jesus did, but if these were to be described individually, I do not think the whole world could contain the books that would be written (John 21:24–25).

The gospel affirms that revelation through the Beloved Disciple, which we understand as a symbol of each member of the community of intimates of Jesus that produced the Gospel of John, will continue until Jesus returns. The revelations abound, so much that no number of books could contain them. And these revelations stand in marked contrast to Peter, who is instructed by Jesus simply to follow him. In essence, the Johannine community says, "Let Peter do his thing, while we hear and respond to the voice of a living Jesus, who continues to speak to us in those among us who are his beloved disciples."

The Voice of Jesus

The heart of revelation for the Johannine community consists of recognizing and honoring the voice of Jesus that comes from various revealers and prophets. The gospel itself, in an important revelatory section, describes the relationship of Jesus, the shepherd, and those who follow him, his sheep:

> "Amen, amen, I say to you, whoever does not enter a sheephold through the gate but climbs over elsewhere is a thief and a robber. But whoever enters through the gate is the shepherd of the sheep. The gatekeeper opens it for him, and the sheep hear his voice, as he calls his own sheep by name and leads them out. When he has driven out all his own, he walks ahead of them, and the sheep follow because they recognize his voice. But they will not follow a stranger; they will run away from him, because they do not recognize the voice of strangers" (John 10:1–5).

Here we find the recognition of Jesus by those who follow him. They know his voice. Jesus calls them by name. The followers associate with Jesus because they know his voice. They do not follow strangers such as those of the Petrine tradition, those whose voice they do not recognize, but they always follow the known voice of Jesus, the shepherd. In John's community, everyone is invited backstage, everyone has access to the band.

The followers recognize that there are other people whom the shepherd Jesus gathers: "I have other sheep that do not belong to this fold. These also I must lead, and they will hear my voice, and there will be one flock, one shepherd" (10:16). The same theme is echoed in the statement "In my Father's house there are many dwelling places" (14:2a). The Johannine community recognizes that diverse understandings of and diverse relationships to Jesus exist among other kinds of believers, and they honor their right to exist and flourish. The Johannine community does not control those who will hear the voice of Jesus, nor do they control those to whom Jesus may speak. Their job, their work, simply is to hear the voice, to respond to the one who knows them each personally by name, and to join the flock of those who recognize the voice of Jesus in their midst, and to remain steadfast and firm in the face of the new voices and revelations.

The Formative Practice: Come and Abide

The gospel also describes the formative process when it frequently refers to "remaining" or "abiding" in Jesus. This is simply staying connected through thick and thin to the revealing conversation (*logos*) with a living Jesus. It is an abiding that begins with someone pointing to Jesus and ends with the simple invitation to "Come and see" (1:36). John the Baptist, the most familiar of these characters, functions as the primary teacher who understands Jesus's true identity and commands his disciples to connect with him: "Behold, the Lamb of God" (John 1:36). Two disciples, Andrew and an anonymous one, obey John's divine utterance and follow Jesus who inquires of them about what they are seeking. Andrew and the other disciple state: "Rabbi" (which translated means Teacher), where are you staying?" (1:38). Here the Greek word is that of "remaining" or "abiding," a theme we discussed above. Jesus commands them to "Come, and you will see" (1:39). The two disciples follow the command. Andrew then finds his brother Simon Peter and brings him into Jesus's presence. The community continues to expand: disciples of John the Baptist begin to function like their teacher and bring others to the fold.

The sense of accepting the invitation to come and see, as well as to abide with Jesus comes through in the gospel most dramatically in the gospel's use of the present tense. Without going into the linguistic arguments, let us simply say that the present tense in Greek signifies simultaneous or present progressive action. This means that someone reading the gospel in Greek experiences the present in what is being narrated. For example, the section with Philip encountering Jesus is usually translated: "The next day he (Jesus) decided to go to Galilee, and he found Philip. And Jesus said to him, 'Follow me'" (1:43), but a truer reading of the Greek would be: "On the next day he (Jesus) desired (past tense) to go to Galilee and is finding (present tense) Philip. Jesus is saying to him, 'Follow me!'" (1:43–44). This is one of many instances in this chapter and throughout the gospel where the present tense is used. We can safely say that the Gospel of John uses the present tense far more than the rest of the gospels. The engagements of the characters in the gospel with Jesus are immediate and ongoing, even for readers centuries later who experience their engagement in the present tense.

But that present tense always takes place in the context of a conversation (*logos*) with Jesus that is taking place right now, whenever that "right now" might be. Jesus's voice in John captures our attention. Jesus really likes to talk with others in John. These conversations are sometimes extensive speeches and at other times, short and simple declarations. In the other gospels, especially Luke and Matthew, the authors used a collection of sayings of Jesus. These sayings were short, pithy, and easily recalled wisdom statements. Matthew refashioned them into speeches. Jesus in the other gospels presents his wisdom in a concise manner, even when it is elaborated in long speeches (as in Matthew) or in parables that portray wisdom in a more succinct manner. Not so in the Gospel of John. Jesus is actively engaged in a wide variety of conversations, both long and short, with almost anyone willing to listen and converse. And there are no parables in John. Even a cursory reading of the gospel shows this difference. John's gospel understands Jesus's voice as crucial to community formation. John's gospel focuses on the conversations (*logos*) of people with Jesus. For example, one way of translating the very first line of the gospel, playing on the various meanings of the word *logos* (which we will explore next) is this: "In the beginning was the conversation, and the conversation was in God's presence, and the conversation was God." The *logos* is a conversation and dialogue always in God's presence and it *becomes* God. The *logos* is the divine utterance within the midst of all conversations and debates. The Johannine community understands this in their unique formative process for all who come into their presence.

The Formative Practice: Hearing the Word of God

In the same first chapter, John affirms that Jesus is the "Word" of God "made flesh" (1:14). Translating *logos* as "word" leads to a very flat reading, which refers merely to a word either spoken or written on a page. But John's gospel has Jesus reveal the "Word of God" and there is much more happening in the "Word made flesh" speaking in the community. The revealing of the Word propels the community to understand God and how to live their lives in this understanding. The "Word made flesh" is revealed as part of a program of reformation. To understand this we need to understand what *logos* means.

The Greek word *logos*, translated as "Word," provides a clue to that formative process. For the Johannine community, the meanings of *logos* are rich and revealing: conversation, discourse, the telling of a story, dramatic narrative, and a rationale for a way of living. The believers in the Gospel of John, and even the opponents and critics, enter a way of living through conversation, a story, a dramatic narrative, a discourse with a living and speaking Jesus, a living and fleshly person. These ways of living where the "Word" continues to be "made flesh," to be a human, the conversation made concrete and real, provide the arena for formation as a follower and believer both then and now. We read this gospel as a formative document where a living and present "Word made flesh" (with all the expansive understandings) speaks, engages in controversial conversation, guides seekers and followers through discourse, and through these means makes it possible for listeners then and now to become children of God (1:12). Becoming a child of God is the desired goal of the formative practice.

Just as *Almost Famous* invites us into the conversation about the meaning of rock and roll, this gospel invites us into the center of the conversation (*logos*) with the founder and promoter of the Empire of God as it unfolds in the present moment. The older tradition points the way to the present moment. One of the recurrent themes in *Almost Famous* is the refrain of the Band Aids whenever they meet each other backstage, in hotels, in parking lots, and at the concerts: "It's all happening." The Band Aids experience the unfolding of the heart and soul of rock and roll in the present moment. They are part of it. They are in the midst of it. It is happening all around them. They abide in it. The voice of Jesus, the revelation of the presence of Jesus to the members of the Johannine community, functions in the same way. These Johannine Christians are saying to each other over and over again in their meeting: "It's all happening. Right here. Right now. To you and to me. The voice of Jesus is still being heard and the revelation of Jesus continues in our conversation. Jesus is still here with us and he's showing us how we are to live our lives and understand who God is. We're living it! It's all happening."

The Beloved Disciple is the one who hears Jesus's voice, who engages Jesus in conversation (*logos*), who remains wherever Jesus's voice is speaking no matter how challenging that voice may be, and who can be any person in the flock of people who recognizes Jesus's voice and follows him. But the Beloved Disciple of Jesus operates in a very diverse community. Like those rock and rollers in the film, there is a wide diversity of perspectives from which to seek the heart of rock and roll. We have the band itself with its connections to other bands performing at the same time and the tie to the bands that made their music possible. We also have the Band Aids and their particular way of supporting the movement. And we have the critics among whom we rank William Miller, Lester Bangs, and the editors of *Rolling Stone*. We also have the innumerable fans whom the band wants "to get off" on their music. Each has a different and yet very immediate connection to rock and roll through Stillwater.

The Production of the Gospel: Gathering Revelations

Likewise in the Gospel of John, we find a wide diversity of perspectives on the revelation in their midst. In John's gospel, this immediate and present experience of believing goes far beyond simply the familiar church tradition about the Twelve to include many other characters who have answered the call. The Samaritan woman, Nicodemus, Mary and Martha, Lazarus, the man born blind, the woman caught in adultery, the woman who anointed Jesus at Bethany—all attest to this. Some of these as well as others play a role in the synoptic gospels, but in those narratives they are invariably acted upon by Jesus; they do not interact with him. Some the gospel names, but most remain anonymous, like the Beloved Disciple. They come to life in John as paradigms of revealers, fully alive and fully engaged with Jesus. Each of these characters opens new avenues of experiencing the reality of Jesus in the present moment, immediately, and without the mediation of any person or religious structure.

We commented earlier that the formative practice of remaining, abiding in the presence of a living Jesus who reveals to his intimates, his sheep who recognize his voice, has been written into the gospel in two kinds of revelatory dynamics: the interactive and the prophetic revelation. The gospel itself maintains a record of these intimate conversations with Jesus and describes various ways, both positive and negative, that they affect those living in the community. For the community, all the revelations are valued and honored, even if they do not agree with one another. Scholars have solved the problem of disagreements and alternative perspectives in the gospel by positing a series of editions of the gospel. Each left its distinctive and perhaps contentious mark on the final edition. In contrast, we understand those alternative perspectives as divergent revelations of one Jesus in the voice of his intimates, and the community values them even if members of the community find them problematic. The community gathers all the voices into the gospel, despite the difficulties such gathering presents them.

The narrative of the gospel unfolds as documenting the various voices, the revelations of Jesus, that enter into the community's story. We understand the community as suspended between tradition and revelation, holding on to both, and yet finding themselves stretched between two seemingly opposite perspectives. But there they hang in the in-between space that connects the past to a living present, an historical Jesus enshrined in familiar narratives and yet still a living voice in their midst; suspended between the old days of rock and roll and the new era of rock and roll bands serving a different generation. The narrative structure serves the purpose of providing Jesus's intimate followers with the occasion to bring new revelations to bear within the community as it lives out its life and its members try to understand themselves and their social and religious locations in relationship to a living Jesus. It is a difficult place for the community, but it demands the practice of remaining and abiding in order to stay connected to the living Jesus who speaks to diverse people in often different and challenging ways.

Now we are in a position to watch the community as it remains steadfast in the face of new revelations from a living Jesus. We look closely at the unfolding of revelation in three long sections of the Gospel of John. We explore interactive revelation through a reading of the Samaritan woman (John 4), the unveiling of prophetic revelation in healing of the man at the pool of Bethsaida (John 5), and the dynamic of revelation in the Bread of Life discourse (John 6). These readings show the way that the gospel as a whole forms its members to be intimate disciples of Jesus, even children of God, and to remain firm in the face of new and challenging revelation.

Interactive Revelation: the Samaritan Woman

The story of the Samaritan woman tells first of Jesus's conversation with a woman concerning the sources of eternal life and then the reactions of his disciples and the woman's neighbors to the resulting revelation. In the film *Almost Famous* the character of Penny Lane plays an important role, a role analogous to the Samaritan woman in John 4. Penny Lane creates the concept of the Band Aids, a group of women who no longer function as mere band "groupies," but as a necessary support for the band in the development of their art. Penny Lane, now retired and yet still very active, becomes William Miller's guide to the inner workings of the relationships within this specific rock and roll community. She is the lover of Stillwater's lead guitarist, whom she clearly loves, and she connects with him in every town in which the band performs. She knows all the members of the band very well, and she is both advisor and leader among the fans.

At one point in the film, the lead guitarist bets and loses Penny Lane for fifty dollars in a card game. It is a devastating moment for her. She experiences the rejection and hurt of being disposable, and she leaves Stillwater and rock and roll. William Miller, who himself has fallen in love with Penny Lane, continues to try to connect with her and to keep ties with her, but Penny Lane remains elusive. At the end of the story, Stillwater rejects William Miller by not confirming the facts of his article for *Rolling Stone*, and the article is not published. But the lead guitarist, in a moment of repentance, contacts Penny Lane and asks to meet with her. Penny gives not her own address for the meeting, but William Miller's home. When the lead guitarist enters William Miller's house, William Miller's mother takes him to William's room. For the first time, the lead guitarist is ready to give William Miller the interview that he has sought throughout the film. The interview and article is written, and Stillwater begins their new tour, now not almost famous, but in fact famous. It was Penny Lane who in her betrayal and disappearance made possible both William Miller's success as a critic and Stillwater's fame as a rock and roll band in the best tradition of the older rock and roll bands. The Samaritan woman performs a similar function in the Johannine gospel.

In the film *Almost Famous*, viewers watch with very mixed emotions the complicated life that Penny Lane lives in her dedication to the work of rock and roll bands and especially in her complex relationship with the lead guitar player. Complications, complexities, and conflicts describe also the Samaritan woman in John's gospel.

Entering the Story

We feature the story of the Samaritan woman because it describes the community's practice of formation: the rules for interactive revelation through conversation or *logos*; as well as the material of revelation from unexpected, unusual, and conflicting sources; and the goal of formation, which is to become an intimate revealer of the living Jesus. Because the production of the Gospel of John itself *is* the formative practice of the Johannine community, as opposed to the synoptic gospels that merely *describe* the formative practices, we have adopted a different approach for reading the text, one in which we reflect on the text as a member of the Johannine community might reflect on the story as the revelations unfold.

The story of this remarkable Samaritan woman and her revelations begins in this way:

> He had to pass through Samaria. So he came to a town of Samaria called Sychar, near the plot of land that Jacob had given to Joseph. Jacob's well was there. Jesus, tired from his journey, sat down there at the well. It was about noon. A woman of Samaria came to draw water (4:4–6).

As Jesus rests at an historic well, a unnamed woman of Samaria approaches to draw water, probably one of her normal, daily-living tasks. This is the context for her interactive revelation. The community hearing this story wonders what will follow. It is the most unlikely place for Jesus to engage in a conversation, and his conversation engages a foreigner, an outsider, just as they (the community) are outsiders. The community's assumptions about the context for revelation have been confirmed: revelation can come anywhere, at any time, to anyone.

The interactive process begins with conversation (*logos*) when Jesus makes a simple demand:

> Jesus said to her, "Give me a drink." His disciples had gone into the town to buy food. The Samaritan woman said to him, "How can you, a Jew, ask me, a Samaritan woman, for a drink?" (For Jews use nothing in common with Samaritans) (4:7–9).

In her response, the Samaritan woman sizes up the request and demonstrates a keen awareness of cultural differences in the request. Interactive revelation often begins when the members recognize the cultural fault lines between them. Their differences become a platform for revelation. The Johannine community watches the unfolding drama of revelation as the woman and Jesus engage in a conversation, and they must be curious about what will follow. In a sense, the Johannine community has staked out new ground for revelation in their differences. Now, as the conversation proceeds, they expect revelation, but cannot imagine the direction that it will take in such unusual circumstances.

The Revelatory Conversation Begins

Conflict and difference inaugurate the revelation and Jesus responds by laying the foundation for a new revelation in God's presence:

> Jesus answered and said to her, "If you knew the gift of God and who is saying to you, 'Give me a drink,' you would have asked him and he would have given you living water." [The woman] said to him, "Sir, you do not even have a bucket and the cistern is deep; where then can you get this living water? Are you greater than

our father Jacob, who gave us this cistern and drank from it himself with his children and his flocks?" Jesus answered and said to her, "Everyone who drinks this water will be thirsty again; but whoever drinks the water I shall give will never thirst; the water I shall give will become in him a spring of water welling up to eternal life" (4:10–15).

Even though the woman does not understand the significance of what Jesus says, she engages further in conversation with him because her interest has been piqued. Interactive revelation often depends upon clarifying some statement that Jesus speaks. It is the engagement and abiding with Jesus that sets the stage for unfolding revelation. Just as the Samaritan woman stands fast in her commitment to remain engaged, the members of the Johannine community must also stand fast as revelation unfolds. The community is demonstrating the primary formative practice of "remaining" and "abiding" with Jesus as he reveals the ways of God to the community.

As the woman continues the conversation with this stranger, not shying away from the conflict and confusion, she addresses him with the honorific "Sir," a formal address from the Greek word *kyrios,* which means Lord or Master. She senses that something significant is about to happen. Even while addressing him honorably she taunts him with the stranger's obvious lack of a bucket, with a saucy question about the living water, and with a pedantic history lesson about the well. She is an active agent in her own revelation. For the Johannine community as it unfolds the revelation, this engagement is meant to startle, because the tone of the interaction seems at once disrespectful and honorific. Revelation does not occur simply in positive and peaceful contexts, it also emerges for this community by direct and forceful engagement. Confusing lines of association and distance among themselves cause the Johannine community to step back, to release their preconceptions, and to listen attentively for the voice of Jesus.

Introducing History, Memory, and Continuing Revelation

And so the Samaritan woman presses forward. She knows what she knows, and her taunting reply shows what she brings to the revelation. Her knowledge of history and her experience of the cultural fault line between Jews and Samaritans paradoxically form her foundation for something new. She reaches back into the history of the well, which held such a primary place in the Samaritan imagination. It was the well that nurtured Jacob, his family, and his flocks and that continued to nurture the surrounding people for generations. She contrasts the still water of the well with a question about Jesus's living water, by questioning the relative authority of Jesus to her forebearer Jacob. She wants to know where Jesus fits in with what she knows. Interactive revelation demands not that a person forget the past, or ignore traditions, or put aside personal or communal concerns, but that history, the past, and traditions all be brought to the fore as an integral part of the revelation. Revelation involves the whole person, including her memory, and the whole community, including its history. Revelation gathers up history and memory as points of departure for new revelation. This is what the Johannine community hears: they, too, have a history and a history that puts them in conflict with the Petrine tradition and the portrayal of Jesus in the synoptic gospels. They, too, bring their collective history and individual memories to bear in the revelation found in the voice of Jesus conversing with this strange woman.

Having set the stage for the Samaritan woman and responding to her engagement with him, Jesus gives a direct revelation of an internal spring of life-giving water. This kind of first-person speech characterizes prophetic revelation, which we will discuss more fully later. In this instance it is important to understand that Jesus makes a pronouncement that reveals important information about the nature of God and how Jesus manifests that nature. Jesus contrasts the still water of the well with the living water that he will give. Jesus plants that living water within the person as an abundant interior well that leads to eternal life. Jesus's water will be so satisfying that those who receive it will never thirst again.

The conversation has shifted significantly with this revelation. Here we see revelation at its clearest point: Jesus tells the woman that he will give her living water so that she will thirst no longer; she will have an interior well that is completely satisfying. The Johannine community seems to revel in dramatic images that portray the surprising works of God. For them, to tell of living waters welling up within the person may not be unusual, but they place the revelation within the context of a conversation with a Samaritan, hoping to challenge their members. They have learned to hear the voice of Jesus even in those other sheepfolds, from other sheep, and from those who live in the many other dwelling places in which God is present. They are formed as a community able to hear revelation from any source and in any context.

In her response to Jesus's challenging and consoling revelations, the woman models the behavior of the Johannine community, confirming the revelation in her life, as she asks for this same wellspring. The interactive revelation, begun with a simple request for a drink, has moved into new levels of interaction. The revelation operates at a number of different levels. The Johannine community sees the cultural antipathy between Jew and Samaritan transformed into a life-giving conversation (*logos*). They also realize something about God, who in this instance does not value the cultural fault lines that separate people, but rather who freely pours forth life to people reaching across human divides. And the community learns something about Jesus as God's messenger and revealer—he engages with everyone, seeking to guide them more fully into relationship with God.

Revelation and Personal Life

Being guided more fully toward God, however, comes with a cost, a high cost of personal honesty and disclosure. Disclosure is at the heart of revelation, and the community begins to experience the cost of revelation in personal disclosure. The next level of interaction forges new avenues for revelation. Just as the woman taunted Jesus earlier, so now Jesus taunts the woman:

> Jesus said to her, "Go call your husband and come back." The woman answered and said to him, "I do not have a husband." Jesus answered her, "You are right in saying, 'I do not have a husband.' For you have had five husbands, and the one you have now is not your husband. What you have said is true." The woman said to him, "Sir, I can see that you are a prophet" (4:16–19).

The arena of revelation has shifted from the ethnic-historical to the personal. Jesus confronts the woman with her past relationships to men. The interactive revelation continues; Jesus functions as a divine seer who knows this woman's life story. The woman agrees wholeheartedly with this revelation. Once again she models the community's deepening response with her own revelation: "Sir, I can see that you are a prophet" (4:19). Through the interactive revelation the woman begins to develop categories in which to put the revealer Jesus. Later she will find other categories, but in the early stages of the interactive revelation settles on the role of the prophet to explain Jesus's personal revelation about herself.

Opening New Patterns of Thought

Revelation as disclosure reaches into every realm of human existence. It is not simply looking to have God revealed; it is also a process of revealing the self to God. The community, as it processes this story shows how to evaluate their categories for understanding God, Jesus, themselves, and revelation. Here, they demonstrate that revelation penetrates to the core of their being, even as they reflect on that revelation and try to understand and articulate their understanding clearly to themselves and to others.

The understanding of the categories leads even further, however. Revelation also includes a reflection, a thinking through, of the reality of God in new and challenging ways. It is not enough to reach back into history; nor is it sufficient to disclose the secrets of your heart. Revelation demands the full engagement of the mind in discovering and revealing the reality of God. The interaction of the Samaritan woman with Jesus in the next section articulates that movement into reflection. The Samaritan woman confronts Jesus with the issue that separated Jews from Samaritans:

> "Our ancestors worshipped on this mountain; but you people say that the place to worship is in Jerusalem." Jesus said to her, "Believe me, woman, the hour is coming

when you will worship the Father neither on this mountain nor in Jerusalem. You people worship what you do not understand; we worship what we understand, because salvation is from the Jews. But the hour is coming, and is now here, when true worshippers will worship the Father in Spirit and truth; and indeed the Father seeks such people to worship him. God is Spirit, and those who worship him must worship in Spirit and truth" (4:20–24).

Here the community emphasizes, once again, that conflict can be revelatory. Indeed, in this case, it generates a theology of worship "in Spirit and truth," which has no geographical bounds. The revelation resolves the conflict by positing that worship can happen anywhere.

The community shows how the mind should reflect on the various human, social, and divine elements that have come into play in a conversation (*logos*) with a living Jesus. Who could have guessed that the conversation would lead to a theology of worship? The members of the community turn their minds to theological issues in order to resolve cultural and historical (and perhaps personal) tensions through reflections on revelation. The story shows how the community makes theology out of conflict, disclosure, and cultural and religious difference. Their persistence in remaining and abiding with Jesus's revelation results in creating a new theology for their own day, one that begins to heal the divisions and hurts of previous generations.

The woman has engaged intently in the conflict with Jesus the Jew. She has held her ground as a Samaritan against the religious hegemony of Jerusalem. She has abided with Jesus. But Jesus also has held his ground as a revealer and as a Jew speaking with a Samaritan. Jesus has abided with the Samaritan woman. Their interaction affects the woman who, as a seeker, pursues knowledge of God with energy and commitment. She brings everything she knows about Samaritans and Jews to the conversation.

As the process of revelation continues, the level of conversation continues to deepen. Now the woman at the well takes the lead in asking for more revelation, and it is startling:

The woman said to him, "I know that the Messiah is coming, the one called the Anointed; when he comes, he will tell us everything." Jesus said to her, "I am he, the one who is speaking with you" (4:25–26).

Two things happen here: the woman asks about the Messiah, and Jesus proclaims himself to be the Messiah. For the Samaritan woman, the category in which she has placed Jesus has expanded: he is no longer simply a prophet, but now the Messiah. The community shows that revelation is not always linear. While Jesus's discussion about her marital status has led her to understand Jesus as a prophet, nothing up until now has prepared the community for her raising of the image of the Messiah. But when she is ready for the deeper revelation, Jesus honors her intuition by speaking directly. The way he phrases this is very important: a literal translation of Jesus's response would be that "I am." You recall that "I am" statements in the Israelite scriptures signify God's immediate presence; so Jesus claims divinity in very strong language. To the Samaritan woman he says: "The one who is speaking to you [is] 'I am.'" The interactive revelation has now hit the apex. The woman at the well understands who Jesus is and has become a true worshipper. The conflict is resolved in the revelation of God as Jesus and Jesus as God. Both Jesus and the Samaritan woman have claimed their realities and moved into direct revelation of God. This would not have been possible without everything that preceded it. The members of the community relating this story know the significance of the "I am" statement and find themselves face-to-face with God and with God's chief revealer, Jesus.

Through conversation (*logos*) the community shows how revelation forces the expansion of categories for understanding Jesus. Revelation comes through conversation, and overcomes—indeed even grows from—conflict and diversity. Revelation deepens with time as the community abides with Jesus.

Responding to Revelation

The community tells an astonishing and disconcerting consequence of revelation: the Samaritan woman becomes an apostle and revealer to her community.

> At that moment his disciples returned, and were amazed that he was talking with a woman, but still no one said, "What are you looking for?" or "Why are you talking with her?" The woman left her water jar and went into the town and said to the people, "Come see a man who told me everything I have done. Could he possibly be the Messiah?" They went out of the town and came to him (4:27–30).

She is just like all the other members of the Johannine community: a revealer and transmitter of the voice of Jesus to her community. While the woman is going out to her neighbors, the disciples are returning from their shopping expedition.

At this point the narration alternately develops the different response to Jesus of the two wider communities: on the one hand, the Samaritans and on the other, the disciples. Through the power of her rhetoric, the Samaritan woman succeeds in drawing her neighbors into a conversation with Jesus. The disciples, on the other hand, display an air of mistrust, misunderstanding, and conflict in their silence about the intimate meeting that they have witnessed. By now the Johannine community has shown how conflict and misunderstanding can lead to ever deeper revelation. We expect that something similar will occur with the disciples. But at this point the quality of the responses is striking: the outsiders are becoming insiders, and in their initial silence, the disciples are endangering their status as insiders. As the Samaritans gather, Jesus interacts with the disciples:

> Meanwhile, the disciples urged him, "Rabbi, eat." But he said to them, "I have food to eat of which you do not know." So the disciples said to one another, "Could someone have brought him something to eat?" Jesus said to them, "My food is to do the will of the one who sent me and to finish his work. Do you not say, 'In four months the harvest will be here'? I tell you, look up and see the fields ripe for the harvest. The reaper is already receiving his payment and gathering crops for eternal life, so that the sower and reaper can rejoice together. For here the saying is verified that 'One sows and another reaps.' I sent you to reap what you have not worked for; others have done the work, and you are sharing the fruits of their work" (4:31–38).

The conversation (*logos*) and discourse in the interactive revelation with the disciples begins with a focus on Jesus's comfort, as it did with the Samaritan woman. The disciples are concerned that Jesus has not eaten. Despite their status as disciples of Jesus, the community, processing the story, relates how the disciples lost sight of the revelatory function of Jesus and turned their minds not to theology and understanding of revelation, but to physical realities. The story warns the members about the perils of losing sight of revelation.

The interaction with the disciples indeed shows how misunderstanding, confusion, and disparate Jesus traditions can lead to revelation. Jesus and the disciples talk at cross-purposes as the disciples focus on material food while Jesus uses this as an opportunity to reveal the true nature of food. Jesus draws nourishment from doing the will of God. And just so, the Johannine community has found that they as disciples draw sustenance from their own missions, reaping from that for which they have not worked. This confirms the revelation embedded in the story of the Samaritan woman, an apostle (one sent) to her own community.

While the revelation seems clear, the methods of delivering the message must not be overlooked. This revelation resonates with so many different traditions and reveals the depths of the revealers' connection to the tradition. We hear echoes from Matthew and Luke of Jesus's sending out his followers because the harvest is ready (Matthew 9:37 and Luke 10:2); Jesus's parable of the sower (Mark 4:1–20, Matthew 13:3, and Luke 8:5); and we hear echoes of Paul's statement about sowing and reaping (2 Corinthians 9:6). The revealers have produced a response that explores many different traditions about apostolic ministry, and they have connected it to the true food that feeds Jesus. What feeds the Johannine community is the missionary work, including the construction of this very gospel. The revealers define the true significance of food by relating it to the tradition of missionary expansion of the community. The community shows how to look deeper into the meaning of things, to look for the revelation in the common activities of the day, like eating or drawing water, to connect with what they know of the traditions about Jesus, and to correlate those common activities to the mission of the church. The community hearing these revelatory words discovers how to look through deflection to the reality of God.

Forming Community Around the Voice

The interaction here, as with the Samaritan woman, starts with a problem: the Samaritan woman and water, the disciples and food. At the level of the story Jesus leads the characters into different understandings. For the Samaritan woman, Jesus leads to an understanding of worship and prophecy that transforms her into an evangelist to the Samaritans, the outsiders whom she brings into the fold. For the disciples, the insiders, Jesus instructs them on the evangelical mission, which is both a feeding for them and a cooperative effort with others. The Johannine community shows how the same conversations can lead to very different understandings. But it also shows that all of the participants, at whatever the level of understanding they have achieved, still remain a part of the community. The diversity and all the conflict it brings, as well as all the conflicting understandings present in it, provide the context for a continuing revelation that knows no bounds, parameters, or firm categories.

In our understanding of the Gospel of John, the voice of Jesus in the narrative of the stories represents the voice of one or more members of the community who are intimate hearers of Jesus. In other words, the voice of "Jesus" really is the voice of the continuing revelation of the Jesus whom the speaker recognizes as the living Jesus, the one sent from God to reveal God to the community. The community recognizes in the speaker's voice the voice of their shepherd. The interactive revelation in this story of the conversation between Jesus and the Samaritan woman and in the story of the responses from the disciples and the Samaritan community opens doors for forming a revelatory lifestyle, to hear the voice of Jesus spoken in the most unpredictable and challenging contexts and from the most unexpected people. Throughout the story, the revealing voice of Jesus leads the community into ever-deepening understandings of themselves and their lives. If a member of the community is an outsider like the Samaritan woman, the revealer guides them into understanding Jesus as a prophet and as the Messiah and brings them into the community. If the member is an insider, a disciple, the revealer instructs them on the missionary work of the community. The two-fold interactive process interweaves the life of Jesus with the issues and problems of the community in order to make them all members of the community, to help them become children of God, and to make them beloved disciples, intimate hearers of the voice of Jesus, the Good Shepherd.

Interactive revelation often begins with a concrete problem, like food and water in chapter 4. Other issues that emerge throughout the gospel have specific concrete problems as well. There are many conflicting problems with theological understandings, differences in worship, ritual, and practice, and issues with how to interpret scripture. These concrete problems lead the community to a deeper revelation and understanding of God. They are teaching moments that guide the community's formation in understanding revelation. This is all achieved through revelation from Jesus's voice, brought forth by the beloved disciples, and maintained by a practice of remaining and abiding in the revelation.

We began this section with the story of Penny Lane from *Almost Famous*. She, too, functions as a kind of revealer and guide to train the Band Aids and William Miller in the ways of the rock and roll community. She is an unlikely guide, especially since she has retired, but throughout the film she opens doors, explains circumstances, and remains steadfastly dedicated, even with her own personal loss and hurt, to the advancement of rock and roll, and her cherished band Stillwater. Revelation has no bounds or limits. It can happen at any time to any person, even —or perhaps especially—when it hurts.

Prophetic Revelation

As we said earlier, the Johannine community engages in two forms of revelation. The story of the woman at the well embodies the first, interactive revelation. In the story of the healing of the paralytic, found in John 5, the Johannine community demonstrates the second form of revelation, prophetic revelation. Here, Jesus is shown as both a healer and the prophetic revealer of the will of the Father. In the film *Almost Famous* the lead guitarist, Russell, at one point finds himself in the midst of conflict with his band, William Miller, the teenage critic, and his own identity. Russell is conflicted about his role as the prophetic voice for Stillwater and, by extension, for the new understanding of rock and roll.

The immediate context is William Miller's attempt to identify a single leader who will speak for the band. Stillwater is conflicted about this, because the band members have a strong sense of group cohesion, and William Miller's seemingly innocent request seems to violate the intimacy that the band experiences in their performances and lives. The band wanted to imitate the Rolling Stones model of two leaders, Keith Richards and Mick Jagger, but the reality of Russell's central role thwarts this model. William Miller recognizes the plain fact that Russell alone stands at the heart of the band. The band's promoter, seeing the same reality, designs a T-shirt for the band. When the band members see the shirt they are angered. The picture on the shirt has only Russell in clear focus; the other members are blurred. The T-shirt incident brings to the surface the inner conflict in the band. Russell sets out in search of what is real; the conflict has collapsed his world. So he and William Miller attend a real Topeka, Kansas, teenage party.

At the party, Russell remembers the reality of his own youth, a reality that he finds sane and rational compared with the appearance of the rock and roll industry. Not surprisingly, he is troubled that this connection with the past will be recorded by William Miller, whose very presence reminds him of the conflict and confusion he faces in the present. After taking LSD in a drink, Russell climbs up on the roof of the house with the adoring teenagers below screaming in joy. He yells, "I love rock and roll!" The teenagers groan at this bland pronouncement. Then he screams, "I'm a golden god. I'm on drugs!" and the crowd erupts in frenzied enthusiasm—because they could connect with this revelation—and Russell dives from the roof of the house into the swimming pool. Afterward, William Miller and Russell return to their familiar life with the band, and they move on to the next concert city. In the midst of the crisis, Russell reveals his deepest loves and desires, and William Miller, taking notes throughout, records the revelation for his article.

William Miller's and Russell's experience in Topeka resonates with the way the Johannine community experienced revelation. We have two perspectives given at once. The lead guitarist speaks in the first person: "I love rock and roll" and "I'm a golden god." William Miller, however, speaks in the third person; he describes the lead guitarist's statements as "he is a lover of rock and roll" and "he is a golden god." Both statements are revelatory, but from different perspectives. We find the same alternation between direct revelatory statements ("I am") and third-person revelation ("the son") in the gospel of John. But in the gospel, these two perspectives are given in the singular voice of Jesus. The site for these revelatory statements is the story of the healing of the paralytic. An earlier version of the story appears in Mark 2:1–13 with parallels in Matthew and Luke.

The Johannine community, then, transforms a familiar story—as familiar as Topeka, Kansas—from the synoptic tradition to demonstrate the work within the community of revealers, prophets from whose lips come the revelation of the living Jesus in the community's midst.

As with the story of the woman at the well, the story of the healing of the paralytic opens with a very physical need: the need to walk.

[T]here was a feast of the Jews, and Jesus went up to Jerusalem. Now there is in Jerusalem at the Sheep (Gate) a pool called in Hebrew Bethesda, with five porticoes. In these lay a large number of ill, blind, lame, and crippled. One man was there who had been ill for thirty-eight years. When Jesus saw him lying there and knew that he had been ill for a long time, he said to him, "Do you want to be well?" The sick man answered him, "Sir, I have no one to put me into the pool when the water is stirred up; while I am on my way, someone else gets down there before me." Jesus said to him, "Rise, take up your mat, and walk." Immediately the man became well, took up his mat, and walked (5:1–9a).

We envision the community beginning the revelatory process, the revelatory conversation (*logos*), by reading the familiar story of the healing of the paralytic in Mark. Quickly this becomes an occasion for the revealers in the community to do their work of bringing forth for the rest of the community the deep revelatory significance of healing.

In Mark's gospel and its parallels, the revelation arising from conflict is Jesus's ability to forgive sins. For the Johannine community, as we shall see, this revelation is deepened to encompass Jesus's power and authorization to reveal the Father.

In the next section of the story, a simple good deed turns into a moment of conflict.

> Now that day was a sabbath. So the Jews said to the man who was cured, "It is the sabbath, and it is not lawful for you to carry your mat." He answered them, "The man who made me well told me, 'Take up your mat and walk.'" They asked him, "Who is the man who told you, 'Take it up and walk'?" The man who was healed did not know who it was, for Jesus had slipped away, since there was a crowd there. After this Jesus found him in the temple area and said to him, "Look, you are well; do not sin any more, so that nothing worse may happen to you." The man went and told the Jews that Jesus was the one who had made him well. Therefore, the Jews began to persecute Jesus because he did this on a sabbath (5:9b–16).

The paralytic following Jesus's command leaves the pool and confronts the wider community. The healed man's response creates a conflict within the community.

Recall the diversity of the Johannine community that we discussed earlier. The community consists of a wide variety of people: Greeks and Romans, Samaritans, Jews, named and unnamed disciples, and people not found in the other gospel stories; they are all part of the Johannine community seeking revelation from Jesus. Clearly some members of the Johannine community are questioning observance of the Sabbath, criticizing Jesus for healing as a forbidden work on the Sabbath. So the conflict in the community focuses on whether members should observe Jewish law strictly or find new ways of understanding their missionary work. The prophetic revelation that follows addresses this issue from a wide variety of perspectives. Building on this conflict, Jesus begins a long prophetic revelation:

> But Jesus answered them, "My Father is at work until now, so I am at work." For this reason the Jews tried all the more to kill him, because he not only broke the sabbath but he also called God his own father, making himself equal to God. Jesus answered and said to them, "Amen, amen, I say to you, a son cannot do anything on his own, but only what he sees his father doing; for what he does, his son will do also. For the Father loves his Son and shows him everything that he himself does, and he will show him greater works than these, so that you may be amazed" (5:17-19).

The Gospel of John is replete with long revelatory speeches by Jesus. Because of the length of this speech, we will break it into parts so that we can see more clearly the way the revealers in the community worked together to open wider contexts for understanding Jesus, the Father, and the mission of the community.

The Voices of Jesus

As we have suggested, prophetic revelation, as distinct from interactive revelation, works primarily through a singular voice that speaks most often in the first person singular ("I am" sayings) or in the third-person singular ("he does") spoken by Jesus to reveal God's message and presence to others. The first-person technique is usually put on Jesus's lips where he speaks as "I" either to God or to characters around him. The third-person voices the revelation at one step removed from the direct first-person revelation, but still in Jesus's speech. The third-person speech generally has Jesus make statements about himself in the third person, using titles such as the Son of God, Messiah, Good Shepherd, true vine, and many other metaphors. This prophetic revelation allows the revealers in the community to explain Jesus's role and significance to others in a self-referential way in the process of giving a direct revelation.

In this discourse, the community revealers use both first person and third person prophetic revelations. Jesus's first statement, for instance, includes both forms: "My Father is at work until now [third-person revelation] so I am at work [first-person]" (5:17b). In the revelatory process, we notice how many topics the revealers introduce: the identification of Jesus with the work of the Father and the mutual relationship between Jesus and the Father that makes Jesus God. We wonder what holds these disparate ideas together and how they are related to the question of the Sabbath. It is at this breaking point that interactive discourse ceases, other voices are silenced, and revelation ensues. What holds the issues together is simply that they are all issues within the community that the revealers are addressing; they are loosely connected to the healing of the man at the pool, which has become the occasion for new revelation. We are privileged to eavesdrop on the Johannine community's discourse on the revelation received on these topics.

The inception of prophetic revelation is marked by the first-person voice on Jesus's lips ("Amen, amen, I say to you.") that moves quickly to a third-person voice ("a son cannot do anything on his own, but only what he sees this father doing; for what he does, his son will do also") (5:19). Here we see clearly the two perspectives on the person of Jesus. We have difficulty seeing how the revelation relates to the question of the Sabbath. The revealers affirm that the only way to understand the Sabbath is to understand Jesus. The revelation shifts the ground of controversy from the breaking of the Sabbath law to Jesus's identity. The immediate switch from Jesus referring to himself as "I" to his referring to himself as "the son" makes the identification explicit: the revealers relate both first-person and third-person perspectives on Jesus. In talking about the son, the revealers explain the basis for Jesus's actions: Jesus does what the Father does. The movement between first person and third person representing the perspectives of various community revealers is seamless, in order to underscore and emphasize this identification. The third person functions as a reflection upon the person and role of Jesus and not on the breaking of Sabbath law, but it is placed on Jesus's lips as though we are hearing Jesus ruminating about himself.

Voice and Revelatory Themes

Then the revelers continue in the third person by introducing new themes not about the Sabbath but elaborating on the person of Jesus:

> For the Father loves his Son and shows him everything that he himself does, and he will show him greater works than these, so that you may be amazed. For just as the Father raises the dead and gives life, so also does the Son give life to whomever he wishes. Nor does the Father judge anyone, but he has given all judgment to his Son, so that all may honor the Son just as they honor the Father. Whoever does not honor the Son does not honor the Father who sent him (5:20–23).

Notice the shift in perspective. This revealer reflects on a number of important aspects of Jesus's work. The revelations do not necessarily follow one upon the other, but rather seem to gather various loosely related topics into one longer revelation: the Father loves Jesus and shows Jesus what to do; Jesus will do greater works to make his followers marvel, including raising the dead and giving life; the Father has made Jesus the judge; and both Jesus and the Father deserve honor.

The only thing that holds these pronouncements together is that they are being spoken in Jesus's voice by the community's revealers. But the two perspectives (first and third person) talk to one another in a seamless fashion. The third-person reflection that the revealers speak in Jesus's voice provides multiple pieces of information about him. Questions about the Sabbath (that so occupy the synoptic gospels) have long been left behind, and Jesus's voice has gathered a number of themes together. These themes do not seem to be related to each other, except that they explore Jesus's identity as the Johannine community understands and experiences him.

This long discourse then is again interrupted by a dramatic revelation in the first-person voice of Jesus:

> "Amen, amen, I say to you, whoever hears my word and believes in the one who sent me has eternal life and will not come to condemnation, but has passed from death into life. Amen, amen, I say to you, the hour is coming and is now here when the dead will hear the voice of the Son of God, and those who hear will live. For just as the Father has life in himself, so also he gave to his Son the possession of life in himself. And he gave him power to exercise judgment, because he is the Son of Man. Do not be amazed at this, because the hour is coming in which all

who are in the tombs will hear his voice and will come out, those who have done good deeds to the resurrection of life, but those who have done wicked deeds to the resurrection of condemnation" (5:24–29).

As the next step in formative practice, the community shows how the members are to receive prophetic revelation; the revealers speak in the voice of Jesus and call the community to a renewed faith in the Father who sent Jesus. The revelation continues with related themes of the identity of Jesus and his relationship to the Father. The revealers affirm that Jesus is the one sent from the Father who gives life, and who judges. The characteristics outlined in the third-person revelation just before this continue in the first person. The voices are merged into a single stream of revelation.

With the return to a first person singular, "Amen, amen, I say to you" (5:25), the community's reflection takes up the question of the implications of the relationship of Jesus to the Father for understanding the future in a number of themes: the question of the dead having life, the right of the Son of Man to judge, and the final judgment of the dead. The revealers build upon one another's visions of the future. They refer to those in the tomb being raised, to the Father and the Son having life, to judgment exercised by the Son of Man, and to the resurrection for judgment. The statements of the various revealers are woven together, some connecting with other elements in the revelation, and yet they do not constitute a cohesive argument. They seem piled one upon another. What holds them together is that the various revelations are given in the voice of Jesus, and the community hears and recognizes their various voices as the voice of Jesus. All the voices have entered the sheep gate.

This section of the revelation that began in the conflict over the healing of the paralytic on the Sabbath ends with a first-person statement that brings it back to the beginning of the revelation in reference to Jesus's deeds. "I cannot do anything on my own; I judge as I hear, and my judgment is just, because I do not seek my own will but the will of the one who sent me" (5:30). This revelation summarizes succinctly the issues presented throughout this discourse. It affirms Jesus's intimate connection to the Father and his role as judge, which the Father has committed him to perform. The various revealers in the community have done their work: they read the scriptures, spoke in the voice of Jesus, and explored the implications of their understanding of Jesus for the community. The Johannine community looks on in amazement at the various revelations, just as one of the revealers indicated they would.

Interpreting Prophetic Revelation and Writing a Gospel
Now we wish to reflect on how we understand that this revelation is used in teaching community formation. First of all, we have pointed out how the

revelation moves from the first to the third person. The first-person voice captures our attention and commands power and authority. It makes Jesus's voice present to the community. Then the third-person voice emerges and offers a reflection about the person of Jesus that, while less dramatic, carries the same power and authority. The immediate presence from the first-person voice placed on Jesus's lips is now articulated in third-person titles describing Jesus's identity: Son, Son of God, and Son of Man. These are some of the titles used for theological reflections by the community of John. The various perspectives offered by the revealers form a complete process of theological reflection and revelation.

What is the significance of these revelations? Unlike all the other gospels, these revelations indicate a Jesus who is real, present, embodied, and speaking directly to the community through the revealers in their midst. Scholars have long recognized that these prolonged revelations set the Gospel of John apart from the other gospels. As the last of the canonical gospels we know that something more than the transmission of the Jesus tradition is taking place. The community experienced the historical Jesus who had lived nearly seventy years before the production of this gospel as an active living presence in their church. The revealers in the community convey the words of this present Jesus to the community. The first-person singular voice makes that presence real. It clearly is not spoken by the historical Jesus, but rather by a voice in the community that spoke the divine voice of Jesus to the community.

As we know from the *Didache*, prophets carrying the word of the Lord were a familiar fixture in earliest Christianity. Here in the Gospel of John we find the evidence of such prophetic revelations on the lips of Jesus to guide and instruct the members of this community. The third-person singular references in these prophetic revelations show the way these prophets applied their prophetic sayings to their understanding of the historical Jesus as Son of God and Son of Man. They also interpreted the historical Jesus in the context of a later community whose questions and concerns differed from those of earlier generations. So the prophetic revelations carry forth the voice of Jesus from the past into the present experience of the community in order to form future members. It models an immediate relationship with a living Jesus as a speaking voice within a community.

The interactive and prophetic revelations present interesting content for the sayings of Jesus that are radically different from the sayings in other gospels. How did this new content come to be? In order to understand it we need to characterize how these revealers functioned in the community as a variation from what we discussed in the *Didache*. The core of the community presenting the Gospel of John consists of revealer prophets who live together and who together give voice to Jesus in the community. They are the living embodiment of the Beloved Disciple. These prophets interact with other members in the community and with other religious communities, and their role requires that they speak the words of the living Jesus in every activity and meeting of the community. These embodied beloved disciples are there whenever the community gathers, when scripture is being read, when problems are being faced, whenever conflict exists, whenever they come together for their sacramental rituals, such as the meal and the foot washing, whenever they incorporate a new member into their community, and whenever the members yearn to know the reality of Jesus in their lives, some seventy years after his resurrection.

But these embodied beloved disciples, the prophets, do not always bring forth the same words of Jesus; sometimes they even disagree. But the community knows that whatever they say comes directly from Jesus through their lips. So the community records their words, their revelations, their insights, and their discernment as the complex revelation of the living Jesus who stands in their midst. The community's work is to abide with all the revelations, to remain constant in receiving and grappling with the revelations through the context of their lives. The written gospel that we are interpreting is their testament to these revelations, their interactions, their disagreements, and their joys and sorrows as they live out their lives in Christ as a community whose core consists of these holy prophets of Jesus. Abiding with the prophets, the embodied beloved disciples, makes for hard work for the members of the community. There is no way to predict where they will go in their revelations; there is no control over the content of the revelation; and there is no authority to mediate between conflicting revelations. So the members must simply abide in the presence of Jesus and attend to his various voices, despite the difficulties of doing so.

Abiding is like the band getting on the tour bus and heading to the next town even as the conflicts and tensions remain unresolved. They have their revealers in their midst in the voice of William Miller and the lead guitarist. They have their mission to display the essence of rock and roll. And they have the community of support, the Band Aids and the fans, who listen eagerly for the revelation that comes from their performances. The band's revealers will guide them through these confusing times, responding to the issues and problems that arise. Revealers work that way, despite the differences in perspective.

The Dynamic of Revelation

The Johannine community presents in the Bread of Life discourse (John 6) a wrenching portrayal of the way revelation of sublime truths brings to consciousness the divisions in a community. These divisions may be canyons, ultimately unbridgeable, leading to often painful separations. *Almost Famous* portrays the impact of a series of revelations on the community that is Stillwater. On their way to a concert, their plane enters an apocalyptic electrical storm. The pilot tells them that they are in serious trouble and he hopes to land safely in a field. The storm rages and the plane loses altitude. They face impending death.

This crisis begins a process of revelation as members of the band disclose the secrets of their hearts, and express the tensions and conflicts within the band. The lead guitarist Russell tells the band that he loves them. Another member of the band confesses that the band has been his only real family. Then one discloses that he has slept with Russell's wife. Many of them reveal that they have slept with the manager's wife. Tensions rise. William Miller angrily confronts the band with the way they misused Penny Lane, and confesses his love for her. The band tells Russell that, although he has been the heart of the band, they have had enormous problems living with him and his erratic ways. The drummer screams, "I'm gay!" (the only words he speaks in the film). The manager apologizes for stealing money from them. The new promoter admits that he might have killed someone in a hit-and-run accident. The moment of crisis has become a moment of revelation, a time of disclosure, conflict, admission, and expressions of strong emotions. The revelations begin to reform the band's practices. In the end, the plane stabilizes and they do not crash. Walking into their hotel room, they are sobered by the depth of conflict and emotion that has been expressed. The fault lines of the band have been exposed and articulated clearly. Pain abounds. It is the revelation of that pain, however, that leads to their eventual healing and reconciliation.

Living in a revelatory community demands fortitude and strength. It is not easy. It demands a formative practice simply to abide, to remain steadfast. The Johannine community, much like Stillwater, lived with such diversity that conflict was inevitable. Revealers did not always agree on the significance of the other revealer's revelations. Jews, Samaritans, Greeks, Romans, opponents and seekers alike—all these find a home in the community aiming to make every member an embodied beloved disciple, a revealer. Conflict was not only inevitable, but it is evident in the gospel's description of the community's life. But their value, their highest aspiration, was to meld every disparate member into a cohesive community through revelations that held them together. Their commitment to remain and to abide with Jesus, to stand steadfast in the face of the revelatory conflict, came to them at a great cost.

In our description of the Samaritan woman at the well, we saw the way revelation occurred in everyday living among people divided by culture and religion, and the misunderstanding and conversion that resulted from that revelation. In the story of the healing of the paralytic at the pool of Bethesda, we experienced the way the many voices of the various revealers in the community guided the community through a revelatory reading of a synoptic gospel healing to new and greater understandings of Jesus and of the Father who sent him. These observations set the stage for examining the cost of living in such a diverse revelatory community in the great discourse on the Bread of Life (John 6). In the discourse on the Bread of Life, we find the most sublime theology of the Eucharist, the Lord's Supper that the other gospels place just before the Passion and crucifixion of Jesus. It is a sublime theology that the church has recognized throughout its history. And at the same time, we find in the same discourse the reality of the conflict and confusion that this very theology created for the diverse members of the Johannine community. Sublimity and conflict call the community to abide, to remain, to stand steadfast with one another even in the midst of difficulty, confusion, disagreement, and discouragement. The revelation, and the formative practice of abiding, come at a great cost.

Honoring Past Revelations

Just as individuals in Stillwater's retinue had to bring forth their checkered past in the moment of crisis, so the Johannine community uses the traditions from the Gospel of Mark to form the basis for their exploration of their community. The Johannine community honors the revelations in the traditions they have received, even when those revelations conflict with their current understandings and visions of Jesus and of the community that the living Jesus forms. These revelations at once form the platform for new revelations and, as a consequence, reveal the fault lines in the community. In this way, the Johannine community bridges tradition and revelation.

One sequence in John's gospel in particular displays the community's process of using the tradition from Mark to develop new revelations, uncover community divisions, and reform the community as Jesus directs it. The sequence includes the testimony of John the Baptist (5:31–47), the miracle of the feeding of the five thousand (6:1–15), the miracle of the walking on water (6:16–21), and the discourse on the Bread of Life (6:22–71). John the Baptist introduces the two miracles, as he does in Mark, but the Johannine revealers frame the miracles as part of a conversation (*logos*) about the testimony and signs. John the Baptist raises the question of testimony; the miracles raise the question of the signs.

Let's first summarize John's sequence. It opens where the revelations associated with the healing of the paralytic end (5:30), as the revealer addresses the continuing authority of John the Baptist for the community. John, we learn, is inferior to Jesus, who has been sent by the Father (5:36). Jesus then performs one of his great signs, the feeding of the five thousand with five barley loaves and two fish (6:1–14). Separately Jesus and the disciples leave the wilderness but Jesus later joins the disciples in their boat as they cross a stormy Sea of Galilee (6:15–21). When the crowds who had witnessed the feeding miracle join Jesus and the disciples, their questions prompt Jesus to declaim the revelatory Bread of Life discourse (6:22–71). As we proceed through this sequence, we will note how the Johannine community wrestled with the traditions from the Gospel of Mark, producing revelatory discourse in the process.

The miracle of the walking on water, with its critique of believing in the wonder-working Jesus, and the feeding of the five thousand both invoke a criticism of yet another important "sign" in the church, the presence of Jesus in the Eucharist, the Lord's Supper. At the crossroads, when John's gospel was produced, Ignatius tried to link the Eucharist to the presence of the bishop. Ignatius argued that the only valid Eucharist was the one celebrated by the bishop. Every other Eucharist was invalid and ineffective. This is not the perspective of the Johannine community, whose prophets ask what a living Jesus would say about the Eucharist in their own time at the beginning of the second century. A living Jesus, to the Johannine prophets and community, would never link the Eucharist to the presence of a church authority. The Johannine Eucharist means much more. Since they have a living Jesus in their midst, with whom they abide and remain steadfast all the time, the Eucharist must mean something else.

To be fair, in later Christian theology, this discourse on the Bread of Life in John forged the church's eucharistic theology. The church took the lead from the Johannine community, which identified this discourse with the Eucharist. John's text reads: "Then Jesus took the loaves, gave thanks, and distributed them to those who were reclining" (6:11). The "gave thanks" here in Greek is "to make Eucharist," and so both the Johannine community and the church identified this discourse with the sacrament. Later Christian theologians merged Johannine theology with the church's practice of the Eucharist as the eating of Jesus's body and drinking his blood as instituted during the Passover meal before Jesus's death. That is how later people read this discourse, but the members of John's community entered a different way of understanding the Bread of Life. It was in its day a startling and dramatic revelatory moment that we need to recapture in our reading. So just as nothing in the church tradition of Mark, Matthew, or Luke paved the way for this discourse in antiquity, nothing should blunt the starkness of the revelatory conflict this discourse presents.

This discourse shows more than any other the suspension of the Johannine community between church tradition and revelation. The discourse invokes the tradition: Jesus is the bread given to the community at a Passover feast. John's gospel underscores the tradition dramatically in this discourse, but the community refracts, reorients, and refines the tradition to make it a platform for revelation of something new, different, and compelling. It is so new and different that it creates conflict in the community—conflict which itself becomes a revelatory platform. The dynamism itself is compelling and challenging. Now more than ever the Johannine community will be challenged by their prophets to practice abiding in the midst of conflict and disagreement about the sacrament.

The Revelation about John the Baptist

So we begin with the discourse material about John the Baptist. Watching how John's gospel deals with John the Baptist instructs us about how the prophets in the Johannine community engage tradition in forming new revelation. In Mark's gospel, the author's recounting of John the Baptist's death by beheading at an imperial meal (Mark 6:17–29) forms a prelude to the feeding story (6:30–44). Mark connects John the Baptist to these miracles. The Johannine community transforms the revelation.

First, the revealers in the voice of Jesus speak to the community about John as one who continues to provide revelation to the community:

> "You sent emissaries to John, and he testified to the truth. I do not accept testimony from a human being, but I say this so that you may be saved. He was a burning and shining lamp, and for a while you were content to rejoice in his light" (5:33–35).

The revealers treat John the Baptist as one who testifies, who provides valid revelation. The Johannine community is not interested in the fact that John the Baptist was beheaded, but rather it is interested in the Baptist's role as the one giving revelation and in holding on to that revelation. The Baptist's revelation actually starts in the first chapter of John's gospel where John points to Jesus and says, "Behold the Lamb of God, who takes away the sin of the world" (1:20). This revelation of the Johannine revealers does not denigrate John the Baptist, but incorporates his testimony into the community's revelation. The revealers shift the significance of John the Baptist from the martyrdom tradition to his revelation of the truly divine mission of Jesus. The revealers upbraid those who do not have John the Baptist's "word remaining in" them. The formative practice of remaining in revelation includes the Baptist's testimony. While the Baptist's testimony is true, the Johannine revealers argue that Jesus has a testimony from the Father that is greater than the Baptist's. Further, the tradition to be reconciled must include the testimony about Jesus in the Israelite scriptures:

> "But I have testimony greater than John's. The works that the Father gave me to accomplish, these works that I perform testify on my behalf that the Father has sent me. Moreover, the Father who sent me has testified on my behalf. But you have never heard his voice nor seen his form, and you do not have his word remaining in you, because you do not believe in the one whom he has sent. You search the scriptures, because you think you have eternal life through them; even they testify on my behalf. But you do not want to come to me to have life. I do not accept human praise; moreover, I know that you do not have the love of God in you. I came in the name of my Father, but you do not accept me; yet if another comes in his own name, you will accept him. How can you believe, when you accept praise from one another and do not seek the praise that comes from the only God? Do not think that I will accuse you before the Father: the one who will

accuse you is Moses, in whom you have placed your hope. For if you had believed
Moses, you would have believed me, because he wrote about me. But if you do not
believe his writings, how will you believe my words?" (John 5:36–47).

Here the revealers explore older sources and traditions that point to Jesus. To
the testimony of John the Baptist, the revealers add the testimony of Moses in
the Israelite scriptures. Both John the Baptist and Moses give testimony to a
community struggling with the traditions about Jesus, the relationship of Jesus
to the scriptures, and the role of Jesus among those who look to John the Baptist
and Moses as guides. The old ways of understanding have ceded to new, revelatory ways. The older traditions have not died; they continue to function within
the Johannine community, but they have become the basis for new revelations
as testimony to Jesus. It is the revelation born in the old tradition that speaks
loudly to the community; it is the way the revealers extend the tradition that
brings new life to the community. The community works to reconcile the two,
steadfast to the past as they have received it, to current revelation and to future
discourse as they will hear them. Their formative practice of remaining and
abiding relates to all the traditions the community has received to the extent
that they reveal Jesus to the community.

The Miracle of the Feeding of the Five Thousand
Abiding and remaining in the tradition and using the tradition as a basis for new
revelation continues with the community's reading of the feeding of the five
thousand. The Gospel of Mark (6:34–44) tells of Jesus and his followers with-
drawing to the wilderness to find respite from the intense ministry of healing and
teaching the crowd around them. The crowd races to follow them. The retreat
that Jesus and his followers sought does not occur. Instead Jesus has compassion
on the crowd and continues to perform his ministry of teaching. This particular
teaching is long and it takes Jesus's close followers to remind Jesus that a break
and a meal would be great at this point. Jesus requests that his followers feed the
people, but they have not enough money to feed such a large crowd. So they go to
the people and discover they have five loaves and two fish. Jesus takes this offering from the people and, looking upward, blesses the food before it is distributed
to the crowd. Miraculously, the people are satisfied and well-fed by the loaves and
fish. This fulfilling meal results in more abundance because baskets are filled after
the meal. As we discussed earlier in the chapter on Mark, this familiar account
bears many connotations of an anti-imperial tale.

The prophets in John's community amplify this familiar account of the feeding of the five thousand:

After this, Jesus went across the Sea of Galilee (of Tiberias). A large crowd followed
him, because they saw the signs he was performing on the sick. Jesus went up on the

mountain, and there he sat down with his disciples. The Jewish feast of Passover was near. When Jesus raised his eyes and saw that a large crowd was coming to him, he said to Philip, "Where can we buy enough food for them to eat?" He said this to test him, because he himself knew what he was going to do. Philip answered him, "Two hundred days' wages worth of food would not be enough for each of them to have a little (bit)." One of his disciples, Andrew, the brother of Simon Peter, said to him, "There is a boy here who has five barley loaves and two fish; but what good are these for so many?" Jesus said, "Have the people recline." Now there was a great deal of grass in that place. So the men reclined, about five thousand in number. Then Jesus took the loaves, gave thanks, and distributed them to those who were reclining, and also as much of the fish as they wanted. When they had had their fill, he said to his disciples, "Gather the fragments left over, so that nothing will be wasted." So they collected them, and filled twelve wicker baskets with fragments from the five barley loaves that had been more than they could eat. When the people saw the sign he had done, they said, "This is truly the Prophet, the one who is to come into the world." Since Jesus knew that they were going to come and carry him off to make him king, he withdrew again to the mountain alone (6:1–15).

The Johannine community knows Mark's story, but must now refract it to meet the needs of their community. We see the refraction begin in making specific that the feeding miracle occurs during the Jewish feast of the Passover, a time only hinted by Mark. As we discussed in the chapter on Mark, the Passover invokes memories of the Exodus for the Jewish members of the community and recalls the Last Supper in Mark when Jesus institutes the sacrament of his body and blood. This will become an important detail in the discourse that follows, and it shows how the Johannine community mixes traditions from the gospels and the wider Israelite scriptures to suit its needs. Since the community consists in all likelihood of observant Jews as well as many other people, this blending of traditions reflects the process of reconciling the very diverse life and perspectives found in the community. The blending of traditions provides the revealer prophets with a challenge to make the voice of the living Jesus present and pertinent to their lives.

We also see how the Johannine revealers read the tradition. They honor the tradition by retaining the Markan sequence of miracles (John the Baptist, feeding the five thousand, walking on water), but they alter the tradition to accommodate their understanding of Jesus. For example, when the Johannine community heard the Markan story they were troubled by how Jesus was portrayed. In the Markan story Jesus seems to be absent-minded in his teaching to the people, unaware of the needs of the people. Unnamed disciples must draw Jesus's attention to the late hour and the need of the gathered people to eat. In contrast, John's gospel portrays Jesus as in complete control, seeing the crowd before they have arrived and initiating a discussion with Philip over feeding the multitude "because he himself knew what he was going to do" (6:6). With this alteration, Jesus now displays knowledge of the revelation that is about to come, purposefully unfolding the divine plan. The gospel will build on this foreknowledge as it explores the meaning of his actions in the discourse that will follow. The revealer prophets in the Johannine community identify with the characters in the Markan account and begin to explore the richness of revelation inherent in the story they tell. The revealers even tell the story emphasizing that Jesus is a prophet, just like them. The crowd's response to the miracle introduces the prophetic dynamic by calling Jesus a prophet. The story itself points toward the presence of the prophets in the singular voice of Jesus.

At the same time, the miracle of the feeding of the five thousand introduces the question of signs: "A large crowd followed him, because they saw the signs he was performing on the sick" (6:2). And the conclusion to the miracle underscores the power of signs: "When the people saw the sign he had done, they said, 'This is truly the Prophet, the one who has come into the world'" (6:14). We will see that the Johannine revealers, while taking up the miracles in the Markan account, frame them in a new context, one critical of believing in Jesus only because he works miracles.

The revelation in the feeding of five thousand carries forward into the ritual practices of the community, for the feeding of the five thousand, as a cipher for the Eucharist, remains an open table. Everyone is fed. In the Markan account and its parallels in Matthew and Luke, the Last Supper is reserved for the circle of the disciples. But for the Johannine community, the Eucharist is open to all who follow Jesus, without regard to their understanding about what it means to follow Jesus. In usual fashion for John's community, however, these various understandings cause conflict and disagreement. It is these conflicts and disagreements that the revealers will address in the discourse that follows. Implicit in this way of approaching the meaning of the Eucharist is a critique of the various traditions of a restricted Eucharist. This will become clearer as we enter the discourse itself where we will see the community suspended between tradition and revelation.

The Miracle of Jesus's Walking on Water: the Problem of Signs

The miracle of walking on the water (6:16–21) reflects the Markan story, but the miracle in John's gospel has shifted focus.

> When it was evening, his disciples went down to the sea, embarked in a boat, and went across the sea to Capernaum. It had already grown dark, and Jesus had not yet come to them. The sea was stirred up because a strong wind was blowing. When they had rowed about three or four miles, they saw Jesus walking on the sea and coming near the boat, and they began to be afraid. But he said to them, "It is I. Do not be afraid." They wanted to take him into the boat, but the boat immediately arrived at the shore to which they were heading (6:16–21).

John's account retains some of the elements from Mark: the storm, the disciples alone in the boat, the disciples' fear, and their inability to recognize Jesus as he walks toward them on the water. Mark emphasizes the power to still the storm, while John uses the story as a basis for revelation. In John's gospel, Jesus says to the disciples: "'I am. Do not fear'" (our translation). Jesus reveals himself with the name of God ("I am"), and he tells them not to be afraid. Again, this is a stunning revelation: Jesus identifies with the God who led the people from Egypt, another bridge to the Passover event.

This revelation forms the introduction to the discourse on the Bread of Life. The revealers take up the meaning of the signs and the significance of the Eucharist at the same time, by fearlessly engaging in a difficult conversation within their community. For the Johannine community, the Markan eucharistic tradition acted as a foundation for revelation. Unlike miraculous deeds that merely display Jesus's remarkable power, signs point to something greater than the miraculous event. When asked by the people how he got to the other side, the revealers in Jesus's voice begin a discourse about signs:

> And when they found him across the sea they said to him, "Rabbi, when did you get here?" Jesus answered them and said, "Amen, amen, I say to you, you are looking for me not because you saw signs but because you ate the loaves and were filled. Do not work for food that perishes but for the food that endures for eternal life, which the Son of Man will give you. For on him the Father, God, has set his seal." So they said to him, "What can we do to accomplish the works of God?" Jesus answered and said to them, "This is the work of God, that you believe in the one he sent." So they said to him, "What sign can you do, that we may see and believe in you? What can you do? Our ancestors ate manna in the desert, as it is written: 'He gave them bread from heaven to eat'" (6:26–31).

The revealers open the discourse by taking up the problem of believing because of the signs and move into further reflection based on the various understandings of the miracle of the feeding. The feeding miracle has set up this opportunity for discourse when Jesus instructs the disciples, "Gather the fragments left over, so that nothing will be wasted" (6:12). The discourse gathers all the fragments of reaction to the miracle, so that nothing is lost.

Some in their community need signs to believe, even more signs than the miracles in Mark provide. But the revealers introduce new themes to expand the horizon of the community's conversation. The revealers begin to weave together the themes that will follow from the feeding of the five thousand. We are given a window into their process. They take up a criticism of believing because of signs, but the sign is that of eating the loaves. They also introduce the distinction between the perishable food of those eating manna in the desert, and the imperishable food. They expand the theological reflection to embrace

belief in Jesus and they reinforce the Passover theme. It is as though the revealers criticize those who believe in miracles and do not make the connections
between the miracles and the wider revelatory context.

This critical reading of tradition through a blending of themes characterizes
the prophets' and community's way of reading the tradition. It presents a challenge to the community: How can anyone remain or abide in the midst of this
blending and weaving of tradition? It forces the community to expand horizons,
to live with diverse kinds of knowledge, and to experience the miracles as part
of a much larger theological frame. By forcing horizons to expand, the revealers
set the stage for a much more conflict-laden set of revelations.

The Bread of Life Discourse Begins

The revealers thrust the community immediately into the disagreements about
the meaning of the miracle of the feeding of the five thousand. The many sign-
seekers taunt Jesus with the sign from Exodus:

> "Our ancestors ate manna in the desert, as it is written: 'He gave them bread from
> heaven to eat.'" Jesus then said to them, "Amen, amen, I say to you, it was not
> Moses who gave the bread from heaven; my Father gives you the true bread from
> heaven. For the bread of God is that which comes down from heaven and gives
> life to the world" (6:31–33).

This is the primary prophetic revelation of the discourse, but the revelation begins
in an exploration of the biblical tradition. The revealers assert that God gave the
bread, not Moses, and the bread of God "comes down from heaven" to feed the
people. The revealers explore the true significance of the manna from heaven
and continue a discourse about the Eucharist through the Israelite scriptures. The
community reveals here that forceful and honest interaction among the community's revealers, so focused on understanding the way God works, marks the way
the members of the Johannine community relate to one another.

The first revelation sets the stage by presenting a series of connections that
the revealers make in Jesus's voice and that are essential to understanding the
discourse:

> So they said to him, "Sir, give us this bread always." Jesus said to them, "I am
> the bread of life; whoever comes to me will never hunger, and whoever believes
> in me will never thirst. But I told you that although you have seen [me], you do
> not believe. Everything that the Father gives me will come to me, and I will not
> reject anyone who comes to me, because I came down from heaven not to do my
> own will but the will of the one who sent me. And this is the will of the one who
> sent me, that I should not lose anything of what he gave me, but that I should
> raise it [on] the last day. For this is the will of my Father, that everyone who sees

the Son and believes in him may have eternal life, and I shall raise him [on] the last day" (34–40).

The revelation responds interactively to the sign-seekers' demand, "Sir, give us this bread always" (6:34), with a stark first-person statement. In words resonating back to the Samaritan woman, Jesus reveals: "I am the bread of life; whoever comes to me will never hunger, and whoever believes in me will never thirst" (6:35; see 4:14 for the parallel with the woman at the well). The revealers make connections between the primary revelation and other revelations. The revelations have no obvious connection with the Bread of Life, but seem rather to extend the revelation into other aspects for the believing community. In order to perceive the Bread of Life a member of the community must both see the Son and believe in him. Those who believe in him know him to be the one who came down from heaven. Seeing and believing describe the status of those whom the Father has chosen and has entrusted to Jesus. Those entrusted to Jesus become the community that Jesus gathers, and Jesus will not reject them. Those whom Jesus gathers are those who will be raised up on the last day. These interlocking statements provide the context within which a member of the community can understand the Bread of Life. The revelation does not present information but a series of connections that extend the specific content of this discourse with major themes found throughout the gospel. It is the connections that make the revelations resonate because revelations in the end come through the details of such connections.

Whether these five connections come from one revealing prophet in the community or five different prophetic voices in the end does not matter. The revealers train the Johannine community to continue an expansive reading of the tradition, to bring previous understandings to bear, to voice questions, and to reveal problems to the community. Like the warning from Stillwater's airplane pilot, the single revelation explodes into many different strands and links them all to the exploration of the meaning of the Eucharist in a community where Jesus continues as a living presence. The community's practice of abiding embraces all these problems and questions, and the revealers weave them together as a model of how to reflect on the meaning of sacraments in their community life.

The Problems Arising from Revelation

The process of bringing forth the problems these revelations create in the community continues immediately with the revealers relating to dissenters in the community. The gospel shows the fault lines in the community in dramatic language:

> The Jews murmured about him because he said, "I am the bread that came down from heaven," and they said, "Is this not Jesus, the son of Joseph? Do we not know

his father and mother? Then how can he say, 'I have come down from heaven'?" (6:41–42).

Here is a real question among some in the Johannine community. It is an important question that the revealers must address, because it broaches the issue of the relationship of the living Jesus to the revealers who give him voice in the community. If a member of the community cannot make that connection, they cannot abide in the community. So it is an important foundation that the revealers must lay for the Johannine community.

The gospel has thrust us into the middle of a conversation (*logos*) within the Johannine community. The revealers insist, as the prologue to the gospel insists, that the Word, the "conversation" in our translation, is in the presence of God and is God. It is often a difficult conversation to have, but the revealers persist in it despite the pain. The revealers affirm the importance of the conversation by linking their revelations to the teaching that comes directly from the Father:

> Jesus answered and said to them, "Stop murmuring among yourselves. No one can come to me unless the Father who sent me draw him, and I will raise him on the last day. It is written in the prophets: 'They shall all be taught by God.' Everyone who listens to my Father and learns from him comes to me. Not that anyone has seen the Father except the one who is from God; he has seen the Father" (6:43–46).

The revealers respond by arguing that it is the Father who gathers people to the living Jesus and the Father is the primary agent for contact with Jesus. The phrase from Isaiah (54:13), "They shall all be taught by God," suggests that it is the Father who does the teaching, even though curiously the revelation ends with a statement that only "the one who is from God . . . has seen the Father" (6:46). The revealers forge links among Israelite scriptures, the Father's teaching, and their revelations. These links establish the authority of the prophets in the community's midst: they understand that the scriptures point to Jesus, that the prophets are sent by God, and they can speak the words of the living Jesus in the community. This resonates with the crash scene in *Almost Famous* in which the band must struggle with who will be their leader and who will speak for them. The revealers faced the same issue in their community at the crossroads of the second century.

The Johannine Eucharist Explored

Having established their authority, the revealers continue with the revelation. Here we see the revealers invoking the Eucharist as the site for understanding how Jesus continues to live and speak in the community:

"Amen, amen, I say to you, whoever believes has eternal life. I am the bread of life. Your ancestors ate the manna in the desert, but they died; this is the bread that comes down from heaven so that one may eat it and not die. I am the living bread that came down from heaven; whoever eats this bread will live forever; and the bread that I will give is my flesh for the life of the world" (6:47–51).

For the revealers of the Johannine community, the significance of the Eucharist is not about the presence of Jesus, but about immortality. The Johannine community experiences Jesus's presence in the community conversations (*logos*), and the Johannine Eucharist, therefore, does not make Jesus present to the community, but rather confers on them the capacity to abide in God forever. The Eucharist for them is an entry into eternal life, a continuation of the eternal presence of Jesus in their midst. The revealers differentiate between those who ate manna in the desert and died and those who eat the living Bread and live forever.

The revealers take the lead on the distinction between the Ignatian and Johannine traditions of the Eucharist in articulating how a person remains and abides in Jesus. The revealers use two different Greek words for eating: one is the common word for eating (*phagein*); the other is a more graphic word that is best translated as "gnawing at" or "munching on" (*trogein*). As you will see in the translation below, the revealers present two different perspectives on eating the flesh of Jesus through these two different words. The revealers use of language invariably gets lost in English translations.

One perspective, that of Ignatius, focuses on regular eating of bread and drinking of wine as the way to make Jesus present and to participate in eternal life (*Letter to the Ephesians*, 20). The more graphic form, gnawing at the flesh of Jesus, seems to describe the Johannine understanding of the sacrament. In other words, the revealers use different words for eating to describe the different ways of understanding the sacrament, retaining the more graphic form with its physical connotations for the Johannine eucharistic tradition. The Johannine community probably had members who were trained in the Ignatian and Petrine tradition, so the question was an important one. In the tradition of the community, these questions were never submerged, but brought into the open. The revealers model this capacity to keep the conversation (*logos*) in God's presence no matter how challenging or painful, and they bring the words of the living Jesus to bear on them:

The Jews quarreled among themselves, saying, "How can this man give us [his] flesh to eat?" Jesus said to them, "Amen, amen, I say to you, unless you eat the flesh of the Son of Man and drink his blood, you do not have life within you. Whoever gnaws at my flesh and drinks my blood has eternal life, and I will raise him on the last day. For my flesh is the true food, and my blood is true drink.

Whoever gnaws at my flesh and drinks my blood remains in me and I in him. Just as the living Father sent me and I have life because of the Father, so also the one who feeds on me will have life because of me. This is the bread that came down from heaven. Unlike your ancestors who ate and still died, whoever eats this bread will live forever." These things he said while teaching in the synagogue in Capernaum (6:52–59; translation altered).

The revealers affirm the Ignatian tradition of the Eucharist: it is indeed the eating of Jesus's flesh and the drinking of his blood. But for the revealers of the Johannine community the issue is not the presence of Jesus, but the capacity to remain in Jesus and Jesus in the person: "Whoever gnaws at my flesh and drinks my blood remains in me and I in him." The community practice of remaining and abiding in Jesus forms the central practice of the Eucharist. The Eucharist is not an instrument of the presence of Jesus, as in the Ignatian tradition, but rather an instrument of abiding. The Eucharist, where all the disparate and diverse members of the Johannine community gather, each of them with a particular relationship to a living Jesus, provides the site for abiding in that difference. Eating the bread come down from heaven confers eternal life upon them all despite their conflicts, disagreements, and divergent understandings. Jews, Samaritans, Greeks, Romans, and everyone who knows the living Jesus gather at the Eucharist to abide, to remain steadfast, to find a place where presence overcomes difference.

Community Responses to the Revelation

But this is a difficult place to remain and abide. The revealers recognize the deep divisions within the community—divisions that all relate to the different relationships with a living Jesus—and they guide the community to remain in the presence of Jesus even when it hurts. And it will hurt everyone. This is made evident in the response of some of the disciples of Jesus: "Then many of his disciples who were listening said, 'This saying is hard; who can accept it?'" (6:60). The eucharistic theology does not receive universal acceptance within the community. This eucharistic revelation becomes a breaking point for the community:

> Then many of his disciples who were listening said, "This saying is hard; who can accept it?" Since Jesus knew that his disciples were murmuring about this, he said to them, "Does this shock you? What if you were to see the Son of Man ascending to where he was before? It is the spirit that gives life, while the flesh is of no avail. The words I have spoken to you are spirit and life" (6:60–63).

The revealers address the difficulty directly. To make room for the divergent understandings in the community, the revealers embrace yet another understanding of the Eucharist. In the previous revelation it is the flesh of Jesus that confers life and immortality, but here the revealers dismiss the flesh as irrelevant. They value spirit and word over flesh. The revealers give voice to different understandings of the Eucharist and of the way of relating to Jesus. The prophetic discourse on the Bread of Life makes room for such dissent. The role of the revealers, in modeling a process of finding union in a living Jesus from diverse and divergent perspectives, is not to exclude, but to gather the different perspectives under the patronage of a living Jesus. The revealers literally "gather up the fragments, so that nothing is wasted" (John 6:12). Difference and conflict propel the Johannine community into a larger theological and spiritual frame of reference, and the revealers make room for all views.

Despite the capacity to make room for greatly divergent views, some members of the community still cannot endure it. Some cannot abide in a living Jesus:

> "But there are some of you who do not believe." Jesus knew from the beginning the ones who would not believe and the one who would betray him. And he said, "For this reason I have told you that no one can come to me unless it is granted him by my Father" (6:64–65).

The revealers recognize that living with a present Jesus is not easy. It takes a calling from the Father to be able to abide in such a community. Some even will betray the community and that, too, becomes part of the revelation. Other members of the community will leave: "As a result of this, many of his disciples returned to their former way of life and no longer accompanied him. Jesus then said to the Twelve, "Do you also want to leave?" (6:66–67). The revealers understand that life in a prophetic community is difficult for everyone, including Jesus's closest followers. They do not disparage those who need to leave; they simply returned to their prior way of living. And the revealers give the same option to the Twelve, those who represent the leadership of the church in the Markan tradition.

And yet for others, the challenge of abiding in such a community offers an opportunity for renewal and renewed commitment. The same conflict prompts Simon Peter's confession of faith: "Simon Peter answered him, 'Master, to whom shall we go? You have the words of eternal life. We have come to believe and are convinced that you are the Holy One of God'" (6:68–69). While some must leave, others find it the occasion of abiding in the conversation (*logos*), of finding life in the revealers' words, of staying connected to the living Jesus, the Holy One of God in their midst.

This extended conversation around the meaning of the Eucharist for the Johannine community, as difficult and expansive as it is, does not occur in a vacuum. The revealers continue to connect this conversation with the passion narrative of the Gospel of Mark by connecting it to the betrayal that will lead to Jesus's crucifixion: "Jesus answered them, 'Did I not choose you twelve? Yet is not one of you a devil?' He was referring to Judas, son of Simon the Iscariot;

it was he who would betray him, one of the Twelve" (6:70–71). The discourse is over. Our attention is turned to events of the future yet to be told. But the connection between Judas and the rejection of the eucharistic theology in the discourse on the Bread of Life will also continue.

The Ritual of Foot Washing as a Substitute for the Last Supper

We describe the Johannine community as bridging church tradition and revelation through the formative practice of abiding. John's community explores the meaning of the Eucharist in the revelation discourse, not as part of the received tradition about the body and blood as it is formed in Mark, Matthew, and Luke. Why? What is John's community doing here?

Two things really complicate what John is doing. First, at the Last Supper when Jesus institutes the Eucharist in Mark, Matthew, and Luke, John substitutes a new sacrament, the washing of feet. What John's community understands as the sacramental act inaugurated at the meal before Jesus's crucifixion is an act of service and humility among the members. Jesus even instructs the community to imitate this washing of feet (13:1–20). Second, at the meal at which this new sacrament of foot washing is instituted, Judas is the only person who eats bread and "Satan enters into him" (13:21–30). His is no communion with the Bread of Life, but a Satanic communion. These two displacements of the church tradition are jarring.

John's community simultaneously tests and invokes the synoptic church tradition. Revelation has led them to a new way of living sacramentally. Their relationship to Jesus does not rely upon tradition or sacraments, but upon an intimate relationship with a living Jesus come down from heaven in the voice of the revealers to feed the people, an intimacy revealed in the washing of the community's feet and in humble service to one another. This constitutes a severe critique of the church's practices. It is as though John's community mistrusts and confronts the direction the church has taken and offers alternatives based on prophetic revelation worked out through interactive revelation.

When the Johannine community produced their gospel, the church of Mark, Matthew, and Luke was making way for the intensely hierarchal organization of the church that we find in the letters of Ignatius, bishop of Antioch. As we explained in the portal, Ignatius argued for a strict hierarchy of bishop, presbyter (priest), and deacon, maintaining that only a bishop could celebrate a valid Eucharist (*Letter to the Smyrneans*, 8). Ignatius conjoined sacraments and hierarchy.

John's community would have nothing of this conjoining. Everyone in John's community lived in close contact with a living Jesus given voice by resident revelers living among them. They were all "beloved disciples" of Jesus. Their feeding took place in revelation—revelation that created conflict, which in turn led to more revelation. Their sacrament of foot washing emphasized the egalitarian prophetic service among the members of the community. Their Eucharist gave them strength to abide with and through the one come down from heaven, the Word made flesh, as well as with those who knew Jesus's voice intimately. It was a very different world in which they lived. Ignatius, his successors in the hierarchy, and even some in the Johannine community, could not value this understanding of God and Jesus, even though later theologians found ways to support the hierarchical sacramental system using the revelations from the Bread of Life discourse. The church would eventually domesticate these radical prophetic revelations while at the same time forbidding both prophetic and interactive revelation as a means of encountering the living Jesus.

Conclusion

We need to remember that all Christian communities—indeed all communities—find organizational issues challenging. All Christian communities seek to develop ways to maintain unity or, more importantly, ways to interpret the tradition in their present times to meet the community needs. John's gospel was written nearly eighty years after the crucifixion of Jesus, or about 110 CE. The world had changed dramatically, and Christianity was at a crucial and critical crossroad. The Christian communities faced questions about the constructions of power and authority. At this time, bishops emerge as the primary leadership in the church in many communities. The bishops claim apostolic authority of the kind that the Acts of the Apostles helped inscribe. Ignatius, bishop of Antioch, is the exemplar. These bishops sharply contrasted to those revealers who continue to carry the "Word of the Lord" from community to community. The Gospel of John shows that they are running into resistance from ecclesiastical authorities. There are more and more communities led by bishops who supersede the revealers and appropriate their authoritative voice. Both kinds of community—those choosing a hierarchy to lead and those oriented toward continual revelation—seek to find ways of making Jesus present, but they disagree about how to accomplish this.

In this critical time of the early second century, the Johannine community emerges as a critical renewal agent. The members organize their lives around a living and present Jesus, and their formation involves the difficult work of remaining or abiding with a living Jesus amidst the great diversity of understandings, practices, and experiences that a living presence produces among the members of the community. The community actively criticizes other Christian community structures, even while honoring the traditions that produced them.

The synoptic tradition follows the Petrine story, the story that focuses on the central role of Peter in the development of the church. We can see the expansion of Peter's and the bishops' roles as we move from Mark to Matthew to Luke/Acts to the letters of Ignatius and *Didache*. John's gospel consistently ignores that trajectory, rendering Peter a less central character. The gospel shows the Johannine community criticizing the pyramidal authority structures having but one representative of Christ in the person of a bishop whose voice is the only authority in a community. The concept of a unitive representative meets with strong resistance in the Johannine community, which understands and works with revelation coming from many sources.

The Johannine community operates through revelation, revelation that not only represents past events, but highlights present concerns. The Johannine community holds on to the tradition and yet reads and experiences it very differently, since revelation is ongoing and unfolding, responding to the needs of a diverse community. It is the revealers who give voice to Jesus present in their midst, providing unity and cohesion for this diverse community. The revealers pray in the voice of Jesus: "And now I will no longer be in the world, but they are in the world, while I am coming to you. Holy Father, keep them in your name that you have given me, so that they may be one just as we are" (17:11). As a consequence of experiencing ongoing revelation from the ever-present Jesus, the Johannine community forms a unity markedly different from the unity described in the Acts of the Apostles (a unity within an idealized empire) or in Ignatius's letters (a unity of an institutionalized hierarchy). The Johannine unity emerges precisely from the different way that the Gospel of John forms its community. It is by abiding in the living words of Jesus in their midst that the community coheres.

The prologue to the gospel provides a window on the formative theology that informed this remarkable community. The practice of abiding in revelation is deeply rooted in the creation of all things by the *logos*, which we have translated *conversation*. Because God is present and incarnate in the conversation, the Johannine community must remain steadfast in it. The conversation is where God abides and works; it is the creative origin of all things. The prologue also affirms that everything is created, and probably recreated, by abiding in the conversation. Listen to how we hear the prologue:

> In the beginning was the conversation (*logos*), and the conversation was with God, and the conversation was God. This (conversation) was in the beginning in God's presence. Everything came to be through it, and without it not one thing that was made existed. In it was life, and the life was the light of humans, and the light shines in the darkness, and the darkness did not comprehend it (John 1:1–5, our translation).

The Johannine community knew that they had nothing to fear: the light of new revelations, the darkness of division, conflict, pain, of contesting views would never overwhelm the light of divine conversation (*logos*) that is in God's presence. But they go much further than that: the community affirms that the conversation in God's presence created all of it. The world exists because God created it in conversation. So they embrace it all as part of God's work. Since everything exists in it, they embrace everything and everyone: the outsiders, the objectors, the prophetic voices, the community members, the dissenters, the conflicting views of the Eucharist, the Petrine and Ignatian tradition, the brilliant revelations, the images of Jesus as Way and Life and Door and Shepherd. God created them all and through the conversation brought them into God's presence. That presence is real life not only for the Johannine community, but for all humanity. It was a way of life—difficult, challenging, and filled with conflict—but at the same time a way of living that brought true life, eternal life. The revealers made this possible through their ongoing revelations that began in the beginning of time and continue until the end of time. All the community needed was to abide in the revelations that brought them eternal life.

This abiding in a conversation made present in Jesus also stands in marked contrast to the other gospels. John's community criticizes Mark, Matthew, and Luke/ Acts, first of all, for presenting Jesus as only an historical figure, and second, as having left the world in the hands of a select few male disciples. John's community continually portrays Jesus as fully present, even many years after his crucifixion. Jesus speaks to the community through a wide variety of people. The story of the woman at the well illustrates how Jesus interacts with many anonymous followers, including women, who become leaders, carrying the voice of Jesus into their communities. As we saw in this story, John's gospel argues that anyone, friend or foe, can be a beloved disciple, a revealer, and that new disciples are always being formed, often out of conflict or disagreement, but always in engagement with a living Jesus brought to the community by prophetic voices within the community.

Thus the Gospel of John uses ongoing revelation as its primary means first to criticize and then to renew the church in the early second century, embracing the formative practice of abiding in new revelations as the primary means of renewal. Because revelation for John's gospel continues a pattern of revelation stemming from Jesus through prophets, carrying the voice of Jesus into their own day, there is no sense in this gospel that revelation ever ends. This is the greatest difference between John and all other gospels. This sense of ongoing revelation has made John's gospel the most compelling theological, liturgical, poetic, sacramental, and evangelical text in the history of the church from the second century until now.

We know that, in the end, the Gospel of John becomes famous. In *Almost Famous* the terrible threat of death in the apparently imminent plane crash, the crisis that provides the space for the members of the band to bare their souls and reveal the fault lines in the community, also created the opportunity for the healing of the community. In the end, *Rolling Stone* publishes William Miller's article "Stillwater Runs Deep," despite the band's denunciation. Then he gets the interview he has been seeking with the lead guitarist. The final scenes show the band beginning their next concert tour, not in a plane, but in their bus Doris. The concert tour's title is "No More Airplanes Tour." They have lived through their trauma and emerged even stronger. In the very last scene, the lead guitarist dances over to the lead singer and kisses him. They still disagree about who will lead and speak for Stillwater, but they have found peace in abiding in the moment and letting the future, the now famous future, unfold as it will. In the end, the Gospel of John has achieved the same peace. With all the con-flicts, disagreements, misunderstandings, and differences, the Gospel of John runs deep: they have found peace in abiding with a living Jesus who continues to speak to them in their troubled times in the voices of the revealers, the truly beloved disciples of the Lord.

Questions for Discussion

1. Living with divergent and conflicting voices in community demands fortitude. Discuss a difficult and controversial subject, one with opposing perspectives, with your colleagues, accepting every position as valued and true. What problems arise from that acceptance? How does the presence of alternative voices and perspectives challenge group process? What ben-efits does the group experience from discussions that include alternative perspectives? Can you relate these reflections to the Gospel of John?
2. Read the front page of a national newspaper. What are the voices that are considered revelatory? What voices hold greater power and authority than other voices? Why are some voices more authoritative than others? What is the basis for establishing the authority of voices? How does this relate to the Gospel of John?
3. Read the feeding of the five thousand in Mark (6:30–44) and in John (6:1–15), and then read the discourse on the Bread of Life (6:22–71). Compare the two readings of the miracles. What are the differences and similarities, and how can you account for them? How does the discourse in John change your understanding of both accounts? How do you read Mark's account differently after reading the discourse in John?

Resources for Further Study

The direction and mode of interpreting the Gospel of John continues the work Richard Valantasis began in a seminar with Dieter Georgi at Harvard over twenty years ago. In that seminar, Georgi read, refracted, and challenged the work of his teacher, Rudolph Bultmann, on the Gospel of John (*Gospel of John: A Commentary*, trans. G. R. Beasley-Murray (Philadelphia: Westminster Press, 1971). Valantasis taught a seminar at Iliff School of Theology, taking up the questions Georgi raised and pursuing them further with his students Douglas Bleyle and Dennis Haugh, coauthors of this book. This replicates the succession of teachers we have discussed in this book, from Bultmann to Georgi to Valantasis and to Bleyle and Haugh.

The most prominent work on the Gospel of John is that of Raymond Brown. His scholarship on John is culminated in two influential books: Raymond E. Brown, *The Community of the Beloved Disciple* (New York: Paulist Press, 1979) and *An Introduction to the Gospel of John*, ed. Francis J. Moloney (New York: Doubleday, 2003) that has Brown's most current perspectives. The significance of Raymond E. Brown's contribution to scholarship on the Gospel of John can be further investigated in a collection of essays *Life in Abundance: Studies of John's Gospel in Tribute to Raymond E. Brown*, ed. John R. Donahue (Collegeville, Minn.: Liturgical Press, 2005).

Other important commentaries on John include: Francis J. Moloney, *The Gospel of John*, Sacra Pagina Series (Collegeville, Minn.: Liturgical Press, 1998); and the less accessible, but still important, Ernst Haenchen, *John: A Commentary on the Gospel of John*, Hermeneia Series, trans. Robert W. Funk (Philadelphia: Fortress, 1984).

Two works address the question of revelation: Wayne Meeks, "The Man from Heaven in Johannine Sectarianism," *Journal of Biblical Literature* 91 (1972), 44–72; and Gail O' Day, "Narrative Mode and Theological Claim: A Study in the Fourth Gospel," *Journal of Biblical Literature* 105 (1986), 657–668.

There has been significant work on the literary structure of John's gospel. The three books of R. Alan Culpepper, *John, the Son of Zebedee: The Life of a Legend* (Columbia: University of South Carolina Press, 1994); *Anatomy of the Fourth Gospel: A Study in Literary Design* (Philadelphia: Fortress, 1983); and *The Johannine School: An Evaluation of the Johannine-School Hypothesis Based on an Investigation of the Nature of Ancient Schools* (Missoula, Mont.: Scholars Press, 1975) provide important analyses of the text. J. Louis Martyn also addresses the structure of the Johannine community in his *History and Theology in the Fourth Gospel*, third edition (Louisville: Westminster John Knox, 2003). Although his argument that the gospel responds to the community's expulsion from the synagogue has been widely criticized, Martyn's reading of the narrative of the gospel on multiple levels has received general acceptance.

CHAPTER TEN

A Theological Conclusion:
Good News Everywhere

Imagine with us again our itinerant Theodore, but now as one who travels through time to the cities in which the gospels have been written. Walking into a community in Rome, Theodore is startled to hear a biography of Jesus so openly read in a public setting. He is startled not only by the way the story is told—with demons understanding while the disciples seem befuddled—but he is also startled by the fact that his understanding of the way various Christians lived could be summarized in one simple story of the founder of the movement called the Empire of God.

Traveling to Matthew's community, Theodore finds himself in a rabbinic school. It is very Jewish compared to Mark's Roman community. He studies the Israelite scriptures in order to find common ground between Jesus and the ancient traditions of Israel. He hears the words and sayings of Jesus refracted through the prophets, Moses, Elisha, and Elijah, and through the Psalms. The Jesus of this community is God's wisdom brought forth to a new age and a new community deeply rooted in a long tradition of revelation and wisdom.

Moving then to Luke/Act's community, Theodore hears of a Jesus who sounds very much like a Roman gentleman. The teaching in this community resembles the teaching of the famous philosophers of Rome. And Theodore learns the history of Jesus in new ways—a history that goes back to Israel, through Jesus, and into the life of the church founded by the apostles. Theodore had never before thought of the history of his church, but now he understands anew where it all began and he imagines where it would lead in the future.

Arriving at John's community, Theodore finds himself in a new world. The historical perspective of Luke/Acts has been supplanted by devotion to a Jesus who still lives in the community. Really lives in the community. He hears Jesus's voice and words in the prophets who carry forth his teaching, bringing the living words of a living Jesus to bear on the circumstances of this church that seems so critical of the way Christianity has developed. Theodore gets a glimpse from John's community of the way the Empire of God got its start—in hearing Jesus speak a living word of God that transformed everything.

Finally, Theodore miraculously arrives in a twenty-first-century urban setting. Here he sees the same diversity expressed. He walks past a Baptist church, a Holiness temple, an Episcopal church, all in a row. He takes the subway downtown to find a Methodist church, next to a Quaker meeting house that stands beside a Roman Catholic church. Theodore wonders at Mormons, Jehovah's Witnesses, Congregationalists. At Christmas, Theodore remarks at how all the stories were put together from the gospels to tell a seamless story of the birth of Jesus that he can see in people's yards as a nativity scene. At Easter, Theodore takes stock of the way all the accounts of the resurrection seem to have been folded into one unified witness to the reality of Jesus's resurrection. Hearing sermons in these various churches that call themselves Christian, he is astounded by the rich diversity of understanding of Jesus's teaching and how differently each community forms a moral code out of them. How can all this be? How could these twenty-first-century Christians do this? Can this all be the same Jesus? Of course, he thinks, it is no different than the communities he has witnessed in his travels to Rome and in his travels through time. God, he thinks, has done a wonderful thing in all these diverse expressions, and certainly God is at work doing new things in different times among diverse peoples and languages.

And so Theodore brings his travels to an end. He understands that his mind simply cannot fathom how strange and complex his religion really is, and yet he rests in the understanding that this is how God has always worked.

Our imaginary Theodore points to something very important about the gospels: they are very different from one another. That difference arises because each gospel responds to the formative needs of a different community. The gospels were malleable, adjustable, interpretable in their historic contexts. This flies in the face of what most modern people understand about the Bible: we have been trained to think of the gospels as different remembrances of the same eyewitness accounts. We have been trained to interpret each gospel as providing information missing from other gospels as each evangelist remembered it. But we now know that such was not the case. The unity of narrative in the gospels, particularly Mark, Matthew, and Luke, does not depend upon their common remembrance of historical events, but rather on Matthew and Luke's use of the first creative gospel, that of Mark. John's gospel does not use Mark's narrative as a basis and therefore does not display the same sort of unity with the others. It was not memory that guided the gospel writers, but community circumstances and a relationship to the Gospel of Mark. The gospels differ because they were written for different purposes, to different communities, under different historical and political circumstances, and with different theological and spiritual aims. These differences are very important. Without understanding the differences, we really cannot understand the gospels at all. So rather than reading the gospels for their similarity, we must read them for their differences, to appreciate the subtlety and brilliance of their revelation about Jesus and the Empire of God that Jesus announced.

For whatever reasons, most religious people seem uncomfortable with reading for differences. We think that something talking about God, or God's work, or the knowledge of God must be consistent throughout all history and for all times. But that perspective masks the fact that God is not limited by our conceptions. In fact, God surpasses all our capacities to understand and articulate, and in surpassing human capacity for understanding, we must understand the limits of our knowledge and of our ways of knowing. This is difficult for us. But theologians in previous generations understood human limitations very well. They articulated two ways of knowing God: one through constructing human categories that describe God and God's activity, and the other through negating those categories by saying that God so surpasses our human categories as not to be the category at all. For example, we can say that God is good, but the human understanding of goodness as a category finds its meaning only in the context of human experience in particular settings and circumstances and therefore God is not good in the fullest sense of our personal and communal knowledge. This does not mean that God is not good, but that God's goodness is of a nature so transcendent and different from our understanding that the category *good* no longer fully explains God. Our human capacity to know is limited to our personal and corporate experiences, and therefore our experience limits our capacity to understand.

God's goodness, for example, is understood differently in each one of the gospels we have studied. Mark's goodness of God is one who is hidden from the Roman authorities and who brings healing to the community. Matthew's goodness of God relates to poverty of spirit and to connections between Jesus and the Israelite scriptures. Luke's goodness relates to God's reflection of the Greco-Roman values that his community reveres. And John's goodness of God relates to intimacy, an intimacy with Jesus that reveals the inner workings of the community and reveals the ever-presence of God in human ways of knowing. Our desire for a consistent view blinds us from seeing these differences as all relating to a God who far surpasses our understanding. We are limited by our desire for uniformity through time when we try to understand God's ways.

Our study of the formative practices in the gospels points us toward different ways of knowing and understanding God, the Empire of God, and Jesus from a place of appreciating and even reveling in the differences. The differences tell us more than the similarities about the diversity of ways of understanding God. And so we encourage our readers to plunge into the differences as a way of approaching the revelation of God in different ways. This is crucial for our age, when different ways of knowing and understanding God have created conflict and wars between peoples and nations, and especially among religious bodies where differences of perspective have caused strife and division over interpretations of the scriptures. Embedded in the Christian scriptures, however, is a very different perspective, where an acceptance of different revelations shows the resiliency and strength of religious traditions, an acceptance that has the potential for transforming community and that may be especially instructive in our times.

If we take a lead from the gospel writers, we should be able to understand how to appreciate differences in religious perspective. Each one of the gospel writers rewrote the narrative in order to address the real-life issues in their various communities. The gospels model how to use the story of Jesus to discover and create the significance of Jesus and the Empire of God in new and different circumstances. The problem in Mark's community, the problem of unity and diversity under an oppressive political regime, differs from Matthew's and Luke's communities, which were situated in more irenic contexts where they could explore the significance of Jesus in language and images appropriate to their communities. Mark's dissimulation no longer applied to them because they were living in different places in the Roman Empire, so they selected from Mark what they could use: the narrative frame of the life of Jesus, the gospel biography, as their frame, while at the same time filling out the story with information important to their communities. For Matthew and Luke, it was important to know the circumstances of Jesus's birth, so they include birth narratives, but different ones, because Matthew's birth narrative relates primarily to Joseph and his response to God's new work in Jesus, while Luke's birth narrative relates to Mary, Jesus's mother, and the story of the miraculous and very imperial sounding circumstances of Jesus's birth. John, on the other hand, needed to place Jesus within the context of a cosmic creation, so he begins his gospel with a hymn about the Word of God existing from before time in God's presence and becoming human by taking on human flesh. If we follow the lead of the gospel writers themselves, we begin to understand that circumstances and contexts change, and therefore the proclamation of the gospel must change as circumstances do.

The need for change goes very deep in the gospels, and all the gospel writers seemed empowered to change the story to fit their needs. Empowerment is important here. Their communities' needs determined how the story of Jesus that Mark created should be told in their communities. Take the example of John the Baptist. Each gospel shifts and adjusts the orientation toward John. For Mark, John the Baptist becomes the platform upon which Jesus begins his ministry after his baptism. For Matthew, John the Baptist becomes Jesus's first teacher and rabbi, bringing ancient knowledge and perspectives to their school environment. For Luke/Acts, John the Baptist functions as a connection between the ancient Israelite prophets and Jesus, creating a lineage of teachers on the model of Greco-Roman schools. For John's gospel, John the Baptist serves as a revealer, someone who points to Jesus as the true leader in the Empire of God, and the true revealer of God's presence in their community.

Similar empowerment to fill in the story that they took from Mark occurs with the resurrection accounts. Mark's gospel has no clear indication of a resurrection, because that did not suit his project of dissimulation. But each of the other gospels presents resurrection accounts that differ from one another and tell different stories of the resurrection. Matthew emphasizes the women, while Luke emphasizes the connection of the resurrection to the descent of the Spirit, and John emphasizes the revelation of Jesus to those who followed him: Mary Magdalene, Thomas, and the disciples. These examples, from the way each community refracted their understanding of John the Baptist and Jesus's resurrection, display for us the deep sense of the gospel writers' empowerment to transform and adapt the life of Jesus to fit the needs of their own communities.

We have the same empowerment, if we follow the gospel writers' lead. We, too, in our own day can begin to shift and change the story to respond to the various and diverse (and even conflicting) needs of communities in our own day. At its heart, the story, or at least the frame of the story, stays the same: Jesus was born, taught, healed, engaged in the world both positively and negatively, was tried, crucified, died, and resurrected. But within that frame, there is as great a diversity possible for us as for the gospel writers. Like those students who created the controversy stories, the *chreiai*, we can begin to apply the sayings of Jesus to new circumstances and, if we follow John, to create new sayings of a living Jesus in our midst that would bring the reality of Jesus's teaching and the reality of the Empire of God to new and different circumstances that the gospel writers could never have anticipated. This is what Matthew, Luke/Acts, and John did with Mark's gospel. We, too, are empowered by the same divine energy to refract and retell the story in language, metaphors, images, and contexts that differ wildly from the Greco-Roman world in which the gospels writers wrote.

Actually there were many more communities of Christians in the ancient world who wrote gospels that suited the needs of their communities. They too experienced empowerment. The recent popularity of newly published ancient gospels witness to the great diversity and creativity in telling the story of Jesus and the Empire of God. The *Gospel of Mary* tells the revelations of Jesus to Mary after his resurrection and instructs that community about the theology of the cosmos and the stages of a person's life after death in the body. The *Gospel of Thomas* collects sayings of Jesus without any narrative of the life of Jesus. For Thomas's gospel the words of Jesus spoke for themselves and functioned as a resource for future generations to make connection with the living words of a living Jesus, a Jesus who is always present in the voice of the members of the community. The newly published *Gospel of Judas* tells a different set of revelations of Jesus from the perspective of the disciple who betrayed Jesus. Although only four gospels made it into what we call the New Testament, these other gospels attest to the empowerment our ancestors had to engage with Jesus in new and different ways. Each of these communities took parts of the story of Jesus, well-known from Mark's gospel, as a platform for creatively engaging with Jesus in ways their communities needed, in order to grow and develop spiritually, intellectually, and religiously. In fact in our own day, the same reframing of the story happens all the time. Whenever a preacher takes a text and begins to expound on it in ways that address the real-life circumstances of the gathered community, the preacher expands and fills in the details so that the community may bridge their experience and the revelation in scripture. The gospel writers model this for us, as they did for Christians throughout history. The gospel writers all direct us to manifest the significant empowerment given to the community to tell the story in their own way.

If we look to the way the gospel writers operated we can learn even more about this empowerment. Imagine Mark's spectacular accomplishment for his community. He gathered all the fragments of knowledge and understanding and united them in a created biographical narrative. He used what information was at hand and began creatively to develop a book that would hold his community all together. Matthew, Luke, and John, under the same impulse of the divine presence and the divine working in their community, used what was at their disposal to create documents that would hold their communities together. In addition to Mark, they had the sayings of Jesus, ritual and sacramental traditions, traditions of hospitality, teaching on the manner of evangelizing others and spreading the good news, oral teaching, and many traditions of their own construction, which they fed into their story. They reorganized the sayings, in Matthew's case into long speeches, and they filled in the story. They used whatever was at hand for them to help their communities. We have even more for our own day. We have the four gospels, new knowledge of the relationship of the church to the Roman society in which it grew, new insights into what it means to be human, two millennia of living with, reflecting on, and being led by these gospels, and much else to help us tell a story that will help us to become the kinds of religious people we yearn and need to become. We, too, are empowered by the gospel writers to use whatever is at hand to transform and form ourselves and our communities. The gospel writers show us the way.

The gospel writers also lead us away from creating a homogenous and uniform Christianity. The four different gospels in the New Testament lead us to value the differences, and to build from the differences, those traditions and ways of living that fit our own circumstances. None of the gospels explicitly reject their predecessors. Their reworking of material simply stands as a testament that religious experience and knowledge shift and change as circumstances change. The gospel writers used earlier material to create different kinds of communities with divergent perspectives, practices, theologies, sacraments, social and political engagements, and concerns for the outcast and poor. These differences, as divergent and conflicting as they might be from one another, underscore how very complex and diverse Christianity was, should be, and will always be. We have smoothed over the differences in our day, hoping to find a single truth and a singular perspective that would apply to all people at all times. But our gospel-writing ancestors knew better. They knew and wrote, and the church affirmed in these four gospels the truth, that Christianity differs and changes as the times and circumstances change. That is difficult for us today to understand, but the gospels speak loudly that there is not a single Christianity, homogeneous and uniform, that fits all people everywhere throughout history. In the short hundred years or so that it took to compose the four gospels in the New Testament, we see the multiform and pluriform perspectives on Jesus and the Empire of God. Since the time of the New Testament, we continue to see multiple and plural kinds of Christianity expressed as denominations, movements, theological frames, and multiple ways of interpreting the scriptures that display the very same complexity and diversity. The gospel writers direct us to affirm and embrace such diversity and complexity in our own times, just as they did in their times.

In our day we experience diversity of expression and divergence of understandings as a threat to true Christianity. Our gospel writers, in doing their work, tell us to relax with that diversity. Our formation as religious people in our day, taking the gospels' lead, should include a deep sense that the working of God simply surpasses our understanding and our ability to make everyone conform to a common perspective. Presbyterians, Lutherans, Episcopalians, Methodists,

Unitarians, Roman Catholics, Eastern Orthodox, Baptists, Jehovah's Witnesses, Mormons—divided as they are internally about what constitutes true Christianity—simply carry on the tradition started by Mark, Matthew, Luke, and John. The gospel writers encourage us to experience diversity and difference not as threat, but as grace, as an occasion for learning more, as a time of refreshment and renewal in the face of a God who simply transcends our capacity to unify, homogenize, and conform. Our divisions and conflicts within Christianity lead us to a knowledge of God, of Jesus, of the Empire of God that reveals the miracle of a God who acts in every human circumstance and context, language and culture, historical period and governmental structure, nation and people in strikingly different and often shockingly divergent ways. And yet it is the same story, the same Jesus, the same Spirit that produces that diversity. Paul knew this when he wrote to the Corinthians. We know this from reading the gospels.

In the end, this is the formative practice of the gospels to which we must attend. Our demon, which the gospel writers would have us expel, is the demon of uniformity and consistency. The difficult work before us in forming ourselves as religious people, as Christians, takes up the mantle of transformation, reframing, and refracting left to us by the four gospel writers. Their creative energy directs us to learn to live with diversity—not simply to live but to love the diversity as reflecting the reality of God's presence. To be formed in such appreciation of difference, of a flexible gospel that responds to different circumstances and needs, of the importance of a gospel message that relates to the real lives of participants in a church, demands our attention. This appreciation of difference equally demands engagement with other Christians and other religions, our serious intellectual study, and our interaction with the sciences and other knowledge of our day. The gospel writers' formation, that is, must become our own in new times. And that takes not only a formation in reading the scriptures, but also a formation in relating to different kinds of religious believers and practitioners. It also requires a humility that acknowledges that no one person or group can ever speak the entirety of God's message for all people and all times.

In the end, we hope that the reader of this book has learned one important lesson about Christianity: that diversity pervaded the beginnings and every subsequent development of Christian revelation through the ages. The formation found in the gospels revolves about a formation to appreciate the diversity, to revel in it, and to apply it to new times and circumstances. The formative challenge is to embrace that difference and to live lives faithful to the revelation in our own times and circumstances, faithful not in the sense of replicating the past, but faithful in the sense of refracting the past and allowing the light of the past to become a kaleidoscope of faithful living to the future. This humble embracing of diversity, we hope, will lead religious people of every stripe and time to living in harmony, peace, mutual respect, and godly love toward all God's creatures and creation.

Index

❊

About the Authors

Richard Valantasis received an MA in Theology and a ThD in New Testament and Christian origins as well as in church history from Harvard University. He has taught at Saint Louis University, Harvard Divinity School, Iliff School of Theology, and is on leave from Emory University where he is professor of ascetical theology and christian practice and director of the Anglican Studies program. He is currently a codirector of the Institute for Contemplative Living in Santa Fe, New Mexico, an institute the promulgates contemplative practice for active people. An ordained Episcopal priest for over thirty-five years, he has served in parishes as well as chaplain to the Sisters of St. Margaret in Boston. He is the author of *The Gospel of Thomas*, *Centuries of Holiness*, *The Beliefnet Guide to Gnositicism and other Lost Christianities*, *Asceticism*, as well as many articles on religious practices ancient and modern.

Douglas K. Bleyle received a BA from Metropolitan State College in Denver, Colorado specializing in anthropology. He earned a MDiv from Iliff School of Theology, and a ThM in contemplative practices from Candler School of Theology at Emory University. Trained as an occupational therapist, he worked children with learning disabilities for over ten years. He is currently a codirector with Richard Valantasis of the Institute for Contemplative Living in Santa Fe, New Mexico. He has written and lectured in ascetical theology and contemplative practice. He has specialized in liturgical contemplation and has led numerous retreats and workshops in churches to teach contemplative practices in worship.

Dennis C. Haugh is and a candidate for the PhD in biblical studies in the joint University of Denver–Iliff School of Theology doctoral program. He serves as adjunct faculty at Iliff, teaching biblical languages and early Christian history. Haugh has also published a text critical study of Codex Washingtonianus. A Roman Catholic lay person, Haugh has extensive practical experience in adult faith formation. Prior to resuming academic studies, Haugh was a financial executive in the extractive industries.